ISBN 978-1-334-97614-8
PIBN 10783582

F. L. LUCAS

Fellow of King's College, Cambridge
University Reader in English

THE SEARCH FOR GOOD SENSE

FOUR EIGHTEENTH-CENTURY CHARACTERS

Johnson

Chesterfield

Boswell

Goldsmith

NEW YORK
THE MACMILLAN COMPANY
1961

Macmillan Paperbacks Edition 1961

The Macmillan Company, New York
Brett-Macmillan Ltd., Galt, Ontario

Printed in the United States of America

TO HARRY AND HILARY HINSLEY

Je lis quelquefois toute une histoire sans faire la moindre attention aux coups donnés dans les batailles ou à l'épaisseur des murs des villes prises; uniquement attentif à regarder les hommes, mon plaisir est de voir cette longue suite de passions et de fantaisies.

Montesquieu

Laisser le bavardage aux bavards, ne prendre que l'essentiel, ne le traduire aux yeux que par les actions probantes, concentrer, abréger, résumer la vie, voilà le but de l'art.

Taine, on Mérimée

PREFACE

THIS book deals with four eighteenth-century figures—Johnson, Boswell, Chesterfield, Goldsmith; it will be followed, I hope, by another, covering Hume, Horace Walpole, Burke, and Benjamin Franklin. It would have been easier, in some ways, to combine both in a single volume; but in this age of growing bustle and mounting prices there is, more often than ever, truth in the adage of Callimachus, librarian of Alexandria—'μέγα βιβλίον, μέγα κακόν'—'a big book is a big evil'.

On all these men there already exist many books—many of them big. One feels embarrassed at adding to the number. Nothing can be a substitute for Boswell's *Johnson*; or for those works on an American scale of magnificence, the *Boswell Papers* and the fifty-volume edition of Walpole's letters. But, given the brevity and busyness of life, many have not time to read these large works, or a series of full-scale biographies; still less, to re-read them. There is a need for both long and short biographies, as for large-scale and small-scale maps. And it is not only a question of time. One reads such things not only for the amusement of reading, but also to remember. For this, I feel, biographies tend to grow too long. Just because one is told far more than one really needs, one remembers far less. The impression is blurred by multitudinousness; just as one could not, says Aristotle (with a flash of imagination rare in his austere pages) grasp as a unity a creature ten thousand furlongs in length.

On the other hand, a life grows lifeless if too short. For vividness depends on detail. The brevity of an encyclopædia can reduce to prosaic boredom even a Cæsar or an Alexander.

Therefore there is often much to be said, I think, for a happy mean—a length of 60–120 pages, which attempts to omit nothing that is really vital, and to include nothing that is not; which can leave a unified impression, but not lay a staggering load upon the memory. (A supreme success at this, to my mind, is Sainte-Beuve.[1])

[1] His *Causeries du Lundi* average about 8,000 words; but he might devote severa *Lundis* in succession to the same person.

This, at all events, was my object in treating these characters in lectures at Cambridge; and in reprinting them here, in somewhat amplified and modified form. Whatever the drawbacks of lecturing, it makes one mind the clock.

If I have made very liberal use of quotations, I trust my readers will not regret it. Better that these remarkable people should speak, where possible, for themselves, than that I should try to speak too much for them. They may speak more vividly: they may speak more truly. Often, I think, one comes to judge those one knows personally less by what they say than by what they do; but with historic characters the reverse may often be true. What, exactly, they did, is frequently disputed; why they did it, more disputed still. But what they wrote or said, is often certain enough; and may prove, by its style and tone, more revealing than all their recorded actions; which may have had a dozen possible motives, now unknowable. The style is the man.

I have chosen these characters, first, because they seem to me fascinating in themselves; secondly, because they seem to me (apart from Boswell who was, in many ways, a pre-Romantic) typical of their fascinating time. It may be said that there are only too many studies of the eighteenth-century mind already. Possibly. But here I have an axe of my own to grind—even though I may lose my head in the process. For though the men of the eighteenth century would have been enchanted to learn a thousand things from us, yet there are also, I think, many things we might still learn from them. They are not only historic curiosities: they can also become our guides and, sometimes, our friends.

My thanks are due to the McGraw-Hill Book Company and to Messrs Heinemann for permission to quote extensively from Boswell's *Private Papers* (privately printed in the USA in nineteen volumes, 1928–37, and since partly re-edited in popular form). And I am grateful for valuable suggestions to Mr John Saltmarsh, Vice-Provost of King's.

Contents

I. *INTRODUCTORY*

The Eighteenth-Century Mind

EVEN the most devoted lover of History may feel, at moments, dismayed by doubts of her. Is she, perhaps, only a loquacious liar, a deceitful baggage, after all?

We can trust History, no doubt, for billions of bare facts. Yet how bare are bare facts! The living interest lies far less in facts than in ideas, in minds, in personalities. Yet can we hope really to grasp the minds of the dead? We stand frustrated like Æneas, face to face in burning Troy with the phantom of the wife he loved:

> Ter conatus ibi collo dare bracchia circum;
> Ter frustra comprensa manus effugit imago,
> Par levibus ventis volucrique simillima somno.

> Three times I threw, in longing, my arms about her neck,
> Three times through my hands vain-clinging the phantom took its flight,
> Like the fleeting winds of Heaven, or the wingèd dreams of night.

Even the yellowed letters or diaries of the generation immediately before us can often contain feelings, beliefs, prejudices, scruples, that now seem fantastic past comprehension, remote as the ideas of Esquimaux. Indeed it can easily occur that we no longer know ourselves in old letters of our own. 'Tout s'en va, tout passe; l'eau coule et le cœur oublie.'[1]

Even with our own contemporaries our contact is largely illusion. No doubt, Proust may have exaggerated when he compared a man talking with his friends to the type of lunatic who holds animated converse with the chairs and tables in his room, imagining that they sympathetically understand him. That seems extreme. For, after all,

[1] Flaubert.

we can *sometimes* foretell the behaviour of those we think we know. And this is at least some sort of test to distinguish false beliefs from true. Astronomy can regularly predict: astrology cannot. And yet, to be honest, try how much you can really predict the reactions even of those you know best; it may prove chastening to find how often one is quite uncertain; how often one is wholly wrong.

So little understanding even our contemporaries—so little understanding even ourselves—how, then, should we hope really to fathom minds long dead?

> If this were true now! But the space, the space
> Between the breast and lips—Tiberius' heart
> Lies a thought further than another man's.[1]

Again, anyone who pictures what his own biography would look like, were it worth writing, must surely realize how much it would infallibly misrepresent, how much it would ignore. What we did would be constantly misunderstood, or overlooked; and still more, why we did it—often we no longer know that ourselves—even if we ever did know.

Even autobiography, however frank and full, remains at best a mere sketch of life's infinite complexity. We forget; we distort—if not consciously, then unconsciously. It is sometimes possible to tell nothing but the truth; but the whole truth—never. Even Montaigne sometimes misleads; even Rousseau, though unblushing in his exhibitionism, is quite untrustworthy. Pepys, indeed, and Boswell, journalizing for themselves alone, do convince us; but they remain almost unique.

Sometimes, it is true, we seem to understand the dead. Indeed we may feel them closer to us than many of the living. We may have far more sense of contact and sympathy with Homer, despite three thousand years, than with Hitler. And yet even with the best loved figures of the past what gulfs can suddenly open, what baffling differences of feeling rise up to sunder age from age!

When, for example, the wise and humane Odysseus, the loyal and affectionate Telemachus, together with their faithful henchmen celebrate their triumph in Ithaca by hanging twelve of Penelope's

[1] Ben Johnson, *Sejanus*.

false handmaidens, 'like netted thrushes', from a ship's cable; when we read how, in vengeance on the goatherd Melanthius, 'with the ruthless edge of bronze they severed his ears and nose, and tore away his genitals for the dogs to eat raw, and hewed off his hands and feet in the fury of their hate'; then indeed the long illusion of perfect understanding is abruptly broken. For a moment—if only for a moment—we are utterly estranged. Such horrors do not bear imagining. We hasten on.

We listen with delight to the liberalism of the Funeral Speech of Pericles, or the charm of Plato's *Symposium*; yet this same brilliant Athens was fatuous enough to take the evidence of slaves under torture, ferocious enough, at times, to massacre the males of conquered cities with the ruthlessness of Himmler. Men are not easy to understand.

We may picture the hero of Agincourt as a type of medieval chivalry—gay prince and knightly king. Yet at the siege of Rouen, for instance, this knightly monarch could leave twelve thousand useless mouths expelled by the besieged to agonize, day after day, between his own lines and the walls, while under the bleak Christmas skies starving infants sucked their dead mothers' breasts, and starving mothers gave birth to doomed infants which were hauled up by ropes to the battlements to be baptized, then lowered again to die.

> War we had waged in other sort
> Upon the field of Agincourt
> On Crispin and Crispinian's day.

The more one knows of Shakespeare's hero-king, the less one really comprehends.[1]

Or there is the age of Shakespeare himself, and Sidney, and Spenser, so full of high aspiration, and courtly idealism, and elaborate art; which yet, by law, could punish malefactors with deaths as hideous as that of Melanthius, while men and women squeezed to watch the ghastly ritual of hanging, castration, and disembowel-

[1] I have tried to discuss this problem in *From Many Times and Lands*, pp. 171–83. For the siege of Rouen see Michelet, *Histoire de France*. Even if this account is overcoloured, there are other instances of Henry's iron ruthlessness.

ment. We imagine history a clear glass through which we see the past; too often it becomes a deceiving mirror giving back our own blurred reflections, our own distorted likenesses.

Yet historians and biographers seem to me constantly to forget this. Dr Emmet will dissect to his own satisfaction the most hidden motives of Charles V or Cæsar—yet show, it may be, very moderate powers of understanding his own colleagues and pupils. Professor Pismire may analyse the most secret machinations of Catherine de' Medici—and wake to find his own wife has run off to the Riviera with some more practical, if less profound, psychologist. Up and down the corridors of history pass Rosencrantz and Guildenstern, playing the 'recorder' with the bones of the dead—'you would seeme to know my stops; you would pluck out the heart of my Mysterie; you would sound mee from my lowest Note, to the top of my Compasse.... Why do you thinke, that I am easier to bee plaid on, then a Pipe?' Historians are seldom sceptical enough.

There is a well-known story that Sir Walter Raleigh once witnessed from his prison-window in the Tower some brawl in the courtyard below; then, discussing it later with a friend who had watched it likewise, was so staggered by their contradictory impressions of what had just happened under their own eyes, that he flung aside in despair his *History of the World*. The story, indeed, appears to be dubiously historical; but that too illustrates the doubts that cling to history.

'What will you read, child?' said Sir Robert Walpole to his son Horace. 'Some history?' 'No, don't read history to me; that *can't* be true!' 'History,' echoes Horace Walpole in his turn, 'is a romance that is believed; romance, a history that is not believed.' Even Wellington was goaded by the legends that quickly gathered round Waterloo, to exclaim—'I begin to believe I was not there myself.'[1] Even the omniscient Macaulay knew moments of chilling doubt:

> That Science is a blind man's guess
> And History a nurse's tale.

Henry Ford, passing beyond doubt, dismissed all history with

[1] There are modern biographies that provoke those who knew the originals personally, to the same cry of humorous despair.

one curt, contemptuous monosyllable.[1] More polished, but still more pessimistic, is the view of Valéry: 'L'Histoire est le produit le plus dangereux que la chimie de l'intellect ait élaboré.... Il fait rêver, il enivre les peuples, leur engendre de faux souvenirs, exagère leurs réflexes, entretient leurs vieilles plaies, les conduit au délire des grandeurs ou à celui de la persécution, et rend les nations amères, superbes, insupportables, et vaines.'

Considering the curse that nationalism has become, even this may not be overdrawn. And we have seen what Marxists make of history. 'Not God Himself,' said the Greek tragedian, 'can make the past undone.' But in Russia they do it every few years.

Perhaps if we knew more of the past, we should not think we knew so much; if we understood it better, we might cease to hope to understand it.

I stress these uncertainties of history because it seems to me essential, for honesty, to preserve the 'mitigated scepticism' of that great and honest thinker, Hume. I do not wish to overstress them. Hume himself wrote history. But I emphasize them here at the outset because one cannot put 'perhaps' or 'I think' or 'I feel' in every sentence. I merely wish to make clear that, though I may sometimes seem to speak dogmatically, I presuppose, from first to last, the vanity of all dogmatizing.

Such doubts apply particularly to that generalizing kind of history which tries to seize the spirit of a whole period. No two individuals since the human race began have ever been exactly alike; great men are still less like their fellows, or we should not call them 'great'; how then, it may be asked, can one talk to any purpose about the spirits of whole ages?

Certainly it is difficult and dangerous. For example, our shelves groan with works on the spirit of the Renaissance; yet now we are asked to doubt if the Renaissance ever existed. A few years ago endless twaddle was talked and printed about 'Victorianism'. For many of the young it became an article of faith that the England of the old Queen was almost wholly populated with Mr Pecksniffs and Mrs Grundys. 'Was he a fraud?' an Oxford youth asked Neville Cardus, with reference to Dr W. G. Grace; 'I fancy there is a bit of fraud in all the Victorians.' Are we to suppose that Dr Grace

[1] 'Bunk.'

bribed the bowlers? 'Nobody living to-day', said W. J. Turner, '—and I deliberately choose the word *living* and not the word *surviving*—has much sympathy with the Victorian age.' Sweeping criticism of this type—like much other criticism—throws less light on the subject than on the critic himself. A light not always impressive.

The eighteenth century, for the moment, is less out of favour than the nineteenth. It is easy enough to form nostalgic visions of an Enlightenment where all was good sense and good taste; where, in Talleyrand's phrase, 'la douceur de vivre' was enjoyed by exquisite marquises and elegant philosophes to the strains of Mozart. But that too is not history.

Indeed, I can well imagine an objector growling: 'You talk of "the eighteenth-century mind". But a century does not have a mind —it has millions of minds—all changing year by year, day by day, hour by hour. The spirit of an age no more exists than the Cock Lane Ghost; and attempts to evoke it are mere table-turning for intellectuals.

'You are asking us,' such a critic might continue, 'to idealize the eighteenth century, or perhaps its latter half. But this is merely the old dream of golden ages, sometimes in the past, sometimes in the future; though they are really to be found only at the foot of the rainbow.

'It has become common enough to romanticize the age of neo-classicism:

Comme vous meurtrissez les cœurs
De vos airs charmants et moqueurs
    Et si tristes,
Menuets à peine entendus,
Sanglots légers, rires fondus,
    Baisers tristes![1]

Your old music, how it stings us!
Charming, mocking—yet it brings us
    Bitterness.
Minuets with cadence dying,
Echoed laugh and whispered sighing,
    Tear and kiss.

[1] Fernand Gregh.

'The same frail delicacy could haunt and sadden even the boisterousness of Browning, as the phantom fingers of Galuppi[1] glided up and down the clavichord:

> Was a lady such a lady, cheeks so round and lips so red,
> On her neck the small face buoyant, like a bell-flower on its bed,
> O'er the breast's superb abundance where a man might base
> his head? . . .
>
> Yes, you, like a ghostly cricket, creaking where a house was
> burned:
> 'Dust and ashes, dead and done with, Venice spent what Venice
> earned.
> 'The soul, doubtless, is immortal—where a soul can be
> discerned.'

'Yet consider,' my objector might add, 'the odious horrors, squalors, and brutalities of your "Age of Reason"—the villagers uprooted by Enclosure Acts; the first pallid victims of the Industrial Revolution herding already into their slums; Governments of cynical place-hunting and brazen corruption; a sluggish and simoniacal Church[2]; indolent and port-swilling Universities[3]; a Navy

[1] Venetian composer (1706–85), particularly of light operas, often in collaboration with Goldoni; popular in England towards the middle of the century.

[2] Cf., for example, Horace Walpole on Edmund Keene, who became Master of Peterhouse, then Bishop of Chester: 'My father gave him a living of seven hundred pounds a year to marry one of his natural daughters: he took the living; and my father dying soon after, he dispensed with himself from taking the wife, but he was so generous as to give her very near one year's income of the living.' (She was reduced to penury, till Horace Walpole heard of her plight and supported her for the rest of her life.)

George Grenville, in his worldly wisdom, distinguished between 'bishoprics of business for men of abilities and learning', and 'bishoprics of ease for men of family and fashion'.

[3] In 1782 the German traveller Moritz sat tippling all night with a number of clerics at The Mitre, Oxford; as dawn approached, one of them, Mr Modd, exclaimed: 'D—n me, I must read prayers this morning at All Souls.'

In 1721, according to Amhurst's *Terrae Filius* (a scurrilous work, it is true), for three years no lectures had been given in any Oxford Faculty, except Poetry and Music; shortly before 1800, says A. D. Godley (*Oxford in the Eighteenth Century*), not more than one Oxford Professor in three ever lectured.

Chesterfield suggests to his son that he might like to become 'Greek Professor at one of our Universities'. 'It is a very pretty sinecure, and requires very little know-where press-ganged wretches, with teeth dropping out from scurvy, gnawed putrid salt meat and weevilly biscuit[1]; an Army no less brutal and far less efficient[2]; a law still more asinine than now, which, often for offences we should not think even worth prosecuting, sent its victims in crowds to the gallows, or in coffin-ships to the colonies[3]. Remember your own Johnson's words, in his hideous picture of London:

> Scarce can our fields, such crowds at Tyburn die,
> With hemp the gallows and the fleet supply.

'Imagine that London with its seventeen thousand gin-shops

ledge (much less than, I hope, you have already) of that language' (January 15, 1748). At this date Philip Stanhope was fifteen!

But not everything can have been so bad. Johnson, for example, always loved Oxford.

For Cambridge, see pp. 12-13.

[1] E.g., for his famous voyage round the world (1740–44) Anson was allotted 500 Chelsea Pensioners, 'the most decrepid and miserable objects,' most of them at least sixty, some over seventy; only 259 were got on board; the rest deserted. (One wretch with a wooden leg is said to have been dragged to the place of embarkation three times over.) A year later, after rounding Cape Horn, *Centurion*, *Gloucester*, and *Tryal* had only 335 men left alive out of 961. 'If blood be the price of admiralty. . . .'

[2] We hear of a soldier, under George II, receiving 30,000 lashes in sixteen years—'yet the man is hearty and well' (which leaves me sceptical). Such things may remind us that the eighteenth century, which we think of as polished, and at times even effeminate, in figures like Lord Hervey, Horace Walpole, Cowper, Jane Austen's Mr Woodhouse ('An egg boiled very soft is not unwholesome'), could yet be incredibly tough.

Again, the expedition, in which Hume took part, to besiege Lorient (1746) sailed with no maps except a small one of all France, which the General's aide-de-camp managed to pick up in a Plymouth shop.

[3] Two hundred offences were capital—even stealing a handkerchief; yet attempted murder was not. If one was *seen* stealing from a shop, one was transported; if not seen, hanged. Yet this judicial butchery became a topic for jokes. It was remarked that nothing got cheaper, except human life; and the hanging judge, Sir Francis Page (who tried Savage for murder—see Johnson's *Savage*), being asked in 1741, at the age of eighty, how he was, could sardonically reply—'My dear sir, you see I keep *hanging on*, *hanging on*.' Burke, leaving the House, was once asked by the Clerk to stay—'What business?'—'Oh, sir, it is *only* a new capital felony.'

Rogers *said* that he recalled seeing a whole cartful of young girls bound for Tyburn after the Gordon Riots, and that Greville heard several boys sentenced to the same fate—'Never did I see boys cry so.' Of twenty-one rioters executed, it seems seventeen were under eighteen years old, three under fifteen. See Yale edition of Horace Walpole, xxix, 75.

"drunk a penny, dead-drunk for twopence"[1]; turn over the engravings of Hogarth, or the novels of Smollett; and then, because your ugly, unwashed Johnson talked as insatiably as he guzzled gallons of tea, or your sleek Gibbon scribbled over declining Rome while scamping his duties at the Board of Trade, or your plutocratic Voltaire capered and sniggered in his manor of Ferney, spin your idealistic phrases about "the eighteenth-century mind". And do not forget to illustrate its graces with the endearments lavished on his daughter by Squire Western, in language that would to-day bring blushes from a drunken bargee; or with the refinements of Burke's queenly Marie Antoinette who, amid the glitter and polish of Versailles, could laugh aloud before her court at a courtier's breaking wind!'[2]

So far as they go—and they certainly go far—such objections are perfectly rational. And I own that there come chill moments of misgiving, as one reads of the darker side, the squalors and horrors, of that brilliant world—moments when I ask myself whether all the good sense and urbanity and grace that I love and admire in it are merely the blue enchantment of distance on a range of hills that prove, on closer approach, to bear indeed a few noble trees, but are otherwise full only of stunted scrub, straggling weeds, broken bottles, scummy pools, and diseased rabbits.

But *that* I cannot believe. When I am beset by doubts whether it makes sense to speak at all of the spirit of an age, or whether our neo-classic age was really, at its best, a period of reason and dignity, of poise and grace, in certain ways unequalled since, then I call to mind the view from the Bridge of King's.[3]

[1] It appears that in some East End parishes the infant-mortality reached 100 per cent; and that at the worst of the gin-orgy London burials doubled the baptisms.

[2] Cf. Queen Caroline's message to Sir Robert Walpole, when he had passed the Civil List, that 'the fat bitch' (as she knew he had called her) 'had forgiven him'. The ladies of Versailles, complained Mrs Thrale, 'hawk and spit . . . without the least attention to delicacy.' Or again there is Lady Louisa Stuart's description of Johnson's aristocratic friend, Topham Beauclerk, great-grandson of Charles II and Nell Gwyn, as 'what the French call "cynique" in personal habits beyond what one could have thought possible in any one but a beggar or a gypsy'—when he stayed at Blenheim, all the company were as plagued with lice as the Egyptians; to the unspeakable distress of the ladies with their elaborate head-dresses. 'What,' said Beauclerk, 'are they as nice as that comes to? Why, I have enough to stock a parish.'

[3] See frontispiece.

For if you stand on King's Bridge, you will see about you buildings that embody the diverse spirits of no less than six English centuries—a visible chronicle in characters of stone.

North-eastward, high above the rest, towers King's Chapel—slowly perfected through six reigns and seventy years (1446–1515), while the stormy sunset of the Middle Ages passed into the stormy dawn of the Renaissance, the England of Henry VI and Margaret of Anjou into the very different England of Henry VIII and Anne Boleyn.[1]

To the classic eye the Chapel exterior may not be wholly happy—too like a gigantic tithe-barn embellished with Gothic prickles or, as a cruder criticism once put it, an inverted sow with legs in air; but, as with its saintly founder, the true beauty lives within.

To west of it stands, in contrast, the quieter grace of the seventeenth century—not towering heavenward, but brooding over the tranquil stream beneath—the College and the Bridge of Clare. Clare Bridge (*c.* 1639–40) recalls the darkening years of a more dubious saint than the founder of King's—that perplexed and shifty person whom his enemies called 'the man Charles Stuart'; and Clare College building, like King's College Chapel a century and a half before, had a long and painful birth amid the throes of civil war. Indeed some of its building materials were seized by the Roundheads to strengthen Cambridge Castle. But to-day, while Cambridge Castle (as old Fuller puts it) 'may seem to have run out of the gatehouse', leaving behind it only a grass-grown mound, Clare still keeps that balanced composure it finally completed in the early eighteenth century, when the last of our erratic Stuart kings had fled across the water, and the Revolution of '88 had ushered in a taciturn Dutchman and a century of sense.[2]

Clare does not strain after grandeur. It does not strive nor cry. But it is gracefully satisfying—as true an embodiment, to me, of one side of the late Renaissance as King's Chapel of the late Middle

[1] Her initials are still discoverable, with some difficulty, here and there among the ubiquitous 'HR's of her husband, on the wooden screen between Chapel and Antechapel. Did her royal daughter, one wonders, notice those traces of bygone tragedy when she sat in King's Chapel to be entertained with plays in 1564?

[2] The east range of Clare is dated *c.* 1638–40; the south range (conspicuous from King's Bridge) belongs to *c.* 1640–42; the north range to *c.* 1683–90; and the west range, begun in 1640, was not finished till 1715.

Age. It brings to mind, not the giant imaginings of the blinded Milton, but rather the neat Herrick, the lovable Dorothy Osborne, the snug, yet musical Pepys, the balanced Halifax, the calm Locke. It has what Herrick loved—'civility'. The shocks of the Civil War have not marred its reposeful lines. Those giants, that Flood, are gone; beside the sleepy glide of its waters, Clare rests like a deftly chiselled, neatly dovetailed, peaceful Ark.

And now a new dynasty arrived from Hanover. South-east of the seventeenth-century charm of Clare, the eighteenth century raised in its turn a fabric, not less harmonious, but prouder, more dignified, more august—as different in spirit as Chatham from Halifax, or Gibbon from Locke.

Only four years had passed since the bursting of the South Sea Bubble; but, in an England steadied by the grasp of that sound and solid Kingsman, Robert Walpole, his college found itself rich enough to begin, with James Gibbs[1] for architect, the magnificence of the Fellows' Building.

On March 25, 1724, after a special sermon and a special anthem, its foundation-stone was laid by Andrew Snape, Provost of King's and Vice-chancellor, in the presence of Noblemen, Heads of Houses, and other members of the University. Yet one figure was missing—the most famous figure of eighteenth-century Cambridge—the great Aristarch, Richard Bentley, Master of Trinity. For six years he had been deprived of all his degrees, and reduced to the status of an undergraduate. And though a *mandamus* from the Court of King's Bench had now ordered his reinstatement, this was cunningly delayed till the day after the foundation. The Grace rehabilitating Bentley was not passed by the Senate till March 26. At least they had barred the ogre from the ceremony at King's.

That too is typical. For it is a vulgar error that the Age of Reason excluded violent passions. It was not so dull.

With its no less typical Greek pediments (originally meant to hold sculptures) and its massive Roman garlands, this Fellows' Building of Gibbs presented an audacious contrast to put within

[1] James Gibbs, by origin a Roman Catholic Jacobite from Aberdeen; in Rome, 1704–9; architect of St. Mary-le-Strand (1714–23), St. Martin-in-the-Fields (1722–6), Senate House at Cambridge (1722–30), Fellows' Building at King's (1724–c. 1732), Radcliffe Library, Oxford (1738–48), etc.

a few feet of the Gothic of King Henry VI's Chapel. Yet even here the English mind worked typically. Its tradition might have changed: yet it cherished tradition.[1] For the foundation-stone of Gibbs's Building, it is said, was a block left half-sawn by the dismayed builders of the Chapel, two and a half centuries earlier, when they downed tools and fled at the news that good King Henry had lost his throne. And if the male splendour of this eighteenth-century pile contrasts also, though less violently, with the more feminine delicacy of seventeenth-century Clare, yet here too there was still continuity—for Gibbs had learnt from the greatest of our seventeenth-century architects—Sir Christopher Wren.[2]

'All this', some may grumble, 'is a lot about architecture. What bearing has it on life, or on the subject? Can these dry stones live?' Yes, I think, they not only live—they speak. They bear witness. There is truth in that poetic title borne by some medieval architect —'magister de vivis lapidibus'—'the master of living stones'. In the masonry of Gibbs', and the Senate House, and hundreds of other English and European buildings from that age, there still *lives* a dignity, an order, a restrained sense of proportion, that modern taste, I feel, has largely lost. They speak for their age as the Parthenon for the grace of Greece, the Pont du Gard for the iron resolution of Rome. These things are civilized. If we are tempted at moments into doubt or disillusion about the eighteenth century, because much of it seems crass, or gross, or dull, let us look back at what it could build. Such things are far from speaking the whole truth; but they speak true.

That century was by no means at its best in our Universities. Gibbon, Gray, Gunning, and many more have left bitter or ludicrous pictures of academic sloth, decadence, and corruption—dumb dogs and unfed sheep. 'Surely', groans Gray in 1736, 'it was of this place, now Cambridge, but formerly known by the name of Babylon, that the prophet spoke when he said, "The wild beasts of the desert shall dwell there, and their houses shall be full of doleful creatures, and owls shall build there, and satyrs shall dance there;

[1] Gibbs thought King's Chapel 'a beautiful building of the Gothic taste, but the finest I ever saw' (a revealing 'but').

[2] Wren himself was approached for plans in 1712; two models were made by Wren's assistant, Hawksmoor; the second of these was taken as a basis by Gibbs.

their forts and towers shall be a den for ever, a joy of wild asses." '[1] And again, seventeen years later, in 1751, Gray warns a Dr Wharton who proposed settling in Cambridge—'You are aware undoubtedly, that a certain Deference, not to say Servility, to the Heads of Colleges is perhaps necessary to a Physician, that means to establish himself here. . . . Another Inconvenience your Wife, rather than you, will feel, the Want of Company of her own Sex; as the Women are few here, squeezy and formal, and little skill'd in amusing themselves or other People. All I can say is, she must try to make up for it among the Men, who are not over-agreeable neither.'[2]

And yet again, pointing out to Wharton the comfortable security, for his nephew, of gaining a King's fellowship for life, Gray adds ominously: 'You must remember, what a thing a fellow of King's is'.[3] Or, if verse is preferred, there is that couplet of Christopher Smart:

> Even gloomiest Kingsmen, pleas'd awhile,
> Grin horribly a ghastly smile.

A letter of the time[4] gives a lively picture of what it could be like, in those days, to elect a Provost of King's—how the Fellows spent over thirty hours on end, in the biting January of 1743, wrangling like a Papal Conclave in the unwarmed Chapel; till at last the two Whig factions combined to down the intransigent Tories. An eye-witness describes the scene there at 2 a.m.—'some wrapped in blankets, erect in their stalls like mummies; others, asleep on cushions, like so many Gothic tombs. Here a red cap over a wig; there a face lost in the cape of a rug. One blowing a chafing dish with a surplice sleeve; another warming a little negus, or sipping Coke upon Littleton, i.e. tent[5] and brandy. Thus did they combat the cold of that frosty night; which has not killed any one of them, to my infinite surprize.'

Gross and grotesque old phantoms, far removed from any Chesterfieldian graces. To tell the truth, the eighteenth century

[1] To West, December 1736.
[2] October 10, 1751.
[3] June 23, 1761.
[4] C. H. Cooper, *Annals of Cambridge*, iv, 244.
[5] A kind of Spanish wine.

was seldom sublime, and quite often ridiculous. And yet, for all its grossness and grotesqueness, a spirit of grace was in the land. Even that queer Cambridge—this is the miracle—has bequeathed us Gibbs' and the Senate House—things, I feel, that put the modern buildings of Cambridge, for all its modern knowledge, completely to shame. Life is extremely odd.

But let us not over-idealize. Gibbs's Building is typical also in its drawbacks—and becomes thereby only the better symbol. With its aristocratic dignity goes also a certain aristocratic chill. How cold its lofty rooms could be, like eighteenth-century peers, until at last, only a few years back, central heating came! The builders of King's Chapel thought more of its interior, where God should be glorified, than of the exterior they showed the world; Gibbs, on the contrary, sacrificed something of inner use and comfort to external magnificence.[1] His building is less a thing to love, perhaps, than to admire. As late as 1750 William Cole was complaining (perhaps with exaggeration) that, during the sixteen years he had lived in it, half its other rooms had stood empty, because the Fellows found all this sumptuous pomp less attractive than the humbler and homelier King's Old Court (north of the Chapel, on the present site of the University Offices. For it must be recalled that the College has performed the athletic feat of jumping right over its Chapel, from north to south).

And so William Cole, antiquarian that he was, felt moved to wonder if something more Gothic might not have been better. Think, and shudder! Imagine, in place of Gibbs', a piece of eighteenth-century 'Gothick'—a first cousin of Strawberry Hill!

But though we may smile at poor Cole, he was being prophetic. Fully to appreciate Gibbs and the eighteenth century, it is worth lingering a moment longer on King's Bridge, to glance at what later ages have achieved. For the work of the two and a half centuries since the Fellows' Building provides a curious contrast to the work of the two and a half centuries before. By its own efforts, and by Royal Commissions, the University may have been

[1] Even so, the actual fabric is less grandiose than Gibbs's design, which has dozens of statues reclining on the pediments or standing along the roof-balustrades; and his plan for a hall facing the Chapel, fronted with a vast pedimented portico of eight Corinthian columns over forty feet high, would have been, I feel, overpowering.

wonderfully reformed and improved; but hardly its architecture.

In 1823, all but a hundred years had passed, mellowing, over the stonework of Gibbs; Keats and Shelley were just dead; but Gothic Romanticism was very much alive. And now Wilkins came.

His nightmare idea of Gothicizing Gibbs's Building remained, luckily, for us, a dream. But to south-west of it Wilkins erected a Gothic Provost's Lodge, with the usual buckram turrets and pasteboard crenellations. His Hall on the other hand remains, in most eyes, a success. But, for me, he was less happily inspired to link his own imitation Gothic to the genuine Gothic of the Founder's chapel by a screen bristling with large stone pepper-pots.[1]

Here, however, it is hardly for the twentieth century to look down its nose at the nineteenth. It has not mended matters much. To the Victorian dullness and mediocrity of Webb's Court it has added a not unpleasant new Provost's Lodge, but also an arid hexagon of knobbly cobbles, where seven squirts of water counterfeit a fountain; and, atop of the College kitchen, a thing like a miniature bandstand, where the Fellows if they chose—but they have never chosen—might conduct Platonic dialogues while snuffing, like ancient deities, the sweet savour of the dinners cooking beneath them, behind a grille symbolically embellished with a single gilt pineapple. Small things; yet typical, in their lack of all sense, or point, or grace. To westward our age has allowed the Backs, where after the First War the nightingales still sang, to become a motor-packed highway, where night is made garish by the City Council with cadaverous sodium-lighting. And, beyond, it has planted a College Hostel in the familiar brick-box style of a war-bled, impoverished generation.[2]

For ours is an age of common men and connoisseurs; and between them, the arts fare ill. Yet, after all, it is unreasonable to expect the arts to be always at their best. The arts cannot rise steadily upward,

[1] In fairness to Wilkins I should add that his work is far more favourably judged by the wise Professor Pevsner (*Cambridgeshire*, 1954).

[2] At this point, however, having allowed myself freely to criticize, I feel bound to add, however inadequately, a word on the other side. Human beings matter even more than buildings. And if King's College seems to me to have failed since 1800 (more by the fault of the age than its own) to maintain the architectural beauty of its earlier centuries, yet never in my experience of half a lifetime has it declined for one moment from that tradition of humanism, tolerance, and freedom in which I believe it unsurpassed throughout the Universities of the world.

like the sciences, on the accumulations of the past. Rather they dance; sometimes divinely, sometimes—as De Quincey describes Wordsworth skating—'like a cow dancing a cotillon'.

But however that may be, I do not think it would be easy to find a group of buildings that symbolize so significantly, in so compact a space, something of the spirits of six centuries. It is worth going to look—perhaps on some evening when the late sun burns reflected in the windows of Gibbs'. There in the Chapel brood the mystery and poetry of the Middle Ages; there in Clare and Gibbs' endures the different grace of *this* world, of good sense and measure and balance—as if, like Ibsen's Master Builder, the architectural genius of the race had here turned from building churches for God to building homes for happy—sometimes happy—men.

Other arts might have served as well to typify the finer side of the Enlightenment—paintings by Reynolds or Gainsborough, music by Handel and Haydn, Gluck and Mozart. But music or pictures cannot stand before us in that striking and permanent contrast with the work of other times, which makes these pieces of architecture symbols unsurpassed. True, all such symbols are imperfect; they only reflect one or two of a multiplicity of aspects. Yet, provided we remember that imperfection, how much life they can add to ideas! A symbol can at least be concrete—something tangible and vivid, amid the fogs of abstraction, the drone of verbiage. Do not let us despise symbols. They can possess strange power—like that statue of Strasbourg in the Place de la Concorde which for half a century after 1871 received from French hands its faithful tribute of flowers, although above Alsace-Lorraine there flapped the eagle-standard of the German Reich.

To say that buildings like Clare or Gibbs' are 'typical', in their grace and dignity, their clarity and proportion, of the neo-classic age, is of course ambiguous. To call a quality 'typical' may mean either that it is common among people or things of a given kind (as good humour seems typical of the English); or it may mean merely that this quality is less uncommon there than elsewhere. It would be a false and flattering view of the eighteenth century to suppose that the qualities of a Reynolds or a Mozart were common then. Such qualities are never common. And yet work like that of

Reynolds or Mozart, Montesquieu or Voltaire, Johnson or Gibbon *is* 'typical' of its age in the sense that one can say at sight, even without knowing the author, '*That* must be eighteenth-century'. Indeed it is a very curious thing about periods in general that, however violently contemporary writers and artists may often loathe or despise one another, in after-ages the critic can generally date their work at a glance. Despite their wranglings, the stamp of their period somehow rests upon them all.

Now the stamp of any period may be largely moulded by vast impersonal forces; but I suspect that it is also largely determined by a few thousands, or ten thousands, of that period's finer personalities, by a few dozens or hundreds of its really original minds. The full charm and grace, courage and intelligence, of the Enlightenment may have been confined to a happy few. But these are here my concern. Their qualities are what really matters to us, the living. For from them we may still learn; where we can only pity the suffering millions of that, as of other ages, who sleep now in an obscurity dim even to the most searching historian. How few, comparatively, those happy few were, they sometimes realized themselves. 'Quelques avantages,' wrote Diderot's clever friend, the German Grimm, 'que nous attribuions à notre siècle, on voit qu'ils ne sont que pour un petit nombre d'élus, et que le petit peuple n'y participe jamais.' But, for us, it is not the smallness of that élite which matters; it is the fact that they existed at all.

Of what they gave their age I know no better summary than that by J. L. and Barbara Hammond, in their *Village Labourer*:[1] 'A row of eighteenth-century houses, or a room of normal eighteenth-century furniture, or a characteristic piece of eighteenth-century literature, conveys at once a sense of satisfaction and completeness. The secret of this charm is not to be found[2] in any special beauty or nobility of design or expression, but simply in an exquisite fitness. The eighteenth-century mind was a unity, an order; it was finished, and it was simple. All[3] literature and art that really belong to the eighteenth century are the language of a little society

[1] Chapter XII.

[2] It might be safer to say, 'is *often* not to be found'. For, even if we ignore eighteenth-century music, surely there is beauty at times in Pope, Gray, or Goldsmith; nobility in Gray, Burke, or Vauvenargues?

[3] 'Much' might be more prudent than 'all'.

of men and women who moved within one set of ideas; who understood each other; who were not tormented by any anxious or bewildering problems; who lived in comfort, and, above all things, in composure. The classics were their freemasonry.'

This graceful picture applies much more, I think, to the second half of the century than to the first, to the Age of Gibbon than to the Age of Swift; parts of it seem to me put too strongly; none the less it is admirably put. Nor is it the praise of a blind, uncritical partiality; it comes at the end of a book devoted to the wrongs inflicted by this polished society on the eighteenth-century villager.

But whether we accept this picture or not; whether we believe that an age has a spirit, or many spirits, or none at all; in any case for those who have not been processed by the whirl of modern life into automata, or mashed by modern politics into some totalitarian lump, what matters ultimately is the individual. And so my main concern is less with generalities about Johnson's age than with the definite characteristics of a few very definite characters in it. And my motive is not merely that curiosity which provides the only impulse for much history and much science.

Curiosity, no doubt, is precious. It can keep men alive who would otherwise—whether buried or not—be dead of ennui; just as the old Mercier said, 'I go on living to see what will become of Napoleon'. All the same, surely life grows rather a poor business when it is reduced to an Old Curiosity Shop.

For Johnson, books were trash unless they helped their readers 'better to enjoy life, or better to endure it'. It is a little mournful to consider, as week by week one reads one's *Times Literary Supplement*, how many books fail to do either. Yet Johnson seems to me profoundly right. Others, indeed, like Housman, have held a mystical faith about learning, which denies any distinction between useful and useless knowledge,[1] and believes any grain of fact, how-

[1] Johnson himself, on occasion, could suggest the same (Boswell, ii, 357); but it was the reverse of his usual view; and he was not always equally wise. He has recorded a curious example of futile investigation in Dr and Mrs Kennedy, who were living in Derbyshire about 1774 and 'were employed as Dr Johnson told me for near 42 long years in the same Study' [computation of the exact season of the creation of the world]. 'My eldest Daughter, then precisely ten Years old, said they looked like Baucis & Philemon, and so they did.' (Note by Mrs Thrale; see Hill-Powell, Boswell's *Johnson*, i, 547.)

ever boring or trifling, to be somehow precious in itself. But, much as I admire Housman, I cannot admire this sort of mysticism. Modern man is daily more in danger of drowning amid the multitudinousness of modern occupations, of modern knowledge, even of modern amusements. Part of the composure of the educated in the eighteenth century came, I suspect, from their power still to digest what was known; but, since then, men have become increasingly plagued with mental dyspepsia. Perhaps our posterity may one day wonder as much at the excess of superfluities we cram into our heads, as we wonder now at the excess of superfluities our ancestors crammed into their bellies. Many of them over-ate: many of us over-read. Few moderns are good mental economists; given the limited capacity of human memory, the limited length of human life, it becomes ever more vital to select; and to find a principle of selection. For to-day more than ever, any person of sense must constantly cry out, like the wise old Cynic at the fair, 'Immortal Gods, what a mass of things that Diogenes does *not* need!' Knowledge too includes a large and crowded Vanity Fair.

It seems to me, then, mere common sense never to undertake a piece of work, or read a book, without asking, 'Is it worth the amount of life it will cost?'; never to pursue any kind of knowledge (apart from practical necessities) without demanding, 'Will it make life more vivid, more intelligent, more complete, more real?' Then one has at least some principle to simplify existence, instead of emulating La Fontaine's dogs who, seeing an appetizing dead mule afloat offshore, tried drinking up the sea to get it—and burst.

It is said that the Emperor Tiberius used to tease scholars by asking them abstruse and futile questions such as the name of Hecuba's mother. (She was, it appears, the dimmest of dim creatures, called Metope.) What was Hecuba to him? Nothing, except an occasion for pedantry. It would doubtless have been suicidal for the scholars to retort to that irritable potentate, 'What does Hecuba's mother matter?' Yet it is important, I think, to keep asking oneself precisely that question, alike in life and in learning. For the learned world is overpopulated with Hecuba's mothers. Nine Ph.D. dissertations in ten are written about her. Her children are Legion; and most of them abortive. It is fatal to get wedded to her; she is both phantom and vampire.

I believe that one should be as difficult about what one admits to one's brain as the American authorities about whom they admit to the United States. To be curious about nothing is to be nearly dead; to be curious about too few things, is to be narrow; to be curious about too many, is to be shallow. The kind of general-knowledge questions beloved by some schoolmasters and journalists are often so pointless, that credit should really go, not to those who know the answers, but to those who do not.[1] Odd details, indeed, can often be delightful; but they must be really odd—and illuminating.[2] Does a book contain even a dozen new facts, or ideas, that will be permanently, and valuably, mine? Excellent! I will go miles for it. But how seldom that happens! 'Wisdom is the principal thing, therefore get wisdom: and with all thy getting get understanding.'

Men like Johnson, Boswell, Goldsmith, Hume, Burke, or Benjamin Franklin are not only fascinating to try to understand; they raise fascinating problems. How far were their lives successful experiments in the art of living? How far not? And why?

No doubt there are many people who dislike and distrust such questions—who hold it impossible, in spite of Johnson, both 'to point a moral' and 'to adorn a tale'. But I cannot see why; provided one does not overdo the moral, or distort the tale. Morals seem to me one of the few topics interesting enough to discuss with zest till two in the morning.

In Western Europe the eighteenth century, like the later part of the twentieth, followed on a ghastly era of wars and revolutions, fanaticisms and ferocities. In consequence, just as severe illness can stimulate an organism to a new strength of resistance, many

[1] One may recall the comment of W. H. Thompson (1810–86), Fellow and later Master of Trinity, to a colleague, Ederson, who had proved ignorant of some triviality —'Oh, I should have thought that unimportant enough to have engaged your attention.' (Whether this snub was deserved, I know not; it certainly proved unwise. For the resentful Ederson revenged himself by searching the statutes, and finding that Thompson had broken them in holding both a Fellowship at Trinity and the Regius Professorship of Greek.)

[2] Unlike the kind of detail that makes some modern books interminable. What pleasure is there, for example, and what profit, in learning that George Washington's epileptic step-daughter Patsy, who vanished from life, poor girl, at seventeen, received at the age of six 'one pair of pack-thread stays', and at twelve 'a toy tea-canister', price one shilling? At this rate one soon fills six volumes.

minds of the Enlightenment acquired a perfect passion for good sense, moderation, balance, order, and intellectual honesty, such as had never, I think, been so prevalent since ancient Greece; and has never, I think, since the coming of Romanticism, been so prevalent again. There is, to me, something most remarkable in their enthusiasm against 'enthusiasm'—or what we should call 'fanaticism'. In human history it is lamentably rare.

For one of the first things Man did when he acquired an intelligence was, it seems, to invent ways of fuddling it with intoxicants. And he has continued to do so ever since. But the worst intoxicants do not come out of bottles. Hitler, for example. And certain periods, such as parts of the Middle Ages, the middle of the seventeenth century, or the first half of our own, have produced mental reelings and ravings that might have horrified Noah, the inventor of wine, and sobered even Dionysus, the god of it.

It might have been hoped that, after what we have gone through in the last fifty years, we should be ripe, by reaction, for something like another Age of Reason. The two World Wars came in part, like much modern literature and art, because men, whose nature is to tire of everything in turn, as the Athenians tired even of the goodness of Aristides, had tired of common sense and civilization;[1] by now they might have been expected to be a little tired of their opposites. There may be some faint signs of this: I wish there were more.

No doubt, from many aspects, the free world in the twentieth century is a vast advance on the eighteenth. There are enormously more justice, decency, health, and happiness, less needless misery, want, and pain, than ever before. Our science has progressed immeasurably. True, our literature and art have not—at least for me. But even so, though the films loved by the great public may be often tawdry, they are at least better than most eighteenth-century drama; and, mediocre (except in music) as the influence of radio and television may be, it is at all events more civilized than watching

[1] Cf., for example, Gauguin's panacea for the world—'rejuvenation through barbarism'; or the explanation given by Barrès for his nationalism—'le principal pour lui avait été de "mettre du charbon sous sa sensibilité qui commencait à fonctionner mollement" '; or Marinetti's idea that war would happily rid us of 'diplomats, professors, philosophers, archæologists, critics, cultural obsessions, Greek, Latin, history, senility, museums, libraries, and the tourist industry'.

eighteenth-century cockfights, pugilists, or hangings at Tyburn.

But when it comes to the happy few—to that intellectual minority which produces the thought and literature of an age—the comparison seems to me much less in our favour. With rare exceptions, such as Bertrand Russell or Somerset Maugham, the intellectuals of the last forty years seem to me far less sane and balanced, less intelligent and civilized, than some of their eighteenth-century predecessors.

One reason for this may be that the eighteenth-century élite, in an aristocratic world where the masses were still largely illiterate, and science had not yet become monstrously specialized, could feel themselves leaders of civilization, in the van of Progress. But to-day Demos is king; he pays the pipers, and calls the tunes—not normally tunes of much inspiration. One should not, I think, grudge this price of the Welfare State—better a few should wince than millions be galled; still one may regret it. To-day the intellectual minority tends to feel impotent and frustrated, ignored by the masses and dwarfed by the portentous growth of science; and thence to develop the vices common in dissident minorities—to become narrow, snobbish, hysterical, and split into jealous little warring factions, like eighteenth-century Jacobites or nineteenth-century French royalists. A hundred years ago Matthew Arnold denounced the literature of his day as 'fantastic and lacking in sanity'; he was, I think, rather prejudiced and premature; but he was curiously prophetic. Many minds, of course, enjoy the fantastic and the insane. That is a matter of taste; and therefore vain to argue over; but one *can* argue that, in the long run, the consequences of such pleasures are apt to be very far from pleasant.

However it is vain to lie awake at night about the state of the world. The course of the future, maybe, was all determined long ago, before the solar system was even formed. Meanwhile one has oneself to improve—usually a more practical and practicable undertaking. I have learnt much from eighteenth-century minds; better, no doubt, if I had learnt still more; and I should like, if possible, to help others to learn from them.

Dempster told Boswell that he had better be palsied at eighteen than miss the company of a man like Johnson. I should be extremely loth to be palsied at any age, for the company of anybody. Still, bating that picturesque exaggeration, I think Dempster not far wrong.

And here we come to the inestimable advantage of books. To keep company with the living Johnson, poor Mrs Thrale had to sit up night after night, dropping with drowsiness, and brew tea at four in the morning.[1] But, for us, the whim of a moment can call the buried Johnson, majestic yet docile, from the dead; with the push of a little finger he retires meekly to his shelf again; and one may go to bed, if one will, 'domestic as a plate,' at eight p.m. Reading, not rapping tables, is the true necromancy.

Let us summon him, then.

[1] 'Whoever thinks of going to bed before twelve o'clock', said Johnson, 'is a scoundrel.' (Hawkins.)

JOHNSON

Of the few innocent pleasures left to men past middle life, the jamming common-sense down the throats of fools is perhaps the keenest.

T. H. HUXLEY

AMONG all English writers, or in all English history and biography, or in all English fiction and drama, it may be doubted if there is any character that has more stamped itself on English memories than Johnson. There have been men with better brains, men who did bigger things, men who wrote greater books; but as a personality he has had, and is long likely to have, few rivals. English literature possesses many writers more original; but no more original character. Johnson remains what the French call—curiously enough, for it is the reverse of typical—'*un vrai type*'.

The personality of Byron, no doubt, may have been for a time more dominant. To Goethe, I suppose, comparison between Johnson and Byron would have seemed absurd. But to-day, though Byron still fascinates us as perhaps the nearest approach in real life to Milton's fallen archangel, in his pride and scorn, indignation and despair, yet Byron's verse-style has tarnished, his ideas have worn thin.

Even among the fictitious characters of our literature there are few that we know so well as Johnson, or find so gripping, so inexhaustible. The Wife of Bath has her portion of Johnson's robustness, frankness, and common sense; but compared with his vast variety, her twin passions for domineering and for amorousness leave her, mentally at least, a rather narrow figure. Falstaff has the charm, summed by Johnson in two admirable words, of 'perpetual gaiety'; Falstaff, like Johnson, is both realist and wit; yet beside Johnson he dwindles, after all, to a jolly, amusing, old roisterer. Hamlet himself is less vivid to many of us than the great Sam. My Uncle Toby and Dr Primrose are both adorable in their generous simplicity; but before Johnson's roaring solidity they fade like frail and gentle phantoms before the confident crowing of the cocks of dawn. Mr Micawber has a kind of ridiculous, pontificating wisdom, a grandiloquence hollow yet booming as a drum, which Dickens's father may have ultimately derived, in part, from the tradition of Johnson's *Rambler*; but Wilkins Micawber remains only a superb figure of fun. Johnson is more living than the liveliest figures of our fiction; and the strangest of them is less extraordinary.

But not only is Johnson one of the most cherished of English characters; he is also one of the most English. It is, you will find, not easy to acclimatize foreigners to him. They are apt to ask wonderingly what on earth we see in such a man. They do not understand what seems to them a sort of bear-worship. Johnson's influence has made no Grand Tour of Europe, like those of Pope or Byron. Only Sweden, so far as I know, has undertaken a full translation of Boswell's *Life*.[1] And Herr Gustav Radbruch in his essay on Johnson[2] frankly admits that, being shown a portrait of the sage at University College, Oxford, he had no notion who on earth he was; 'which, as I was later forced to recognize, is normally the case even with cultivated Germans'.

Not long since, I have been told (though this may be only gossip), some Russian emissary was entertained at Johnson's old college in Oxford. For his diversion they produced a sacred relic—'This is Dr Johnson's teapot.' They were a trifle surprised to see the Russian's face light up with sudden interest. Still, after all, *Rasselas* in its day was translated into Russian; and Muscovites might be expected to feel a special interest in bears. But the Russian's comment shattered their illusions. 'Ah!' said he, 'the Dean of Canterbury?' Very flattering for the Red Dean. Less flattering for the dons of Pembroke.

Similarly even in France; for the brilliant, though erratic Taine, Johnson is 'respectable et insupportable'. Taine cannot see that Johnson is also lovable. 'Nous demandons aux gens, ce qui peut leur plaire dans cet ours bourru, qui a des habitudes de bedeau et des inclinations de constable. On nous répond qu'à Londres on est moins exigeant qu'à Paris en fait d'agrément et de politesse, qu'on permet à l'énergie d'être rude et à la vertu d'être bizarre. . . . Reste à savoir quelles idées l'ont rendu populaire. C'est ici que l'étonnement d'un Français redouble. . . . Nous baîllons. Ses vérités sont trop vraies; nous savions d'avance ses préceptes par cœur. . . . Nous nous rappelons alors qu'en Angleterre les sermons plaisent.'

This taste for sermons is hardly conspicuous in the English of to-day. Yet our taste for Johnson persists. We still relish him both as a realist, and as an eccentric. That we should like his realism is

[1] Four volumes 1926–30; but apparently not completed.

[2] *Gestalten und Gedanken*, 1944.

natural enough. For the English still remain, I think, temperamentally practical, with all their ancestral distrust for theories and ideologies. Yet is it not a paradox that our conventionality should so enjoy his eccentricities?—eccentricities which outraged many of his contemporaries, and were deplored by many of his friends?

But this paradox seems to me only apparent. Just as the English, though often maddeningly prosaic, have produced an unsurpassed share of the world's poetry, and, though maddeningly unintellectual, have bred an unsurpassed share of the world's most impressive thinkers, so, though often maddeningly conventional, they have thrown up some of the world's most astonishing eccentrics. In all three cases the reason may be partly the same. The flora and fauna of deserts have to be uncommonly hardy to survive; but those which do survive are uncommonly hardy.

And just because we are so traditional and conservative, once an eccentric has established himself among us, he has a chance of becoming in his turn an institution, a tradition, an ancient monument, as much cherished by our conservatism as he was at first resented by our conventionality. (This is sometimes observable with the older inhabitants of University towns.)

Even in his lifetime Johnson had become such an institution. To foreigners he may seem grotesque as a Beefeater. But just try proposing to the English the abolition of Beefeaters!

Yet it is not merely that Johnson was himself remarkable; it is hardly less remarkable that we seem to know him so intimately. Horace Walpole, I think, wrote far better letters even than Johnson's; yet with Walpole we cannot feel quite the same intimacy. For even in letters a man's pen seldom runs as frankly and truly as his tongue. The letter-writer, even when he demands (how often in vain!) that his letters be burnt, can seldom have the casual talker's easy sense of speaking 'off the record'.

As Johnson himself well and wisely observes of Pope's too artificial correspondence, 'It has been so long said as to be commonly believed, that the true characters of men may be found in their letters, and that he who writes to his friend lays his heart open before him. But the truth is, that such were the simple friendships of the Golden Age, and are now the friendships only of children. Very few can boast of hearts which they dare lay open to themselves, and of which, by whatever accident exposed, they do not shun a distinct and continued view; and certainly what we hide from ourselves, we do not show to our friends. There is, indeed, no transaction[1] which offers stronger temptations to fallacy and sophistication than epistolary intercourse. In the eagerness of conversation the first emotions of the mind often burst out before they are considered; in the tumult of business, interest and passion have their genuine effect; but a friendly letter is a calm and deliberate performance in the cool of leisure, in the stillness of solitude, and surely no man sits down to depreciate by design his own character.'[2]

Journals or autobiographies might seem to offer more scope than letters for real intimacy. But even Montaigne, whose essays are so full of autobiography and who would have been quite happy, he said, to paint himself naked, is in some ways less vivid to us than Johnson, because we lack a real portrait of Montaigne by anyone else. Pepys, for all his charming garrulity as a diarist and his sterling worth as a public servant, remains a less remarkable person than Johnson, and far less remarkably illumined. And Rousseau, though an exhibitionist, was that particularly deceptive type of liar who lies, above all, to himself.

Curious, indeed, that one and the same period—the late eighteenth century—should have produced three of the figures we know best in all human history—Rousseau, Boswell, Johnson. But Boswell we know more intimately than Rousseau; for Rousseau was writing propaganda for publication, whereas Boswell wrote his journal at first for his friend Johnston, later for himself alone. Indeed, we know Boswell more intimately than we know even Johnson. Still most of our knowledge of Boswell comes from Boswell himself. Now it is hard for a man to portray himself at full-length. There is much of him that only his contemporaries can see. And Johnson stands portrayed for us both by himself, in his talk and writings, and by others, particularly Boswell, who observed him vividly in real life. Familiar talk, in fine, provided a man *can* talk,

[1] 'No transaction' seems a little strong.

[2] Boswell indeed, especially in his letters to Temple, often behaves, in his artless outspokenness, as if he had sat down with this very purpose of self-depreciation. He remains, however, an extreme exception. Letters in general, though they often reveal a great deal, do it to a large extent involuntarily, and only to the reader between the lines.

seems the most revealing medium of all. A journal lacks what Johnson calls, in the passage quoted above, 'the eagerness of conversation,' the 'first emotions' of the mind. Further, in Boswell there is less to know, less that seems worth knowing. He was a shallower personality. Often he revealed himself because he was too naïve to realize what others would think; but often Johnson did it because he cared not a rap what others thought.

Unfortunately the talk of great men is seldom preserved. We have, it is true, such books as Coleridge's *Table-talk*, or Goethe's conversations with Eckermann. But, even there, the talk is less well recorded than in Boswell's *Johnson*; and less worth recording.

Johnson, in short, was not only great, he was incredibly lucky. He not only had Reynolds to paint him, he had Boswell. And, beside Boswell, what is even Reynolds? And we too are incredibly lucky. It seems almost miraculous that one of the best talkers that ever lived should have chanced to encounter one of the best recorders of talk that ever lived—and to encounter him just at the right moment, when Johnson was fifty-three and Boswell twenty-two. For had Boswell been born, and died, earlier than Johnson, we should have missed those crowning years of leisure when the old man could at last fold his legs and talk. Had Boswell been an exact contemporary, or had Boswell lived all the time in London, his book might have grown too unwieldy. And had they never met at all, Johnson might well have remained to-day, instead of the still dominating figure of his century, a name less famous than the Sterne he disapproved, or the Gray he despised. Even Boswell was made by his *Corsica* more of a European name at twenty-eight than Johnson was even at seventy-five.

After all, Johnson produced no poetry equal to the *Elegy in a Country Churchyard*, no political utterances equal to Burke's. *A Journey to the Western Islands* cannot compete with *A Sentimental Journey*; nor *The Rambler* and *The Idler* with *The Spectator*; nor *Rasselas* with *The Vicar of Wakefield*; nor *Irene* with *She Stoops to Conquer* or *The School for Scandal.* Time has inevitably superseded Johnson's *Dictionary*, and his *Shakespeare*—though not its splendid Preface, nor *The Lives of the Poets*. Yet even these fine pieces of criticism probably interest most modern readers less for the light they throw on the poets criticized than for the light they throw on the critic. They interest us largely because of our interest in Johnson himself.

For he is an exception to the general rule that writers often seem not only oddly different from their books, but also markedly inferior to their books.[1] As Johnson himself has put it, with an image characteristically vivid: 'A transition from an author's book to his conversation is too often like an entrance into a large city, after a distant prospect. Remotely, we see nothing but spires of temples, and turrets of palaces, and imagine it the residence of splendour, grandeur, and magnificence; but when we have passed the gates, we find it perplexed with narrow passages, disgraced with despicable cottages, embarrassed with obstructions, and clouded with smoke.' But Johnson himself is still further remarkable, not only in being more intimately known to us than most writers, but in gaining, not losing, from that intimacy. Johnson impresses us by what he is, but still more by what he says. Take the talk out of Boswell's *Life*, and it would collapse like an animal deprived of its heart; take the talk out of Boswell's *Hebrides*, and it would be little superior to Johnson's own account of the same tour. Johnson is, above all, a dramatic character—the infinitely versatile protagonist of a series of dramatic scenes, where the distinguished figures of his day serve only, in Burke's phrase, to 'ring the bell to him'. Johnson in his armchair, or at table, rises far higher than Johnson at his desk.[2]

And as Johnson is more interesting than his works, so he is more interesting than the actions of his life. It was, indeed, no very exciting or eventful life. Like Shakespeare, he had for father a Midland tradesman who, after making some figure in his native place, came down in the world. Johnson was born at Lichfield on September 18, 1709, in a house with eleven bedrooms (of a kind); yet his inheritance, when his father died in 1731, was only twenty pounds.

[1] Addison, for example, shy and silent except with intimates, said of himself—'I have only ninepence in my pocket, but I can draw for a thousand pounds.' So, at times, with Goldsmith. So with Corneille; who, like some other poets, did not even know how to read his own verses.

[2] Contrast Horace Walpole's view of Hume, as so superior in his books to his talk 'that I frequently said he understood nothing till he had written upon it'. (A view, however, that I find hard to believe.) Whereas Hogarth thought Johnson as superior to other men in talk as Titian to Hudson in painting.

This father, Michael Johnson, bookseller and high-church Jacobite, was at the time of Samuel's birth Sheriff of Lichfield; a few years later he was humorously described as one who 'propagates learning all over this diocese . . . all the clergy here are his pupils'; but he is also less flatteringly recorded as given to vanity, wrong-headedness, and 'a vile melancholy'—in fine, to use his own son's blunt phrase, 'a foolish old man'. All his 'propagation of learning' failed to bring prosperity. 'He got something, but not enough.'

Johnson's physical burliness is familiar; but his father was even burlier; and his uncle Andrew, later a bookseller too, had for a year kept the ring in Smithfield, as unconquered in boxing and wrestling as his pugnacious nephew, half a century later, in the ring of conversation. Indeed, according to Mrs Thrale, 'Mr Johnson was very conversant in the art of attack and defence by boxing, which science he had learned from his uncle Andrew, I believe'.

Johnson's mother, Sarah Ford, was praised by him in a belated epitaph of 1784, as 'sprung from the ancient house of Ford', and 'eminent for acuteness of mind and subtlety of judgment'[1]; and credited by Boswell with a 'distinguished understanding'. But this was perhaps flattering. For, apart from birth, she seems to have been her husband's inferior, and no very happy wife. She wished, it appears, only to talk of her husband's affairs, and did so 'with complaint, fear, and suspicion'; whereas Michael Johnson loathed his affairs, and preferred books; of which his wife knew nothing. In short, 'they seldom conversed'. Her son loved, but did not respect, her—'one day, when in anger she called me a puppy, I asked her if she knew what they called a puppy's mother.' It appears that Johnson acquired at a tender age his lifelong gift for the 'countercheck quarrelsome'.

But in other ways the boy was burdened from birth. He had scrofula (tuberculosis of lymphatic glands, bones, and joints), which his mother thought inherited from her side, though it may have been caught from a nurse; and from his father, so Johnson himself believed, he inherited the still heavier curse of melancholia. He was also to acquire, perhaps as the child of a none too happy home, an acute obsessional neurosis. All his life he was to show those violent

[1] 'Antiqua Fordorum gente oriunda'—'mentis acumine et judicii subtilitate praecellentem.'

oscillations between wild gaiety and crippling gloom that mark the manic-depressive, who represses now his hopes, now his fears. These were ills past curing by the royal touch, in his third year, of poor Queen Anne.

In addition, he was deaf in his left ear, nearly blind in his left eye, and short-sighted in the other.[1] Hence his terse retort, when asked whether he were a botanist—'Sir, I must first turn myself into a reptile.' In fine, he did not know—so he told Hawkins—what it was to be totally free from pain; and in old age he wrote to Hector that, since twenty, his health had seldom given him a single day of ease. Few men can have triumphed against heavier handicaps. Even the deformed Pope was in some ways more fortunate than Johnson.

Latin he had well flogged into him at school. But in the main, perhaps, he educated himself. And yet by nature he was idle. He did not believe in reading books one dislikes. Even if he liked them, he could not be bothered to read them through—'Sir, do *you* read books through?'[2] To this curious rule the Bible seems to have been an exception; and Lady Mary Wortley Montagu's Letters. So, presumably, was the Shakespeare he edited. So perhaps was Fielding's *Amelia*, which he read at a sitting (but did he skip?). Fanny Burney's *Cecilia* (despite his fond admiration for the authoress) was not. John Opie, asking if it were true that he had sat up all night to finish it, got the bluff answer—'I never read it through at all; though I don't wish this to be known.' True, in 1783 he had 'great delight' in reading the twelve books of the *Æneid* in twelve nights. But in his lonely last years he could 'apply better' to books.

This refusal to read books through seems an eccentric principle; though, since most books are too long, it may not, after all, have been an unwise one. All the same, from twelve to eighteen, he must have read omnivorously ('like a Turk'), if he knew, as he affirmed, almost as much at eighteen as at fifty-three. For Adam Smith considered that 'Johnson knew more books than any man alive'. Perhaps like some other reputedly omniscient readers, he

[1] Though, like the short-sighted Tennyson, he at times astonished people by showing himself minutely observant.

[2] Cf. his comment on Twiss's *Travels in Spain*: 'I have not, indeed, cut the leaves yet; but I have read in them where the pages are open, and I do not suppose that what is in the pages that are closed is worse than what is in the open pages.'

did not so much read more than other men, as remember more. For many of us cannot recall so much as the titles of half the books we read two years ago.

But, unlike most bibliophagi, who easily become stuffed animals, Johnson early showed himself a supreme talker. Even at sixteen, according to Percy, though poor, ugly, uncouth, and 'little better than a schoolboy', he made himself welcome in the best society of Stourbridge.

At nineteen, in 1728, he entered Pembroke, Oxford. 'A nest of singing birds,' he later called it; but he was hardly a very tuneful nestling, this turbulent, insolent freshman, so 'frolicksome' on the surface, who cut his tutor to slide on the ice in Christchurch Meadows and, with 'stark insensibility', told him so; or still more starkly commented that he had been fined twopence for missing a lecture not worth a penny; or lounged about the college gateway, stirring up rebellion as if he had been a Whig dog.

Still he can hardly have been quite as indolent as he afterwards pretended. For he admits to reading Greek 'solidly'; his Latin verses won him a University reputation, and the approval of Pope; and there can never have been many freshmen given to quoting the obscure Macrobius.

In any case, beneath this 'frolicksome' exterior, the young Johnson remained melancholy, 'mad and violent,' with an acute sensitiveness about his poverty (so that he angrily flung away a pair of shoes left by charitable hands at his door). In December 1729 that poverty drove him from Oxford.[1] His hypochondria reached a crisis,[2] which he vainly tried to cure by thirty-mile walks. There followed five desultory years given to schoolmastering,[3] tutoring, and a hack

[1] In 1731, the year of his death (at seventy-four), Michael Johnson was granted ten guineas as 'a decayed tradesman'.

[2] Attributed by R. M. Ladell ('The Neurosis of Dr Samuel Johnson', *British Journal of Medical Psychology*, ix (1929), 314 ff.) to a realization that he was impotent. This I see no reason for believing, and many for not believing.

[3] His brief experience (1732) as usher at Market Bosworth and Chaplain to Sir Wolstan Dixie, 'an abandoned, brutal rascal', was particularly bitter. This was the Sir Wolstan Dixie to whom Queen Caroline observed, meaning to be gracious—'Oh, Sir, it has been related to me, your connexion with Bosworth Field, and the memorable battle fought there.' Sir Wolstan was furious, supposing, in his illiteracy, that she was alluding to his having been thrashed there by a provoked tinker; which his neighbours jeered at as 'The Battle of Bosworth'. (Another version of the story substitutes George II for Queen Caroline.)

translation of a Spanish Jesuit's *Voyage to Abyssinia*, characteristically dictated from bed, and provided with a preface already no less characteristic both in its style (unlike the text), and in its contempt for 'romantick absurdity'. This author, it proclaims, 'meets with no basilisks that destroy with their eyes, his crocodiles devour their prey without tears, and his cataracts fall from the rocks without deafening the neighbouring inhabitants'.

Then in 1735, at twenty-five, came his curious marriage to a widow of forty-six,[1] Mrs Porter, the daughter of a Warwickshire squire, and more familiar to us as 'dear Tetty'—'pretty thing'—'pretty charmer'—'pretty dear creature'. Thanks to the mischievous Garrick, generations have smiled at visions of the Great Cham of classicism becoming—and, still odder, remaining—'romantick' over a little fat widow with three almost adult children; florid in dress and affected in manner; her face red with cosmetics and alcohol (to which she added a taste for opium)—in fact, 'a little painted puppet'. Yet other, less lively accounts suggest that 'Tetty' had not, at this date, so badly lost her looks. And she was no mere fool, if we can trust the story that she remarked, on first meeting Johnson, 'This is the most sensible man that I ever saw in my life'; or again that, when her suitor honestly confessed to having no birth, no money, and an uncle hanged, she replied that this was no obstacle—she had herself fifty relatives who needed hanging. Johnson himself, who did not hesitate to correct even Garrick's emphasis on wrong words, considered that Tetty, though in tragedy she mouthed, 'read comedy better than anybody I ever heard.' Nor did he forget her judicious comment, years later, on *The Rambler*: 'I thought well of you before; but I did not imagine you could have written anything equal to this.'

In any case, though Mrs Porter possessed seven or eight hundred pounds, it was, in Johnson's phrase long afterwards, 'a love-marriage on both sides'; and indeed a sufficiently romantic attitude on her part is suggested by his account of how the bride, having imbibed from romances the notion that 'a woman of spirit should use her lover like a dog', showed on their ride to Derby for the wedding a domineering capriciousness about their speed which the bridegroom, Petruchio-like, was driven to cure promptly and

[1] In the marriage-bond her age appears more politely as 'forty'.

drastically by spurring right out of sight, and then waiting till she caught him up, in tears.

In spite of this brusque beginning, it seems to have been a happy marriage. True, they disputed (so he told Mrs Thrale) 'perpetually'. Tetty was too fussy for Samuel about tidiness—a slave to her own besom; so that one day, weary of her praises of clean floors, he suggested they should 'have a touch at the ceiling'. Samuel, on his side, was too fussy for Tetty about food; so that one day she protested against the farce of his saying grace before a meal he would next moment damn as uneatable. Mrs Desmoulins told Boswell that, in general, Tetty lacked 'that complacency which is the most engaging quality of a wife'.[1] On the other hand, it might have taxed Griselda herself to be always complacent to Johnson; who, incidentally, began by losing most of his wife's capital on his abortive school at Edial.

The fact remains that her death at sixty-three, after seventeen years of marriage (in his words to Edwards a quarter of a century later) 'almost broke my heart'. Stoical even his agony, he might quote Euripides:

οἴμοι. τί δ'οἴμοι; θνῆτα γὰρ πεπόνθαμεν.

Alas! Yet why 'alas!'? Man's life is such.

But when he saw the sea at Brighthelmstone (so he writes in 1770) the wish rose in him that *she* could have seen it. At Paris in 1773 (twenty-one years after his bereavement) the thought of her was still vivid—'she would have been pleased'. Even in 1782, only a little before his own death, he was still lamenting the anniversary of hers, now thirty years ago. 'Couldest thou have lived!' By then, Tetty would have been ninety-three! But it is not the less touching.

Johnson, long poor, always ugly, always ailing, was the loneliest, though the most sociable, of men. Indeed he was so sociable, because so lonely. But society could not cure his solitude; it was, at best, only a palliative. In 1753, a year after Tetty's death, Johnson

[1] For other indications that Johnson's marriage was not always so happy as his fond memories might suggest, see J. L. Clifford, *Young Samuel Johnson*, pp. 298–300. After all, it is very human that spouses far from saintly should sometimes come, after their deaths, to seem 'late espousèd saints'—as with Hardy and his first wife.

actually planned remarriage. But it came to nothing. Little wonder that he remembered with anguish the years when he had possessed a wife, a real home, of his own. If he delayed giving her a tombstone till a few months before his own end in 1784, that procrastination was perhaps due to his horror of the grave; in the epitaph he then wrote, he still celebrated his Tetty in sonorous Latin as 'formosa, culta, ingeniosa, pia'—'comely, cultivated, gifted, religious'.

At the time, however, his marriage brought little relief to Johnson's thirty years' war with poverty. His 'academy' at Edial failed—no doubt this uncouth eccentric, with his tics and grimaces, seemed too forbidding even to eighteenth-century parents.[1] Hence in 1737 his venture to London in the company of his pupil Garrick (then twenty), 'with two pence half-penny in *my* pocket, and thou, Davy, with three half-pence in thine.' Half a century more, and both of them would be lying together in Poets' Corner, near the statue of that Shakespeare whom they served more brilliantly than any others in their age.[2]

But meanwhile there ensued another dreary period of hack-work—translations, biographies, a catalogue of the Harleian Library for Osborne the bookseller, on whom his exasperated employee conferred a grotesque immortality by once beating him, or smiting him down, with a folio.[3] At times Johnson's subsistence is

[1] Compare the objections raised in August 1735, just after the marriage, when Gilbert Walmesley tried to get Johnson a school at Solihull—he was, the Governors admitted, an excellent scholar; but 'he has ye Caracter of being a very haughty, ill natured Gent. & y[t] he has such a way of distorting his Face (wch. though he can't help) ye Gent. think it may affect some Young Ladds.'

In all, Johnson made schoolmastering attempts in, or on, seven different schools. Cf. Lord Auchinleck's contemptuous description of Johnson (according to Scott)—'a dominie, mon—an auld dominie; he keeped a schule, and cau'd it an acaadamy.'

[2] Though Johnson was not prepared to admit this of Garrick. '*Boswell.* "But has he not brought Shakespeare into notice?" *Johnson.* "Sir, to allow that, would be to lampoon the age."'

[3] Sir John Hawkins gives a list of literary projects dreamed of by Johnson at different times, which is both interesting and tantalizing. It includes a 'History of Criticism . . . from Aristotle to the present age' (*that* might have been fascinating); an edition of Chaucer; 'Lives of the Philosophers, written with a polite air' (one wonders how 'polite'); 'A Body of Chronology, in verse, with historical notes'; 'Lives of illustrious persons . . . in imitation of Plutarch'; a 'Hymn to Ignorance'; 'The Palace of Sloth—a vision'; 'Prejudice—a poetical essay.' His enemies would have admitted him specially qualified for the last two.

said to have been fourpence halfpenny a day. In 1738 *London* brought him a pittance of ten guineas and, again, the notice of Pope; in 1749 *The Vanity of Human Wishes* brought another pittance of fifteen. Yet the success of these poems was less niggardly than the pay. *London* reached a second edition in a week, and a fourth in the following year.

From 1741 to 1744 Johnson also composed for the *Gentleman's Magazine* those extraordinary Parliamentary debates (covering the period November 1740–February 1743) which form one of his largest works—some thousand pages—and the least read.[1]

In April 1738 the reporting of Commons debates had again been pronounced breach of privilege. But the public had a passion for political oratory hard for the listless newspaper-reader of to-day even to conceive. So the demand was quickly met by subterfuge. Next month (May 1738) the *London Magazine* simply disguised its Parliamentary reports as 'Proceedings of the Political Club' (a supposed club of young noblemen and gentry dining thrice weekly); veiling the speakers under such Roman names as 'the Hon. Scipio Africanus' (Lord Noel Somerset), 'M. Cato' (Pulteney), 'M. Tullius Cicero' (Sir Robert Walpole). More ingeniously, Cave's *Gentleman's Magazine* took to publishing, from June 1738, 'Debates in the Senate of Magna Lilliputia,' supposedly reported by Gulliver's grandson; with such audaciously transparent masks as 'Gorgenti the Second' for George II, 'Walelop' for Walpole, 'Ptit' for Pitt, 'Vinena' for Vienna, 'Iberia' for Spain (France was rather better disguised as 'Blefuscu'). As a further precaution, debates were not published during the current session, but delayed for months, sometimes over a year. No matter; readers devoured them. It is a fantastic story. Parliament was flouted by childish evasions; and its members saw fathered on them utterances largely or wholly imaginary. 'Entirely false,' runs a comment of Horace Walpole's, 'and had not one paragraph of my real speech in it.'[2] 'Leave them alone,' said the ironic Henry Pelham, 'they make better speeches

[1] They were republished as supplementary volumes to Johnson's *Works* in 1787, 1811, and 1825.

[2] *Short Notes of my Life.* Cf. to Mann, March 24, 1742, note: 'There is a fictitious speech printed for this in several magazines . . . which does not contain one sentence of the true one.'

for us than we can ourselves.' For nearly ten years this aristocratic indolence and indifference allowed the mice to play.[1]

From 1738 to 1741 the Lilliputian debates seem to have been compiled by the Scot Guthrie, with some revision by Johnson; in 1741 Johnson took over. As materials, he had the subject under discussion, names of speakers, and sometimes, though not always, a

[1] The long struggle over Parliamentary reporting is curiously English in its medley of inconsistency and illogicality, stubbornness and saving compromise. Under Elizabeth and Charles I, members were jealous for secrecy from fear of the Crown; in the eighteenth century, from fear of the public.

1628. Order of the Commons that their Journals should say nothing of speeches made.

1641. A speech published by Lord Digby ordered to be burnt by the hangman.

1642. Sir Edward Dering expelled and sent to the Tower for publishing a collection of his speeches.

1680–1. *Votes and Proceedings* of the Commons begin to be officially published (a record of things done, but *not* of things said).

1694. John Dyer brought to the Bar of the Commons for reports in his Newsletter. (He was repeatedly in trouble during the next decade.)

1698. John Churchill brought to the Bar of the Lords for a book, *Cases in Parliament.*

1711. A. Boyer starts his *Political State of Great Britain*, which gave, down to 1737, accounts of Parliamentary proceedings and occasional summaries of debates. These were plagiarized by the *Historical Register* (founded 1716), the *Gentleman's Magazine* (founded 1731), and the *London Magazine* (founded 1732).

1722. Commons resolution that 'no News Writers do presume . . . to intermeddle with the Debates'.

1728–9. Measures against the *Gloucester Journal* for this.

1738. The Commons again pronounce against reporting debates.

1741. The Lords send John Torbuck to Newgate for a collection of debates.

1747. Cave (of *Gentleman's Magazine*) and Astley (of *London Magazine*) brought to the Bar of the Lords for reporting Lord Lovat's trial there.

1771. Eight printers summoned before the Commons. The Lord Mayor, Alderman Wilkes, and Alderman Oliver sign a warrant for commitment of the House-of-Commons messenger who had arrested one of these printers within the City. Riots. The coach of Lord North, the Prime Minister, is torn to pieces, and he weeps in the House. The Lord Mayor and Oliver sent to the Tower, but automatically released at the end of the session. Parliament might seem victorious; yet from this moment it tacitly accepted defeat.

1801. Printer and publisher of the *Morning Herald* brought to the Bar of the Lords for *mis*reporting debate.

1803. Beginning of Cobbett's *Parliamentary Debates*, printed by T. C. Hansard, who later became publisher.

1819. The publisher of *The Times* and his reporter John Payne Collier brought to the Bar of the Commons for *mis*reporting.

1831. Reporters' Gallery established in the Lords.

1835. Reporters' Gallery established in the Commons.

(See M. Macdonagh, *The Reporters' Gallery*, 1912.)

few notes taken by Cave, the editor,[1] or Cave's employees. (Johnson himself was only once in his life, if that, in the House of Commons.) On this flimsy foundation he constructed, like Thucydides or Livy, imaginary speeches. The style is ponderous Johnsonese—polysyllabic, antithetic, elaborately balanced with pairs and triplets. The speakers become as monotonously alike in manner as the characters of *Irene*. It is the spouting of a school of whales. True, there were persons who professed to recognize the distinctive style of various orators. But they must have had strong imaginations. Johnson said he 'took care the Whig dogs should not have the best of it': but in practice he appears to do his thunderous best for both sides.

The general effect is sometimes robust, passionate, dignified; but, in bulk, too pompous and nebulous. Few but specialists would care now to flounder through it all. Yet it remains a prodigy of labour.

Full of generalities though the speeches are, none the less to fabricate debates on so many topics—home and foreign affairs, matters naval, military, and financial—without tumbling into gross absurdities, required formidable ingenuity and general knowledge. Further, Johnson says he often wrote three columns (1,350 words) an hour. That is over twenty-two words a minute. Let anyone try keeping it up. For an hour's work, even Trollope was content with 1,000 words: and 1,000 words could cost Flaubert weeks. Writing *Ramblers* might well seem to Johnson child's play in comparison.

According to Hawkins, Johnson's debates raised the monthly sale of the *Gentleman's Magazine* (extraordinary as it may seem to *us*) from 10,000 to 15,000. Yet for him it was a thankless form of drudgery. Its creative effort was taken by readers as mere reporting; and it proved seriously misleading. But the public was determined to be deceived. Johnson's fabrications got incorporated in the collections of Parliamentary debates published by Torbuck (1741–2), Chandler (1742–4), and Timberland (1742–3). One of his debates spread deception abroad by being translated into French, German, and Spanish. Two speeches he had put in the mouth of Chesterfield were reprinted as genuine a generation later by Dr Maty (whom

[1] Edward Cave (1691–1754), son of a Rugby cobbler, and expelled from Rugby School for robbing the hen-roost of the headmaster's wife, conducted the *Gentleman's Magazine* from 1731 to 1754.

Johnson called 'the little black dog') in his lordship's *Miscellaneous Works* (1777). Johnson laughed—'the best of it is they have found out that one is like Demosthenes,[1] and the other like Cicero'. Smollett, though warned by Johnson, used the speeches as authentic in his history. And even in the nineteenth and twentieth centuries historians and editors have sometimes fallen into Johnson's trap.

The most famous instance however occurred, probably in the seventeen-sixties, at a dinner given by Foote, when Dr Philip Francis, translator of Demosthenes, praised a certain speech of Pitt's as superior to anything by the Athenian, and 'the best he had ever read'—only to be floored by Johnson's calm remark: 'That speech I wrote in a garret in Exeter Street.'[2]

In the end Johnson's own honesty grew uneasy at 'the propagation of falsehood'; and the eloquence of Lilliput was handed over to his admirer Hawkesworth, later editor of *The Adventurer* (to which Johnson contributed) and of Swift. It was as well; though history may regret that when, in 1747, Cave was summoned to the Bar of

[1] Actually the speech praised by Dr Maty as Demosthenic was a third oration, not invented by Johnson.

[2] This seems wrong—perhaps a slip by Murphy who tells the story. Johnson lived in Exeter Street, Strand, only on his first coming to London, in March-July 1737.

Presumably Dr Francis was referring to Pitt's share in the debate on the Seamen's Bill (March 4, 1741). Its most famous passage, Pitt's retort to Horatio Walpole, may be quoted as an example of Johnson in Parliament. (Urg = Esquire.)

'*The Urg*; Ptit *replied.*

SIR,

The atrocious Crime of being a young Man, which the honourable Gentleman has with such Spirit and Decency charged upon me, I shall neither attempt to palliate, nor deny, but content myself with wishing that I may be one of those whose Follies may cease with their Youth, and not of that Number, who are ignorant in spite of Experience.

Whether Youth can be imputed to any Man as a Reproach, I will not, Sir, assume the Province of determining; but surely Age may become justly contemptible, if the Opportunities which it brings have past away without Improvement, and Vice appears to prevail when the Passions have subsided. The Wretch that, after having seen the Consequences of a thousand Errors, continues still to blunder, and whose Age has only added Obstinacy to Stupidity, is surely the Object of either Abhorrence or Contempt, and deserves not that his grey Head should secure him from Insults.

Much more, Sir, is he to be abhorr'd, who, as he has advanced in Age, has receded from Virtue, and becomes more wicked with less Temptation; who prostitutes himself for Money which he cannot enjoy, and spends the Remains of his Life in the Ruin of his Country.'

I think Dr Francis was a little 'enthusiastick' in his admiration.

the Lords, he was not accompanied by his burly contributor. That would have made a 'scene' for Boswell![1]

In 1744 Johnson produced his *Life of Savage*,[2] which so enthralled Reynolds that he numbed his arm on the mantelpiece where he leant to read the book through at a standing. In 1749 Johnson's *Irene* ran for nine nights (the modern reader may wonder how), but without real success. Now nearly forty, despite all his brave efforts he had still not really arrived. It took another eight years of drudgery, from 1747 to 1755, 'beating the track of the alphabet with sluggish resolution,' before he was at last established by his *Dictionary*.[3] And even in 1756 he had to be rescued by Samuel Richardson after arrest for debt.

In the intervals of lexicography, indeed, he produced *The Rambler* (1750–2); yet this, though Samuel Rogers records Johnson's judgment that 'my other works are wine and water, but my *Rambler* is pure wine', can hardly be said to have intoxicated contemporaries; still less has it excited posterity. It impressed, however, even if it did not inebriate. And though, at the price of twopence, its circulation seems to have been less than five hundred, as a book it reached ten editions during Johnson's life, and was, it is said, even translated into Russian.[4]

The Idler (1758–60), though often less ponderous reading, to-day is even less read. *Rasselas* (1759) scribbled in the evenings of a single week, to pay for his mother's funeral, is a prose counterpart of Johnson's *Vanity of Human Wishes*. However, not the least strong of human wishes is to read about their vanity; and *Rasselas*, though eclipsed in brilliance by its twin, Voltaire's *Candide*, which

[1] For the whole subject, see B. B. Hoover, *Samuel Johnson's Parliamentary Reporting* (University of California Press), 1953.

[2] For Savage, see C. Tracy, *The Artificial Bastard* (1953). Whether, in claiming to be the natural son of Earl Rivers and the Countess of Macclesfield, Savage was telling the truth, or deluded, or (least probably) lying, remains still obscure.

[3] This great work (begun 1746) is exhaustively treated in J. H. Sledd and G. J. Kolb, *Dr Johnson's Dictionary* (1955). See especially Chapter 3, on the quarrel between Johnson and Chesterfield, culminating in the famous letters. My feeling is that Chesterfield was too negligent; Johnson, perhaps, too truculent. Had he *written* to Chesterfield earlier, instead of calling vainly at his lordship's door, one wonders if the clash need ever have occurred. But this is guessing. Johnson would never have proved easy to patronize.

[4] If this translation was ever really made, it seems to have left no trace—though there *is* a Russian translation of *Rasselas*.

by a strange coincidence appeared only a few weeks earlier, remains perhaps Johnson's most interesting book, outside his criticism. Now, admirable as parts of *Rasselas* are, I find this a quite astonishing reflection. Was ever man, who wrote so much, so much bigger than his books?

At last, in 1762, came official recognition, with the pension conferred by a more effectual patron than Lord Chesterfield—Lord Bute. After fifty-three years of life, Johnson was at last independent; twenty-two more remained for him to be happy in that independence—had it been possible for Johnson to be happy. Ironically enough, Bute can little have dreamed what a good turn he was doing himself as well as Johnson; for it is the one action that posterity remembers to the poor man's credit.[1]

The next year, 1763, brought the old 'Scot-hater' his meeting with a third Scot who served him yet better than Bute who bestowed his pension, or Wedderburn who suggested it—James Boswell. Two years later still, in 1765, he was taken up by the rich brewer, Henry Thrale, whose gay, rattling little wife[2]—Carlyle's 'bright papilionaceous creature'—thirty-two years Johnson's junior, as Tetty had been twenty-one his senior—perhaps did more than anyone else to brighten those last twenty years while Johnson talked himself into immortality. That talk had thus acquired its two chief chroniclers.

Further, in 1764, Johnson had found a new field for his talk, with the formation of The Club, whose original members included Reynolds (who had first proposed it), Burke, Goldsmith, Beauclerk, Langton, and Hawkins.

Henceforth Johnson's publications of importance appear only at long intervals—*Shakespeare* in 1765, the *Journey to the Western Islands* in 1775, *The Lives of the Poets*[3] in 1779–81. His tongue had grown mightier than his pen.

Probably this long Indian summer was the least unhappy period

[1] Cf. Thurlow's remark forty years later, on hearing that someone was writing a biography of Bute, 'The life of a fly would be as interesting.'

[2] She stood only four feet eleven.

[3] It is typical of his generous indifference to money that he asked only £200 for them, whereas Malone thought he could have got £1,500. He might hold that only blockheads wrote for anything but money: but he was content to write for very little of it.

of that unhappy life; but, just before the end, 'inspissated gloom' returned. In 1781 'my master', Thrale, succeeded, after prolonged efforts, in eating himself to death. And Mrs Thrale, with forty years behind her, but forty more to come—a little vulgar perhaps, but clever, charming, bouncing with vitality—felt a very human impulse to taste at last that real love which she had never found in seventeen years with the stodgy, flirtatious Thrale, to whom she had been married off at twenty-two without ever being more than five minutes alone with him.[1] So now she yielded to that passion for honest Gabriel Piozzi,[2] which neither Johnson, nor her children, nor—with less excuse—posterity could ever forgive. I have never understood why critics should still stamp on her grave for it; as if we could still, like her contemporaries, regard Piozzi as impossible for the four not very valid reasons that he was obscure, a musician, an Italian, and a Papist.

[1] It had been one of the rather too rational marriages of the Age of Reason. 'Our mutual preference,' Hester wrote at the time to an aunt, '... not founded on Passion, but on Reason, gives us some Right to expect some happiness.' Unfortunately, Henry Thrale considered he had some Right to some Passion elsewhere, with persons like Sophy Streatfield and others; his wife he forbade to ride, because that was too masculine; and to cook, because that was too important—for an epicure like himself. So Hester never knew what was for dinner, till it was served on the table.

[2] Here a little chronology may help.

1778. Piozzi sings at Dr Burney's party and is mimicked behind his back by Mrs Thrale. (This was the famous occasion when the pompous Fulke Greville warmed himself in stubborn silence before the mantelpiece, till Johnson observed: 'If it were not for depriving the ladies of the fire, I should like to stand upon the hearth myself.' Whereupon Mr Greville, in high displeasure, rang for his carriage.)

1780 (July). Mrs Thrale, meeting Piozzi at Brighton, asks him to teach her daughter music. A few weeks later he 'is become a prodigious Favourite with me'.

1781 (April). Henry Thrale dies. Only the day before, Mrs Byron observes to Mrs Thrale that Piozzi is clearly in love with her.

(July-November). Piozzi in France and Italy.

1782 (April). As possible matches for Mrs Thrale, newspaper gossip mentions Lord Loughborough, Sir Richard Jebb, Piozzi, Selwyn, and Johnson.

(October.) Mrs Thrale in her diary weighs whether to marry Piozzi.

(November 4.) She has confessed her passion to Fanny Burney and to her daughter Queeney.

(November 27.) 'I have given my Piozzi some hopes.'

1783 (January). She gives him up, owing to the furious opposition of her family and friends.

(April.) He goes to Italy.

(November.) She is so ill and wretched that he is summoned back.

1784 (July). Reunion at Bath. Marriage.

(December 13.) Johnson dies.

One of the few rational comments by anyone really in a position to judge seems that of the waspish Samuel Rogers: 'The world was most unjust in blaming Mrs Thrale for marrying Piozzi; he was a very handsome, gentlemanly, and amiable person, and made her a very good husband.' Perhaps Rogers, author in his old age of a now long forgotten poem on Italy, was able to take a more human view of mere Italians.

But, at the time, the topic roused frenzies of the kind that sometimes makes our 'Age of Reason' seem far more passionate in real life than it was in its poetry. Mrs Montagu thought Hester 'mad', and 'fallen below pity'—'I bring in my verdict lunacy'. 'There must,' echoes Mrs Chapone, 'be really some degree of *Insanity*.' Fanny Burney, with unpleasant unction,[1] wrote to Queeney Thrale of 'your poor fallen Mother'; and referred to the situation as 'this horrible affair'. Later she recorded that 'the outcry of surprise and censure raised throughout the metropolis . . . was almost stunning in its jarring noise of general reprobation'. One would have thought people might have found more serious themes for worry, when they had just lost a major war, and an empire in America. Yet they howled as if Hester Thrale had been another Queen Gertrude of Denmark; to me she seems more like the poor Duchess of Malfi with her Antonio.[2]

To-day the battle still rages between Thralites, Johnsonites, and Boswellites. One might have wished that poor Hester and her Gabriel could be allowed to rest in peace in Tremeirchion churchyard; but the matter has still some historic importance, because it darkened the close of Johnson's days; and because it throws light on the volcanic intensity of the old man's feelings to the last. Yet who shall judge now what was in essence a lovers' quarrel? In lovers' quarrels, only the lovers know all the facts, but cannot judge them dispassionately; while those who might judge them

[1] At times Fanny Burney reminds one of her own description of Sophy Streatfield —'caressing, amiable, sweet, and—fatiguing.'

[2] There is a curious similarity between Queeney Thrale's warning to her mother (January 1783) about marrying Piozzi—'You are going you know not whither, I believe'—and the Duchess's words before wooing Antonio—

I am going into a wildernesse,
Where I shall find nor path, nor friendly clewe
To be my guide.

dispassionately, cannot possibly know all the facts.

In common fairness, however, a few general points seem worth making. It was hardly for Johnson to denounce Mrs Thrale's marriage so brutally, when his own marriage had been even odder. For he had himself been obscure, like Piozzi; Tetty had been socially and financially his superior, old enough to be his mother, and the actual mother of three children; of whom her eldest son resented the match, all his life, as passionately as Mrs Thrale's eldest daughter resented *hers*. Yet surely adults may be allowed to marry without being vetoed either by their parents or by their children. As Johnson had himself so sanely said, of adult daughters—'When I may suffer for my own crimes, when I may be sued for my own debts, I may judge by parity of reasoning for my own happiness.' And to Mrs Thrale herself he had once expressed his contempt for Cyrus because he asked his father's leave to marry—'a matter which concerns no man's happiness but his own'.

But it is much easier to be rational about things remote. Very humanly, his own judgments seem to have been forgotten by Johnson then; and, less excusably, by his biographers since. Could he only have accepted Piozzi as he had accepted Henry Thrale, the breach might have been spared. But jealousy is not reasonable;[1] and we know too little for any final judgment. There is no verdict but pity. For all of them suffered.

Well indeed for Johnson, probably, had he died before Henry Thrale. Yet not so well for us; for his talk kept its vigour to the end, But the shadows thicken over his last three years. Levett, his doctor. died, 'the single talent well employed'; the blind Miss Williams died, who for thirty years had at least given him 'domestick amusement'. His house grew desolate. Gout, asthma, dropsy, fastened on him. By July 1784, he had at last learnt of Mrs Thrale's marriage. In his rage, he became monstrous—'Madam, if I interpret your letter right, you are ignominiously married. . . .' Her answer was much more dignified. 'You have always commanded my esteem, and have enjoyed the fruits of a friendship never infringed by one harsh expression on

[1] It seems curious that in the summer of 1782 Johnson took quite calmly the idea that Mrs Thrale might go away with her girls to Italy for two or three whole years. It was she (according to *Thraliana*) who was upset because he was not upset. Was he in an unimaginative mood? Or was it jealousy that made the sudden difference?

my part[1] during twenty years of familiar talk. Never did I oppose your will, or control your wish, nor can your unmerited severity itself lessen my regard;[2] but till you have changed your opinion of Mr Piozzi let us converse no more. God bless you.' It is as if for a moment she had learnt from Johnson something of his own trenchant honesty.

Perhaps the old man himself felt that; at least he became honest enough to admit part of the truth. 'Dear Madam, What you have done, however I may lament it, I have no pretence to resent, as it has not been injurious to me. . . .' Then follows his famous and pathetic comparison of himself to the Archbishop of St Andrew's vainly warning Mary Stuart not to trust herself across the Solway in foreign England—not to cross 'the irremeable stream'.[3] 'The Queen went forward. If the parallel reaches thus far, may it go no further. The tears stand in my eyes.'

It is one of Johnson's most revealing and most moving moments. Hester Thrale had indeed been his queen for twenty years. And yet —so often is tragedy intertwined with the comic—it is hard not to smile a little at this fantasy worthy of Mrs Radcliffe, about the risks of wedding the perilous Piozzi—as if he were some captain of Italian banditti with a sinister den in the Apennines, where Hester Thrale might find awaiting her a prison-cell and a headsman's axe.

But Johnson hardened his heart as implacably as Mr Barrett when Elizabeth Browning likewise fled with a husband to Italy. 'I drive her quite from my mind. If I meet with one of her letters, I burn it instantly. . . . I never speak of her, and I desire never to hear of her name. I drive her, as I said, wholly from my mind.'

But perhaps it was easier said than done.

Five months later, on December 13, 1784 (after previously stabbing his dropsical legs in desperation with lancet and scissors, but

[1] Both knew (though she wisely refrained from saying so) that this was more than could be claimed for Johnson. He had been no easy guest; he had kept her up till 4 a.m. to make him tea and beguile his sleeplessness; but this had not prevented him, at times, from harshly rending both her guests and herself.

[2] This, indeed, one may doubt.

[3] It is curious that in his unspeakable *Ode, by Dr Samuel Johnson, to Mrs Thrale upon their supposed approaching nuptials* (written 1781, published 1788) Boswell had already made the Doctor compare Piozzi to Mary's Italian favourite, Rizzio.

refusing to cloud his dying spirit with opiates) 'the old lion'[1] died; more calmly, in the end, than he had ever thought about death.

But earthly immortality was already his. A week later he was laid at Westminster, beside his old pupil Garrick, at whom in his scorn of actors he had carped so often, yet suffered none else to carp. And now as 'Peter Pindar' put it,

> From beggars, to the great who hold the helm,
> One Johnso-mania raged through all the realm.

In the next year, 1785, appeared Boswell's *Tour*; in 1786, Mrs Thrale's *Anecdotes*; in 1787, Hawkins's *Life*; in 1788, Mrs Thrale's *Letters to and from Dr Johnson*; and in 1791, the crowning work of Boswell. For a time, after 1800, Romantics might growl at his fame.[2] But in the English tradition Johnson's niche, though far narrower, seems almost as solidly hewn as even Shakespeare's.

But why? Though one may count some eleven editions of his works between 1787 and 1825, yet in the hundred and thirty years since then there seem to have been only two more—London, 1850, and New York, 1903. (Another is in preparation now.) Strange that one of the most famous of English authors should be an author so comparatively unread. In what then, exactly, does the fascination of Johnson lie?

Taine, as we have seen, found that fascination an unaccountable whimsy of the English. And, after all, a Devil's Advocate could draw up against Johnson quite a lengthy indictment. It may be worth considering the faults that can be, and have been, found in him. For this may better bring out his real features than a mere smothering of his effigy with the conventional flowers.

First of all, to many of his contemporaries, he seemed positively

[1] So he was called by the absurd Irishman, Mr Murphy (later Sir Richard), in Fanny Burney's *Early Diary*.

[2] Coleridge, for example, with his girdings at Johnson's verse and prose style, or that curious comparison in a marginal note (T. M. Raysor, *Coleridge's Shakespearean Criticism*, i, 82), 'Johnson, the Frog-Critic. How nimbly it leaps, how excellently it swims—only the fore-legs (it must be admitted) are too long and the hind ones too short.' Even if the hind legs of frogs *were* short, the point of the comparison escapes me.

Wordsworth, again, denied Johnson style or poetry; Hazlitt thought him 'always upon stilts'.

repellent; for Dean Barnard,[1] 'no gentleman'; for Gray and Lord Auchinleck, 'Ursa Major', 'the Great Bear'. Indeed that shaggy beast recurs like a *Leitmotiv* in descriptions of Johnson.

'I have seen many a bear led by a man,' observed Margaret Boswell[2] of her husband and his master, 'but I never before saw a man led by a bear.' Henry Erskine, introduced to Johnson at Edinburgh, slipped a shilling into Boswell's hand 'for the sight of his bear'. Wits coupled Johnson as 'He-bear' with his fellow Jacobite and fellow pensioner Dr Shebbeare. 'Peter Pindar' writes of

> The lengthen'd lip of scorn, the forehead's scowl,
> The lowering eye's contempt, and bear-like growl.

Then there is Churchill's tribute:[3]

> Pomposo, insolent and loud,
> Vain idol of a scribbling crowd,
> Whose very name inspires an awe,
> Whose every word is sense and law . . .
> Who scorns those common wares to trade in—
> Reasoning, convincing, and persuading,
> But makes each sentence current pass
> With puppy, coxcomb, scoundrel, ass;
> For 'tis with him a certain rule
> That folly's proved when he calls fool;
> Who to increase his native strength,
> Draws words six syllables in length,

[1] Not to be confused with Dr Barnard, Provost of Eton, who (said Johnson, according to Mrs Thrale) 'was the only man that did justice to my good breeding; and you may observe that I am well-bred to a degree of needless scrupulosity.' ' "No man," continued he, not observing the amazement of his hearers, "no man is so cautious not to interrupt another; no man thinks it so necessary to appear attentive when others are speaking; no man so steadily refuses preference to himself, or so willingly bestows it on another, as I do; no man holds so strongly as I do the necessity of ceremony, and the ill effects which follow the breach of it; yet people think me rude; but Barnard did me justice." '

I doubt if Mrs Thrale could have invented this marvellous speech. But, from Bottom, with his claims to roar gently as a sucking dove, to old King Gama in *Princess Ida*, unable to conceive for what mysterious reason no one likes him, it would be hard to match this jewel of unconscious humour.

[2] I do not know why this hardly used and unhappy woman has been called 'dull'.

[3] *The Ghost* (1762).

With which, assisted with a frown
By way of club, he knocks us down . . .
Pomposo, form'd on doubtful plan,
Not quite a beast, not quite a man.

Similarly, Soame Jenyns (who had felt the bear's claws at their sharpest, in Johnson's superbly disdainful review of his *Nature and Origin of Evil*) revenged himself with an epitaph:

Here lies Sam Johnson: Reader, have a care,
Tread lightly, lest you wake a sleeping Bear.
Religious, moral, generous, and humane
He was; but self-sufficient, proud, and vain;
Fond of, and overbearing in dispute,
A Christian, and a Scholar—but a Brute.

When Johnson one day, discoursing of bears, proceeded, 'We are told that the black bear is innocent; but I should not like to trust myself with him', Gibbon was heard to murmur, 'I should not like to trust myself with *you*'. (And he did not.) Even in defending Johnson, as a man fundamentally kind, Goldsmith neatly summed the matter with the comment, 'He has nothing of the bear but his skin'.

Lord Chesterfield's phrase 'a respectable Hottentot', though actually referring to Lord Lyttelton,[1] was repeatedly mistaken by contemporaries for an allusion to Johnson; nor is it likely that Chesterfield would have disputed Johnson's fitness for the title. Horace Walpole, son of a Whig Prime Minister and embittered by Johnson's scorn for Gray, was more scathing still—'unfortunate monster'—'saucy Caliban'—'lettered elephant'. This loathing was not, indeed, founded on personal acquaintance; the two men, accord-

[1] George Lyttelton (1709–73), a lord of the treasury 1744–54, brilliantly but mercilessly sketched by Horace Walpole: 'With the figure of a spectre and the gesticulations of a puppet, he talked heroics through his nose, made declamations on a visit, and played cards with scraps of history or sentences of Pindar. He had set out a poetical love plan, though with nothing of a lover but absence of mind and nothing of a poet but absence of meaning. Yet he was far from wanting parts.' See also Johnson's biography in *Lives of the Poets* (which got him into such hot water with Mrs Montagu's set); Chesterfield to his son, September 22, 1749; and S. C. Roberts, *An Eighteenth-century Gentleman.*

ing to Walpole, were less than half-a-dozen times in the same room, and never exchanged one syllable; but Johnson's writings were provocation enough. 'With a lumber of learning,' writes Walpole, 'and some strong parts, Johnson was an odious and mean character. By principle a Jacobite, arrogant, self-sufficient, and overbearing by nature, ungrateful through pride and of feminine bigotry, he had prostituted his pen to party even in a dictionary, and had afterwards, for a pension, contradicted his own definitions. His manners were sordid, supercilious, and brutal, his style ridiculously bombastic and vicious; and, in one word, with all his pedantry he had all the gigantic littleness of a country schoolmaster.'

It is surprising what a lot of truth one can tell in detail, only to reach a general verdict that seems wildly false.

But perhaps the most vivid witness for the Devil's Advocate would be Macaulay, with his brilliant, journalistic flair for bizarre, yet typical details—Johnson's 'rolling walk, his blinking eye, the outward signs which too clearly marked his approbation of his dinner, his insatiable appetite for fish-sauce and veal-pie with plums, his inextinguishable thirst for tea, his trick of touching the posts as he walked, his mysterious practice of treasuring up scraps of orange-peel,[1] his morning slumbers, his midnight disputations, his contortions, his mutterings, his gruntings, his puffings.'[2] 'The roughness and violence which he showed in society were to be expected from a man whose temper, not naturally gentle, had been long tried by the bitterest of calamities, by the want of meat, of fire, and of clothes, by the importunity of creditors, by the insolence of booksellers, by the derision of fools, by the insincerity of patrons, by that bread which is the bitterest of all food, by those stairs which are the most toilsome of all paths, by that deferred hope which makes the heart sick. Through all these things the ill-dressed, coarse, ungainly pedant had struggled manfully up to eminence and command.'

[1] Even Boswell failed to plumb this mystery (which, says Dr Campbell, made him quite unhappy—'I verily believe he is as anxious to know the secret as a green love-sick girl'). Actually the orange-peel seems to have been nothing more sinister than a nostrum (when powdered) for indigestion.

[2] From other sources may be added the piercing, sometimes terrifying glance of his light-grey eyes; the rotatory motion of his head, inclining towards one shoulder; his brown greatcoat with 'two huge Patagonian pockets'.

A curious pair, the English Johnson and the Scot Macaulay—at opposite poles in so many tastes and convictions, yet linked inseparably, for me, by one common quality—the vital intensity and sledge-hammer vigour with which they both can wield the English tongue. But I suspect that, while Johnson talked even better than he wrote, Macaulay wrote even better than he talked. For he seems to have monologued too much.

Here even Macaulay, exaggerated though he could often be, does not seem to have exaggerated Johnson's physical uncouthness. We may recall Garrick's impersonation of him, saying in his Midland accent, 'Who's for poonsh?' and squeezing the lemon for it with unappetizing hands—a detail supported by the old lady who once outraged Tennyson by her description of Johnson stirring his lemonade with a finger not overclean. Further, he appears to have habitually eaten fish with his fingers, for fear of bones. All this does not lose in irony when we recall his indignation with French or Scottish waiters who dared to paw his sugar; though I suppose he might have retorted that any man may be allowed to dislike another's fingers more than his own.

Even that plea, however, would hardly cover his genial little trick of pouring the wax from burning candles on the carpet, to improve the light; for he did not confine this form of illumination to his own carpets; and it did not endear him to Mrs Boswell.

As for Mrs Harris of Salisbury, wife of 'Hermes' Harris, her disapproval was much more outspoken—'dreadful voice and manner . . . more beastly in his dress and person than anything I ever beheld. He feeds nastily and ferociously.'[1]

Indeed, along with more enviable claims to pre-eminence, I suppose it *could* be argued that Johnson was the rudest man, except Whistler, in recorded history. What made it still more intolerable for his victims was that his sharpness of wit, his vigour of language, his vehemence of ridicule, the terrifying intensity of his grey eyes, and his 'bow-wow' tone, all made him almost impossible to answer. 'There's an end on't,' he would roar—and there usually was. People who minded being thus manhandled, he thought weak-nerved; if some rare victim counter-attacked, as did Reynolds on one famous

[1] By the same severe lady, Boswell is dismissed as 'a low-bred kind of being' (1775).

occasion, Johnson might be honest enough to take it; but, like Lamb's Mrs Battle, he was all for 'the rigour of the game'. 'Well,' he observed after a typical evening, 'we had a good talk.' 'Yes, Sir,' replied Boswell, 'you tossed and gored several persons.'

No one, indeed, was more 'tossed and gored' than poor Boswell himself; till even his convinced self-satisfaction and indiarubber resiliency gave way at times to sulks.

He is told, for example, that he deserves a place in Pope's *Dunciad*—'Ah, Sir, hadst *thou* lived in those days!' He is told that, if he cannot talk better as a man, 'I'd have you bellow like a cow.' (Boswell had just artlessly related how he once diverted Drury Lane by mooing, in the pit, like a cow.[1]) He asks pleadingly if a man may not be allowed to drink for the sake of forgetting 'whatever is disagreeable'; and duly the thunder falls—'Yes, Sir, if he sat next *you*.' Or again Boswell high-spiritedly exclaims that Langton's friends, since he is ruining himself in London, must quarrel with him to drive him back to the country. Perhaps Johnson resented this remark as uppish. Again the thunder falls—'Nay, Sir, we'll send *you* to him. If your company does not drive a man out of his house, nothing will.'[2]

Boswell quotes Hamlet in an argument—'Nay, if you are to bring in gabble, I'll talk no more.' Boswell confesses that martial music makes him long to rush into the thick of the fight—'Sir, I should never hear it, if it made me such a fool.' And then there is that crowning snub—'Sir, you have but two subjects—yourself and me. I am sick of both.'

But perhaps most outrageous of all is that Streatham scene in 1779, still hard to read without vicarious embarrassment, when Boswell, displaced from Johnson's side at dinner by the new favourite, Fanny Burney, planted his chair in the sage's rear, only

[1] Not the least ludicrous episode in the comedy of Boswell's life (see p. 191). And yet, without this passion for mimicry, his *Life of Johnson* would be less living. We may laugh at his imitating the cow; but remember how well he imitated the Bear—so well, indeed, that he could compete at it, not unsuccessfully, with Garrick himself.

[2] This ruthless suggestion of Boswell's powers as a bore is not confined to Johnson. Topham Beauclerk humorously threatens a friend that, if he does not come back from Ireland, 'I will bring all the Club over to Ireland to live with you, and that will drive you here in your own defence. Johnson shall spoil your books, Goldsmith pull your flowers, and Boswell talk to you: stay then if you can.'

to be discovered and ignominiously hounded back to the table—'What do you there, Sir?—Go to the table, Sir!' When poor Boswell again endeavoured to stir thence, the storm redoubled: 'What are you thinking of, Sir! Why do you get up before the cloth is removed? Come back to your place, Sir! . . . Running about in the middle of meals!—One would take you for a Branghton!'[1]—'A Branghton, Sir? What is a Branghton, Sir?' 'Where have you lived, Sir, and what company have you kept, not to know that?'

It caused great mirth at Streatham; it makes high comedy to read; but it would have made one hot to witness.

No doubt Boswell fared worse than most. He was a born whipping-boy, constantly running to get slapped; where the wary Gibbon, for example, lay low. But Goldsmith, too, was repeatedly shattered—like the earthenware pot, says Mrs Thrale, that kept rash company with an iron one. Garrick was mauled—Johnson could not forget that this public idol had once been his own obscure pupil.[2] When Garrick complained that Johnson's loud talk in the wings destroyed his feelings in playing Lear, all the satisfaction he got was—'Prithee, do not talk of feelings, Punch has no feelings.' Seldom can monosyllable have been so loaded with contempt as that 'Punch'—or rather, I suppose, 'Poonsh'.

Percy was mauled—accused of a 'narrow mind' for disliking Pennant.

> *Percy*. 'Sir, you may be as rude as you please.'
> *Johnson*. 'Hold, Sir! Don't talk of rudeness; remember, Sir, you told me' (puffing hard with passion struggling for a vent) 'I was short-sighted. We have done with civility. We are to be as rude as we please.' (*That* would be saying a good deal.)

Even Reynolds was mauled; though he, for once, seems to have made Johnson blush.

[1] A disagreeable, vulgar family in Fanny Burney's *Evelina*. Poor Boswell was reduced to asking Mrs Thrale (aside), 'Pray, Ma'am, what's a Branghton? . . . Is it some animal hereabouts?'

[2] Cf. his answer in Skye when Boswell asked why he had omitted to mention Garrick in the Preface to his *Shakespeare*: 'Garrick has been liberally paid for any thing he has done for Shakespeare'; which in Boswell's original version runs, more contemptuously, 'for mouthing Shakespeare.'

> *Johnson* (who, from drinking only water, supposed everybody who drank wine to be elevated). 'I won't argue any more with you, Sir. You are too far gone.'
> *Sir Joshua.* 'I should have thought so indeed, Sir, had I made such a speech as you have now done.'
> *Johnson* (drawing himself in and, I really thought, blushing). 'Nay, don't be angry. I did not mean to offend you.'

And even Burke, whom Johnson so much admired, despite his Whig ideas, as to keep off the perilous ground of politics in his presence, had yet suffered enough from Johnson's tongue to talk of its 'oil of vitriol'.

But, as one would expect, it was usually outsiders, and not Johnson's friends, that received the most merciless taps of the bear's paw. There was, for example, the young man[1] who asked, in tones of inadequate respect, 'Mr Johnson, would you advise me to marry?' and was duly crushed—'I would advise no man to marry, Sir, who is not likely to propagate understanding.' There was that unfortunate whose conversational spasms Johnson encouraged with the growl—'Pray, Sir, what you are going to say, let it be better worth hearing than what you have already said.' There was that other unfortunate, who 'over-fondled' the Doctor and was duly bitten—'What provokes your risibility, Sir? Have I said anything that you understand? Then I ask pardon of the rest of the company.'[2]

Then there was the Mayor of Windsor, who gave Johnson a hearty dinner, but a still heartier flow of talk. 'So, after he had spoke a great deal of clumsy nonsense, he told me that at the last Sessions he had transported three people to the Plantations. I was so provoked with the fellow's dullness and impertinence that I exclaimed, "I wish to God, Sir, I was the fourth." '

[1] Probably Sir John Lade, the subject of Johnson's Housman-like ballad *One-and-Twenty:*

Loosen'd from the Minor's tether,
Free to mortgage or to sell,
Wild as wind, and light as feather,
Bid the sons of thrift farewell.

Lade's uncle, Henry Thrale, wanted him to wed Fanny Burney; but Sir John married a woman of the town, and ran through all his wealth before he died in 1838. Johnson had not misjudged.

[2] Recorded by Cumberland, who cannot vouch for it. But it would have taken a clever mind to invent.

There was Barnard, Dean of Derry, who had rashly asserted that no man improved after forty-five—'You, who perhaps are forty-eight, may still improve if you will try . . . there is great room for it.'

But perhaps as fantastic an example as any, considering its sacred scene and occasion, is Johnson's reported outburst on emerging from a service in Lichfield Cathedral, to a pompous gentleman who purred, 'Doctor Johnson, we had a most excellent discourse to-day'—'That may be; but it is impossible that *you* should know it.'

Men have been murdered for less.

Almost worse, for they were addressed to a gentle Quakeress, Mrs Knowles, are Johnson's fulminations, as recorded by Anna Seward, over a young heiress converted to Quakerism. True, Anna Seward is less reliable than Boswell, and the conversation is long: but if she invented, she invented very Johnsonianly, up to the climax—'Madam, I pretend not to set bounds to the mercy of the Deity; but I hate the wench, and shall ever hate her. I hate all impudence, but the impudence of a chit's apostasy I *nauseate*.' Seldom can any Christian church have been defended less Christianly.

Again, one of his most brutal and wanton explosions, which really shocked observers, was his onslaught (not the only one) on Mr (later Sir) William Pepys[1] at Brighton in October 1782. Pepys had quoted Pope on wit.

> True Wit is Nature to advantage dress'd,
> What oft was thought, but ne'er so well express'd.

> ' "That, Sir," cried Dr Johnson, "is a definition both false and foolish. Let wit be dressed how it will, it will equally be wit, and neither the more nor the less for any advantage dress can give it." '
> *Mr Pepys*. "But, Sir, may not wit be so ill expressed, and so obscure(ly), by a bad speaker, as to be lost?"

[1] William Weller Pepys (1740–1825; apparently pronounced 'Peppis'), Master in Chancery 1775–1805, seems to have been a worthy, but somewhat stuffy and starchy person. However, he had the kindly generosity, on hearing of Johnson's despondency in his last days, to write him an anonymous letter of reassurance, dwelling on the good done by Johnson's books. This was the more generous as Johnson had savaged him on other occasions also—particularly (June 1781) over the character of Lyttelton, recently trampled on in the *Lives of the Poets*.

Dr. Johnson. "The fault, then, Sir, must be with the hearer. If a man cannot distinguish wit from words, he little deserves to hear it."
Mr Pepys. "But, Sir, what Pope means—"
Dr Johnson. "Sir, what Pope means, if he means what he says, is both false and foolish. In the first place, 'what oft was thought' is all the worse for being often thought, because, to be wit, it ought to be newly thought."
Mr Pepys. "But, Sir, 'tis the expression makes it new."
Dr Johnson. "How can the expression make it new? It may make it clear, or may make it elegant; but how new? You are confounding words with things."

'This was the summary; the various contemptuous sarcasms intermixed would fill, and very unpleasantly, a quire.'[1] One can well understand Mrs Thrale's saying that, for persons used to deference, Johnson's manner was 'mustard in a young child's mouth'.

Nor was that terrible tongue his only weapon; he could crush, also, by merely shutting his mouth. At Cumberland's house Reynolds reminded Johnson that he had already drunk eleven cups of tea. Johnson retorted that he had not counted Reynolds's glasses of wine; and defiantly asked Mrs Cumberland for a twelfth cup. When she promptly obeyed, with a 'kind and cheerful look' he continued: 'Madam, I must tell you for your comfort you have escaped much better than a certain lady did awhile ago, upon whose patience I intruded greatly more than I have done on yours; but the lady asked me for no other purpose but to make a zany of me, and set me gabbling to a parcel of people I knew nothing of; so,

[1] C. B. Tinker, *Dr Johnson and Fanny Burney*, 1912, pp. 151–2.

It seems a futile enough quarrel. It depends what you mean by 'thought' and 'expressed'. Take Swift's remarks, that marriages are often unhappy because young ladies are better at making nets than cages; or that old gentlemen and comets are alike in having long beards and pretensions to foretell the future. Surely it has long been known that marriages are often unhappy, and old men often pretentious prophets. It is only the images of nets, cages, and comets that are new and witty. No one had 'thought' of these before; in that sense they are part of the thought: but they are also mere illustrations used to 'express' general statements; in that sense they are merely methods of expression.

It is all part of the hoary dispute where, in writing, form ends and content begins. Poor Pepys seems to me here less unreasonable than Johnson, who had himself praised Pope for making 'familiar things new'. (Cf. Johnson's own comment on the *Essay on Man*: 'The reader feels his mind full, though he learns nothing: and when he meets it in its new array, no longer knows the talk of his mother and his nurse.')

madam, I had my revenge of her; for I swallowed five and twenty cups of her tea, and did not treat her with as many words.'

Yet, even so, the full extent of Johnson's capacity for rudeness will remain, perhaps, for ever unknown. For at Auchinleck he made some retort to Boswell's father which even Boswell could not bear, or dare, to record. And when, in Skye, Boswell himself 'laughed immoderately' at Johnson's curious observation that, had he a seraglio,[1] the ladies should all wear linen, Johnson 'instantly retaliated with such keen sarcastick wit, and such a variety of degrading images . . . that I would gladly expunge from my mind every trace of this severe retort'.[2]

In fine, when Johnson once growled to Joseph Warton at Reynolds's house—'Sir, I am not used to be contradicted', there was force in Warton's answer—'Better for yourself and friends, Sir, if you were; our admiration could not be increased, but our love might be.'

At all events, it becomes easy to understand some of the marks awarded to Johnson (out of a maximum of 20) by Mrs Thrale—'Religion, Morality, General Knowledge, 20; Scholarship, 19;[3] Humour, 16; Wit, 15;[4] Person, Voice,[5] Manners, Good Humour, 0.'

Secondly, an anti-Johnsonian might argue, not only was Johnson, as Taine said, an 'ours bourru'. He was also, by his own confession, hardly sane. He laboured under acute melancholia and obsessional neurosis. The first time that Hogarth's quick eye fell upon Johnson,

[1] A topic on which Boswell, who had entertained such dreams himself, was perhaps liable to become somewhat hysterical, when it was broached by the revered Johnson, from whom he kept that side of his life discreetly veiled.

[2] In the MS of the *Tour* (September 16, 1773) Boswell recorded Johnson as saying 'he'd make a very good eunuch'. Which strange notion he then proceeded to amplify in detail. Boswell seems to have writhed much more at these peculiar pleasantries than at the serious insults of Johnson's anger.

[3] To which Johnson might, I suppose, have replied, as to the poor gentleman outside Lichfield Cathedral, 'That may be; but it is impossible that *you* should know.'

[4] Most of us, perhaps, think of Johnson as having *more* wit than humour. But this may be because his gaiety was often less easy to record, and was certainly less recorded by Boswell, than his sharpness of tongue. We form a false picture of Johnson if we forget how often the lion laughed, as well as roared.

[5] This low estimate of Johnson's voice does not tally with some other evidence. 'His speaking,' says Boswell, 'was indeed very impressive; and I wish it could be preserved as musick is written.' Similarly M'Leod of Ulinish, in Skye—'He is a great orator, Sir; it is musick to hear this man speak.' (At his first meeting with Johnson, however, Boswell did think he had 'a most uncouth voice'.)

in the house of the novelist Richardson, he concluded this strange figure shaking and rolling itself by the window to be some idiot kindly cared for by Richardson. Then, suddenly, the unknown burst into so tremendous an invective against George II that the astounded Hogarth thought the idiot momentarily inspired.

But perhaps the most vivid picture of this side of Johnson comes from Miss Reynolds. In her *Recollections* she has described how he would whirl the blind Miss Williams round with him on the steps outside Sir Joshua's door, or stalk with a sudden spring across the threshold, as if seeing to what length he could stride; how he would make triangles with his feet (heels together and toes wide apart, and *vice versa*), or hold his hands, like a jockey, before his breast, or lift them, for minutes, high over his head; how he would terrify ladies for their dresses by wheeling a cup of tea about him at arm's length, or twist round, breathing hard, to drink it facing the back of his chair; how he would violently see-saw while reading; how his antics, when with her, once collected a laughing crowd in Twickenham meadows; how he would retire from company, dive behind a window-curtain, and pray aloud; how Garrick trod thrice on his toes to stop him disparaging a gentleman whose presence in the room Johnson was too short-sighted to notice—only to provoke the injured question, 'David, David, is it you? What makes you tread on my toes so?'

More familiar are his other rituals and tics, his touching of posts, his twitching off ladies' shoes at table. He was indeed a classical type of the obsessional neurotic, who averts impulses he dare not face by magic acts he does not understand.

More mysterious still is what Johnson himself refers to as *de pedicis et manicis insana cogitatio*—'mad thoughts about fetters and manacles'. An object called 'Johnson's padlock', committed to Mrs Thrale's care in 1768, was auctioned in 1823. And there exists a bizarre letter of his to Mrs Thrale (May 1773?), written in French (because of the servants?) and suggesting that he be daily locked in his room. These strange facts have been explained as due to fear of mental disturbance; but they look to me more like symptoms of it—whether simple masochism, or symbolic attempts, like his tics, to chain dreaded impulses.[1]

[1] See *Johnson's Letters*, ed. R. W. Chapman, iii, 323–4. Strange, too, is Mrs

Of his melancholia he has spoken often and vehemently enough himself. 'I inherited a vile melancholy from my father, which has made me mad all my life, at least not sober'—'gloomy discontent or importunate distress'—'tristis et atra quies et tardae taedia vitae'—'thus pass my days and nights in morbid wakefulness, in unseasonable sleepiness, in gloomy solitude with unwelcome visitors, or ungrateful exclusions, in variety of wretchedness.' True, this last sentence comes from the closing year of his life; yet what a contrast with the stoic cheerfulness preserved by the sceptic Hume, or the ironic Gibbon, or the realistic Franklin, to the very end!

Now it must be admitted that these inner conflicts jaundiced and distorted Johnson's wisdom about life in general, just as the violence of his passions misled him into particular prejudices. Unhappy himself, he belittled the happiness of others. He might, in one of his more balanced moments, propound the view—obvious, yet in practice constantly forgotten—that 'it is the business of a wise man to be happy'. But he generally took a poor view even of the sage's chance of success. He would mournfully proclaim that a man was happy only in his schooldays, or only when drunk,[1] or only when lying awake in bed in the morning;[2] or, it might be, when enthroned in a tavern, or filling up the day with petty business, or driving fast in a chaise with a pretty and intelligent woman. But however his views might vary about details, they remained gloomily constant in the conviction that happiness was an exceptional, fleeting, momentary thing. 'No man is happy but as he is compared with the miserable.' 'Human life is everywhere a state in which much is to be endured, and little to be enjoyed.' 'Philosophers there are,' he wrote to Mrs Thrale from Skye, 'who try to make themselves believe that this life is happy, but they believe it only while they are saying it, and never yet produced conviction in a single mind.' *Never* in a *single* mind? It is something that Johnson admitted the 'philosophers' to believe it even while they were saying it. And even this he could not always do.

Thrale's note—'How many Times has this great, this formidable Dr Johnson kissed my hand, ay and my foot too, upon his knees!'

[1] 'He who makes a *beast* of himself gets rid of the pain of being a man.'

[2] 'I may perhaps have said this: for nobody, at times, talks more loosely than I do.'

'It is all *cant*,' he would growl when someone claimed happiness, 'the dog knows he is miserable all the time.' Indeed this mania provoked one of the grossest even of Johnson's outbursts. A dear friend dared to assert that his own wife's sister was happy: 'If your sister-in-law,' retorted the angry sage (the wife herself being present), 'is really the contented being she professes herself, Sir, her life gives the lie to every research of humanity; for she is happy without health, without beauty, without money, and without understanding.' So at least the horrified Mrs Thrale reports. And I see no good reason to doubt her. A strange 'research of humanity'!

For himself, he said that not even the invitation of an angel would induce him (once more, unlike Franklin) to live a single week of his life again. Garrick's display of his fine house could only bring from Johnson the mournful comment, 'All these things, David, make death very terrible.' And, as Xerxes wept to reflect that the myriads of his army would all be dust in a hundred years, so, Johnson said, it went to his heart amid the gaieties of Ranelagh 'to consider that there was not one in all that brilliant circle that was not afraid to go home and think.'[1]

Now this, it must be owned, is a most dubious proposition. For, first, it is optimistic to suppose that many of these social butterflies would 'think', even when they did get home. Secondly, one may doubt whether even those who did 'think' would all have thoughts so dismal.

Johnson's life seems sometimes a kind of *Paradise Lost*, full of laments for happiness never to be regained, full of battles between better spirits and worse; and, beneath, gapes the horror of Hell. At times he is like another *Samson Agonistes*, blind, lonely, heroic, with no joy left but crushing Philistines.

'You see,' the Devil's Advocate might continue, 'not only was your Johnson, firstly, a bear and, secondly, half-crazy; in the third place he was a biased and unbalanced thinker. Admittedly, madmen have sometimes been geniuses, like Blake or Nietzsche; but John-

[1] Cf. Imlac to Rasselas (ch. xvi): 'In the assembly, where you passed last night, there appeared such sprightliness of air, and volatility of fancy, as might have suited beings of an higher order, formed to inhabit serener regions, inaccessible to care or sorrow: yet, believe me, prince, there was not one who did not dread the moment when solitude should deliver him to the tyranny of reflection.' (An interesting example of the difference between Johnson's spoken and his written style.)

son, that irrational figure-head of your Age of Reason, was, in his reasoning, very far from profound.'

Now no doubt Johnson's admirers have too often treated him as a complete oracle of wisdom. Sir Archibald Alison called him 'the strongest intellect and the most profound observer of the eighteenth century'. (Ah, these rash superlatives beloved of critics!) And then there is Ruskin: 'I never for an instant compared Johnson to Scott, Pope, Byron, or any of the really great writers whom I loved. But I at once and for ever recognized in him a man entirely sincere, and infallibly wise in the view and estimate he gave of the common questions, business, and ways of the world.'

Was this 'wisdom', it may be asked, really so 'infallible'? Even if we accept, as few will, Johnson's sombre, overloaded view of man's universal misery, how can we respect his ideas of philosophy? Is a man intellectually above the level of Squire Western at moments when he indulges in cross remarks like 'we know our will is free, and there's an end on't'; or 'no honest man can be a Deist; for no man *can* be so after a fair examination of the proofs of Christianity'? And what are we to think of one who imagines Berkeley's idealism sufficiently refuted by kicking stones;[1] or Hume's scepticism by calling it 'bull's milk'?

Indeed the name of Hume always roused what is least admirable in Johnson: 'I know not indeed whether he has first been a blockhead and that has made him a rogue, or first been a rogue and that has made him a blockhead.' And what could be feebler than Johnson's assertion that the dying Hume must have lied in saying he had no fears of the hereafter? Unless it be Johnson's argument for it—that, believing in no hereafter, Hume had no motive not to lie. Clearly Johnson cannot have it both ways. Either Hume believed in survival, or he did not. If he did not believe, then he was not lying. If he did believe, then he *did* have a motive not to lie.

Again, Johnson's own form of religion seems as unconvincing and disastrous as poor Cowper's—its intolerance left him narrowed, its morbid sense of guilt stuffed his pillow with prickles, its terror

[1] *Life*, i, 471; it has, indeed, been suggested by H. F. Hallett (*Mind*, lvi (1947), 132–47) that Johnson's objection was philosophically profounder than it looks; but I remain doubtful if so much subtlety can be read into four words ('I refute it *thus*') and a kick.

of the after-life proved a lifelong nightmare. That it made him a better man, may well be doubted; it did not restrain his ferocity, nor his idleness. And had he been as gaily sceptical as Hume or Voltaire, there seems no reason to believe that he would have become any less generous or compassionate; though he might have ceased to be so prudish as to scold Hannah More for having read *Tom Jones*.

It may, of course, be pleaded that many eminent minds have staggered in matters philosophical or religious; though they have usually staggered more discreetly. But even in fields more mundane Johnson could become, at moments, positively dense.

He might distract his hours of solitude with measuring the rate of growth of his hair and fingernails, or the loss of weight in dried vineleaves; with chemical pastimes or the distillation of horrible concoctions, 'which all,' says Hawkins, 'might smell, but few chose to taste'; but his thinking was no more scientific than it was philosophic. 'Swallows certainly sleep all the winter. A number of them conglobulate together, by flying round and round, and then all in a heap throw themselves under water and lye in the bed of a river.'[1] Or again—'Births at all times bear the same proportion to the same number of people.' After such biological fantasies[2] one may wonder how much right Johnson had to mock at poor Goldsmith—'if he can distinguish a cow from a horse, that, I believe, may be the extent of his knowledge of natural history'.

Nor again is it easy to find much logic in that review of Dr Lucas's *Essay on Waters* where Johnson attacks cold baths. That a man who so little loved clean linen should have no great passion

[1] This was in 1768 (*Life*, ii, 55); by 1773 he had perhaps dropped this pleasant fancy, for he did not contradict Goldsmith's statement that swallows in part migrate (*Life*, ii, 248). Perhaps, as suggested by R. D. Spector in *Notes and Queries*, vol. 196 (1951), 564–5, he had meanwhile read Pennant's *British Zoology* (2nd ed. 1768), which says that believers in 'the submersion of swallows' 'must provoke a smile'.

[2] One still more extraordinary is recorded in Boswell's journal (May 29, 1783). Boswell remarked, he says, to Johnson, of Langton, that he was 'the reverse of the Insect which is first snail then butterfly, for he was first Butterfly, then Snail'. 'Who said this of him?' 'I say it now.' 'It is very well said.' 'I say very good things sometimes.'

But it remains very hard to believe that Johnson really supposed snails to be insects, or to turn into butterflies. One wonders, even, if Boswell was quite sober when he wrote it. ('Snail' in older English could mean 'slug'; but it seems doubtful if even in Scottish it could mean 'caterpillar'.)

for baths, hot or cold, is hardly surprising;[1] but the argument becomes so. 'It is incident to physicians, I am afraid, beyond all other men, to mistake subsequence for consequence. "The old gentleman," says Dr Lucas, "that uses the cold bath, enjoys in return an uninterrupted state of health."[2] This instance does not prove that the cold bath produces health, but only that it will not always destroy it. He is well with the bath, he would have been well without it.' But how could Johnson know that?

No less extraordinary at times were Johnson's ideas on mechanics. He jeered at the idea of a machine on which one could propel oneself along the road, as fundamentally preposterous. 'Then, Sir, what is gained is, the man has his choice whether he will move himself, or himself and the machine too.' At that rate one would have thought all machines employing human strength, like the lever or the pulley, must be equally chimerical. A pity that Johnson never lived to see the first bicycle of 1839.

Nor is it impressive to find him recommending to Sophia Thrale 'a curious calculation' in Wilkins's *Real Character*, 'to show that Noah's ark was capable of holding all the known animals of the world, with provision for all the time in which the earth was under water'.

Nor was he much better informed in many other branches of thought or knowledge. His Greek was somewhat superficial; his French, when he writes it, is surprisingly poor. For history, except its biographical parts, he expressed frequent contempt. On politics he was amusing but often grotesque. There seems to me no great exaggeration in Macaulay's phrase about 'the torrents of raving abuse which he poured forth against the Long Parliament and the American Congress'. For even in 1781 Johnson thought that the towns in America should have been razed to the ground—'let them enjoy their forests'. And though a man is not on oath in talk, Johnson's repeated references to William III as a 'scoundrel', or 'one of the most worthless scoundrels that ever existed', could damage no one but himself. (It is interesting to note a much more

[1] 'I hate immersion.' However he bathed at Brighton in 1766; and was complimented by the attendant—'Why, Sir, you must have been a stout-hearted gentleman forty years ago!'

[2] This, it must be owned, seems a little sweeping.

moderate reference to the great Dutchman in the *Life of Prior*.)

On education his views could be monstrous, even for that flogging age. When Boswell had to defend a Scottish schoolmaster accused of brutality, Johnson was emphatic in the brute's favour. 'This man has maimed none of his boys. They are left with the full exercise of their corporeal faculties. In our schools in England many boys have been maimed; yet I never heard of an action against a schoolmaster on that account.' Lucky that Johnson's own schoolmastering failed early, so that for the rest of his life he had to vent his fierceness on adults, not children—though perhaps with schoolboys his practice was less ferocious than his theories. For, in a milder mood, he once stated that schoolmasters were worse than Egyptian taskmasters. And he could plead for a remission of holiday-tasks. None the less he opposed any diminution of flogging—what the children gained at one end, they would lose at the other.

No doubt there were also some social and political questions on which Johnson took the side of light. He denounced the Slave Trade, while Boswell made himself its foolish and flippant defender; indeed, in grave company at Oxford, Johnson even drank 'to the next insurrection of the negroes in the West Indies'. But it can be argued that this was the effect of outraged heart and conscience, rather than of studied thought. Similarly, Johnson shared Montaigne's hatred for white exploitation of coloured peoples—'I do not wish well to discoveries, for I am always afraid they will end in conquest and robbery.'

Again, he was among the minority of Englishmen who condemned the oppression of Ireland—'Let the authority of the English government perish, rather than be maintained by iniquity.... Better to hang or drown people at once, than by an unrelenting persecution to beggar and starve them.' But he was not always so liberal towards Ireland. Here too passion would break in. Talking in 1781 to Dr Thomas Campbell about the Irish volunteers, he burst out, 'had I been a minister ... I would have done as Oliver Cromwell did, I would have burned your cities, and roasted you in the fires or flames of them.' Campbell pointed out that these drastic methods had not worked very well in America. Regretfully Johnson admitted that 'the times are altered, for *Power* is now nowhere'. Still, he persisted, the towns of America *should* have been razed.

'After this wild rant,' Campbell comments, 'argument would but have enraged him, I therefore let him vibrate into calmness.' This succeeded. Johnson smiled in the end, and owned that the Irish were not 'so very wrong'. A typically Johnsonian struggle between passionate vehemence and honest fairness.

It is true, also, that *Idlers* 22 and 38 boldly and sensibly attack the system of imprisoning debtors, which was to endure another eighty years, into the days of Pickwick. 'It appears that more than twenty thousand are at this time prisoners for debt. . . . It seems to be the opinion of the later computists, that the inhabitants of *England* do not exceed six millions, of which twenty thousand is the three-hundredth part. What shall we say of the humanity or the wisdom of a nation, that voluntarily sacrifices one in every three hundred to lingering destruction!'

Again, Johnson put his practical finger on the supreme importance for the individual Englishman of having his personal freedom safeguarded by *Habeas Corpus*. And he never shared the follies of Rousseauism, or canted about savages. But, in general, his political ideas do not seem more than a blend of prejudices, commonsense, and (sometimes) humanity; just as his religious ideas seem largely a blend of forlorn hope and nightmare.

Of the arts Johnson knew little, apart from literature. For painting and sculpture, he was too blind; even if he had not been, he might have cared as little for them as he cared for music.[1] Literature was another matter. His critical powers we can consider later; yet it is generally agreed that even here, though his feeling for some poetry was intense, and his incisiveness of judgment sometimes superb, his ear was often defective and his sympathies somewhat narrow.

In fine, an accuser might say, Johnson was no great thinker. Ruskin's praise of him as 'infallibly wise' only illustrates how right was Madox Brown's phrase for Ruskin himself—'the incarnation of exaggeration'; or Carlyle's—'a bottle of beautiful soda-water'.

[1] 'Surely,' he wrote to Baretti, of the Royal Academy Exhibition, 'life, if it be not long, is tedious, since we are forced to call in the assistance of so many trifles to rid us of our time, of that time which can never return.' Of music he complained, 'it excites in my mind no ideas, and hinders me from contemplating my own.' A player or singer 'has the merit of a Canary-bird'. And most of us remember his retort to the remark that a certain violin performance he had just heard was 'very difficult'—'Difficult do you call it, Sir? I wish it were impossible.'

There was little enough in common between Adam Smith and Blake; but about Johnson, for once, they agreed. For Adam Smith called him 'of all writers ancient and modern, the one who kept off the greatest distance from common sense'.[1] And, in his different manner, Blake thought the same:

> Lo, the Bat with leathern wing,
> Winking and blinking,
> Winking and blinking,
> Winking and blinking,
> Like Dr Johnson.

Indeed, Blake's further remarks on Johnson are not quotable in decent print.

In fine, Johnson was never a profound thinker in comparison with men like Montesquieu, Diderot, or Buffon, Hume, Berkeley, or Burke.

Fourthly, an anti-Johnsonian might claim, he was not really a great writer any more than he was a profound thinker. Over a century has passed without Johnson's Works being reprinted, even in his own country. There is no very remarkable achievement, it might be urged, in producing an unreadable tragedy, some ponderous essays, and a mass of hackwork. The Dictionary and the *Shakespeare* are obsolete. *Rasselas*, though sometimes praised, is seldom read. And even Johnson's criticism remains, it may be urged, chiefly of historic interest. Above all, the style particularly associated with Johnson is a laborious, sterile hybrid between English and Latin. 'Johnson,' it has been said (though I passionately disagree), 'represents all the vices of eighteenth-century prose, as Pope represents all the vices of eighteenth-century verse'.[2]

His pompous grandiloquence, which often attempts rather than attains impressiveness, maddened readers like Horace Walpole,[3] provoked Churchill to his satire on 'Pomposo', and made Archibald Campbell jeer in *Lexiphanes* that Johnson 'might write his *Ramblers*

[1] But see pp. 34, 101 footnote.

[2] H. Bett, *Some Secrets of Style* (1932), p. 260.

[3] *E.g.* to Mason, April 14, 1781: 'The machinery in *The Rape of the Lock* he calls "combination of skilful genius with happy casualty", in English, I guess, "a lucky thought".'

to make a dictionary necessary, and afterwards compile his Dictionary to explain his *Ramblers*'.[1]

It would be mere waste of time to quote and analyse at length this bad style of Johnson's, which welters along like his description of the Foyers river—'frequently obstructed by protuberances and exasperated by reverberation'. At times it shows clearly enough the influence of Sir Thomas Browne,[2] and a love of Latin and Latinisms equal to Sir Thomas's—a love, no doubt, partly disinterested, but not without a touch of self-importance. As Wordsworth bound *The White Doe* in quarto to show how much he thought of it, so at times Johnson liked to speak his thoughts in polysyllables to show how much *he* thought of *them*. None the less one cannot doubt his love of Latin for its own sake. In it he recorded events of his own life; in it, and no other tongue, would he commemorate Goldsmith; touring France, he was 'resolute in speaking Latin'; speechless with a stroke, he still composed Latin verses; and his last recorded words on earth (by one account) were still Latin—'Iam moriturus.'

And yet it seems a little paradoxical in a man who vehemently denounced Gallicisms in English style, thus to overload it himself with Latinisms. Indeed one might argue that French prose has proved in practice a far safer and healthier influence for English, than Latin prose has, or German.

No doubt, like an old Roman draping himself in his toga, Johnson thought he was thus adding dignity both to his country

[1] Cf. the parody, suspected by Mrs Thrale to be by Soame Jenyns, in which Johnson woos Thrale's widow to become his wife:

> Cervisial coctor's viduate dame, (*i.e.* brewer's widow)
> Opin'st thou this gigantick frame,
> Procumbing at thy shrine,
> Shall, catenated by thy charms,
> A captive in thy ambient arms
> Perennially be thine?

Like most Johnsonian parodies, this is abject; but it shows one side of Johnson's reputation.

[2] The famous definition of 'cough', however, in the *Dictionary*—'a convulsion of the lungs, vellicated by some sharp serosity'—which looks a typical Brownism, turns out to be an abbreviated borrowing from Johnson's predecessors, Benjamin Martin and Chambers—'a disease affecting the lungs, occasioned by a sharp serous humour vellicating the fibrous coat thereof, and urging it to a discharge by spitting'. (See J. H. Sledd and G. J. Kolb, *Dr Johnson's Dictionary*, p. 36.) Still one must own that only a man over-tolerant of Latinisms could have endured such jargon.

and to himself. But nothing more exposed him to criticism than sentences like this—'In cities, and yet more in courts, the minute discriminations which distinguish one from another are for the most part effaced, the peculiarities of temper and opinion are gradually worn away by promiscuous converse, as angular bodies and uneven surfaces lose their points and asperities by frequent attrition against one another, and approach by degrees to uniform rotundity'[1] —in short, as pebbles are rounded.

Or, again, there is that design for conversation in *The Idler*—'I will instruct the modest by easy generalities and repress the ostentatious by seasonable superciliousness.' We smile.[2]

At times, indeed, Johnson could laugh at this mania in himself, as when he referred to Foote's loss of a leg as 'the depeditation of Foote'. But only towards the end of his life did he largely clear his written style of this kind of lumber. And even in his last year, 1784, everyone knows how he corrected, in conversation, his own verdict on *The Rehearsal*, 'It has not wit enough to keep it sweet,' by the 'more round sentence'—'It has not vitality enough to preserve it from putrefaction'.

This too abstract and latinate diction was aggravated by overfondness also for devices of Roman rhetoric like personified abstractions, antitheses, and triplets—such as 'assist the struggles of endeavour, dissipate the blush of diffidence, and still the flutter of timidity'.

And yet at Oxford he had refused to allow his fellow-undergraduates to use the epithet 'prodigious'. He had warned Boswell—'Don't, Sir, accustom yourself to use big words for little matters.' He had mocked Gray because 'he has a kind of strutting dignity and is tall by walking on tiptoe'. Was it for the author of *The*

[1] *Rambler*, 138.

[2] As one would expect, since faults are usually easier to copy than virtues, Johnson's worse style, like Milton's, had a detestable influence on imitators; such as Sir James Mackintosh or Sir William Scott, Professor of Ancient History at Oxford (1773–85), whose lectures are amusingly described by one of his undergraduates: 'He has a good deal of the Doctor's manner. . . . He turned, doubled, and practised all the windings of a hunted hare, in order to avoid that odious word butter, or cheese, and talked with great ingenuity about shoes for several minutes without naming them. Describing the houses of the Athenians, he acquainted his audience that "they had no conveniences by which the volatile parts of fire could be conveyed into the open air".' (Hill–Powell, Boswell's *Johnson*, iv, 490.)

Rambler to find fault with 'cumbrous splendour'? Or to tax Milton with 'forming his style by a perverse and pedantic principle'? Again, it seems a curious kind of correction when, to Boswell calling a Highland peak 'immense', Johnson retorted, 'No; it is no more than a considerable protuberance.' I suppose Johnson's defence might have been that he objected, not to words bulky in size, but to words extravagant in meaning. Still, it might have been better to object to both.

Finally, the Devil's Advocate might conclude, Johnson wasted in indolence and frivolity those talents that he did possess. By his own admission he was fundamentally indolent. Further, he devoted a great deal of his energy and mental power to mere talk. This charge has been brought with special vehemence by Bernard Shaw. 'I,' wrote Shaw, 'have not wasted my time like Johnson trifling with literary fools in taverns, when he should have been shaking England with the thunder of his spirit.' On this view, Johnson was only a ponderous drone, preserved in amber for posterity by the gossiping assiduity of a Scottish squireen.

To sum up this long indictment, it is possible to question whether Johnson was either wise, or profound, or a good writer, or an admirable man. On the contrary, he can be taxed with bearishness, craziness, superficial thinking, inflated writing, indolent triviality. What, then, can justice urge in answer, on Johnson's side? Why does he still delight, if not the world, at least the English-speaking part of it?

The first charge, of bearishness, is of course true. But even this remains a one-sided truth. The best answer is Goldsmith's 'Johnson has nothing of the bear but his skin'. Knowing him so much better, we have less excuse than his contemporaries (who suffered from his rudeness, as we do not) for forgetting what exceptional goodness and humanity lay beneath that rough exterior. On the other hand, we may easily get an exaggerated impression of his explosiveness. The eruptions of the volcano were naturally much more recorded than its long intervals of sunny, or clouded, quiescence. But these intervals did exist. 'Dr Johnson,' writes Fanny Burney to Mrs Thrale on August 24, 1779, 'was very sweet and delightful indeed; I think he grows more and more so, or at least, I grow more and more fond of him.'

His had been a grim career, that might well have left him embittered and devitalized. Virgil's Dido could, indeed, exclaim

> Non ignara mali, miseris succurrere disco.
>
> I have known sorrow—and learned to aid the sad.

And yet prolonged unhappiness can easily sink men, on the contrary, into a soured and sullen egoism that retains neither the sympathy, nor the energy, to bestir itself for others. But with Johnson it was not so.

Everyone knows how he turned his house into a home for incurables—Mrs Desmoulins, the blind Miss Williams, Poll Carmichael (the lady who, he said, was 'wiggle-waggle'), and Levett the surgeon;[1] how he carried home in his arms a destitute streetwalker, or thrust pennies he could ill afford into the paws of sleeping street-urchins; how he went out himself to buy oysters for his cat Hodge, lest his servants should grow to hate the poor beast; how at Gwynagag, when his host's gardener caught a hare among the potatoes, he saved the poor victim on its way to the kitchen by popping it out of a window. Vivisection he denounced in *The Idler*, and even in a note on *Cymbeline*; and he would never sit down to a table that had among its dishes a lobster cooked alive.

'Madam,' he replied to a lady asking why he gave money to beggars, 'to enable them to beg on.' He lent his aid to a subscription for clothing French prisoners-of-war. He pleaded for Admiral Byng. He pleaded for Dr Dodd. And it was Goldsmith, with all his own Irish generosity to the needy, that best summed up this humanity of the blunt Englishman who had so often snubbed him. 'He is poor and honest,' said Goldsmith of Levett, 'which is recom-

[1] Levett, a thin being, with visage 'swarthy, adust, and corrugated', whose looks, said Johnson, 'disgusted the rich and terrified the poor,' had picked up part of his medical knowledge as waiter in a Paris café frequented by surgeons, who found him attentive to their talk, and generously subscribed for his further education. At nearly sixty he married a pocket-picking prostitute whom he had been used to meet in a coalshed; supposing her an heiress, while she imagined him a successful doctor. Fortunately she ran away. With Johnson he regularly breakfasted; but usually in silence. None the less his death in 1782 occasioned one of Johnson's finest poems.

According to Hawkins, however, 'Levett would sometimes insult him, and Mrs Williams, in her paroxysms of rage, has been known to drive him from her presence'.

mendation enough to Johnson. He is now become miserable and that ensures the protection of Johnson.'

There is, indeed, no denying Johnson's conversational brutality. But though it cannot be explained away, it can perhaps be explained. And, once understood, it may no longer seem, after all, very heinous, or even very regrettable. Why was this man of active and fundamental kindness towards real suffering, this devout believer in that creed which blesses the meek, none the less so often a blunt and blustering curmudgeon?

All this is not only a problem in literary history; it is a problem in something still more important—human nature. It was lack of knowledge of human nature that made Plato's *Republic* a Cloud-cuckoo-town, and caused Marx, with all his good intentions, to pave the way to a dozen hells on earth; it is lack of knowledge of human nature that helps to fill the world with unhappy marriages and warped children. It matters more than the study of atoms or animals, of metaphysics or linguistics. And here is a fragment of it.

The first reason, I think, for Johnson's violence is the obvious one that, like most energetic characters, he was tensely passionate. As he wrote to Mrs Thrale—'my *genius* is always in extremes.' 'I can't drink a *little*, child,' he said to Hannah More, urging him to take a little wine; 'therefore I never touch it.' 'I find it does a man good,' he reflects, after his interview with George III,[1] 'to be talked to by his sovereign. In the first place he cannot be in a passion.' Not a reason that would ever occur to most of us; but Johnson's intensity was like an almost ungovernable horse, always ready to take the bit in its teeth and bolt.

His lapses were not due to savagery, or callousness, so much as to momentary force of feeling. Reynolds noted how often, after these outbursts, he was the first to seek reconciliation; and Boswell

[1] It is said that George III was more nervous about this interview than Johnson, and 'went to it as a schoolboy to his task'.

It also appears that George (though finding a great part of Shakespeare 'sad stuff') yet used to enter in notebooks Shakespearian quotations appropriate to persons or happenings he had known; and in 1778 he applied to Johnson the lines from *Love's Labour's Lost* (v, 1)—'He draweth out the thread of his verbosity finer than the staple of his argument. I abhor such phanatical phantasms, such insociable and point-devise companions, such rackers of orthography.' The application may have been humorous: but Johnson would hardly have been amused. (See Arthur Sherbo in *Notes and Queries*, vol. 197 (1952), 37–8.)

has recorded some charming examples of such olive branches. 'When I am musing alone,' wrote Johnson to Taylor in 1756, 'I feel a pang for every moment that any human being has by my peevishness or obstinacy spent in uneasiness.' And Fanny Burney notes his saying, 'I am always sorry when I make bitter speeches, and I never do it but when I am insufferably vexed.' Unluckily he was not seldom 'insufferably vexed'.

Thus his passion caused him remorse—till new passion goaded him into new remorselessness. One can actually watch the process in that scene of high comedy when the gaunt and gawky Langton, in answer to Johnson's humble request to be told his faults, brought him in 1784 a paper filled with various scriptural texts on meekness and long-suffering; which the penitent proceeded to glance through with deepening fury, till he finally bellowed, 'What is your drift, Sir?' (One may conjecture that poor Langton's[1] drift was in the direction of the door.)

Secondly, Johnson had battled long years through the Gehenna of Grub Street;[2] he had lived rough among rough characters and rough tongues; he had been recommended by one bookseller to find himself a porter's knot, and had knocked down another with a folio; he had smitten the aristocratic condescension of Lord Chesterfield with a letter like a sledgehammer; he had stood amid the abuse of his *Irene*, 'like the Monument'. Johnson had, perforce, grown tough-minded. Why, after seeing and feeling so much misery, should he temper the wind of his irritation to 'weak-nerved' persons, who whined over metaphysical troubles or mere bluntness of speech? Who was, in any real sense, the worse for being spoken of, or to, uncharitably? No doubt this did not prevent his being sensitive enough himself to the least trace of incivility. That was inconsistent. But it was human.

Thirdly, Johnson had been from birth poor, obscure, deformed, short-sighted, neurotic. Yet he had fought his way up by his wits

[1] Langton seems to have been of an improving disposition. He presented Boswell with a work called *The Government of the Tongue* (1693); in which Boswell wrote: 'He gave me the Book and hoped I would read that treatise; but said no more. . . . It was a delicate Admonition.' (Some may feel more doubtful of the delicacy.)

[2] Though only in a metaphorical sense; for, oddly enough, as he owned to Fanny Burney in 1780, he had never been there; so that he gaily suggested to her a joint expedition to 'visit the mansions of our progenitors'.

and character alone. Now he had become in a sense, a beggar on horseback, a dictator called from the plough, a peasant of the Danube raised by his own energies to the purple. None the less, for many, he was still 'no gentleman'. And he knew it.

Besides, greatly as he had succeeded, he could feel that he ought by rights to have succeeded still more. Poverty had cramped and curtailed his Oxford career; he had seen his intellectual inferiors rise to rank and fame above him; what wonder if at times he had a bitter sense of injustice and frustration?

At all events, he would not be put upon now, even by peers. As guest of Lord Shelburne at Bowood, he is said to have repeated at dinner part of his letter to Lord Chesterfield. Shortly after, for the sake of a late-arrived guest, Shelburne politely suggested, 'I dare say the Doctor will be kind enough to give it us again.' But Shelburne should have been warned by the fate of Chesterfield. 'Indeed, my Lord,' came the surly answer, 'I will not. I told the circumstance first for my own amusement, but I will not be dragged in as a story-teller to a company.'

To-day the term 'inferiority-complex' is too loosely bandied about. But, in some degree, it may really apply to Johnson. Boswell seems feeling after something of the sort, when he notes in 1784—'Dr Johnson's harsh attacks on his friends arise from uneasiness within. There is an insurrection aboard. His loud explosions are guns of distress.' In fine, Johnson's offensiveness may often have been, in his own phrase, 'defensive pride'. On religious topics, however, his explosiveness was, I take it, due less to lurking doubts of himself than to lurking doubts of his religious creed; for, though his dread of death was morbidly excessive, his faith was by no means perfectly assured.

Fourthly, Johnson had not only the inferiority of his origin and his physique to overcome; he had also his painfully won superiority to maintain. For the last third of his life his main profession was talk. In that he had succeeded, partly because he cared so intensely to succeed. He may have been, at times, indolent as a writer; but as a talker he spared no effort to talk his very best. Rossetti once wrote to a friend about literary success—'What you lack is simply ambition—*i.e.* the feeling of pure rage and self-hatred when anyone else does better than you do. . . . You comfort yourself with other things, whereas Art must be its own comforter, or comfortless.' So Johnson felt. He had risen both by his pen and by his tongue. Even young, he had deliberately studied the art of contradiction. And now he must maintain his supremacy by tongue alone. Yet he was growing old; a younger generation was at the door. He felt perhaps a little like the ancient priest of Nemi, the escaped slave who had won by assassination the priesthood of the Golden Bough, till assassination should extinguish him in turn.[1] We may recall how Dr Parr, when Johnson stamped at him, stamped back; explaining that he would not concede to his opponent the advantage even of a stamp. This was a feeling that Johnson could well have understood. It was the same policy as made him once (so he told Reynolds) endure to be nearly roasted by the fire in a room full of booksellers, rather than quit the head of the table 'and let one of them sit above him'. His broadsides, in short, were not only, in Boswell's phrase, 'guns of distress'; they were also fired to repel possible boarders. He was like a buccaneer, always cleared for action.

At the same time, it must, I think, be owned that Johnson was not only 'defensive', but also aggressive. There was no lack of primitive aggressiveness and joy in battle about the man who answered the menaces of Macpherson by arming himself with a six-foot ash sapling, worthy of Hercules; who, finding his seat taken at a Lichfield play, tossed the intruder, chair and all, into the pit;[2] who threatened, if Foote guyed him in a London theatre, to go from the boxes and chastise him before the whole audience; who could battle single-handed with four footpads in nocturnal London, till the arrival of the watch to the rescue. Naturally, a man so pugnacious and courageous was tempted at times to abuse his powers. For his tongue was as formidable as his fists. He had a quicker wit than most, and a more forcible energy of speech. If his rapier failed, he could bring up a battering-ram. He was fearlessly unhampered by the least regard for persons, politeness, or public opinion. No holds were barred. Small wonder then if, be-

[1] Cf. his remarks to Fanny Burney when she was to meet Mrs Montagu: 'Down with her, Burney!—down with her!—spare her not!—attack her, fight her, and down with her at once! You are a rising wit, and she is at the top; and when I was beginning the world, and was nothing and nobody, the joy of my life was to fire at all the established wits.'

[2] Or, in another version, across the stage.

coming a dictator, his power at moments corrupted him; if, like other champion duellists, he became sometimes a bully; if he learnt to stalk in society like some majestic chanticleer about a barnyard, who dared peck anybody (except a bishop), and whom hardly anybody dared peck.

Lastly Johnson was fanatically sincere. Cant was his abomination. But politeness often involves some degree of insincerity. 'L'art de plaire est l'art de tromper.' Yet of that Johnson remained as incapable as Cordelia. He would not—he simply could not—pretend to be convinced, or impressed, or sympathetic, when he felt none of these things.

It can, of course, be retorted—'You may have explained Johnson's boorish rudeness; you may have excused it; but it remains, none the less, an odious and repellent blemish, like the snarling savagery of Swift.'

But I do not think the parallel holds. To me, the moments when Swift becomes himself a yahoo are ugly and jarring; but Johnson's rudeness is amusing. Ethically, no doubt, he would have been a better man had he possessed a better humour, like Hume; but æsthetically we should be the losers now. Had he given less pain to his associates, he would give less pleasure to his readers. It is an odd example of Mandeville's 'private vices, publick benefits'. Here is rudeness raised to an art; it is an essential element of that rugged, vital character; it produced some of the most vivid and forcible of all his sayings; and we watch it with a fearful joy.

There are decadent intellectuals in our day who have celebrated the beauties of bull-fights. This seems to me a particularly disgusting *trahison des clercs*. If anything in the world is foul, it is the infliction of pain for mere amusement. But here the bull and his victims are all long dead; and one can surely enjoy without brutality the creature's strength, his agility, the sharpness of the horns with which he 'tosses and gores'. Indeed a cynic might suggest that many are fascinated by this very unseraphic Doctor because he dared to be as rude in reality as they long to be in their daydreams.

Let us face it—up to a point Johnson can be excused and justified; yet this process can be overdone. The passionate admirers of great men are often tempted to march up with whole buckets of whitewash. But a good painting is not improved by whitewash. Biography, history, fiction have an æsthetic as well as an ethical side. Johnson would have been a better man, had he been better-tempered, more courteous, gentler, cleaner; but he would be less picturesque, less amusing, less known and valued to-day. Johnson lives for us not so much as a remarkable writer, but rather as an extraordinary dramatic character in the great drama of life—often tragic, still more often comic. We treasure his memory partly because he was often wise and good, but partly—let us own it—because he could also resemble an intoxicated hippopotamus.

The 'pious' Æneas, no doubt, was a better character than Achilles, Octavia than Cleopatra, Sir Galahad than Sir Lancelot, the Chief Justice than Falstaff. But it is not the better characters that men care about. Often they are even bores. So with Johnson—he at least was no bore.

Hamlet, again, would have been a happier man, had he possessed the resolution of Fortinbras. Falstaff would have been a finer figure, if less fat and less cowardly. Don Quixote would have been a healthier person, if less lean and lunatic. Yet, as characters, they would only lose by these improvements in their characters. Ninnies, indeed, have tried to clear Falstaff of his cowardice. But they only deserve Johnson's own contemptuous comment on Maurice Morgann—that as he had proved Falstaff no coward, doubtless he would come forth again to establish the virtues of Iago.

In short, one can no more wish Samuel Johnson politer than one can wish Wilkins Micawber less feckless, or Mrs Proudie less domineering, or Uncle Toby more worldly-wise.

In the real world Montesquieu, Hume, or Franklin were probably as gifted as Johnson. They led far more enviable lives. But their good sense and health of mind can never fascinate like his oddities and eccentricities. Again, what a tedious person was George Washington! Johnson himself, paradoxically, interests posterity less by his kindness than by his unkindness. Faults may be a far better ladder to fame than virtues. Indeed the best lives may often be lived by men who are never heard of.

Johnson, I repeat, is much more important as a personality than as a maker of books—less like Sophocles or Euripides than that Heracles they both wrote of—a violent, brutal, sometimes demented hero, yet all the more human in his heroism for his failings. There is, then, no occasion for whitewash. Truth is better.

Secondly, there is the question of Johnson's mental maladies. Here, I think, there are several answers.

No doubt, with better mental health, as with better manners, he might have been a more rational, better, and happier man. But though his own life might well have gained, his memory would not. It would have lost some of that picturesque, mysterious strangeness which marks him out all the more strikingly in that balanced, reason-loving age.

Further, it surely deserves our admiration that despite such burdens he should have made his way so gallantly and so far. Melancholia is no laughing matter. He might have let himself sink into mere apathy and inertia. He perpetually cursed his own indolence; yet he proved, again and again, by his own example that a man can always write if he sets himself to it 'doggedly'. The Dictionary, the Shakespeare, and a dozen volumes of works are not, after all, the output of an idler. Even when he ceased to write much, he resolutely talked and jested even at times when, as he said, his heart like Milton's Satan might be cursing the sun.

Above all, whatever his gloom, he did not whine. He consumed his own smoke. He had indeed thought, in 1768, of composing 'the history of my melancholy'. But he did not. Perhaps it was indolence; but perhaps it was, rather, that stoic good sense which made him write so sternly, yet wisely to the lamenting Boswell in 1780: 'You are always complaining of melancholy, and I conclude from those complaints that you are fond of it . . . make it an invariable and obligatory law to yourself, never to mention your own mental diseases. . . . When you talk of them, it is plain that you want either praise or pity; for praise there is no room, and pity will do you no good.' Johnson suffered; but, as a rule, in silence.

As with his melancholia, so with his other neurotic quirks. With these too he battled. He did not, like some later decadents, parade them with the vanity of being different—though he well knew the temptation. 'There is in a human nature a general inclination to make people stare, and every wise man has to cure himself of it and does cure himself of it.' One cannot conceive Johnson dyeing his hair green like Baudelaire. Nor did he in his work exploit his mental maladies, like some more modern writers, who have used the bees in their bonnets to produce sticky oozings of poisonous honey; and who sometimes make one think of Goldsmith's poem—

The dog, to gain some private ends,
Went mad.

All his life, on the contrary, Johnson wrestled with himself for sanity and decency. That is one lesson to be learnt from him, and from the Age of Reason. It is not the least.

Johnson, in fine, was a very sick as well as vigorous man; both in body and in mind. Little wonder that Boswell saw him as 'a mighty gladiator', contending always in the Coliseum with wild beasts which he could never kill, only drive back for the moment to their dens; little wonder that Johnson himself could say to Dr Adams, 'I would consent to have a limb amputated, to recover my spirits.'

Even so, of course, it can be answered: 'In this no doubt Johnson was admirable—courageous, resolute, kind, and generous. But men like John Howard, or the good Lord Shaftesbury, did far more to lessen human suffering and sorrow than Johnson; yet twenty books are written about Johnson for one about them. The essential point at issue is the quality of your Johnson's intellect. Now that has justly been questioned.'

This third charge against Johnson—of being as a thinker often unsound, and never profound—cannot, I think, be honestly denied. In matters philosophic, scientific, political, he often flounders; and it can only be said for him, as he said of Warburton, that 'he flounders well'—that is, vigorously and (far more than Warburton) amusingly.

But, after all, it is not only profound minds that are remarkable. Indeed they can sometimes be intolerably tedious—the deeper, the duller. And in other ways Johnson's brain seems to me very remarkable indeed. It is not merely that he had an amazing memory. Good memories can go with very second-rate minds; and good minds can have memories like sieves. Montaigne, for example. The four great qualities of Johnson's mind seem to me its range, its quickness and wit, its honesty, and its power (above all, in talk) of clear and decisive utterance.

Johnson's mind was hardly broad; but it was unusually wide.

When he was a boy of sixteen, his cousin Cornelius Ford (a disreputable person, at one time chaplain to Lord Chesterfield, and supposed, though this is dubious, to figure in Hogarth's *Modern Midnight Conversation*) gave him a piece of excellent advice—'to obtain some general principles in every science; he who can talk only on one subject, or act only in one department, is seldom wanted and, perhaps, never wished for'.

For many, such counsel might be dangerous. One remembers Macaulay's Lord Brougham, that 'slovenly Solomon', 'half knowing everything from the cedar to the hyssop'. Such a course might produce a dilettante, *Reader's Digest* type of mind. But for an original and active intellect, resolute to distinguish between mere idle curiosities and what has a bearing on the real values of life, there can be great advantages in avoiding that over-specialization which even Darwin came so bitterly to regret. Schopenhauer took the same view as Cornelius Ford; and Johnson is a supreme example of the profit such a policy can yield.

> Deign on the passing world to turn thine eyes
> And pause awhile from letters to be wise.

When a clergyman complained to Mrs Thrale's mother that his neighbours talked of nothing but 'runts',[1] she replied, 'Mr Johnson would learn to talk about runts.' And, in effect, Mr M'Queen listening to Johnson in Skye at first thought he must have been bred in the Mint; then in a brewery. At the Thrales' again, he gave a similar impression of inside knowledge to a dancing-master; which is the more remarkable as few men can have looked less like a dancer. He would discourse on tanning, or on butchery, or, to the officers at Fort George in the Highlands, on the making of gunpowder. (One is reminded of the technical versatility of Diderot.) Arkwright thought him the only man to understand at once the complications of the spinning-jenny. Similarly the nephew of Reynolds wrote, 'His knowledge is infinite and my Aunt says that She never found him ignorant of one thing but the method of splitting Pease (for his knowledge descends to all mechanical arts, even to the making of Custards).'

[1] Small breeds of horses or cattle.

Whether, indeed, it is really worth extending one's interest even to the making of custards, seems to me dubious. Though Arnold may be right in saying 'Not deep the poet sees, but wide,' perhaps Johnson's eye wandered in some directions a little too widely; as too narrowly in others. Still in his multifarious interests he kept at least one principle of selection—knowledge, unless it were to be a futile vanity, must bear on human life. 'He that would travel for the entertainment of others, should remember that the great object of remark is human life.' 'As gold which he cannot spend will make no man rich, so knowledge which he cannot apply will make no man wise.' Perhaps this too much disregards that simple curiosity which has led men, surely with advantage, into pure science. Still, it may well be that most men (especially intellectuals), remember too little, rather than too much, Johnson's principle of asking—'What use in knowing that?' There are plenty of industrious pedants who might gain by keeping framed above their mantelpieces those other words of his—'Life is surely given us for higher purposes than to gather what our ancestors have wisely thrown away, and to learn what is of no value but because it has been forgotten.'

For Johnson, the main thing we have to do in life was to live it. Hence his passion for biography was only equalled by his contempt for the brute, impersonal facts of history. He would have agreed with Goldsmith's 'ingenious gentleman' who, when asked what was the best reading for the young, replied 'The life of a good man'; and, when asked the next best, replied 'The life of a bad one'. But he refused to disguise his boredom at topics more impersonal, like the Punic Wars, or Catiline's conspiracy. Here he reminds one of that Socrates who turned away from the physical studies of his youth, to pursue the great problems of human life and ethics. Like Socrates, or Confucius, or Montaigne, Johnson was a practical thinker, a moralist, a sage—often, indeed, blinded by passion, but still a sage.

It is partly because he was so wide in his interests, yet so scornful of the inhuman curiosity of the mere pedant, that Johnson has himself remained so interesting to his fellow human beings. Curiously enough, Wordsworth with all his stress on contact with common men and common speech, remained often more remote than the Johnson he reacted against, from the thoughts and concerns of common men. Grasmere rustics thought Wordsworth forbiddingly odd. But even simple Highlanders were entranced by 'the big Sassenach'. Typically, Fanny Burney records that 'Dr Johnson almost always prefers the company of an intelligent man of the world to that of a scholar'. Intense men have often been narrow men; but Johnson, though otherwise so remote in character from Shakespeare, has something of the multitudinous variety of Shakespeare's world. In him tragedy blends with comedy, gloom with gaiety, gentleness with brutality, affection with pugnacity, grace with grossness, self-indulgence with self-restraint, wisdom with childishness, honesty of mind with reckless sophistry, courage with terror, energy with indolence, love of poetry with moods of Philistine prosiness.

Another of Johnson's most attractive qualities is his dazzling quickness of mind. This, of course, reveals itself only in his talk. Here he was the reverse of Goldsmith. It was, doubtless, poetic licence to say that Goldsmith 'wrote like an angel, and talked like poor Poll'. To see the exaggeration it suffices to read some of Goldsmith's remarks in Boswell. Still it does appear that Goldsmith's wit, so delightful in his books, was largely *esprit d'escalier*. No one, on the other hand, would claim that Johnson talked 'like an angel'. But one might perhaps say that he talked 'like a demon'. For few things are as amazing about him as that gift of extempore analogy, imagery, and wit which, together with his browbeating manner, made him so formidable in debate.

The imagery of Johnson can be better discussed as part of his style. But a word must here be said of Johnson's wit; which found few equals even in that wittiest of centuries. For even to-day it is perhaps not always realized how much of Johnson's true appeal lies simply in this.

Sometimes it was an unexpectedly ingratiating wit, as when there was no chair for Mrs Siddons, visiting him in illness—'Madam, you who so often occasion a want of seats to other people, will more readily excuse the want of one yourself.'[1] Even that Tragic Muse, who would ask for a cup of tea in tones more suitable to a cup of hemlock, must surely have smiled.

Or, again, he writes to Mrs Garrick on her husband's death:

[1] *Aliter*, 'You see, Madam, wherever *you* go, there are no seats to be got.'

'Dr Johnson sends most respectful condolence to Mrs Garrick, and wishes that any endeavour of his could enable her to support a loss which the world cannot repair.'

Sometimes, on the other hand, it was a ferocious wit (as, for example, at the expense of the Scots, who had not encountered such a *malleus Scotorum* since Edward Longshanks).

(On a bad inn at Bristol.) 'Describe it, Sir?—Why, it was so bad that Boswell wished to be in Scotland.'

(To one saying England was lost.) 'Sir, it is not so much to be lamented that Old England is lost as that the Scotch have found it.'

(Unlike the Scotch) 'The Irish are a fair people; they never speak well of one another.'

(Of Chesterfield.) 'This man I thought had been a Lord among wits, but, I find, he is only a wit among Lords.'

(To a fond father bringing two small sons to recite alternate stanzas of Gray's *Elegy*.) 'No, pray Sir, let the little dears both speak it at once. More noise will by that means be made, and the noise will be the sooner over.'[1]

(On two highly derivative poems by Ogilvie.) '*Boswell.* "Is there not imagination in them, Sir?" *Johnson.* "Why, Sir, there is in them what *was* imagination." '

(On angling or float-fishing.) 'A stick and a string, with a worm at one end and a fool at the other.'

As Reynolds observed, 'his conversation not only supported his character as an author, but, in the opinion of many, was superior. Those who have lived with the wits of the age know how rarely this happens.'

Then, again, there is that honesty of mind which remains one of

[1] Johnson had derived a rooted dislike of performing children from his own childhood, when he had resented his proud father's passion for showing him off.

the finest of all Johnson's qualities. He might often be ferociously prejudiced; he might at times talk with sophistry, merely for verbal triumph; but few men seem to me to have struggled more against the constant human temptation to say and believe, or pretend to believe, what is comfortable, conventional, lazy, or pleasant. No five words make a more characteristic motto for Johnson's whole life and personality than 'Clear your *mind* of cant'.

This passion for realistic honesty is, inevitably, rare among Romantics (though, at his best, Byron often had it)—for it would often sweep their cloud-castles out of the sky. Realists, on the other hand, make such honesty their ideal—but often they too miss it, by becoming cynics, till they see only the corruptions of Sodom, not its few righteous; or, like a sort of human woodpecker, interested in nothing but grubs and maggots, give the impression that every tree in the forest is somewhere rotten. This too can become a form of cant; and a particularly unpleasant one. But, from that, Johnson's realism was saved by his sense of poetry, by his religion, by his warmth of heart.

This honesty, far more than any special profundity, seems to me the really distinctive thing about Johnson's mind.

Most people, for example, know that the best remedy for painful emotion is active distraction. Long ago Euripides wrote:

> Love does not vex the man that begs his bread.

But in Johnson this truism gains a new vigour and concreteness. When he heard of people pitying young Lady Tavistock who was dying broken-hearted for her husband, killed in a riding accident, 'So do not I,' he retorted. 'She was rich and wanted employment, so she cried till she lost the power of restraining her tears: putting her into a small shop, and giving her a nurse child to tend, would have saved her life now.'

Others, again, have preached the danger that thistles and thorns will grow rank in a mind left fallow: but few have uttered it as vehemently as Johnson to the fussy clerk who came to him in torments of conscience over certain petty thefts from his employer —'Five hours of the four-and-twenty unemployed are enough for a man to go mad in; so I would advise you, Sir, to study algebra . . .

your head would get less muddy, and you will leave off tormenting your neighbours about paper and packthread, while we all live together in a world that is bursting with sin and sorrow.'

That ideas of *l'amour unique*—of 'the only woman in the world'—are over-romantic, has also become a platitude. But this chestnut of a truth sprouts with new life when, in reply to Boswell's question whether there are not in the world at any time fifty women with any one of whom a man might be equally happy, the Master snorts—'Ay, Sir, fifty thousand!' (And no doubt Boswell would have liked to try.)

A similar example from politics is, again, platitudinous in itself; but Johnsonian in its energy. 'Sir, there is one Mrs Macaulay[1] in this town, a great republican. I came to her one day and said I was quite a convert to her republican system, and thought mankind all upon a footing; and I begged that her footman might be allowed to dine with us. She has never liked me since.' 'What oft was thought, but ne'er so well express'd.' Poor Pepys was not so wrong.[2]

Similarly, whether or no it be authentic, there is much that is typical in his reported rebuke of Mrs Thrale's announcement, over a lark-supper, that her cousin had been decapitated by a cannon-ball: 'Madam, it would give *you* very little concern if all your relations were spitted like these larks and drest for Presto's supper.'

It is not that Johnson was hard. He was capable of bursting into tears in a way that most of us to-day would find embarrassing. But he despised mere 'feelers'. He did not splash about in sentiment like Richardson or Sterne. 'We must either outlive our friends, you

[1] Boswell, *London Journal*, July 22, 1763; fuller version in *Life of Johnson*, i, 447. Catherine Macaulay (1731–91) was called by Mary Wollstonecraft 'the woman of the greatest abilities that this country has ever produced'. She was at all events a determined person, who made the acquaintance of Washington, criticized Burke over the French Revolution, and at forty-eight took for second husband a youth of twenty-one. Her *History of England* (published 1763–83) is forgotten; it too was very republican. (Hannah More records asking Mrs Macaulay's daughter if she did not find fine things in Shakespeare's *King John*—only to be answered, 'I never read the *Kings*, ma'am.')

It has, however, been pointed out by C. Fortescue-Brickdale (*Notes and Queries*, vol. 159 (1930), 111–2) that Mrs Macaulay gave a different version in her *Letters on Education* (1790), 167. She says she told Johnson she was an advocate, *not* of social or economic levelling, but only of political equality; and that the discussion was conducted 'with great good humour on both sides'.

[2] See p. 57.

know, or our friends must outlive us; and I see no man that would hesitate about the choice.' *No* man? This is perhaps running from one exaggeration into another. But it remains interesting to find him thus echoing, without knowing it, that stoic proverb of the Icelandic Sagas—'Man must outlive man.'

Again, Johnson was a rigid moralist about sexual relations; one is therefore surprised by the frank honesty of his comment on Prior —'I do, however, think that some of Prior's tales are rather too wanton for *modest women*, according to established opinion. But I have my own private notions as to modesty, of which I would only value the appearance; for unless a woman has amorous heat she is a dull companion, and to have amorous heat in elegant perfection' (what a phrase!), 'the *fancy* should be warmed with lively ideas.'

So Boswell recorded in his *Ashbourne Journal*; but he dared not include this in the *Life*. A hundred years ago it would have produced groans of horror; but to some, at least, to-day it may seem not the least striking instance of Johnson's resoluteness in clearing his mind of cant.[1]

The same honesty made sham admiration as hateful to him as sham sorrow. 'The reciprocal civility of authors is one of the most risible scenes in the farce of life.' For this kind of insincerity Mrs Thrale got into trouble. She had rashly praised a Mr Long. Then the whip cracked. ' "Nay," said the Doctor, "my dear Lady, don't talk so. Mr *Long's* character is very *short*. It is nothing. He fills a chair. He is a Man of a genteel appearance, and that is all. I know nobody who blasts by praise as you do. For whenever there is exaggerated praise, every body is set against a character. They are roused to attack it. Now there is Pepys.[2] You praised that man with such disproportion that I was incited to lessen him perhaps more than he deserves. His blood is upon your head. So now, Mr Long. And by the same principle, your malice defeats itself. For your censure is too violent.... And yet" (with a pleasing pause and leering smile) "She is the first woman in the World. Could she but restrain that wicked tongue of her's, she would be the only Woman in the World. Could she but command that little whirligig...." '[3]

[1] Yet he was shocked at Hannah More's having read *Tom Jones*.

[2] See note on p. 57.

[3] This version from the *Boswell Papers* (xiv, 186) differs slightly—and I think for the better—from that in the *Life of Johnson* (iv, 81–2).

How the scene lives! I know no moment when the Doctor and his mistress rise more dramatically from the grave. It embodies so vividly Johnson's combination of honesty and harshness, yet also of tenderness and affection. Pepys, I suspect, was doubly odious to Johnson: first, because, in Mrs Thrale's phrase elsewhere, his artificiality disgusted 'a Man who has seen all sorts of Tricks and who can be pleased with nothing but Nature'; secondly, I suspect, because Johnson was jealous of his intimacy with Mrs Thrale. But the whole episode is a living instance of Johnson's principle that 'scarce any man becomes eminently disagreeable, but by departing from his real character'. Johnson could not repress his healthy nausea at 'Tricks'.

Similarly with his dislike of religious poetry. It jarred his sincerity. Religion was too solemn a subject for literary frills, and clevernesses, and affectations. The addresses of poets to the Deity seemed to him, one suspects, too like 'the reciprocal civility of authors'. And it is often true. Again and again, the pomp of *Paradise Lost* rings a little false when it embellishes the grave simplicities of the Old Testament. Still Johnson forgot Herbert and Vaughan; nor do his strictures touch Christina Rossetti.

The same passionate sincerity of mind and heart led him to scent out the lack of genuine grief in *Lycidas*, and so to condemn it.[1] Let us frankly admit that Milton does not give the impression that he really ate a slice of pudding the less when the news came that Edward King was at the bottom of the Irish Sea. What Johnson failed to grasp was that the poem did not thereby become really insincere. For King was merely its occasion; its real theme was Milton and England—about both of which Milton felt with passionate intensity. 'Sir,' Johnson might have retorted, 'a man can speak

After 'She is the first woman in the World', the *Life* has a comma instead of a full stop. Mrs Thrale no longer *is* the first of women; she only *would* be, if. . . . This change has been ascribed to malice in Boswell. Surely an over-subtle notion? It would have been so simple to omit this tribute to Mrs Thrale altogether.

[1] Bridges explained that Johnson could not like *Lycidas* because he had an 'unpoetic mind'; and thereby showed himself as prejudiced as Johnson. There is abundant evidence that Johnson was passionately moved by some kinds of poetry. His mind was stocked with it. It could reduce him to terror, or to tears. Bridges, for that matter, could see nothing in the poetry of Hardy. Not every kind of match will strike on every kind of matchbox. Yet critics constantly persist in remaining as intolerant as Nazis or Marxists.

his heart without playing crocodile, with smock and crook, above a grave.' But that seems arguing too precisely. Milton was really in the position of a Laureate, called to write for an occasion and obeying a convention, yet using both occasion and convention to utter his own sincerest passions and beliefs.

Even about his own literary efforts Johnson kept the same blunt candour. In the *Lives* he is almost shamelessly frank in admitting that a whole generation has passed since he read this or that, or that he has not read it at all.[1] When he had misdefined 'pastern' in the Dictionary, everyone knows his answer—'Ignorance, Madam, pure ignorance.' But it was less rational of him to refuse, even so, to correct his error. He remained, as often, more forceful than wise.

There are, perhaps, three degrees in human deception. There is the hypocrisy that simulates what it wishes others to believe it thinks or feels; from this Johnson was finely free. (He could never have sunk to the fulsome grovellings, at moments, of Dryden or Coleridge.) Secondly, there is the intellectual dishonesty which timidly or lazily persuades itself, more or less unconsciously, that it thinks or feels what it wishes to think or feel; here too Johnson was usually above reproach. But there is also, thirdly, that type of highly emotional delusion which passion or neurosis forces on the mind; here Johnson was less fortunate. He seems to me lacking in that calm, free poise with which Hume moves among the problems of philosophy; in religious matters, indeed, Johnson is more like an agonized Laocoön, writhing and bellowing amid the coils of serpents.

Johnson, then, strikes me as an admirably honest and candid mind rather than a profound one. If Johnson had never lived, the world might not have been the poorer by a single important idea; though one may gladly own that, without Johnson, many ideas would have been far less forcibly hammered into the thickness of the human skull.

Why, then, did Reynolds say (and very possibly with truth) of this often confused and prejudiced thinker: 'No man had like him

[1] E.g. on Congreve: 'Of his plays I cannot speak distinctly, for since I inspected them many years have passed.' As for Rowe, Johnson owned to Nichols that he had not read any of Rowe's plays for thirty years! And his unchecked quotations depend to a rash degree on his amazing, but by no means infallible, memory.

the faculty of teaching inferior minds to think'? This faculty came, I believe, not from the depth of his reason, but from his passion for reasoning and his mastery of debate. It is again a question of style. He could put things so clearly, so forcibly, so tellingly, he could produce arguments and analogies with such lightning promptitude that, quite apart from his air of Jupiter Tonans, he was extremely hard to argue with. He had a natural gift for retort; and he trained it by yearlong effort in the prize-ring of dispute.

'We had *talk* enough,' he growled after some insipid evening like a modern sherry-party, 'but no *conversation*; there was nothing *discussed*.'

Indeed to this great debater, as to the ancient sophists, discussion at moments became more important than truth. It was a shrewd hit of Garrick's, when Johnson had begun rumbling, 'Why, Sir, as to the good or evil of card-playing—' to interject, 'Now he is thinking which side he should take.'

Socrates claimed to know only that he knew nothing: Johnson thought he knew a great deal. But both men, in their opposite ways, were masters of dialectic; both reasoned perpetually, if sometimes unreasonably; and so, as Reynolds said, Johnson too may indeed have been an excellent master at teaching men to think. For, fantastic as he could often become, still one understands the exclamation of Dr Alexander McLean in Mull, unconsciously echoing what Mrs Johnson had said at her first meeting with her future husband, 'This man is just a hogshead of sense.'

I have suggested, then, that Johnson's mind, if not particularly deep, and frequently warped, was yet extraordinary in its range, its quickness, its integrity, and its power of expression. But how eminent, in fact, *was* his power of expression? This brings us to the fourth indictment against him—turgid and pompous style.

Now it may be granted at once that his heavier manner is not of much value to most of us, except as an amusing curiosity. But it is a vulgar error, perhaps still not uncommon, to suppose that Johnson expressed himself always in 'Johnsonese'. He had, in fact, two main styles[1]—one plain, and one over-coloured. (There are also, of

[1] Contrast Hazlitt: 'What most distinguishes Dr Johnson from other writers is the pomp and uniformity of his style. All his periods are cast in the same mould . . . the author is always upon stilts.' 'Always!'

course, intermediate variations.) And the two correspond to two sides of Johnson's personality—the formal and solemn on the one hand, the direct and unfettered on the other. It is a curious paradox—but true, I think—that the style commonly associated with Johnson's memory is often the extreme opposite of the style that has really made him memorable.

The faults of Johnson's grandiose manner are clear enough; and of these enough has been said. Influenced partly by Sir Thomas Browne, partly perhaps by Johnson's own work on the Dictionary, they were in their turn to exert a disastrous influence on writers like Fanny Burney or Sir James Mackintosh. Even to-day, among the pretentious—especially in literary criticism—the pompous influence of Johnsonese is perhaps not wholly extinct.

All the same it would be sweeping, I think, to dismiss even Johnson's too formal manner as always unimpressive. There is, for example, that famous peroration on Marathon and Iona; or that burst of unexpectedly romantic zest which describes the scenery of Hawkestone—'the ideas which it forces upon the mind are, the sublime, the dreadful, and the vast. Above is inaccessible altitude, below is horrible profundity'; or his still more romantic picture of a Highland storm—'the wind was loud, the rain was heavy, and the whistling of the blast, the fall of the shower, the rush of the cataracts, and the roar of the torrent, made a nobler chorus of the rough music of nature than it had ever been my chance to hear before.'[1] Or, again, there is that other passage, on the less romantic theme of Shakespearian scholars—'The various readings of copies, and different interpretations of a passage, seem to be questions that might exercise the wit without engaging the passions. But whether it be that *small things make mean men proud*, and vanity catches small occasions; or that all contrariety of opinion, even in those that can defend it no longer, makes proud men angry; there is often found in commentators a spontaneous strain of invective and contempt, more eager and venomous than is vented by the most furious controvertist in politics against those whom he is hired to defame.'

[1] There is a particularly happy phrase in his account to Mrs Thrale of the journey to Iona—'the silent solemnity of faint moonshine'. Johnson was not always so blind or dumb about nature as some suppose.

But indeed this passage is already half-way towards Johnson's other, plainer, finer style.

There are also times when Johnson's exalted turgidity succeeds by an amusingly mock-heroic effect, in ironic contrast to the trivialities it treats of; like the burlesque epic style in Pope's *Rape of the Lock*. Some mouse becomes comical by being installed under a canopy of state. 'What provokes your risibility, Sir? Have I said anything that you understand?' To say 'Why do you laugh, Sir?' would have been far less pulverizing. The poor insect is much more overwhelmingly squashed beneath this portentous verbal jackboot.

Similarly in another passage on critics the very ponderousness of the style gives Johnson's contempt still greater power to crush: 'Much mischief is done in the world with very little interest or design. He that assumes the character of a critick, and justifies his claim by perpetual censure, imagines that he is hurting none but the author, and him he considers as a pestilent animal, whom every other being has a right to persecute; little does he think how many harmless men he involves in his own guilt, by teaching them to be noxious without malignity, and to repeat objections which they do not understand; or how many honest minds he debars from pleasure, by exciting an artificial fastidiousness, and making them too wise to concur with their own sensations.'[1] Never was that wisdom more needed than in some critical circles of to-day.

Or again, on the dullness of travel-books—'This is the common style of those sons of enterprise, who visit savage countries, and range through solitude and desolation; who pass a desert, and tell that it is sandy; who cross a valley, and find that it is green.'

None the less I feel that the style in which Johnson really finds himself, and reveals himself, is his other, very different manner—terse, trenchant, abrupt. For it is one of the strangest paradoxes about him that he can be, not only amazingly wordy, but also amazingly terse—that a man derided by his enemies as an elephantine circumlocutionist, should yet have left us some of the most pointed brevities in English. And this seems to me a far rarer and far more valuable gift.

Take some examples:

[1] Cf. Goldsmith's little widow at Vauxhall, p. 310.

(A Mr Pot had praised Johnson's *Irene* as the finest tragedy of modern times.) 'If Pot says so, Pot lies.'

(After leaving the room, years later, at a reading of *Irene.*) 'I thought it had been better.'

'No man but a blockhead ever wrote except for money.'

(To a bookseller bringing a gentleman's subscription to the *Shakespeare*, with a request that his name be added to the list.) 'I shall print no list of subscribers. Sir, I have two very cogent reasons for not printing any list of subscribers—one, that I have lost all the names—the other, that I have spent all the money.'

(Of Gray.) 'Sir, he was dull in company, dull in his closet, dull everywhere. He was dull in a new way.'

(Of the American rebels.) 'How is it we always hear the loudest yelps for liberty among the drivers of negroes?'

'Who eats a slice of plum-pudding the less because a friend is hanged?'

'Perhaps the best advice to authors would be that they should keep out of the way of one another.'

(Of other biographers.) 'The dogs don't know how to write trifles with dignity.'

'Allow children to be happy in their own way, for what better way will they ever find?'

'There is now, I have heard, a body of men, not less decent or virtuous than the Scottish Council, longing to melt the lead of an English Cathedral. What they shall melt, it were just that they should swallow.' (This was finally omitted, for reasons of tact, from the *Journey to the Western Islands.*)

(Of the advantage of primogeniture.) 'It makes but one fool in a family.'[1]

(To Boswell.) 'Don't cant in defence of savages.'

(In reply to an abusive Thames boatman.) 'Sir, your wife, under pretence of keeping a bawdy-house, is a receiver of stolen goods.' (The rest, one imagines, must have been awed silence. It far outshines even the professor who silenced the fishwife by calling her an 'isosceles triangle'.)

(To Mrs Thrale, complaining of a foolish visitor.) 'Madam, why do you blame the woman for the only sensible thing she could do—talking of her family and her affairs? For how should a woman who is as empty as a drum, talk upon any other subject? If you speak to her of the sun, she does not know it rises in the east; if you speak to her of the moon, she does not know it changes at the full; if you speak to her of the Queen, she does not know she is the King's wife; how, then, can you blame her for talking of her family and affairs?' (Absolutely simple language. Yet note the artful repetition which comes back full circle, in the final sentence, to part of the wording that opened the first.)

(Of Joseph Warton.) 'Sir, he is an enthusiast by rule.'

'Harris is a sound sullen scholar. . . . Harris, however, is a prig, and a bad prig.'

(On the absence of Erse MSS to support Macpherson.) 'If there are men with tails, catch an *homo caudatus*.'

(To Cumberland, who had deprecated his harshness towards the Scots.) 'Do you think so, Cumbey? Then I give you leave to say, and you may quote me for it, that there are more gentlemen in Scotland than there are shoes.'

[1] Contrast the far less forcible diffuseness of Paley: 'If the estate was divided equally amongst the sons, it would probably make them all idle; whereas by the present rule of descent it makes only one so; which is the lesser evil of the two.' Much more Johnsonian is the adage I once heard from my assistant librarian at King's—'An only child makes three fools.'

(Of Metaphysical poets.) 'If their conceits were far-fetched, they were often worth the carriage.'

(Of Milton.) 'He thought woman made only for obedience and man only for rebellion.'

(Of Gray's *Bard.*) 'Suicide is always to be had, without expense of thought.'

(On Akenside.) 'One bad ode may be suffered; but a number of them together makes one sick.'

Some of the above quotations come from Johnson's writing, some from his talk; note that they are not always easy to distinguish.

Writing can, indeed, become too colloquial; that is only too common in the vulgarer kind of literature to-day. Johnson, however, who made it a principle even in conversation to talk his best, seldom, if ever, became crudely colloquial. On the contrary he might talk, at times, like a book—but usually like a good book. People exclaimed that he 'talked essays'. His written style, on the other hand, improved as it more clearly approached his easier talk. The average length of sentences becomes much less in the *Lives* than in *The Rambler*; and so does the average length of words. The Roman toga is largely flung aside—and in Johnson's grip there flashes the short, stabbing sword of the Roman legionary.

Indeed we know that he came to wonder if books would not one day be compressed into series of aphorisms (somewhat like Nietzsche's *Zarathustra*, or Butler's *Notebooks*).

Passion can often lose its power in mere wordiness; but Johnson's explosive force is often seen at its deadliest when it is packed into a single word.

(Of Ossian.) 'Sir, a man might write such stuff for ever, if he would *abandon* his mind to it.' (If you think 'abandon' could be bettered, try.)

(Of Restoration dramatists, in a prologue for Garrick.)

Yet bards like these aspir'd to lasting praise,
And proudly hop'd to *pimp* in future days.

(Of Garrick's funeral, when Mrs Burney asked if there were not six horses to every coach.) 'Madam, there were no more six horses than six *phœnixes*.'[1]

(Of the hopelessness of recovering his oak stick, lost in treeless Mull.) 'Consider, Sir, the value of such a piece of *timber* here.'

No less important in Johnson's best style is that gift for imagery —for simile and metaphor—which made Boswell justly remark that he might have been 'perpetually a poet'. Thus, by another paradox, he who had been at times one of the most abstract of writers, becomes one of the most concrete. Abstract personifications stagger lamely about the pages of *The Rambler*; but Johnson's concrete images leap straight at the throat. It is this gift for imagery that gives his best style not only the virtue of vigour but also that other prime virtue—clarity. And not only clarity—life.

Obscurity, indeed, had never been a marked fault of his. He might often marshal and march his sentences in too processional dignity; yet even at their most ceremonious it remained pretty clear where they were going, and what they meant. But in his briefer manner Johnson's clarity becomes one of the joys of reading him—it is such a contrast to that woolly, misty vagueness which often adds an atmosphere of often illusory depth to the prose of Coleridge or Pater. Like Gustave Doré, Johnson is a supreme illustrator.

No doubt some of the clarity he gained by images and analogies was a false clarity. It could oversimplify. It could become sophistical. No doubt he was overfond of argument from analogy. I do not see how analogy can ever prove anything. It always seems to beg the question and argue in a circle. To urge that because A resembles B in six respects, A must resemble B in a seventh, assumes the very point that it is sought to prove.

But though analogy cannot prove the truth of a statement, it can

[1] It is hard to think of any other word to equal 'phœnixes'. 'Six unicorns' would have expressed the absurdity; but it would still remain less absurd, for unicorns are not unique, and phœnixes *are*—there being only one in the world at a time.

add wonderful life and light to it. It can give body and understanding to the grey drifting ghosts of abstractions, as the draught of sacrificial blood lent utterance to the fleeting wraiths that Odysseus met beside the Ocean-stream.

For example:

(Of Levett's way of taking from his poor clients payment in kind.) 'Had all his patients maliciously combined to reward him with meat and strong liquor instead of money, he would either have burst, like the dragon in the Apocrypha, through repletion, or been scorched up, like Portia, by swallowing fire.'

(Of Rousseauism.) 'If a bull could speak, he might as well exclaim—"Here am I with this cow and this grass; what being can enjoy greater felicity?" '

(Of Hume.) 'Truth, Sir, is a cow which will yield such people no more milk, and so they are gone to milk the bull.'

(Of Henry Hervey, who had been good to him.) 'If you call a dog Hervey, I shall love him.'

(Of Chesterfield's belated patronage of him with two articles in *The World*.) 'I have sailed a long and painful voyage round the world of the English language; and does he now send out two cockboats to tow me into harbour?'

(To the suggestion that in the election of bishops the king's *congé d'elire* was only 'a strong recommendation'.) 'Sir, it is such a recommendation as if I should throw you out of a two-pair-of-stairs window, and recommend you to fall soft.'

(Of Lady Macdonald.) 'This woman would sink a ninety-gun ship. She is so dull—so heavy.'

(Of a certain M.P.) 'A mind as narrow as the neck of a vinegar cruet.'

(Of sending a shy boy to a public school.) 'Placing him at a publick school is forcing an owl upon day.'

(Of a young author.) 'Sir, there is not a young sapling upon Parnassus more severely blown about by every wind of criticism'

(To Mrs Thrale, suggesting that a lady would be sorry at her friend's missing a fortune.) 'She will suffer as much, perhaps, as your horse did when your cow miscarried.'

(To Mrs Thrale pointing out that there were five Cambridge men in the room, where he had just been giving various instances of the superiority of Oxford.) 'I did not think of that till you told me; but the wolf does not count the sheep.'

(Of six Methodist students expelled from Oxford.) 'I believe they might be good beings, but they were not fit to be in the University of Oxford. A cow is a very good animal in the field, but we turn her out of a garden.'

(A good example, also, of the weakness of analogy misused as argument.)

(Of the abilities of Capell, a rival Shakespearian editor.) 'They are just sufficient, Sir, to enable him to select the black hairs from the white ones, for the use of periwig-makers. Were he and I to count the grains in a bushel of wheat for a wager, he would certainly prove the winner.'

(To Langton, after hearing him, with some impatience, read an act of Dodsley's *Cleone*.) 'Come, let's have some more, let's go into the slaughter-house again, Lanky. But I am afraid there is more blood than brains.'

(Of how many Senecan or Elizabethan plays might that be said!)

(Of Dryden.) 'He delighted to tread upon the brink of meaning.'

(Of Congreve.) 'His personages are a kind of intellectual gladiators: every sentence is to ward or strike.'

(Of Shakespeare.) 'A quibble was to him the fatal Cleopatra for which[1] he lost the world and was content to lose it.'

(On literary innovation.) 'Buckinger had no hands, and he wrote his name with his toes at Charing Cross, for half a crown apiece; that was a new manner of writing!'

(Of Edwards on Warburton.) 'Nay, he has given him some smart hits to be sure; but there is no proportion between the two men. . . . A fly, Sir, may sting a stately horse and make him wince; but one is but an insect, and the other is a horse still.'

(Against quixotries of romantic virtue.) 'A plank that is tilted up at one end must of course fall down on the other.'

'Sir, a woman's preaching is like a dog's walking on his hind legs. It is not done well, but you are surprised to find it done at all.'

(In answer to the plea that at least some players were better than others.) 'Yes, Sir, as some dogs dance better than others.'

(Of his bad eye.) 'The dog was never good for anything.'

'Tom Birch is brisk as a bee in conversation, but no sooner does he take a pen in his hand, than it becomes a torpedo to him, and benumbs all his faculties.'

Even on his deathbed this faculty did not fail him. Of the male nurse given him he remarked—'He is an idiot as awkward as a turnspit (*i.e.* a dog—his fondness for comparisons with dogs survives to his dying hour) just put into the wheel; and as sleepy as a dormouse.'

Why do I find all these passages delightful? Not only because they are clear, brief, strong, imaginative in themselves; but also because there ring through them the very voice and personality of

[1] One might have expected 'for *whom*'.

their author. In his more elaborate manner these become muffled; but here speaks the man himself.

A living style and its author's personality are only two sides of the same thing. And Johnson's real style vibrates with that energy which pulses through his whole career. Here is a being, tormented by illness from childhood; assailed by pain, sleeplessness, hardship, and melancholy; mauled by doctors who knew little, and little realized how little they knew, and by still more foolhardy attempts to doctor himself; yet living to seventy-five, with a vitality rare even in our days of balanced diet, vitamins, and scientific hygiene. Misshapen, half-blind and half-deaf, he was ready, till late in life, to ride fifty miles, to leap stocks or railings, to empty his pockets and roll down hills, to challenge young ladies to run races, or Oxford dons to climb walls.[1] In his fifties he electrified a party of ladies and gentlemen at Gunnersbury House by swarming up a large tree, and had to be 'very earnestly entreated' not to scale the higher boughs. At sixty-six he outran Baretti; and once when racing a little man called John Payne, he picked up his small rival half-way, perched him in a tree, and charged on furiously alone. 'I have beat many a fellow,' he observed of his affray with Osborne the bookseller, 'but the rest had the wit to hold their tongues.' At sixty-four he faced the discomforts of the Highlands as calmly as a professional explorer; and at an Inverness supper (on the Sabbath, too!) gave astonished Scots an imitation of the gait of a kangaroo. Earlier, he contemplated Iceland; later still, the Baltic. Indeed, at near sixty-six, he wrote to Mrs Thrale that, were he free and rich enough, 'I might go to Cairo, and down the Red Sea to Bengal, and take a ramble in India.'

But what matters now is not Johnson's physical energy, curiously coupled as it was with indolence, but his accompanying vigour of mind—a vigour both active, as force, and passive, as fortitude. He was not one of those sensitive writers who have sighed in shades, or wilted under criticism—delicate as Rilke dying of the scratch of a rose.

Just as the critics of his *Irene* had left him unmoved as the Monument, so he writes characteristically to Thomas Warton of the

[1] Dr Robert Vansittart, at Oxford in 1759; when Johnson was fifty and Vansittart only thirty.

reception awaiting his Dictionary: 'What reception I shall meet upon the shore, I know not; . . . whether I shall find upon the coast a Calypso that will court, or a Polypheme that will eat me. But if a Polypheme comes to me, have at his eye.'[1]

No doubt a man may have the physique of Hercules, and the energy of Charles XII, without leaving words that enrich the world. Nor is it quite true, as Voltaire said it was, that 'le diable au corps' is necessary to success in all the arts. There was, for instance, not much devil in the polite Addison, nor in the shy Gray, whom Johnson despised, nor in the unhappy Coleridge, nor in the inhibited Amiel, nor in the sensitive Walter Pater. But it *is* perhaps true that writers not thus diabolically inspired are likely to remain minor; and certainly a devil of this kind in an author can cover a multitude of sins. Johnson's *diable au corps* is very different from Voltaire's; but, for the joy of posterity, each was possessed by one.

Typical, then, is Johnson's comment on a Mr Riddock at Aberdeen, 'Sir, he has no vigour in his talk'; or on Carte's *Life of Ormond*, 'The matter is diffused in too many words; there is no animation, no compression, no vigour.' The charge of lacking animation or compression might sometimes be brought against Johnson's own *Ramblers*; but hardly against his *Lives of the Poets*; still less, against his talk.

Typical too, in its small way, is Johnson's own approving use of the word 'manly'. The appearance of Collins he found 'decent and manly'; or, again, in his own youth he had read, 'not voyages and travels, but all literature, Sir, all ancient writers, all manly.'[2]

Irene, as a play, may be a poor thing; but in its prologue there is a new note of defiant sternness towards the audience, as uncompromising as Ben Jonson's:

Unmov'd tho' Witlings sneer and Rivals rail;
Studious to please, yet not asham'd to fail,
He scorns the meek Address, the suppliant Strain,

[1] 'Eyes' is the actual reading; but is surely a slip of Johnson's pen. How, in the very act of comparing himself to Ulysses, should he credit a Cyclops with more eyes than one?

[2] Cf. the praise of Adam Smith (by no means a Johnsonian) for Johnson's Shakespeare *Preface*: 'The most manly piece of criticism that was ever published in any country.'

With Merit needless, and without it vain.
In Reason, Nature, Truth he dares to trust:
Ye Fops be silent! and ye Wits be just!

That must have caused some astonishment in the theatre—'Ye Fops be silent! and ye Wits be just!'

But there is also another quality that adds much, I think, to the appeal of the real Johnson and of his true style—humour and gaiety.

I suspect that no man can be really wise who is never gay. For constant seriousness implies that he takes many things far more seriously than they really deserve. The body that loses the power to relax, grows sick; so too the mind. '*Vive la bagatelle!*'

'In the talent of humour,' says Sir John Hawkins, 'there was hardly ever his equal, except perhaps among the old comedians.' Now on this point the 'unclubable' Sir John may appear an incongruous and questionable witness; but he is confirmed by Arthur Murphy, who calls Johnson 'incomparable at buffoonery'; and by Fanny Burney—'he has more fun and comical humour and love of nonsense about him than anybody I ever saw'.

No doubt this makes a queer contrast with the pessimism of the author of *Rasselas*; the subject of which Hannah More called 'as cheerful as the Dead Sea'. And it is not the side which comes out most evidently in Boswell. But then Mrs Thrale, though she gave Boswell 19 marks out of 20 for good humour, for humour gave him only 3 (as against Johnson's 16 for humour, and 0 for good humour). And indeed, if Boswell had had much humour, Boswell would have become different—he would have found himself impossibly absurd.

All the same, Boswell was quite aware that he had not been able to do full justice to this lighter side of Johnson. That was why he so badgered the embarrassed Miss Burney at Windsor—'Grave Sam, and great Sam, and solemn Sam, and learned Sam—all these he has appeared over and over.... I want to show him as gay Sam, agreeable Sam, pleasant Sam.' But not even Boswell's seven Sams could soften the heart of Miss Burney, who was in a fever to get rid of him before the Royal Family should appear.

'I fancy,' Johnson writes to Mrs Thrale in 1779, 'that I grow light and airy. A man that does not begin to grow light and airy at seventy is certainly losing time if he intends ever to be light and airy.'[1] Alas, had he known it, his days of lightness and airiness were even then almost over—two years later Thrale's death was the prelude to his own last sombre phase.

But certainly there was no lack of fun in the Johnson who 'frisked' with Beauclerk and Langton in Covent Garden at 3 a.m. in 1752; or made Fleet Street echo with his nocturnal laughter over Langton's will; or mischievously discomfited the snobbish Miss Cotterells, who were simultaneously entertaining Her Grace the Duchess of Argyll, by loudly remarking to Reynolds, as if they were both artisans, 'I wonder which of us two could get most money by his trade in one week, were we to work hard at it'; or, after rebuking Sir Robert Chambers at Oxford, for tossing snails into his neighbour's garden, completely changed his tune on hearing the said neighbour to be a dissenter—'Oh, if so, Chambers, toss away, toss away.'[2] In this respect too Johnson, who could laugh 'like a rhinoceros', was the exact opposite of Chesterfield, who never laughed at all. One can understand why Johnson spoke, in praising Falstaff, of 'the most pleasing of all qualities, perpetual gaiety'. Johnson could laugh even at himself, and even at those infirmities over which he was at times so sensitive. 'Ah, ha! Sam Johnson!' he cried, peering over Fanny Burney's shoulder at an engraving of himself, 'I see thee!—and an ugly dog thou art!'

Yet in him, even more than in most men, laughter and gloom could alternate with bewildering abruptness. On March 14, 1768, he writes to Mrs. Thrale: 'I hope all our friends at Streatham are well; and am glad to hope that the poor maid will recover. When the mind is drawn towards a dying bed, how small a thing is an

[1] A good example of what Johnson's friend, Dr Taylor of Ashbourne, called 'the ridiculous Vanities and fulsome Weakness's which he always betray'd in his conversation and Address with his amiable female friends'. (Letter to Mrs Piozzi, October 13, 1787; *Bulletin of John Rylands Library*, xx, 279.) How vividly this censorious phrase paints the character of its writer—that heavy, unclerical cleric, whose idol was his 'great bull'!

[2] Cf. too (for, though it may not be very humorous, it is curiously light-hearted) his mystification of the foolish youth, Rose Fuller, who asked, 'Pray, Sir, what is Palmyra?'—'Palmyra, Sir? Why, it is a hill in Ireland, situated in a bog, and has palm-trees on top, whence it is called "palm-mire".' (But, with characteristic love of truth, Johnson took care afterwards to disabuse the young man.)

election! But on death we cannot always be thinking, and, I suppose we need not. The thought is very dreadful.' Then, without any transition, the very next paragraph runs on: 'This little Dog does nothing, but I hope he will mend; he is now reading Jack the Giant Killer. Perhaps so noble a narrative may rouse in him the soul of enterprise.

I am, etc.'

At times, too, through his very laughter there breaks his underlying bitterness; as in his burlesque lines on Queeney Thrale's new dress:

Wear the Gown, and wear the Hat,
Snatch your pleasures while they last;
Hadst thou nine lives like a Cat,
Soon those nine lives would be past.

Such hectic extremes of gloom and gaiety are, indeed, characteristic of the manic-depressive, as with poor Crabbe's wife; in such persons the superego sits, as it were, like a great baleful cat, while the poor cowed little mouse of an ego creeps about with its tail between its legs; but at intervals the cat drowses off, and then the little ego frolics itself almost into frenzy. But without this gaiety Johnson, and Johnson's style, would lose a great part of their charm.

As he wrote of himself at seventy to Mrs Thrale, 'did you never hear nor read, dear Madam, that every Man has his *genius*, and that the great rule by which all excellence is attained, and all success procured, is to follow *genius*, and have you not observed in all our conversations that my *genius* is always in extremes, that I am very noisy, or very silent; very gloomy, or very merry; very sour, or very kind?'

Candour must add that Johnson's humour was also, at times, unconscious. He remains so amusing, not only because he was often gay, and often clever, but also because he was often absurd. We laugh by turns with and at him. And the comedy in him is made the more poignant by the tragedy. Johnson became himself a living example of that tragi-comedy he defended so well in Shakespeare—he too is at times an agonized, yet jesting Hamlet.

But I still think that the impressiveness of Johnson's mind comes less from the quality of his ideas in themselves, than from the skill with which they were put, and the force of the passionate personality behind. And this is why, compared with his talk where he was most spontaneously himself, his written works remain, as has been said, 'mere outworks.'

To sum up—it can be objected to Johnson that he was often bearish and brutal. But it can be answered, first, that in these very defects he often shows himself astonishingly vivid and vital; secondly, that he redeemed them by a no less astonishing charity and kindliness. It can be objected that he was so neurotic and bizarre as at times to be hardly sane; it can be answered that this only makes more admirably heroic his lifelong effort to think clearly, honestly, rationally, and without cant. It can be objected that he was no deep thinker—too passionate, too prejudiced, too indolent, too multifarious; it can be answered that, indolent as he was, he yet remained indefatigable in talking his best, thinking his best, and teaching others to think; with a passion for reason that, despite his own lapses into prejudice and fury, remains a lasting pattern for all those who value at its true worth our good fortune, and our privilege, in knowing so well a human being in many ways so faulty, and yet in many ways so fine.

Finally, there is the indictment of indolently wasting his talent, of 'trifling', in Shaw's phrase, 'with literary fools in taverns'.

But to this Johnson has already replied in advance: 'Sir, I am not obliged to do any more. No man is obliged to do as much as he can do. A man is to have part of his life to himself. If a soldier has fought a good many campaigns, he is not to be blamed if he retires to ease and tranquillity. A physician, who has practised long in a great city, may be excused if he retires to a small town, and takes less practice. Now, Sir, the good I can do by my conversation bears the same proportion to the good I can do by my writings, that the practice of a physician, retired to a small town, does to his practice in a great city.' *Boswell.* 'But I wonder, Sir, you have not more pleasure in writing than in not writing.' *Johnson.* 'Sir, you *may* wonder.'

After all, Johnson's talk was far more than merely 'idle'. He hated that empty discursiveness which passes with most men, especially to-day, as conversation. For him it was a serious intellectual exercise. Remember his grumble—'We had *talk* enough, but no *conversation*; there was nothing *discussed*.'

And so Johnson was even more justified in his defence than he realized. He would have been vastly astonished, could he have known that, in effectiveness, his writings would actually be far exceeded by his 'idle' talk.

It is true that Johnson spent much of his existence taxing himself, as bitterly as Shaw taxed him, with indolence—'I have been trying to cure my laziness all my life, and could not do it.'[1] (Though he also thought, quite irrationally, that other men were the same—'we would all be idle if we could.'[2]) But even if he talked till two in the morning, and lay abed till two in the afternoon, and hardly ever read books through, it remains an unusual sort of 'idleness' that could produce the *Dictionary*, the *Shakespeare*, and a dozen volumes of works. He could well have concluded, like Chateaubriand: 'I have written enough if my name will last; too much, if it will not.'

It remains to say something of Johnson's books; even though his real appeal—as an extraordinary personality with an extraordinary power of speech—appears far less in them than in his talk; so that Johnson is really bigger in Boswell's works than in his own. That this should be so may surprise us moderns, who are often book-ridden, and have largely lost the art of conversation. But after all it has been pointed out that Socrates wrote nothing; and Christ only one sentence, in the dust. Again, the founder of Islam, at least according to Islamic tradition, could not even write or read at all. Johnson himself once observed to Mrs Thrale, 'There is in this world no real delight (excepting those of sensuality) but exchange of ideas in conversation.' It is a characteristic exaggeration, ignoring as it does the happiness to be found in nature, the arts, travel, affection, parenthood, or the service of some cause worth serving. But it remains at least true enough that his own personality comes out less in books, where he stood always on his dignity, than in speech where he was spontaneously—sometimes too spon-

[1] One may compare the similar self-reproaches of Carlyle: '*Nondum*, should be my motto, with Poppies argent and three Sloths dormant on a tree disleaved.'

[2] Contrast Voltaire's view that it was as much in the nature of man to work, as of fire to rise. So hard is it for men not to generalize about mankind merely from their own temperaments.

taneously—himself. Still, if his works remain 'outworks', let us briefly tour these outworks; especially his criticism.

It was as a poet, with *London*,[1] that Johnson first drew attention. It is a poem both typical of him, and untypical—typical in phrases like 'surly virtue' (in a good sense), or the irony, concentrated in a single word, of—

> The sober trader at a tatter'd cloak
> Wakes from his dream, and *labours* for a joke.

On the other hand, nothing could be less typical of this incorrigible Londoner than the whole theme of a poem which praises 'Thales' (possibly Savage) for turning away from a sordid metropolis to pastoral bliss in South Wales:

> There prune thy walks, support thy drooping flow'rs,
> Direct thy rivulets, and twine thy bow'rs . . .
> There ev'ry bush with Nature's musick rings,
> There ev'ry breeze bears health upon its wings.

Much Johnson cared for directing rivulets! In real life his nearest approach to that is the occasion when, with Boswell's aid, he pushed a dead cat down Taylor's waterfall at Ashbourne. Johnson denouncing London is as out of character as an Athenian decrying Athens—even if we allow that in 1738 he may not yet have acquired all his later passion for the capital.

Johnson's second adaptation from Juvenal, *The Vanity of Human Wishes*, was free at least from this element of the fictitious. For, if there was anything Johnson never doubted, it was precisely this 'vanity of vanities'. Here at least he could really unload his heart.

> Yet hope not life from grief or danger free,
> Nor think the doom of man revers'd for thee.

(How often in life one may quote that to oneself!)

[1] An adaptation of Juvenal, *Satire III* (on Rome), already adapted by Boileau (to Paris) and by Oldham (to London).

There mark what ills the scholar's life assail,
Toil, envy, want, the patron,[1] and the jail.

Year chases year, decay pursues decay,
Still drops some joy from with'ring life away.

(In all poetry it would not be easy to find two lines of more 'inspissated gloom'.)

From Marlb'rough's eyes the streams of dotage flow,
And Swift expires a driv'ler and a show.

(One should remember that these last lines were written by a man in constant fear of insanity.) No wonder that, reading the poem aloud, Johnson himself was at moments moved to tears.

On the other hand, I do wonder at Scott's verdict on these two poems—'that he had more pleasure in reading *London* and *The Vanity of Human Wishes* than any other poetical composition he could mention.' It was the sympathy, no doubt, of one supremely honest man for another; but, to me, there are moments when Scott himself seems a finer poet; for example, in *Proud Maisie*:

'Tell me, thou bonny bird,
  When shall I marry me?'
'When six braw gentlemen
  Kirkward shall carry ye . . .

'The glow-worm o'er grave and stone
  Shall light thee steady;
The owl from the steeple sing
  Welcome, proud lady!'

Or again in those lines on the dead William Pitt:

Now is the stately column broke,
The beacon-light is quench'd in smoke,

[1] Again the characteristic concentration on one vital word. (In the original version of 1749 'patron' had, of course, been 'Garret'—with a mere fraction of the vigour.) The letter to Chesterfield was written in February, 1755; the revised *Vanity of Human Wishes* appeared in March, 1755; the *Dictionary* in April, 1755, with its definition of 'Patron' as 'commonly a wretch who supports with insolence, and is paid with flattery'. Three buffets in three months!

The trumpet's silver voice is still,
The warder silent on the hill!

These quicken my pulses more; as the wind across the Lammermuirs quickens them more than the gusts of Fleet Street.

For that matter Johnson's original, the snarling old Juvenal, seems to me really more interesting than Johnson's adaptations. Indeed, fine as the rhetoric of Johnson's heroic couplets can be, I doubt if his verse ever ran so high as in one stanza of his more lyrical lines on poor Levett, dead in obscurity (1782):

His virtues walk'd their narrow round,
  Nor made a pause, nor left a void;
And sure th' Eternal Master found
  The single talent well employ'd.

The second line of this is curiously neat; the third and fourth, masterly in compression. All the same, Johnson's true gift was strength, not magic. He could turn a witty prologue:

The Drama's Laws the Drama's Patrons give,
For we that live to please, must please to live.

He could trumpet forth a defiant one:

Unmov'd tho' Witlings sneer and Rivals rail;
Studious to please, yet not asham'd to fail.

But he could no more enchant than a trumpet can. Nor could he write a play.

Irene is intolerable. The characters are dull, and from their lips falls sawdust:

There shall soft Leisure wing th' excursive Soul,
And Peace propitious smile on fond Desire.

This sort of writing would wing my excursive soul straight for the exit. Here, to be fair, is the best passage I can find in *Irene* (on the Islamic view of women):

Mahomet. Vain Raptures all—For your inferiour Natures
Form'd to delight, and happy by delighting,
Heav'n has reserv'd no future Paradise,
But bids you rove the Paths of Bliss, secure
Of total Death, and careless of Hereafter;
While Heav'n's high Minister, whose awful Volume
Records each Act, each Thought of sov'reign Man,
Surveys your Plays with inattentive Glance,
And leaves the lovely Trifler unregarded.

Here for a moment the verse gains a certain life. We seem to catch the voice of him who was in raptures talking to Molly Aston; who lived for years under the spell of Hester Thrale; who enjoyed perching Methodist or Highland lasses on his great knee.[1] But, for the most part, the plot of *Irene* is tedious, the characters have no ideas, and one has little idea of the characters. Johnson doubtless thought poorly of Gibbon; but he was no match for that ugly little historian under the walls of Constantinople.

The *Ramblers*, now read by few, are at least possible to read, though we no longer find them, like Johnson himself, 'pure wine', and are readier to agree with his other comment after reading one of them in later years—'too wordy'; or with Lady Mary Wortley Montagu's complaint that *The Rambler* followed *The Spectator* 'with the same grace that a pack-horse would a hunter'. But perhaps *The Rambler* is more like an elephant—intelligent, sometimes playful, but always ponderous.

The modern reader tends to weary of polysyllables; and to wonder that Johnson, who said he would prefer the portrait of a dog he knew to all the allegorical pictures in the world, should yet here be so fond of allegorical writing. All the same, on a winter evening, by a good fire, *The Rambler* is not unpleasant fare—and perhaps more profitable (to the reader, at least) than some bright modern weeklies.

There are, for example, such characteristic pieces as *Rambler* 94, on fitting sound to sense in verse; where, as in his *Life of Pope*, Johnson makes ironic fun of a type of critical over-subtlety too

[1] Young Mrs Alexander Macdonald of Gillen for a wager sat on his knee at Corrichatachin, and kissed him—to which he replied: 'Do it again, and let us see who will tire first.'

common still. He illustrates by quoting (in one case, misquoting) three Latin hexameters,[1] all of which have been admired for their expressive rhythm, which is essentially the same in each case. 'If all these observations are just,' Johnson ironically concludes, 'there must be some remarkable conformity between the sudden succession of night to day, the fall of an ox under a blow, and the birth of a mouse from a mountain.' This is amusing; but not perhaps wholly fair. It might be replied that there *is* in all three lines one common element—sudden surprise. And this abruptness is expressed by the highly unusual rhythm (in Latin) of the final monosyllable. No doubt such devices succeed up to a point. If, however, I am asked to indulge in excessive raptures at them (as we now so often *are*), I must own that my sympathies side with Johnson.

Interesting, again, is that memorable instance (*Rambler* 168) of the subjectivity and relativity of taste—Johnson's criticism of one of the greatest speeches in *Macbeth*;[2] where 'knife' is condemned because it suggests cooks, and 'dun' because it smells of the stable—'*dun* night may come or go without any other notice than contempt'; while 'I scarce can check my risibility' at 'the avengers of guilt *peeping through a blanket*'.

It is also amusing that Johnson could not in these pages of *The Rambler* keep his pen off patrons, although his meeting with Chesterfield came several years earlier, his letter to Chesterfield several years later. And so *The Rambler* ironically conjectures that it was a poet's experiences with a patron that first suggested the infernal tortures of Tantalus. Then we meet the type of supercilious nobleman who is perpetually proposing—or rather

[1] Each ends, exceptionally, with a monosyllable.

Vertitur interea cælum, et ruit Oceano nox.
(The vault of Heaven wheels, and from Ocean rushes night.)

Sternitur, exanimisque tremens procumbit humi bos.
(Earthward there falls, and quivering, lifeless, lies the ox.)

Parturiunt montes, nascitur (it should be 'nascetur') ridiculus mus.
(In travail heave the mountains—to bear, absurd, a mouse.)

[2] Come, thick Night,
And pall thee in the dunnest smoake of Hell,
That my keene knife see not the Wound it makes
Nor Heaven peepe through the Blanket of the darke
To cry 'Hold, hold!'

commanding—alterations in his victims' works. And there are also two somewhat frigid allegories (Nos. 91 and 105). In the first Patronage builds herself an antechamber called the Hall of Expectation, to which petitioners are introduced by Impudence and Flattery, though access to Patronage herself is controlled by Caprice. 'The Sciences, after a thousand indignities, retired from the palace of Patronage, and having long wandered over the world in grief and distress, were led at last to the cottage of Independence, the daughter of Fortitude, etc.' But all this is not very lively; though a very curious relic of medievalism and the Morality play.

In the second allegory (*Rambler* 105) a person applies to Justice and Truth for registration as a patron. 'Justice heard his confession, and ordered his name to be posted upon the gate among cheats and robbers, and publick nuisances.' It becomes odd, after all this, that Chesterfield ever dared to write his two conciliatory papers in *The World.*

Stock characters are at least livelier than personifications devoid of all personality; and though Johnson could not approach Addison's Sir Roger de Coverley or Goldsmith's Man in Black, we can still smile at his lodger who turns out to be a false coiner, and only escapes the constable by crawling along the roof, 'much to the joy of my landlady, who declares him a very honest man, and wonders why any body should be hanged for making money when such numbers are in want of it.'

Or again *The Rambler* is quite amusing about the typical virtuoso (this may have irritated Horace Walpole) whose treasures include 'the longest blade of grass upon record'; 'a turf with five daisies from the field of *Pharsalia*'; 'a snail that has crawled upon the wall of *China*'; and various phials of water, containing a melted icicle from 'the crags of *Caucasus*', or 'dew brushed from a banana in the gardens of *Ispahan*'.

But always the effect remains a little elephantine. And after such pale gleams of sunshine the clouds of Johnsonian gloom are swift to return. 'We know that the schemes of man are quickly at an end, that we must soon lie down in the grave with the forgotten multitudes of former ages, and yield our place to others, who, like us, shall be driven a while by hope or fear about the surface of the earth, and then like us be lost in the shades of death.'

From such sombre passages one can well understand that Johnson should have been ready to write sermons for clergymen to preach—some forty, it appears; though he seems to have kept to his principle of not being 'blockhead' enough to write them for nothing, and duly charged his guinea, or two.

At least, however, he can also laugh very pleasantly at his own gloom. 'Sir,' begins an imaginary correspondent in *Rambler* 109, 'though you seem to have taken a view sufficiently extensive of the miseries of life, and have employed much of your speculation on mournful subjects, you have not yet exhausted the whole stock of human infelicity....

'I cannot but imagine the start of attention awakened by this welcome hint; and at this instant see the Rambler snuffing his candle, rubbing his spectacles, stirring his fire, locking out interruption, and settling himself in his easy chair, that he may enjoy a new calamity without disturbance . . . whether you intend your writings as antidotal to the levity and merriment with which your rivals endeavour to attract the favour of the publick; or fancy that you have some particular powers of dolorous declamation, and *warble out your groans* with uncommon elegance or energy.'

Here there is at least a delightful touch of humorous self-satire; on the other hand the humour seems curiously unconscious when (No. 11) Johnson writes of the passionate man who 'can give no security to himself that he shall not, at the next interview, alienate by some sudden transport his dearest friend; or break out, upon some slight contradiction, into such terms of rudeness as can never be perfectly forgotten. Whoever converses with him, lives with the suspicion and solicitude of a man that plays with a tame tiger, always under a necessity of watching the moment in which the capricious savage shall begin to growl.'

'How,' asks the astonished reader, 'could Johnson fail to see this self-portrait?' Did he? Such blindness is, no doubt, proverbially easy. I remember the head of a college who, after the appearance of a novel about Eton full of scandalous portraits of the living, himself included, one day electrified his hearers by blandly remarking, 'Well, thank God, at least he has left *me* out of it!' Certainly it seems hard to believe that, had Johnson recognized that he was drawing his own likeness, he could ever have called himself a 'capricious savage'.

On the other hand, had some rash spirit taxed him with not practising his own precepts, he would doubtless, after the first explosion of passion, have replied in the same strain as he did to Lady Macleod at Dunvegan: 'I have, all my life long, been lying till noon; yet I tell all young men, and tell them with great sincerity, that nobody who does not rise early will ever do any good.' One may see the better, yet lack the power to choose it.

At its close, *The Rambler* becomes very typically Johnsonian.

'The essays professedly serious, if I have been able to execute my own intentions, will be found exactly conformable to the precepts of Christianity, without any accommodation to the licentiousness and levity of the present age. I therefore look back on this part of my work with pleasure, which no blame or praise of man shall diminish or augment.' (There speaks the proud old Roman.) 'I shall never envy the honour which wit and learning obtain in any other cause, if I can be numbered among the writers who have given ardour to virtue, and confidence to truth.'

Few readers in this century, it is to be feared, will have gained from *The Rambler* much 'ardour' towards virtue, or indeed much ardour towards anything else. Yet the last sentence is not without its impressiveness; especially when one thinks how many writers, not least in our own day, have set themselves to do exactly the reverse—to weaken faith in decency and confidence in truth; and how few critics ever stir now amid their frivolous æsthetic dreams to tax them with it.

The Idler (1758-60) idles less heavily than *The Rambler* rambles. It is still possible to smile over Lady Biddy Porpoise, that 'lethargick virgin of seventy-six, whom all the families in the square visited very punctually when she was not at home'; over Johnson's evident self-portrait as poor Mr Sober, the perpetual talker, who 'trembles at the thought' of the hours when other men have gone to bed, or are not yet risen, and trifles away these doleful interims in playing at distillation—'sits and counts the drops as they come from his retort, and forgets that, whilst a drop is falling, a moment flies away'; or over Dick Minim 'the critick', who has discovered, like many another since, that 'criticism is a study by which men grow important and formidable at very small expense'. For 'criticism is a goddess easy of access and forward of advance . . . the want of meaning she supplies with words, and the want of spirit she recompenses with malignity'. Dick also belongs to that still popular school which loves to discover in a poem hidden beauties unknown to the common reader, and indeed to the poet himself. He has detected a remarkable corrcspondence of sound to sense in *Hudibras*:

> Honour is like the glassy bubble[1]
> Which costs philosophers such trouble;
> Where, one part crack'd, the whole does fly,
> And wits are crack'd to find out why.

Not only, says Dick, do the first two lines inflate the utterer's cheeks as if he were actually blowing bubbles; 'the greatest excellence is in the third line, which is *crack'd* in the middle to express a crack, and then shivers into monosyllables. Yet has this diamond lain neglected with common stones, and among the innumerable admirers of *Hudibras* the observation of this superlative passage has been reserved for the sagacity of *Minim*.' Evidently in our day *Minim* would have writtten six volumes on Shakespeare, in which Shakespeare would be wholly rewritten.

Rasselas (1759), finished in the evenings of a January week to pay for his mother's funeral, is a prose *Vanity of Human Wishes*. But it is not, after all, funereal to read. Indeed, taking it up again recently, I did not find it easy to put down. It too is redeemed from sheer gloom by its pleasant irony; so that, if sometimes one smiles at the author, still more often one smiles with him.

Rasselas, it will be remembered, is confined in a Happy Valley of Abyssinian Amhara, along with other princes and princesses of the royal house, to keep them from troubling the succession to the throne. But it is a Johnsonian Happy Valley, where desire is gratified, yet none finds happiness—'I have already enjoyed too much; give me something to desire.' Rasselas plans escape.

At first his hopes are raised by an inventor who thinks he has found the secret of flight. And then follows a passage now become famous (to our bitter cost).

'If men were all virtuous, returned the artist, I should with great alacrity teach them all to fly. But what would be the security of the

[1] Prince Rupert's drops.

good, if the bad could at pleasure invade them from the sky? Against an army sailing through the clouds, neither walls, nor mountains, nor seas, could afford any security. A flight of northern savages might hover in the wind, and light at once with irresistible violence upon the capital of a fruitful region that was rolling under them. Even this valley, the retreat of princes, might be violated by the sudden descent of some of the naked nations that swarm on the coast of the southern sea.' (Apart from the one word 'naked' it would be hard to find a more exact prophecy than this Abyssinian fantasy, of the Italian bombing of Abyssinia two hundred years later.)

The inventor, however, having 'waved his pinions a while to gather air', merely crashes ludicrously into a lake. After this scientist, Rasselas next encounters a poet, Imlac, who informs him, in another famous passage, that poetry must be general, not concerning itself with minutiae like numbering the streaks of the tulip; and recites such a list of qualifications indispensable for a poet as to convince Rasselas that no man can ever hope to be one. Imlac has sojourned in the outer world; but his report of it is gloomy. Even the white race, though it has found dominance, has not found felicity. 'The Europeans are less unhappy than we, but they are not happy. Human life is everywhere a state in which much is to be endured, and little to be enjoyed.'

With Imlac, Rasselas and his sister Nekayah finally escape through a chasm, and reach Cairo. But the gay assemblies of Cairo prove like those of Ranelagh—places whither men flock only to escape from thought. Rasselas meets a stoic sage who lectures on the happiness to be attained by quelling all human passions; but, visiting him soon after, finds him prostrate with sorrow himself for a dead daughter. So much for the lectures of philosophers!

Next Rasselas and his sister seek a famous hermit up the Nile. On the way they encounter some shepherds, in order that Johnson may once again hurl his realist contempt at the illusions of the pastoral. 'It was evident that their hearts were cankered with discontent; that they considered themselves as condemned to labour for the luxury of the rich, and looked up with stupid malevolence towards those that were placed above them.'

The hermit himself proves no more satisfactory. Johnson once impressed a Mother Superior by remarking that she was in her convent, not from love of goodness, but from fear of evil. His hermit feels the same; and, after fifteen years of solitude, has just decided to re-enter the world. He accompanies them back to Cairo; 'on which, as he approached it, he gazed with rapture'.

Next comes another philosopher—this time a nature-philosopher, whose principle is simply 'that deviation from nature is deviation from happiness'. 'When he had spoken, he looked round him with a placid air, and enjoyed the consciousness of his own beneficence.'

But what, exactly, asks Rasselas, does the philosopher mean? 'To live according to nature,' comes the pompous response, 'is to act always with due regard to the fitness arising from the relations and qualities of causes and effects; to concur with the great and unchangeable scheme of universal felicity; to co-operate with the general disposition and tendency of the present system of things.'

Johnson was unaware that he might here have been parodying by anticipation the poet-philosopher whom he would probably have regarded as a crowning example of pastoral cant—Wordsworth. Yet it seems doubtful if, as early as this, Johnson can have been much concerned even with Wordsworth's master, Rousseau. But, after all, Rousseau was not the first to bid men, if they would find wisdom, 'observe the hind of the forest, and the linnet of the grove'. 'I need not trace,' Johnson might have retorted, 'the pedigree of nonsense.'

'The prince soon found that this was one of the sages whom he should understand less as he heard him longer. He therefore bowed and was silent, and the philosopher, supposing him satisfied, and the rest vanquished, rose up and departed with the air of a man that had co-operated with the present system.'

The prince and princess now agree to pursue their sociology separately; but when they meet to compare results, they have but few and sorrowful results to compare. The powerful, they find, live under the sword of Damocles; private life is torn by domestic discord; 'marriage has many pains, but celibacy has no pleasures'.

They visit the Pyramids. But these too are vanity—useless mountains of stone, 'erected only in compliance with that hunger of imagination' (admirable phrase!) 'which preys incessantly upon life, and must be always appeased by some employment'. In short, the pyramids were really built because men are fools, and must kill time, until time kills *them*.

Worse follows. During the visit, roving Arabs kidnap the princess Nekayah's lady-in-waiting, Pekuah. The princess languishes awhile for her favourite. But finally the lady is ransomed.

The search for a happy man is resumed. Imlac has now unearthed an astronomer whose 'integrity and benevolence are equal to his learning'. His head may be in the stars; but his hands and heart are busy with human sympathy. ' "Surely," said the princess, "this man is happy." '

But no, he is not. As Johnson always dreaded for himself, the astronomer turns out to have gone mad—to believe that he controls the weather. 'The sun has listened to my dictates, and passed from tropick to tropick by my direction; the clouds, at my call, have poured their waters, and the Nile has overflowed at my command; I have restrained the rage of the Dog-star, and mitigated the fervours of the Crab.' (Curious how Johnson can fall, at times, into the rhythmical, antithetical poetry of the Old Testament.)

'The prince heard this narration with very serious regard; but the princess smiled, and Pekuah convulsed herself with laughter. "Ladies," said Imlac, "to mock the heaviest of human afflictions is neither charitable nor wise." '

Sobered, they confess that they too have always day-dreamed: Pekuah, of being Queen of Abyssinia; Nekayah, of being a shepherdess; Rasselas himself, of a Utopian government conducted by his own benevolent despotism. But henceforth they will indulge such dangerous fantasies no more. Always Johnson distrusted rapturists, and detested rhapsodies. Here speaks the authentic voice of the eighteenth century, with its courageous, sober realism.

Next, they meet a wise old man, in the evening of a well-spent life. Here one half dreads some edifying moral. But no, Johnson is too honest. Even the wise old man is not happy. ' "Praise," said the sage with a sigh, "is to an old man an empty sound." ' 'I rest against a tree, and consider, that in the same shade I once disputed on the annual overflow of the Nile with a friend who is now silent in the grave.' His only hope lies in happiness beyond. 'He rose and went away, leaving his audience not much elated with the hope of long life.' (Such sadly ironic understatement is one of Johnson's favourite, and most effective, devices.)

The mad astronomer, however, is gradually restored to reason by resuming the simple human pleasures of converse with Rasselas, his sister, and Pekuah—who become for him something of what Mrs Thrale and Fanny Burney were to be for Johnson. The star-gazer realizes his error—'I have missed the endearing elegance of female friendship, and the happy commerce of domestick tenderness.'

But even this, after all, can only be a temporary palliative. They visit the Egyptian catacombs, and edifyingly reflect on the frailty of mortal life—nothing really matters but eternity. And so to the final chapter—'The Conclusion, in which nothing is concluded.' They return to where they began—to Abyssinia.

Rasselas has not the wit, the high spirits, the *diablerie* of Voltaire's[1] *Candide*. For me, *Rasselas* contains not only less wit but, in its conclusion, less wisdom. 'Vanity of vanities' may be true; but, in practice, it seems to me a less wise and healthy conclusion than Voltaire's—'Il faut cultiver son jardin.' Johnson too, no doubt, held that a man should cultivate his garden; but only as a prelude to eternity. God has bidden us labour on this petty plot; if we labour well, we may be immortally rewarded; yet no man can know, however great his efforts, that he will not be immortally punished.

This idea that God should bid man forgive his brother unto seventy times seven, but should consider Himself at liberty to punish His children infinitely and unendingly for a single offence, or even for an offence committed by others, seems to me the strangest, perhaps, of all human manias. And so I cannot but prefer *Candide* with its disillusioned, yet gay concentration on *this* life, without regard for dreams, or nightmares, about 'I know not what, I know not where'.

[1] For Voltaire, of course, Johnson had little use; finding it hard to 'settle the proportion of iniquity' between him and Rousseau (whom Johnson would have been delighted to sentence to transportation as a felon). Voltaire, however, repaid Johnson with a singular tribute. Naturally he had attacked Johnson's defence of Shakespeare; but in May 1778, at eighty-three, he urged the French Academy in a long and passionate speech to compile a new dictionary similar to those of the Accademia della Crusca and of Johnson. Against great opposition he carried his proposal, and would not allow the assembly to separate till they had distributed the various letters of the alphabet—'he himself took A, as the most copious'. But the incredible old man had overestimated, at last, his own vitality. By the end of the month he was dead.

Had Johnson's own funeral followed *Rasselas*, he would remain to-day a writer comparatively unknown. True, *Rasselas* reached seven editions in his lifetime, and has been translated into French, German, Italian, Spanish, Dutch, Hungarian, Polish, Russian, modern Greek, and Bengali. But nearly all Johnson's still remembered writings, nearly all his recorded talk, date from after 1760, when he was fifty-one—from the last twenty-five years of his life. And most of these remembered writings, apart from his account of the Hebrides, are criticism.

'Johnson's æsthetic judgments,' wrote Lytton Strachey, 'are almost invariably subtle, or solid, or bold; they have always some good quality to recommend them—except one: they are never right.' This epigram is amusing enough; yet it seems to me naughty. 'Never', particularly in criticism, is a terribly dangerous word.

There is no need to take up time discussing whether æsthetic judgments on particular works of art can ever be described as 'right' or 'wrong'. I do not myself believe that they can. If Shakespeare seemed to Tolstoy unpleasing, or Dante to Nietzsche, or Jane Austen to Alice Meynell, or Ibsen to William Morris, then unpleasing, to them, they were. Tolstoy, Nietzsche, and the others had, no doubt, exceptional tastes in these matters; but a taste is not made 'wrong' by being exceptional. Whether a book, or a landscape, or a wine pleases or displeases, remains a matter not of reasoning, but of feeling. True, though one cannot argue about æsthetic effects, one *can* argue about after-effects—that a given book, or a given wine, is unhealthy. Even this, however, is extremely hard to establish.

Yet hardly any critics have ever admitted, or perhaps ever will admit, even in theory, what seems to me this simple truth—that æsthetic tastes are merely subjective. Men's desire of forcing their own opinions on other men remains too incorrigible. I cannot believe that Johnson himself would ever have accepted this view. True, he goes some way in that direction when he says of Pomfret, 'he pleases many; and he who pleases many must have some species of merit.' But the tolerance of reasoned subjectivity was opposed to the whole nature of a man who could reply to one lady, who liked Sterne, that it was because she was 'a dunce'; and to another, who owned knowing *Lycidas* by heart, that nothing remained for her but to 'die in a surfeit of bad taste'.

There are, however, some critical questions where it becomes possible to give an answer that *is* 'right' or 'wrong', because they concern matters, not of opinion, but of fact. The pleasure to be gained from Gerard Manley Hopkins or James Joyce is a matter of opinion; but whether intelligent men can or cannot gain pleasure from a play whose action lasts over ten years, or shifts over a thousand miles, is a matter of psychological fact and simple observation.

Now there are questions of this second kind which have been solidly discussed by Johnson; and it seems to me highly unjust to say his answers to them were 'never right'.

His attack on the Three Unities, for example, in his Preface to Shakespeare, has not only become the generally accepted view; its dialectic skill is such that Stendhal plagiarized from it in his own attack on the French classical drama. It seems to me, indeed, a superbly written piece of argument. True, its main plea (that the only way to decide how much an audience's imagination can stand, is to try) might have been considerably strengthened by further pointing out that the Unities of Time and Place are a mere historical accident due to Greek use of a Chorus. Because drama arose from group ritual, the group survived in the ancient Chorus; because the Chorus was there, changes of time and place were automatically limited (for clearly it is impossible for a dozen damsels, still more for a dozen aged elders, to form an inseparable and immortal party, to-day at Troy, and ten years later at Argos, as if they had chartered a winged chariot). But this simple truth had not occurred to the supporters of the Unities; and it is not surprising that it did not occur, either, to Johnson in attacking them.[1] But essentially his view has prevailed. With the disappearance of the Chorus has disappeared the need for the unities of time and place; though a work which observes them may still gain æsthetically in compactness and intensity (like some plays of Ibsen).

Similarly with Johnson's defence of comic relief in serious drama. No doubt Mr T. S. Eliot has ordained otherwise—'The desire for "comic relief" on the part of an audience is, I believe, a permanent craving of human nature; but that does not mean that it is a craving that ought to be gratified. It springs from a lack of the capacity for

[1] It had, however, occurred to Lord Kames (*Elements of Criticism*, 1762).

concentration. . . . The doctrine of *Unity of Sentiment*, in fact, happens to be right.' Most modern dramatists, however, including Ibsen, being less omniscient, and less puritanical, have continued to use comic relief. So, indeed, has Mr Eliot.

Again, there is Johnson's conclusion that 'words too familiar, or too remote, defeat the purpose of a poet'. True, Aristotle had said the same long before, adding further details very much to the purpose. But at least this piece of commonsense seems to me far nearer the general truth than the blundering logic and rambling abstractions with which the question was debated a generation later, at unconscionable length, by Wordsworth and Coleridge.

Similarly with Strachey's other indictments. It is not true that 'Johnson never inquired what poets were trying to do'; for he inquired when dealing with the Metaphysicals, and when dealing with Pope. It is not true that 'he could see nothing in the splendour and elevation of Gray, but "glittering accumulations of ungraceful ornaments" '; for no one has more splendidly praised Gray's *Elegy* (though Johnson was less kind to it in conversation).[1] To say that 'Johnson had no ear, and he had no imagination' seems to me confuted by many a passage in his prose, his poetry, and his talk. All this means only that Strachey had forgotten them, or that he happened to have a different kind of ear, a different kind of imagination. He could himself be a most admirable critic; but not, I feel, of Johnson's criticism.

Consider, again, some of Johnson's particular judgments. Surely many will agree that Shakespeare's jests do often seem tawdry, and his quibbles often tedious; that the key-quality of Falstaff is excellently summarized as 'perpetual gaiety'; that Morgann's defence of Falstaff's courage is grotesque—'Why, Sir, we shall have the man come forth again; and as he has proved Falstaff no coward, he may prove Iago to be a very good character.' Sometimes Johnson's criticism could be comically practical, as when he read a long passage of Thomson to Shiels, omitting every other line—and Shiels expressed the highest admiration. Nor do I see reason to

[1] Though they never met, Johnson in judging Gray seems to have had to contend with a stronger personal dislike than is usually realized. There is a curious passage in the *Boswell Papers* (April 2, 1775). Boswell, speaking of Pope's Dunces, said: 'They could not have a malignity against Pope without knowing him.' *Johnson.* 'Yes, Sir, very well. I hate Gray and Mason, though I do not know them.'

quarrel with Johnson's view that Milton knew human nature 'only in the gross'; that *Hudibras* with all its wit, grows boring, because 'from what is unnatural we can derive only the pleasure which novelty produces . . . the spectator turns away from a second exhibition of those tricks of which the only use is to show that they can be played'; that Pope's *Essay on Man* preaches a very shallow optimism; that in Gray's odes 'there is a kind of cumbrous splendour which we wish away'; that *Ossian* is poor stuff; and that the only sane object of writing 'is to enable the reader better to enjoy life, or better to endure it'. Nor let it be forgotten that Johnson recognized at once the powers of the unknown Crabbe.

True, there are also many judgments of Johnson's that may make us stare. The Nun's Priest's tale, for example (Chauntecleer and Pertelote), which many besides Housman and Bridges may think one of the very best things in Chaucer, seemed to Johnson hardly worthy of revival by Dryden. How, again, could Johnson find the diction of *Lycidas*, or of the songs of *Comus* 'harsh'? 'Harsh', for some odd reason, he employed to mean 'strained, forced, unnatural', not 'unmelodious'; and, I suppose, there *is* a strained artificiality in language like

> But now my oat proceeds
> And listens to the herald of the sea.

All the same. . . . And then to call the versification of *Lycidas* 'unpleasing', the songs of *Comus* 'unmusical'!

Clearly, however, to Johnson the versification of *Lycidas was* unpleasing; and he had as good a right to his ear as we to ours. One may count ears; but that does not confute him.

When, however, he says, 'Nothing odd will do long. *Tristram Shandy* did not last,' then he clearly spoke too soon. Critics are rash to speak for anyone but themselves. Nor does Johnson persuade many of us when he says of *The Vicar of Wakefield* (to which he preferred *The Traveller*): 'No, madam, it is very faulty; there is nothing of real life in it, and very little of nature. It is a mere fanciful performance.' (Perhaps it was too close to Johnson's prime abomination, the pastoral.) It remains, too, a little startling to be told that Gray is inferior to Akenside; and that Akenside in the general fabric of his blank verse is 'perhaps superior to any other writer'. Finally, when Boswell's question 'Who can repeat Hamlet's soliloquy, "To be or not to be" as Garrick does it?' only brings the retort, 'Anybody may. Jemmy[1] there will do it as well in a week,' then one realizes that, though cautious up to a point on paper, in the passion of conversation Johnson was capable of anything.

Again, when it comes to a generalized dictum like the ban on numbering the streaks of the tulip, though it is certainly common enough for poetry to overdo minute details (like many a tedious novel), still legions of poets rise up to testify on the opposite side—Homer with the delicate observation in his similes; Shakespeare counting the spots in cowslips to visualize Imogen's mole; Wordsworth with his daisy's star-shaped shadow on the stone; Tennyson with his 'blackest ashbuds in the front of March'; Rossetti numbering the triple cups of the woodspurge.

Johnson's criticism, in fine, does not add poetry to poetry like Gilbert Murray's *Ancient Greek Literature*; it does not light up old masterpieces with new knowledge, like Eileen Power on Chaucer's Prioress, or Livingstone Lowes on *The Ancient Mariner*; it has not the breadth and sanity of Sainte-Beuve, the penetration of Emile Faguet, the charm of Anatole France. None the less, for me, it remains enormously readable, because Johnson wrote so well, and because he knew so much of real life. The power of his criticism springs not only from his intellect, but also from his vitality. Being physically full-blooded, he loved the concrete—metaphor, simile, analogy. This makes him not only delightful to read, but also far easier than most critics to remember. And what real use, except to kill time (which is a form of murder), is reading that one does *not* remember? Beside Johnson, Dryden seems to me often thin; Coleridge, sometimes woolly; Arnold, frequently puritanic and pedagogic. Johnson may mistake the truth: but he does not fog it. He marches straight ahead, even when wrong; he does not stagger in circles, like a man lost in mist; and so we at least arrive somewhere. Among his best things are his comments on episodes or aspects of his poets' lives. They are the comments of a man who had himself lived intensely. And, after all, one does not really read him to learn more about poetry; one reads him to learn, and enjoy,

[1] A boy of eight.

more about himself. As Whitman said of his own work:

> Camerado, this is no book,
> Who touches this, touches a man.

In short, the virtue of Johnson's criticism, like the virtue of his original writing and his talk, lies mainly in the same two things (which are largely one)—personality and style.

What, then, can one learn from Johnson in general? First, I think, the inestimable value of individuality. This we seem at times to risk forgetting, in our grossly overpopulated world of overgrown states. Partly these are totalitarian, and therefore preach that the individual must lose himself in the mass (as if there were some mystic value in massed rabbits); partly they are democratic, and therefore preach too often a deadening kind of egalitarianism, dreaming of uniformity in income, uniformity in education, uniformity in status, even if this should mean, in the end, uniformity in stupidity. Nothing matters finally but the states of mind of individuals; if the individuals lack individuality, their states of mind are likely to be cheap, brutish, and nasty. Jonah mattered more than the whale; the individual matters more than Leviathan. Johnson is a supreme example of the wisdom of Montaigne, only confirmed by modern psychology, that a man should 'Jouir loyalement de son être'—'find honest enjoyment in his own nature'—in short, be himself. 'Werde was du bist'[1]—'become what thou really art.' No doubt, if one has more than one self (like most of us), it had better be one's better self that one tries to become. Again, it may be said that all of us have two selves—one egoistic and self-centred, one gregarious and social. And to stifle this second, altruistic self is to poison the whole being. That truth Nietzsche, for instance, forgot; but Johnson did not forget it. Again and again he insisted on the duty for every man, especially for the writer, of trying to leave the world slightly happier, wiser, or better.

Secondly, individuality grows warped if it loses honesty. 'Clear your *mind* of cant.' There are two kinds of humbug—a man may pretend to think and feel as others would wish, or to think and feel as he would wish himself. Johnson was singularly free from the first kind of falsity—hypocrisy; he was not wholly successful in

[1] Nietzsche.

escaping from the second kind—self-deception. But who is? Yet he constantly made the effort to think straight.

The English are perhaps specially prone to self-deception. We have a reputation for mental dishonesty. And it is an unpleasant one. Still this vice may be, in part, due to a virtue. It could be argued that there is more public and private conscience in England than in some countries; and that this develops greater skill in lulling conscience asleep, subtler forms of cant. And again this vice may have in it a certain utility—the English often behave as shabbily as any other civilized nation; but, because they so successfully convince themselves that they are behaving well, they do, in fact, become less demoralized, less cynical, from behaving badly.

Be that as it may, few men have done as much to counteract this English tendency to sham and cant, as Johnson. In comparison, Swift was too malignant; Carlyle, too preposterous; Ruskin, too febrile; Samuel Butler and Shaw, too impish. They were, in fact, not English enough. But Johnson came by temperament, as well as by birth, from the heart of England. The very name of 'Johnson' was a happy chance. At times he might be John Bull in person, if only John Bull had better brains. Indeed Heine called him 'der John Bull der Gelehrsamkeit'. We laugh at him; but we feel him one of *us*; and so we are more willing to listen to him, and to learn.

Thirdly, one cannot hope to escape humbug of either kind—the humbug of deception or the humbug of self-deception—without courage—the courage to ignore, when necessary, hostile opinion, and the courage to face unpleasant facts. That courage is another of Johnson's greatest qualities.

Fourthly, helped by his honesty and his courage, Johnson was one of the great champions of reason. Our rather seedy century has often lost faith in reason, as in individual liberty. We have had Bergsonian intuitionism, and the ravings of D. H. Lawrence about dark loins of Egypt, and the Nazi nostrum of 'thinking with the blood'. A pretty dance *that* was to lead our world, and blood enough it cost. We have had, too, the obscurantism of neo-medievalists, who deplore or deny the Renaissance, and would like to replace it by a Resenescence which would dodder back into what that wiser medievalist, William Morris, called 'the maundering side of the Middle Ages'.

No doubt some eighteenth-century characters trusted too exclusively to reason; but that was because they failed to reason enough. It was Freud, not Bergson or neo-Thomists, who, by reasoning and observation, discovered the irrational Unconscious, with its terrible powers of distorting and misleading the rational part of the mind. And the only hope I can see for the future depends on a wiser and braver use of the reason, not a panic flight from it. 'Intellectuals', no doubt, are often tiresome enough, because they are often pseudo-intellectuals—ingenious fools, too clever to be wise, though brilliant at inventing the most ingenious reasons for the most fatuous beliefs. But, tiresome as intellectuals can be, even they are probably much less menacing and pernicious to the world than anti-intellectuals.

Fifthly, there are Johnson's vitality and gaiety. He would never hold the place he does, had he been as over-earnest as Carlyle, as humourless as Ruskin, as languid as Walter Pater.

Lastly, he is a monument to the magic power of style. He might savage poor William Pepys over Pope's epigram on 'what oft was thought, but ne'er so well express'd';[1] but his own career is a supreme illustration of its truth. His originality and his strength lie, not in his views, but in his power to state them with vigour and vividness unsurpassed. His horse-sense is delivered with the kick of a horse; his spoken style had the weight of a hammer, and the edge of a sword.

There are also, perhaps, certain warnings to be learnt from Johnson. First the supreme importance of health in mind and body. When he wrote *The Vanity of Human Wishes*, he replaced Juvenal's five words '*mens sana in corpore sano*'—very much for the worse—by 'a healthful mind, Obedient passions and a will resign'd'. Curious of him thus to omit that health of body which he so sorely lacked himself. But, because his own mind and body were both sick, through all his years there ran a streak of blackness which marks him off tragically from healthier, saner contemporaries, like Hume, Reynolds, or Gibbon, Montesquieu, Diderot, or Benjamin Franklin.

Secondly, the 'obedient passions' Johnson craved were far from being his. To us, probably, he would be far less interesting and amusing if he had kept pride, passion, and prejudice under better

[1] P. 57.

control. But it would have been better for him. For they cost him, and his contemporaries, a good deal; they made his states of mind a good deal less valuable and enviable, if much more picturesque.

Thirdly, he is an example of bad style, as well as of good. At times his heavier writings become a dreary landscape measured only by longitude and platitude. But these, after all, remain minor matters. His best epitaph was perhaps uttered by William Gerard Hamilton:[1] 'Johnson is dead. Let us go to the next best. There is nobody; no man can be said to put you in mind of Johnson.' Essentially, after nearly two hundred years, that is still true.

Science may change past recognition the face of the world; history may redraw every frontier on the earth; but while men value integrity of thought and trenchancy of speech, they will, I believe, look back at moments to that strange bear-like figure shuffling along the pavements of eighteenth-century London, and they will still hear, across the thickening fogs of time, an indomitable voice that thunders—'Sir. . . .'

[1] He was called 'single-speech Hamilton' because his maiden-speech was his best; but to-day his words on Johnson's death are perhaps the single utterance by which he lives. (Unless we add his comment, which so pleased Johnson once on Brighton Downs—'Why, Johnson rides as well, for aught I see, as the most illiterate fellow in England.')

LORD CHESTERFIELD

Let me remind you what happened to the child from Shou-ling who was sent to Han-tan to acquire the Han-tan Walk. He failed to learn the steps, but spent so long trying, that he ended by forgetting how one usually walks, and came home to Shou-ling on all fours.

'CHUANG TZU' (3rd century B.C.)

ONE of the queerest figures in the whole eighteenth century (though at such an idea he might have smiled disdainfully, and taken snuff)—indeed, one of the queerest in any century—seems to me Lord Chesterfield. To some of his contemporaries he appeared a pattern; but perhaps he is, rather, a warning. Endlessly though he preached on grace and 'the Graces', such endless preaching became in itself not very graceful. Much more real grace was shown in practice, I think, by other figures of eighteenth-century England, such as Horace Walpole, Goldsmith, or Sheridan—to say nothing of many men and women in eighteenth-century France. However, to the theory of the Graces no man, surely, in human history can have devoted more single-minded thought and perseverance. In himself, then, Chesterfield remains of interest as an oddity; and in the history of manners, as a fantastic aberration of exaggeration. For no fop ever believed more fervently that a man is made, or marred, by his manners; and few theologians can ever have wrestled more ardently with the problems of divine grace than this worldling with the problems of a grace much more earthly.

Chesterfield and Johnson form a pair as antithetical as a sentence of Johnson's own. One can picture them as two figures symmetrically opposed on some mantelpiece of the period. On one side stands the rich Whig peer, typical of that confident aristocracy which dominated the course of the whole age; sceptical and irreligious (except for a tenuous theism, and his far more fervent worship of the Graces); strict in manners, but often loose in morals; light in style, yet never laughing, never losing his temper, never except in closest intimacy (if even then) giving away his private thoughts. And opposite him rises that needy, uncouth son of a provincial bookseller, who remained in his politics a fanatical Tory, and whose class in the coming century was to wrest supremacy from the heirs of Chesterfield; a man imbued with violent prejudices and gloomy piety; rigid in morals, yet reckless at moments of every canon of courtesy; often elephantine in style, yet a rhinoceros in laughter; with a temper perpetually exploding, and an outspokenness that thundered forth its views on almost any topic before a world partly awed, partly outraged, partly fascinated.

And yet Chesterfield and Johnson had also qualities in common. Both were ugly, and grew infirm, yet triumphed over physical defects by force of mind and brilliance of tongue; both were impassioned educators; both were intensely, often bleakly, rational and realist; both were disillusioned, sombre, and haunted by the same melancholy lines on human life from Dryden's *Aurengzebe*.[1] Both were, in essence, lonely figures; and each found that the person on whom he had long centred his affection, had preferred, in secret, a marriage most unwelcome. Yet both, as life darkened over them, faced its deepening shadows, to the end, with stoic fortitude.[2]

The first Earl of Chesterfield (1584–1656) had been a loyal Royalist; the second Earl, his grandson, the 'handsome Earl' (1633–1714), was a character of 'exceeding wildness', loved by Barbara Villiers, Countess of Castlemaine, and by Lady Elizabeth Howard (afterwards married off to Dryden, who dedicated his *Georgics* (1697) to his wife's old lover). The third Earl (1673–1726), a morose and passionate person, married the daughter of the famous Marquis of Halifax; and on September 22, 1694, she bore him the fourth Earl, our Chesterfield. After little over a year (1712–4) at Trinity Hall, in 1715 the youth entered Parliament, though still some weeks under twenty-one.

For his maiden speech, attacking the makers of the Treaty of Utrecht, he was congratulated by a Tory M.P., but reminded that, being not yet twenty-one, he had exposed himself to a fine of £500 for taking his place in the House. Chesterfield withdrew for the necessary month to Paris.

Succeeding his father as earl in 1726, he became in 1728 Ambassador at The Hague; where, in March 1732, a French governess of thirty, Mlle du Bouchet,[3] bore him a natural son, Philip Stanhope, the destined victim of Chesterfield's most famous letters.

In 1733, after being dismissed from office for opposing Walpole's Excise Bill (a sensible measure which roused tumults of popular

[1] See p. 167.

[2] Oddly enough Chesterfield and Johnson seem to have been distant relatives. Johnson's cousin, Cornelius Ford, was Chesterfield's chaplain, and married a certain Judith Crowley; her great-niece, about 1740–5, married Chesterfield's brother, Sir William Stanhope. (See A. L. Reade, *Johnsonian Gleanings*, iii, 151–3.)

[3] Chesterfield later brought her to England, where she was naturalized in 1734.

hysteria), he married his King's half-sister, Melusina von der Schulenburg, Countess of Walsingham, daughter of George I and that Duchess of Kendal whom Chesterfield once summed up as 'very little above an idiot'. He may have been prejudiced against his mother-in-law. Still, according to Horace Walpole she was capable of believing that the soul of the dead George I appeared to her in the shape of a large black raven.

Poor Melusina seems to have had nothing fairy-like about her but her name, and she was nearly forty; but she had the solid virtues of a £50,000 portion and £3,000 a year. Chesterfield wanted, as he calmly explained to a Dutch friend, a wife 'qui fournisse un peu à l'entretien de la Bouchet et de son enfant'. And Mlle du Bouchet herself, he frankly observes, 'me connaît trop bien pour vouloir de moi.' The married pair, it is said, long lived next door to each other in Grosvenor Square (for Melusina remained under her mother's roof); in amity but not, it would appear, on his lordship's side at least, with much warmth of affection.

In 1737 Chesterfield delivered one of his most admired speeches, against the restrictions on the stage introduced by Walpole's Licensing Bill in retaliation for the dramatic attacks of Fielding. In the same year, little Philip Stanhope being now five, his father began writing to him, or at him, those letters which have mainly kept alive the name of Chesterfield.

After Walpole's fall, the Earl returned to public office, with a second mission to The Hague (1745), a successful Lord-Lieutenancy of Ireland (July 1745–April 1746), and a Secretaryship of State (1746–8). But he disliked the war with France; he disliked the Duke of Newcastle; and so resigned, refusing a dukedom.

In 1751 he made another famous speech, on Calendar Reform; but after 1755 deafness began to cut him off from public life (though even in 1757 he did real and tactful service in reconciling Pitt and Newcastle). He had pushed his son into Parliament (1754), where the lad was a failure; then (1756) into the post of British Resident at Hamburg, whence he later moved to Dresden (1764), only to die in 1768. But meanwhile there had arrived a second candidate for education, Chesterfield's godson and successor, another Philip Stanhope, nicknamed 'Sturdy' (1755–1815), who was already being written to, at the age of six, in 1761. In 1773, five years after his own son, Lord Chesterfield himself died at the age of seventy-eight. But the very next year he rose again into notice, with the publication of his letters to that son; for which Dodsley paid the son's widow[1] a handsome price of 1,500 guineas.

Nature and Fortune partly forwarded, partly hampered, Chesterfield's vocation as the Apostle of Grace. Nature gave him quick wits, but counterbalanced them with an unimposing physique—short trunk and neck, large head and nose; or, in Sir Paul Methuen's affable description, a head bigger than his body, and a nose bigger than his head. His half-brother-in-law, George II, no less affable, called him 'a little tea-table scoundrel', 'a dwarf-baboon', and 'a little chattering cur'.

But a fuller portrait comes from the deadlier pen of Lord Hervey, Pope's 'Sporus': 'With a person as disagreeable as it was possible for a human figure to be without being deformed, he affected following many women of the first beauty and the most in fashion, and, if you would have taken his word for it, not without success; whilst in fact and in truth he never gained any one above the venal rank of those whom an Adonis or a Vulcan might be equally well with, for an equal sum of money. He was very short, disproportioned, thick, and clumsily made; had a broad, rough-featured, ugly face, with black teeth, and a head big enough for Polyphemus. One Ben Ashurst . . . told Lord Chesterfield once that he was like a stunted giant, which was a humorous idea and really apposite.'

Add to these charms a shrill, croaking voice and, with advancing life, a serious deafness. But it would be wise to discount something in such picturesque portraits; they were not drawn by Chesterfield's friends. In Gainsborough's painting of him the lips, though twisted, look sensitive; the eyes, though pouched and melancholy, are keen; it is not a handsome face, nor a happy one; but it remains distinguished.

In any case it is possible that his physical defects in part even stimulated him to over-compensate them by dogged effort; as the stuttering Demosthenes yet made himself by sheer perseverance the most famous of orators.

[1] Mrs Stanhope tried to get the letters edited first by Gibbon, then by Horace Walpole (Walpole to Lady Louisa Lennox, October 14, 1773); but in the end she did it herself.

Fortune, at first, was kinder to Chesterfield than Nature had been. He came of good family, in an age when family mattered. And it was something to be grandson of the great Halifax. Chesterfield could become M.P. before he was twenty-one.

And yet, despite natural endowments and family fortunes, there remains something frustrated about Chesterfield's whole career. Indeed, his kinsman, James Earl Stanhope (1673–1721), proved a more effective servant of his country. Why?

To his contemporaries Chesterfield seemed brilliant. True, his reputation rested largely on mere wit. And wit, like humour, does not always wear well. The wits of history are sometimes like the wits of Meredith's fiction. We are constantly assured they were wonderful; yet the specimens provided are apt to disappoint. However let us first have specimens of the wit of Chesterfield. There is no other way to judge.

(To Miss Chudleigh, complaining that the world credited her with having had twins.) 'Does it! I make a point of only believing one-half of what it says.'

(To a young lady at a Dublin Ball, during his Lord-Lieutenancy.)

Pretty Tory, where's the jest
Of wearing Orange on thy breast,
While that breast upheaving shows
The whiteness of the rebel rose?[1]

(On a report at the same period that the people of Connaught were rising—with a glance at his watch.)
'It's nine o'clock and certainly time for them to rise; I therefore believe your news to be true.' (This might have been better if briefer. Its levity is said to have so scandalized the Archbishop of Tuam, to whom it was addressed, that he never visited Chesterfield again.)

(On a full-length portrait of Beau Nash, placed at Bath between busts of Newton and Pope.)

[1] There are variant versions.

The picture plac'd the busts between
  Adds to the thought much strength;
Wisdom and Wit are little seen,
  But Folly's at full length.

(On a marriage between some son of obscurity and the daughter of a mother tarnished in reputation.) 'Nobody's son has married Everybody's daughter.'

(Of translations.) 'Everything suffers by translation, except a bishop.'

(To his sister and Lady Huntingdon, trying to lure him, in later life, to some Methodist seminary in Wales.) 'I do not love such tremendous prospects. When the faith of your ladyships has removed the mountains, I will go to Wales.'[1]

(Near his end.) 'Tyrawley and I have been dead two years; but we don't choose to have it known.'

Similarly he withdrew from a thinly attended oratorio of Handel's, patronized by George II and Queen Caroline, because 'he did not wish to intrude on the privacy of his sovereign'. And he proposed that the best way to keep out the Pretender was to make him Elector of Hanover; for England, after her experiences with the House of Hanover, would certainly never endure to take another sovereign thence.

As wit, some of these seem well enough. Yet to-day Chesterfield's journalistic writings seem to me a little flat. And even in his own time there were critics who questioned his fame for epigram.

'It was not his fault,' says Horace Walpole, 'if he had not wit; nothing exceeded his efforts in that point. . . . He was so accustomed to see people laugh at the most trifling things he said, that he would be disappointed at finding nobody smile before they knew what he was going to say. His speeches were fine, but as much laboured as his extempore sayings.'

[1] So Mérimée, when a pious lady urged him to be baptized, stipulated only that she should be godmother 'and carry me, dressed in a white frock, in your arms'.

Johnson's verdict was equally crushing—not 'a lord among wits', but 'a wit among lords'.

Yet perhaps both are a little harsh. Chesterfield seems at all events to have had enough wit to frighten others and, as wits so often do, to damage himself.

'Lord Chesterfield,' says the bitter Hervey, 'was allowed by everybody to have more conversable entertaining table-wit than any man of his time. His propensity to ridicule, in which he indulged himself with infinite humour and no distinction, and with inexhaustible spirits and no discretion, made him sought and feared, liked and not loved by most of his acquaintance.[1] No sex, no relation, no rank, no power, no profession, no friendship, no obligation, was a shield from those pointed, glittering weapons, that seemed to shine only to a stander-by, but cut deep in those they touched.... And as his Lordship, for want of principle, often sacrificed his character to his interest, so by these means he often, for want of prudence, sacrificed his interest to his vanity.'

Hervey, as an ally of Sir Robert Walpole, was no doubt prejudiced; but a good deal of this rings true, and may help to explain the partial failure of Chesterfield's career. It all makes a curious contrast with that invariable tact he assiduously preached to his son. 'A wit,' he writes, 'is a very unpopular denomination, as it carries terror along with it, and people in general are as much afraid of a live wit in company, as a woman is of a gun, which she thinks may go off of itself, and do her a mischief.' 'If God gives you wit, which I am not sure that I wish you, unless he gives you at the same time an equal portion at least of judgment to keep it in good order, wear it like your sword in the scabbard, and do not brandish it to the terror of the whole company.' Still, it was human enough that Chesterfield, while preaching tact, should sometimes fail to practise it; and that he did not always practise it is no proof that his preaching was not sincere.[2]

[1] Cf., for example, his early annoyance of Walpole (1725) by a satirical ballad on the Order of the Bath:

Though I a bauble call it,
It must not thus be slighted;
'Twas one of the toys
Bob gave his boys
When first the chits were knighted.

[2] Cf. the story of Chesterfield's warning a young nobleman at Bath not to play

Yet, besides wit, Chesterfield had also wisdom. In 1765 he foresaw (though, of course, he was not alone) the folly of quarrelling with America—of risking a trade worth £2,000,000 for a Stamp Act yielding £100,000! He shrewdly summarized in a remark to Montesquieu that recurrent weakness in French politics for centuries—'Vous savez faire des barricades, mais vous n'éléverez jamais des barrières.'[1] He foresaw, too, the French Revolution (though in this too he was by no means alone)—'all the symptoms which I have ever met with in history, previous to great changes and revolutions, now exist and daily increase in France'. He was, indeed, wildly mistaken in his prophecy about the effects of that Revolution—'the rest of Europe will be the quieter' (December 25, 1753). But others made the same mistake even after the fall of the French Monarchy had actually begun. And that does not invalidate his wider prevision—'before the end of this century the trade of both King and priest will not be half as good as it has been'. He also foretold the ruin of Poland and the partition, within a century, of the Papal States. On the other hand, his doubts (1762) whether the Papacy itself would long survive were premature. And the decline of his own aristocracy he did not, I think, foresee.

Similarly, like his old enemy Johnson, he did not mince his words about that oppression of Ireland which was also to bring its harvest of whirlwinds—'I see,' he writes to the Bishop of Waterford on October 1, 1764, 'that you are in fears again from your White Boys and have destroyed a good many of them; but I believe that if the military force had killed half as many landlords, it would have contributed more effectually to restore quiet. The poor people in Ireland are used worse than negroes by their Lords and Masters, and their Deputies of Deputies of Deputies.' He had himself dealt far more liberally with the Irish; he had tried to encourage their manufactures, seeing that Poverty was a greater danger than Popery; and he had wished to be remembered, not as the Lord-Lieutenant of Ireland but as the Irish Lord-Lieutenant.

No less keen-eyed are some of his comments on individuals.

with certain card-sharpers; a little later the grateful youth was much astonished to see his lordship busily gaming with 'those very harpies'.

[1] In another version: 'Vos Parlements pourront bien faire encore des barricades, mais ils ne feront jamais de barrière.'

'Pope in conversation was below himself; he was seldom easy and natural, and seemed afraid that the man should degrade the poet, which made him attempt wit and humour, often unsuccessfully, and too often unseasonably.' One can well believe *that* from Pope's letters (though, ironically, this same charge was brought against the wit of Chesterfield himself).

The fussy Newcastle, again, is polished off in a single sentence—'He was as jealous of his power as an impotent lover of his mistress, without activity of mind enough to enjoy or exert it.' Bute fares no better—'His name was Stuart, he called himself a descendant of that Royal House, and was humble enough to be proud of it.'[1] 'Every man who is new in business, is at first either too rash or too timorous; but he was both.' These sentences are not only admirably terse and pointed; they convince.

Even the British Constitution is viewed by his lordship with cool irreverence. He is encouraging his son (in vain, it proved) to succeed in the House of Common by the simple, perhaps too simple, device of despising it: 'I discovered that of the five hundred and sixty, not above thirty could understand reason, and that all the rest were *peuple*; that those thirty only required plain common sense, dressed up in good language; and that all the others only required flowing and harmonious periods, whether they conveyed any meaning or not; having ears to hear, but not sense enough to judge.'

As for the House of Lords, that was 'a mob' and 'a Hospital of Incurables'. One of the most amusing passages in the letters to his son is Chesterfield's description of his own speech to the Lords on his bill for Calendar Reform[2] (March 18, 1751). Chesterfield was himself 'an utter stranger' to the legal and astronomical subtleties involved. But did that matter? Not in the least. 'For my own part I could just as soon have talked Celtic or Sclavonian to them as

[1] About his own descent Chesterfield was proud of *not* being proud. Cf. H. Walpole to Mann, September 1, 1750: 'I am now grown to bear no descent but my Lord Chesterfield's, who has placed among the portraits of his ancestors two old heads, inscribed *Adam de Stanhope* and *Eve de Stanhope*; the ridicule is admirable.' (According to another version it was a painting.)

[2] This measure highly alarmed the Duke of Newcastle, who 'entreated me not to stir matters that had long been quiet; adding, that he did not love new-fangled things!'

astronomy, and they would have understood me full as well! So I resolved to do better than speak to the purpose, and to please instead of informing them. . . . This succeeded, and ever will succeed.' (Is that quite so certain?) 'They thought I informed, because I pleased them; and many of them said, that I had made the whole very clear to them, when, God knows, I had not even attempted it.'

And so the ensuing speech by Lord Macclesfield, who was an eminent mathematician, and really did know what he was talking about, gained no such sparkling success.

All this is clever and entertaining. Yet a Greek might have trembled to read it. What perilous pride! Men who go their ways with eyes half-shut in disdain are apt to trip and fall. And do really superior minds adopt a tone quite so superior?

Chesterfield, indeed, was well aware of the dangers of showing arrogance. 'Were I to make my way to favour in a court, I would neither wilfully, nor by negligence, give a dog or a cat there reason to dislike me.' 'There is nothing that people bear more impatiently, or forgive less, than contempt.' But men with a pride like his may not always deceive others about the disdain they hide; though they may deceive themselves about their power to hide it. They may even be deceived (as we shall see Chesterfield was) by the very men they despise.

Still, apart from his wit, and his penetrating observations, Chesterfield had also practical gifts. He won diplomatic successes. One of Chesterfield's speeches was in Horace Walpole's judgment the best he had ever heard. Perhaps the best Irish Viceroy of the century was, again, Lord Chesterfield. Indeed he succeeded better with the people he governed than with the young men he polished. Perhaps that is hardly surprising. Not only was he incorruptible, in an age when clean hands were far from common. More important still, he did not spend his time improving and reproving the Irish; he tried to amuse them, do them justice, and make them happier. And the Irish responded.

Similarly, after the '45, though at first he breathed fire and slaughter, and would have had the rebels transported wholesale to the West Indies, by 1747 he was more wisely and humanely advocating 'schools and villages to civilize the Highlands'.

In general, however, Chesterfield's political judgment seems to me less sound in the short run than in the long. He was apt to misjudge situations, and then, when things went amiss, to be a too quick despairer, a premature pessimist. A man of few beliefs needs, if he is not to prove ineffectual, a passionate energy of character—like, for instance, Frederick of Prussia.

Not that Chesterfield lacked courage. He kept his head, and his jests, in the insecure Dublin of the '45. And one of the things I most admire about him is his stoic, joking endurance of a deaf and lonely old age at Blackheath, as he 'hobbled' towards his grave. 'Il faut,' he observed to Suard in 1769 before his daily drive, 'que j'aille faire la répétition de mon enterrement.' And again, inviting Mallet and a Monsieur de Bussy to dinner, he desired Mallet 'to inform M. de B. that Lord Chesterfield has been dead these twelve years, and has lost all the advantages of the flesh without acquiring any of the singular privileges of a spirit'. It is a macabre humour; but it was brave.

Nor did Chesterfield lack, in certain respects, perseverance and energy. Even in his dissipated youth he had forced himself to rise early—'I have not for more than forty years ever been in bed at nine o'clock in the morning.' Indeed he was usually up by eight, even if he only went to bed at six. 'Never think any portion of time whatsoever, too short to be employed; something or other may always be done in it.' And, to the end of his long life, no trouble was too great for him to take in educating the young he cared for.

And yet, in spite of all this, there still clings to the career of this gifted figure a touch of frustration. This clever cynic was repeatedly worsted by blunter, cruder, more determined men. It was not merely that he made an early mistake in offending the future Queen Caroline, and failing, it is said, to foresee that George II would be ruled, not by his mistress, Lady Suffolk, but by his shrewd wife. It was not merely that his activity was prematurely closed by ill health. The real causes of failure seem to lie deeper.

In politics Chesterfield lacked, I think, both conviction and tenacity. He was too ready to throw up the game, to retire loftily within his tent, to isolate himself in his eminence as *grand seigneur* and *grand esprit*. Yet even when he had retired from active life and devoted himself only too obstinately to education, there also the practical results were hardly a success.

True, after his death the letters to his son went through five editions in the one year 1774, and eight editions by 1777, besides being translated into French and German. They have remained a minor classic ever since; and even in remote Japan, one is told, they had an influence in the later nineteenth century. Thanks to his pen the name of Chesterfield is still, if not famous, yet familiar; whereas without that he would be now only a name—a shadowy eighteenth-century wit like George Selwyn, and a minor eighteenth-century statesman like Pulteney or Carteret (whom many of us remember only for his quoting Sarpedon's speech from the *Iliad* on his deathbed). Stendhal records that in the campaign of 1812 he looted a volume of Chesterfield from a country house outside Moscow, belonging to the Governor, Rostopchin. That, at least, was fame.[1]

But if Lord Chesterfield is now remembered as an eighteenth-century educationalist, along with Rousseau and Pestalozzi, this success came only posthumously, with the publication of his letters; the chief failure had grown to manhood before his sharp, disillusioned old eyes.

Philip Stanhope, the natural son whom he bred up so unnaturally, whom he had tied so hard to the apron-strings of the Graces, ended, we are told, as a young bear who on one occasion started eating baked gooseberries out of the dish before a startled dinner-party at Chesterfield House.[2] Even if Philip's boobyishness has been exaggerated by malicious gossip, still the young man's maiden

[1] On the other hand the Cambridge University Library copy of Lord Carnarvon's edition of Chesterfield's letters to his godson (1890) was still uncut in 1951.

[2] It is also related that in 1751, when Philip Stanhope, aged nineteen, was newly returned from being polished round Europe, the boy leapt up from his father's table in curiosity to see the cause of some sudden noise in the courtyard; unfortunately he had attached to his buttonhole the tablecloth instead of his napkin; so that the soup and dishes followed him to the window, 'to the utter consternation,' says Lord Charlemont, 'of his distressed father.' But would Lord Chesterfield have shown 'consternation'? I should have expected him merely to take snuff.

Boswell, however, in 1764 was 'mighty well' with Stanhope at Dresden. He described him as 'little and young' (presumably young in behaviour, since he was eight years older than Boswell); 'but much of a gentleman', though, by Boswell's exalted standards, 'not quite the formal man'.

Johnson, on the other hand, once seeing Stanhope in Dodsley's shop, 'was so much struck with his aukward [*sic*] manners and appearance, that he could not help asking Mr Dodsley who he was'.

speech in the House of Commons was a halting failure, like that so vividly described by Trollope in *Phineas Finn*. And when he died, in his mid-forties, he had become merely a worthy, kindly, but dim diplomatic official at Dresden—not, as his father once dreamed, a Secretary of State.

Further, there is some suspicion that Philip Stanhope died (at Avignon) in a religion that Lord Chesterfield particularly disliked—the Church of Rome. At all events, his son's death in 1768, five years before his own, suddenly revealed to my lord the existence of an unsuspected daughter-in-law, likewise illegitimate,[1] and of two small grandsons. Of all the lessons Chesterfield had lavished, day in, day out, Philip Stanhope seems to have really learnt only one—the virtue of secretiveness. '*Volto sciolto, pensieri stretti*,' had been one of his father's most incessant adages—'an open countenance, thoughts close concealed.'[2] That precept, at least, had sunk in.

However, the old peer of seventy-two took this unlooked-for revelation with his usual calm. Perhaps, in secret, he was even consoled by the prospect of two more victims to educate.

[1] Lord Charlemont, who met her in Rome before her marriage, described Miss Peters as carefully educated 'with all the choicest accomplishments', though 'plain almost to ugliness'; her mother, on the contrary, 'was a true English goody, vulgar and unbred'. Her father was supposed to be a wealthy Mr Domville in Ireland.

Further details on this clandestine romance have been given by Willard Connely in the *Times Literary Supplement*, November 11, 1939, p. 660.

Spring, 1750. Philip Stanhope (aged 18) and Eugenia Peters (aged 20) meet in Rome.

1757–9. Philip Resident at Hamburg.

July, 1759. Philip returns in ill-health to England and lodges (near Chesterfield House, South Audley Street) in St James's Street. He kept his wife (married 1758–60?) in the house of a coal-dealer, Mr Phillips.

October 18, 1761. Charles 'Russelas' born there. Mother and child were later moved to the house of a Mr Backwell, gardener, in South Lambeth.

January 21, 1763. Philip 'Russelas' born.

March 18, 1763. Philip Stanhope appointed Resident at Ratisbon (departure thither June, 1763).

November, 1763. Return to England.

April, 1764. Appointed Envoy at Dresden.

January, 1768. Leaves Dresden (ill-health). Settles finally near Avignon.

November 16, 1768. Dies of dropsy.

After Chesterfield's death Eugenia settled at Limpsfield, Surrey; sent both her sons to Oxford; and died in 1783.

[2] It is quoted, according to Birkbeck Hill, no less than eight times in the letters to Chesterfield's son; and twice more in those to his godson—even in the epistle to be delivered him after Chesterfield's death.

Already, indeed, he had turned himself to licking into shape a second cub—a second Philip Stanhope, twenty-three years younger than the first; but, this time, a remote cousin, Chesterfield's godson and the heir to his earldom. Yet Philip the Second (1755–1815), nicknamed 'Sturdy', proved hardly more teachable than Philip the First. He grew up a worthy peer, but by no means in Lord Chesterfield's style.

For this fifth Earl loved the country as much as our Chesterfield the town; took interest, not in high life, but in field sports and fat bullocks; and crowned an undistinguished career with the appropriate eminence of Master of the Horse.

He too survives in a Gainsborough portrait, but as a somewhat lumpish gentleman, who looks fonder of foxes than of Graces. He had, says Fanny Burney, much 'humour and good humour', but 'as little breeding as any man I ever met with'—'how would that quintessence of high *ton*, the late Lord Chesterfield, blush to behold his successor!'

Perhaps, after all, 'Sturdy' was a happier man than his Mentor, however deplorable his manners. However, the sight of all that was spared to Lord Chesterfield.

But even a son and a godson did not exhaust his lordship's pedagogic zeal. He devoted similar attentions to his grandsons, to his friend Dayrolles's son, to Edward Eliot, to Lord Huntingdon, to Lord Bolingbroke. Even ladies taking the waters at Bath had to swallow, in addition, salutary advice from Lord Chesterfield.

'Some years ago, at the Bath,' writes the acid Mrs Montagu, 'I took a particular course of study that he had recommended to a Lady; if I had continued it for six months, I should have been fit for nothing but playing at pictures and mottoes with boarding-school Misses.'

Indeed life itself was not long enough for Chesterfield's educational zeal. He arranged that, even after his death, his godson should receive a final letter of admonition from beyond the grave. And not only was he resolved to go on educating even after he was dead; he would have like to educate the dead as well—Shakespeare for instance. 'If Shakespeare's genius,' he observes, 'had been cultivated, those beauties, which we so justly admire in him, would have been undisguised by those extravagancies and that nonsense with which they are frequently accompanied.' It did not occur to Chesterfield to wonder whether a better educated Shakespeare would necessarily have produced all the beauties whose unlaboured spontaneity we admire.

But from Chesterfield's pedagogic zeal not even vegetables were safe. Of his melons, grapes, and pineapples at Blackheath he writes to Dayrolles—'The growth, the education and the perfection of these vegetable children engage my care and attention next to my corporal one.' Pleasant vision of Lord Chesterfield trotting his hobby-horse even round his glass-houses. Here, indeed, he was perhaps more successful. Melons are patient.

At times Chesterfield's faith in upbringing recalls his younger contemporary Thomas Day (1748–89), disciple of Rousseau and author of *Sandford and Merton*, who took in hand two young girls, a blonde orphan and a brunette foundling, with the hope of training himself a perfect wife; tested the fortitude of the more hopeful candidate by pouring hot sealing-wax on her bare arm, and firing a pistol through her skirts; tried to marry another young lady, who sent him to France to learn the graces, and laughed at those he acquired; finally won a devoted heiress; and was killed by a young horse which was able to resent more efficiently the benevolent burden of Mr Day.

At times, too, one feels that a better match for Chesterfield than Melusina (except that two of a trade so often disagree) would have been Mme. de Genlis (1746–1830), who in her 'verve de pédagogie poussée jusqu'à la manie', as Sainte-Beuve well calls it, began at the age of seven to teach little peasants from the terrace of her château; instructed a dairy-woman's daughter of ten in playing the harp till the victim began to develop a hump, which the youthful instructress remedied with a lead plate and whalebone bodice; fascinated for a while the pedantic La Harpe; and rose by her persistence to become 'governor' of the children of Philippe Egalité—in which capacity she made the young princes garden in German, dine in English, sup in Italian, and subjected the eldest in particular, the future Louis-Philippe, to a Spartan régime including ten or twelve mile walks in shoes with leaden soles!

Indeed one begins almost to wonder if Mlle du Bouchet, Philip Stanhope's mother, may not have won Chesterfield's heart at The

Hague by the simple fascination of being—a governess.

Two questions arise. How did Chesterfield catch this pedagogomania? And why, though his educational precepts sold so well after his death, did his own attempts to educate so largely fail?

First, why did Chesterfield take such a flatly opposite view to that later Whig peer, Lord Melbourne, who opined that it is boring to be educated, boring to educate, and boring to talk about education? Ultimately, I suppose, it is one of the inexplicable differences of human temperament. Luckily for mankind, each generation seems to breed a number of disinterested enthusiasts for teaching the next. But we may also guess at certain contributory causes for Chesterfield's pedagogic ardour.

First, there was a precedent in the family. Chesterfield's grandfather, the famous Lord Halifax, had written for his daughter, Chesterfield's mother, his well-known *Advice to a Daughter*. On that daughter's own copy of the *Advice*, her father-in-law, the second Earl of Chesterfield had written, with sardonic brevity—'Labour in vain!' For the second Earl was a blunt John Bull, and quarrelled with Halifax, protesting he would rather be 'a plain, honest country-gentleman than a cunning, false court-knave'. However, his grandson, our Chesterfield, clearly shared neither the old Earl's scepticism nor his antipathies. It was, indeed, natural that he should side with his mother's family. For his father had disliked his mother, and ignored *him*; leaving him to be brought up (since his mother died young) by his grandmother, old Lady Halifax, though with sullen forebodings of the result—that the boy would 'be bred up an ignorant, worthless, amorous fop'.

Here, then, is perhaps a second reason. Chesterfield, neglected by his father, may have been provoked, in reaction, to over-educate his son.

Thirdly, he had done a good deal to educate himself. Physically unattractive, yet ambitious, he had trained himself, by sheer willpower, to compensate his own defects. An aristocrat by birth, in character he felt that he was largely self-made. He might thus be tempted to imagine that what he had done in educating himself, he could do in educating others. That idea is frequently a fallacy; none the less it is frequently believed.

Still all these remain guesses. It is more profitable, if possible, to make out why Chesterfield's educational efforts proved so ineffective. Did he teach the wrong things? Or teach the wrong way? Or both?

First, what did he teach? Above all, his own philosophy of life—the creed of Mr Worldly Wiseman (who dwelt, it may be remembered, in the town of Carnal Policy, and recommended to Christian the services of Legality, 'a very judicious man,' with 'a pretty young man to his son, whose name is Civility'). Now Mr Wiseman had acquired, between Bunyan's day and Chesterfield's, a good deal more polish, and more acquaintance with the Graces; but he remained, in essentials, much the same.

The true end of existence, Chesterfield seems often to imply, is to make 'a figure in the world'. A pretty worthless world, no doubt, in my lord's serene opinion; yet, somehow, it was absolutely vital to make a figure in it. He seems curiously little concerned to ask what the figures one makes are, in the end, to add up to. If he ever saw that the only real point, or justification, of gaining power and position is to use them well and usefully, he said strangely little about it.

He by no means shared the view of his enemy Johnson that the ultimate object of all ambition is to be happy at home. Life, for Chesterfield, seems rather like an elegant game of cards, in which the trumps are certainly not hearts. Spades or clubs he would have thought 'low'. He would doubtless have preferred the hard, sharp, polished, and brilliant diamonds.

Religion? Chesterfield says not a great deal about that. 'Sensible men,' as Disraeli put it, 'never tell.' He was, I take it, a convinced Whig in religion, as in politics. Chesterfield's God is a kind of Hanoverian monarch, on a loftier throne—an august and necessary part of the constitution of the Universe; but not permitted to interfere too much in its practical affairs. As for the Church, that, to be sure, is an excellent profession for 'a good, dull, and decent boy'.

Morals? Here we shall be unjust to the Letters, if we forget that Chesterfield considered ethics the province of his son's tutor and bear-leader. What he does say on the subject is, as a rule, quite respectable. 'To do as you would be done by, is the plain, sure, and undisputed rule of morality and justice.' A young man, he thinks, must from the start 'establish, and really deserve, a character of truth, probity, good manners and good morals'. 'Conscious virtue is the only solid foundation of all happiness.'

To be more precise, one should not tell lies (except in diplomacy, where they become a duty). One should not drink too much. (Chesterfield was surprisingly temperate, in that age of topers, and wished 'it would but please God, by his lightning, to blast all the vines in the world, and by his thunder to turn all the wines now in Ireland sour'.) One should not play too much. (Chesterfield had burned his own fingers, 'for thirty of the best years of my life', at the gaming-table.) One should not hunt or shoot—gentlemen do not kill their own meat—leave that to English bumpkins, 'the most unlicked creatures in the world, unless sometimes by their hounds'. One should not go in for racing. Under Chesterfield's will, if 'Sturdy' should even 'reside one night at Newmarket, that infamous seminary of iniquity and ill-manners' (note the climax—another might have said 'ill-manners and iniquity'), 'during the course of the races there', he was to forfeit £5,000 to the Dean and Chapter of Westminster. (His lordship chose this Dean and Chapter because he thought they had dealt avariciously with him over the site of Chesterfield House; and so would be sure to claim any penalty incurred—a subtle snub from beyond the grave.) And lastly one should not become an indiscriminate rake—confine yourself to affairs with cultivated women, who can polish you, and push you.

On bribery and corruption, Chesterfield is surprisingly in advance of Robert Walpole's age. 'I call corruption,' says his posthumous letter to his godson, 'the taking of a sixpence more than the just and known salary of your employment, under any pretence whatever.' This does not, however, preclude bribing others. Chesterfield feels annoyed that he can no longer buy his son a parliamentary borough for £2,500, since nabobs and plutocrats from East or West Indies have unfortunately raised the general price of such seats to £3,000, or even £5,000. Again, a letter from him to Marchmont, of June 15, 1734, contains a curious proposal for bribing certain Scottish peers to say they had previously been bribed by Lord Islay. (It looks as if the Scottish peers might have made a good thing out of it.)

Finally, energy and industry are essential. 'Six, or at the most seven hours' sleep is, for a constancy, as much as you or anybody can want.' (This is not at all my experience. It varies with individual physique. It varies with climate. It varies with the amount of hard work, especially mental work, that men do.) 'More is only laziness and dozing; and is, I am persuaded, both unwholesome and stupefying. . . . I have very often gone to bed at six in the morning, and rose, notwithstanding, at eight; by which means I got many hours in the morning, that my companions lost; and the want of sleep obliged me to keep good hours the next, or at least the third night. . . . Know the true value of time; snatch, seize, and enjoy every moment of it. No idleness, no laziness, no procrastination.'

In all these moral preachments there seems much that is true, though not much that is new—except the singular insistence on love-affairs as a means to polish and promotion. Of the time-dishonoured Seven Deadly Sins, Chesterfield concurred with the orthodox in denouncing Sloth, Gluttony, and Avarice; Anger and Envy he would have considered foolish, except as a useful spur to action; Pride, I imagine, he thought in many of its forms a virtue (and I think it *is*), though it might be a folly to show it; and Concupiscence, in his view, could be made highly serviceable.

But I repeat that Chesterfield regarded his son's morals as the concern of his son's tutor—the Rev. Mr Harte—a confidence in Mr Harte[1] which seems a little queer, and proved in fact a good deal

[1] Walter Harte (1709–74) became in 1740 Vice-principal of St Mary Hall, Oxford, and gained reputation as a tutor. In 1745 he was chosen by Chesterfield as bear-leader for his son; and in 1750 (perhaps by Chesterfield's influence) became Canon of Windsor. His works include a verse *Essay on Satire* (1730); an *Essay on Reason* (1735; imitating the *Essay on Man* of his friend Pope); a history of Gustavus Adolphus (1759); *Essays on Husbandry* (1764; praised by Johnson); and *The Amaranth, or Religious Poems* (1767).

He figures in a vivid tale of Johnson's obscurity. 'You made a man,' said Edward Cave to him, 'very happy t'other day.' Harte, praising the *Life of Savage*, had been overheard by Johnson, who was eating in the room behind a screen, because too shabby to appear.

It may, then, have been partly gratitude that made Johnson later commend him 'as a scholar, and a man of the most companionable talents he had ever known'. For others described Mr Harte as handicapped by college rust, a stammer, and a total lack of ear. He also seemed overfond of Greek and Latin, German law and Gothic erudition. 'Il ne sera guère propre à donner des manières,' wrote Chesterfield, who later shared the general view that the style of Harte's *Gustavus* was 'execrable'—sometimes pompous, sometimes vulgar. (It does not seem to me quite so bad as all that.) Similarly another pupil of Harte's, the future Lord Eliot, called it 'a good book

misplaced. And why, after all, should a father think his son's morals a matter to be safely left to someone else? 'You know what virtue is,' he tells his son; 'you may have it if you will; it is in every man's power; and miserable in the man who has it not.' Virtue 'in every man's power'? This seems to me very odd psychology. Few, even of the saints, can have thought goodness so easy.

It was, however, the subject of airs and graces, manners and accomplishments, that attracted Chesterfield's real concern. And here we pass from the trite to the astounding. Chesterfield's pursuit of the Graces was not art for art's sake, but art with a relentless purpose. Manners, for him, were the grand staircase to wordly success. In this vital matter Lord Chesterfield felt that the real expert, guide, and philosopher must be himself.

Indeed, what Faith, Hope, and Charity were to St Paul, the Three Graces were to Lord Chesterfield. At times he talks as if the Three Graces were the Three Fates. 'Senza di noi ogni fatica è vana,' he imagines them proclaiming. 'Without us all labour is in vain.'

But how preposterous!

The standing and shining example, for Chesterfield, of this great truth was the Duke of Marlborough; who, he says, 'could refuse more gracefully than other people could grant.'

Now this art of refusing gracefully is certainly a great gift, still too often neglected. No doubt, too, Marlborough's charm played a considerable part in the brilliance of his career—both in his disreputable youth, when he won Barbara Palmer, Duchess of Cleveland, and a gift from her of £5,000, which, invested by the prudent youth in an annuity, formed the foundation of his subsequent

—in the German translation'. Even Harte's bookseller tried to make him change phrases in it, only to be answered—'George, that's what we call *writing*!' Johnson could only say that the book's faults came 'not from imbecility, but from foppery'. On the eve of publication, it is said, poor Harte withdrew into the country to escape the deluge of praise he anticipated; and when none came, was ashamed to return.

A somewhat strange choice for the elegant Chesterfield. But Chesterfield was still less lucky in entrusting his godson 'Sturdy' to 'a man of unexceptional character and very great learning'—Dr Dodd. For Dodd was hanged. (In 1777 he was convicted of forging a bond for £4,200 in the name of his old pupil. Seemingly he hoped that 'Sturdy', now fifth Earl, would pity him; but 'Sturdy' appeared against him; and, despite Johnson's help, Dodd went to the gallows.) Can it be that Chesterfield, with all his critical subtleties, was not in practice a very good judge of character?

fortune; and later, when in supreme command against France, he had to manage the difficult Dutch, and our other irritable allies.

But when Chesterfield goes to the length of ascribing the better half of Marlborough's greatness simply and solely to these graces, one grows restive. Was it, one asks, the mere suavity of Marlborough's tone and the elegance of his bow, coupled only with 'an excellent good plain understanding', that won Blenheim, Ramillies, Oudenarde, Lille, Mons, Douai, Béthune, and Bouchain? 'An excellent good plain understanding!' Tolstoy was hardly more perverse and wrong-headed about the military unimportance of the genius of Napoleon.

Could all the Graces of Versailles save Marlborough's opponent, Louis XIV, from ending his days as the broken master of a broken France; could the Graces hold back the brilliant court of his successor from sliding, as Chesterfield himself foresaw, slowly but surely towards the red pit of the Revolution? Was it by their graces that our own iron-sided Oliver, or the jack-booted Charles XII of Sweden, or the uncouth Tsar Peter, or the brusque, shabby, Frederick of Prussia, each in his turn awed Europe?

It may be that the young Chesterfield of twenty had been ineffaceably impressed, when, in 1714, he was entertained at Antwerp by the old Marlborough of sixty-four. But nothing seems to me to justify Chesterfield's fantasy that the Graces hold so completely the key to any successful career; or his equally fantastic proposition that 'nobody was ever loved that was not well-bred'. Such are Chesterfield's words to his godson 'Sturdy'; followed by the ugly and most ungraceful threat—'and to tell you the truth, neither your Papa nor I shall love you, if you are not well-bred'.

'Nobody was ever loved that was not well-bred'! What an enormous and disgusting hyperbole! Surely there rises in answer that proud and angry cry of Homer's Achilles against the eternal arrogance of the great:

> 'Is it only the Atridae, of all men born on earth,
> That love their wives!'

But Chesterfield thought the language of Homer's heroes 'porter-like'. Or there is that well-remembered line of Wordsworth:

Love had he found in huts where poor men lie.

But Chesterfield would have thought Wordsworth's characters lower even than porters. As for their hearts, 'whatever Poets may write, or fools believe, of rural innocence and truth', Chesterfield held cottagers to be just as false and perfidious as courtiers—'only with worse manners'.

Here lies perhaps the fundamental error, as well as the ruling passion, of Chesterfield's whole life. He cared far too much for mere appearances and externals (important though these often are). 'To be very well dressed is of much more importance to you, than all the Greek you know will be of, these thirty years.' 'Awkwardness and ill-breeding shock me, to that degree, that where I meet with them, I cannot find in my heart to inquire into the intrinsic merit of that person; I hastily decide in myself, that he can have none; and am not sure, I should not even be sorry to know that he had any.' Chesterfield was far from that Aristides whom Æschylus is said to have had in mind when he wrote, in his *Seven against Thebes*:

His will is not to *seem* the best, but *be* it.

This eighteenth-century sage, who talked so much of reason, was oddly blinded by his odd passion. He seems incapable of learning even from experience, though the polished Bolinbroke and his polished self had both been foiled in the fight for power by the bluff, blunt Walpole, and by the grotesque but indefatigable Newcastle. So, too, the future of the eighteenth century was to be moulded, in politics, by men as graceless as the cold William Pitt, or Edmund Burke, with his awkward gestures and his Irish brogue, or the homely Benjamin Franklin; in thought, by men whom Chesterfield might have lumped together as '*peuple*' or 'Hottentots' —the naïve David Hume, the boorish Johnson, the ugly Goldsmith, the scandalous Sterne, the ungainly Gibbon, the lonely and daemonic Blake.

Even the gruff old Chancellor Thurlow gave sounder advice to 'the First Gentleman of Europe', with all his airs and graces—'Sir, your father will continue to be a popular king as long as he continues to go to church every Sunday, and to be faithful to that ugly woman, your mother; but you, Sir, will never be popular.'

Indeed, even in the polished society of Paris Chesterfield himself never approached the success of Hume or Franklin, whom he would probably have considered clowns; even in so social an activity as letter-writing he seems a far less vivid correspondent than some of his contemporaries. To be written to by Johnson would be impressive; by Boswell, comical; by Walpole, Hume, Goldsmith, or Franklin, in different ways delightful; but correspondence with Chesterfield, I think, might soon become a laborious bore. His letters to his son are interesting because astounding; but his letters to others have, for me, too much the air of dropping from some machine as smooth, polished, but chilly, as a refrigerator.

Chaucer spoke truth:

> Swiche salutaciouns and contenaunces
> Passen as dooth a shadwe upon the wal.

However, having chosen this strange idea of the Kingdom of God—'a man who does not generally please is nobody'—Chesterfield was at least unflinchingly faithful to it, in his own queer fashion. One may discount something in the reminiscences of elderly gentlemen improving young ones; but I suppose what Chesterfield says of his own youth *is* substantially true—'My passion for pleasing was so strong (and I am very glad it was so), that I own to you fairly, I wished to make every woman I saw in love with me, and every man I met with admire me.' And again, of his youthful vanity—'it made me attentive and civil to the women I disliked, and to the men I despised, in hopes of the applause of both; though I neither desired, nor would I have accepted, the favours of the one nor the friendship of the other'. In short, he was possessed by 'an insatiable thirst, a rage of popularity, applause, and admiration'. Strange to be so clear-sighted, yet so uncritical. He mistook being civil for being civilized. But, to his life's end, he at least remained true to this curious creed of resting one's happiness on being thought much of by people of whom one thinks nothing at all.

And to this most peculiar end what, then, are the means?

First, sound knowledge (Chesterfield is at least clear that one cannot keep up appearances by appearances alone). One must have a knowledge of languages; of the best literature, ancient and modern; of history and politics; and of the human heart. 'Approfondissez!' At times poor little Philip's curriculum seems to leave him hardly a free moment in the day. From Leipzig, 'his tutor writes me word that he has barely time to eat, drink, and sleep'. One is reminded of the Quaker's simple, but devastating comment on the breathless daily routine of Southey: 'But, friend Southey, when dost thee think?'

However, graver educators, like Milton, have also fallen into this same error of trying to rear prodigies in forcing-houses, by a degree of overwork more calculated to breed monsters. And yet one gasps at Chesterfield's strange notion of the human mind—'Every quarter of an hour well or ill employed, will do it essential and lasting good or harm.' Believe it, who can!

Still, it is not pedantry that Chesterfield wants, but sensible knowledge and sound taste. His aim is a combination of 'the profoundest learning and the politest manners' (as, he felt, they had been combined in Bolingbroke). He is extremely sensible about hypercriticism—'You French critics seek for a fault as eagerly as I do for a beauty; you consider things in the worst light, to show your skill, at the expense of your pleasure; I view them in the best, that I may have more pleasure, at the expense of my judgment.' There are modern critics who might well take that to heart.

Unfortunately, when we come to Chesterfield's own literary opinions, their oddity once more illustrates the amazing subjectivity of human taste. Plato and Cicero, thinks his lordship, have no merit but their style—'the philosophy of them is wretched and the reasoning part miserable' (not, some may think, always untrue). Homer contains beauties; but 'when he slumbers, I sleep'. The language of his heroes is, as we have heard, 'porter-like'; Achilles was 'both a brute and a scoundrel'; and his divine armour is absurd —for he needed only a horseshoe clapped to his vulnerable heel. (This was a rash judgment: for the vulnerable heel of Achilles is post-Homeric.) Virgil is, indeed, better than Homer, being 'all sense'; but the later books of the *Æneid* are 'often languid'—'I am obliged to take a good deal of snuff.' Dante is curtly dismissed—'I had done with him, convinced that he was not worth the pains necessary to understand him.' Milton, too, remains for Chesterfield unreadable—'the characters and speeches of a dozen or two of angels, and of as many devils, are as much above my reach as my entertainment. Keep this secret for me.' (Some more modern judges have shared this view; but surely, for most readers, the devils' speeches are at all events among Milton's best things, not his worst.)

What Chesterfield really admires is—Voltaire's *Henriade*! For *that* is 'all sense from beginning to end'. And in harmony Voltaire surpasses all French poets, except perhaps Racine. As for the drama, no theatre is 'comparable to the French'.

Towards history, Chesterfield shows a scepticism that seems to me not unsound; especially towards those 'refining and sagacious historians' who see in every act of their characters deep calculation and subtle policy, underestimating the importance of the trivial, the capricious, and the irrational. 'A man who has been concerned in a transaction, will not write it fairly; and a man who has not, cannot.'

Towards book-collecting also he is contemptuous. One should not get too interested in first editions—'beware of the Bibliomanie'. (This, too, may not be wholly foolish.)

Yet it is perhaps worth noting that Chesterfield, while so zealous to instruct the young on literary matters, betrays at times an ignorance that would have shocked schoolboys far less erudite than Macaulay's. 'Αγχίνοια does not mean 'industry', but 'quick wit'; ευφονια is a strange solecism for 'εὐφωνία'; 'nihil conscire sibi nullaque pallescere culpa'[1] is not merely a misquotation, but, in two places, a metrically impossible misquotation; though 'les honnêtes gens ne se boudent jamais'[2] is an excellent maxim, the 'se' seems a mistaken addition; nor finally, does it quite become a purist about correct English to write 'let you and *I*'.

Again, though it may be agreed that 'The letter *which* I received from you, *which* you referred to in your last, *that* came by Lord Albemarle's messenger, and *which* I showed to such one' is abominable, it does not seem much improved by his lordship's improve-

[1] For 'nil conscire sibi, nulla pallescere culpa'. (Horace, *Epistles*, i, 1, 61.)
[2] 'Gentlemen never sulk.'

ments—'The letter *that* I received from you, *which* you referred to in your last, *that* came by Lord Albemarle's messenger, and *which* I showed to such-a-one.'

On Art, also, Chesterfield takes a somewhat curious line. About music the main thing is on no account to play it oneself. 'I declare that I would rather be reckoned the best barber than the best fiddler in England. . . . A glaring example how pernicious an intimacy is with those jackanapeses may be seen in the Duke of Devonshire, who passes most of his evenings with only Signior di Geordino and Signior Bach.' So he wrote to his godson in February 1773. And he had been no less emphatic to his son—'Few things would mortify me more, than to see you bearing a part in a concert, with a fiddle under your chin, or a pipe in your mouth.' True, Frederick of Prussia played the flute; but that '*stupor mundi*' was capable of anything.

Similarly with the visual arts—at Rome, for example, for every minute spent on Capitol, Vatican, or Pantheon, let Philip spend ten days on Papal politics and 'the tricks of the Conclaves'. And when Chesterfield considers taking his godson to see the Tower and Westminster Abbey, it is because 'I would willingly teach him early the *Nil Admirari*'.[1]

Could the ancient Graces have returned to life, they might have been a little astonished at this eighteenth-century noble's ways of wooing them.[2]

Next, there are bodily accomplishments and graceful deportment. 'The dancing-master is at this time the man in all Europe of the greatest importance to you. Learn to loll genteelly.' Every motion should be made at the right tempo—in minuet time. Clean your teeth properly; cut your nails properly; use your handkerchief properly; and never laugh. (A gentleman never laughs; the noise is 'disagreeable', and the distortion 'shocking'. Chesterfield himself has never laughed since he had full use of his reason.[3])

[1] 'To be astonished or staggered by nothing'; not 'to admire nothing'.

[2] It is also, I think, very odd, even allowing for changes in taste, that this Apostle of the Graces could write anything as ungracefully gross as the verses *On a Lady's Drinking the Bath Waters.*

[3] Chesterfield is not alone in this strange and dismal peculiarity. La Rochefoucauld avers that, being melancholic, he has hardly laughed three or four times in as many years; Swift, Pope, and Fontenelle were said never to laugh. Chatham, writing

Never use a word without thinking if you could not find a better. (Chesterfield has done so for forty years, and deserves Horace Walpole's comment: 'How agreeably he passed his time!')

In fact, this part of Chesterfield's teaching is not unfairly summed up in George Colman's mocking prologue to Garrick's *Bon Ton*:

> Keep your teeth clean—and grin if small talk fails—
> But never *laugh*, whatever jest prevails.
> Nothing but nonsense e'er gave laughter birth,
> The vulgar way the vulgar show their mirth....
> Hearts may be black, but all should wear clean faces;
> The Graces, boy! The Graces, Graces, Graces!

Finally, after all this coaching, a man should be ready to use and improve his knowledge of human nature. This is the most important part of Chesterfield's teaching; but perhaps its least engaging part.

Men are to be despised and flattered; women are to be despised, flattered, and, if young enough, flirted with. Princes, in general, are 'about the pitch of women'. Of the House of Lords we have already heard as that 'Hospital of Incurables'; and of the House of Commons, as a place where thirty out of five hundred and sixty members may be supposed to comprehend reason.

To conclude, 'every man is to be had one way or another, and every woman almost any way'—'every woman is infallibly to be gained by every sort of flattery, and every man by one sort or another'.

A gloomy view of human nature; and not, I should have thought, very intelligent.

For Chesterfield is not speaking only of his own society, of

to his nephew Thomas Pitt, says that laughter is rarely graceful—'it is generally better to smile'. And this principle, though to me ridiculous, is ancient—cf. *Ecclesiasticus*, xxi, 20; 'A fool lifteth up his voice with laughter, but a wise man doth scarce smile a little.' There is a tediously priggish passage on the subject in Plato, *Republic* iii, 388E. And Addison records (*Spectator*, 249) reading a Romish sermon which averred that 'laughter was the effect of original sin, and that Adam could not laugh before the fall'.

Such prim objections to laughter seem to have been sometimes because it was unæsthetic, sometimes because it was too uncontrolled, sometimes because it was frivolous, sometimes because it was vulgar. For Chesterfield it was especially the first and the last of these.

England, or of Europe. 'Human nature,' he says, with that generalizing mania which so often blinded the eighteenth century, 'is the same all over the world'—though its externals may be varied by 'education and habit'. Let us not imagine, either, that the Ancients were any better than the Moderns—'I cannot suppose,' he argues, 'that the animals or vegetables were better then than now.' So why human beings?

In fact, for Chesterfield, the human race has always consisted mainly of geese and peacocks. The logical conclusions follow. Seem open; but dissimulate. 'Fish for facts; but fish judiciously.' Find out everybody's special excellence, 'if they have one', and their special weakness, 'which everybody has'; 'do justice to the one and something more than justice to the other'. Show contempt to nobody; be polite even to servants—'a chamber-maid has sometimes caused revolutions'; smile at your enemies, when you cannot strike. 'Were I in Africa, I would pay flattery to a negro for his good-will.'

And so Philip Stanhope is given special hints how, at Turin, to flatter the House of Savoy. He is to admire the galaxies of great men produced by that princely line; to marvel that Nature, instead of being exhausted by such efforts, has redoubled them to create the present King, and the Duke of Savoy; to 'wonder, at this rate, where it will end; and conclude that it must end in the government of all Europe'. The House of Savoy, one feels, must have had strong stomachs if they could swallow butter laid on in such nauseous excess.

At Berlin, again, Philip is to make flattering comments on the King, in the presence of persons likely to repeat them. At Versailles and St Cloud, it is essential 'to insinuate and wriggle yourself into favour'. Similarly young Lord Huntingdon is counselled to make up to Lord Rockingham—'cultivate at present in order to govern hereafter'.

At this point two questions perplex me. First, how does one reconcile all this 'wriggling and insinuating' with that absolute veracity, that doing as you would be done by, which Chesterfield elsewhere enjoins? Admirers, indeed, have persistently defended his lordship with the plea that he preached only prudent dissimulation, not actual simulation. 'It is *simulation*,' he wrote (May 22, 1749), 'that is false, mean, and criminal.' 'Lies and perfidy,' he says elsewhere, 'are the refuge of fools and cowards.' Very good. Yet how can one flatter without lying, without simulating feelings which one does not really feel, and thoughts which one does not really think? The fulsome eulogies which Chesterfield wished his son to lavish on the Court of Turin, he neither believed himself nor expected his son to believe. Was that not 'simulation'? One can, of course, quote from him fine general principles, especially in the letters to his godson—'Humanity inclines, religion requires, and our moral duty obliges us to relieve, as far as we are able, the distresses and miseries of our fellow-creatures; but this is not all, for a true heartfelt benevolence and tenderness will prompt us to contribute what we can to their ease, their amusement, and their pleasure, as far as we innocently may. Let us then not only scatter benefits, but even strew flowers for our fellow-travellers, in the rugged ways of this wretched world.' One has no right to call this 'insincere'. Such things are unknowable. And men's moods are multiple. But one *can* fairly ask whether Chesterfield would have counted it among 'benefits' to study a man's weaknesses the better to twist him round one's finger—whether he would have felt grateful if some youth had, as he counselled Huntingdon to do with Rockingham, 'cultivated him at present in order to govern hereafter'.

Secondly, if the world is thus composed of fools and knaves, why labour like a galley-slave to 'make a figure' among such ciphers, and to win the applause of such noodles? Why not prefer, like Candide, to cultivate one's own garden? I do not know the answer. Nor, I suspect, did Chesterfield. Indeed he was destined, at fifty-four, himself to retire from the world; and a few years later, in 1752, to dismiss worldly ambitions with the disillusioned sentence: 'I know their futility, and I know now that one can only find happiness in oneself.' But the wisdom of China had known that two thousand years before—'The point is not that you have succeeded in attracting the attention of mankind; it is that you have failed in distracting it. What good can *they* possibly do you? None can both be admired and be at peace.' The last sentence is perhaps exaggerated; but at least it seems far wiser than knowing no peace *unless* one is admired.

However, if in Chesterfield's eyes men are poor fish, women are even worse. They are, he observes elsewhere, 'only children of a larger growth. . . . For solid, reasoning good sense I never in my life knew one that had it'. (One wonders whether the sixteen-year old Philip realized, and resented, the implied inclusion of his mother in this universal condemnation. And what a contrast to Horace Walpole's comments on the good sense of Mme Geoffrin or Mme du Deffand!)

As for marriage—'I have at last done the best office that can be done, to most married people; that is, I have fixed the separation between my brother and his wife.'[1] And again—'to take a wife merely as an agreeable and rational companion will commonly be found to be a grand mistake.' (Poor Melusina!)[2] 'Shakespeare seems to be a good deal of my opinion, when he allows them only this department,

To suckle fools and chronicle small beer.'

Chesterfield forgot for the moment, apparently, that those words were put by Shakespeare in the mouth of the amiable Iago.

On the other hand, I must add that I find better sense, as well as wit, in his advice to Lord Huntingdon against marrying too young —'Read men and women, but read the latter unbound for several years at least.'

But though women are dust beneath Lord Chesterfield's gaze, they are none the less indispensable. Dust polishes diamonds—or, to use that favourite word of his, there is nothing so effective to *décrotter* a young man, to scrape off the mud of his rusticity. (A *décrottoir* is a 'door-scraper'.) The dancing-master must be followed by the mistress.

To this form of education (which was exemplified for him in Dryden's *Cymon and Iphigenia*) Chesterfield was passionately attached. Indeed he finds fault with Van Dyke's 'Venus and Adonis' because in that picture Adonis looks angry. No doubt the young man should have been delighted at this chance to be *décrotté*.

[1] Cf. p. 170, footnote.

[2] Cf. his letter to Arthur Charles Stanhope, dissuading remarriage (October 12, 1765): 'I may possibly be in the wrong, but I tell you very sincerely, with all due regard to the sex, that I never thought a woman good company for a man *tête-à-tête*, unless for one purpose, which, I presume, is not yours now.'

Philip begins receiving this sort of advice, to polish himself by gallantries, at what many will feel the somewhat premature age of fifteen. At nineteen he is told, 'I had much rather you were passionately in love with some determined coquette of condition . . . than that you knew all Plato and Aristotle by heart.' And again—'A propos on m'assure que Mme de Blot,[1] sans avoir des traits, est jolie comme un cœur, et que nonobstant cela, elle s'en est tenue jusqu'ici scrupuleusement à son mari, quoiqu'il y ait déjà plus d'un an qu'elle est mariée. Elle n'y pense pas; il faut décrotter cette femme-là. Décrottez-vous donc tous les deux réciproquement.' Mme de Blot was fifteen at marriage, and sixteen now! Philip Stanhope himself was near his nineteenth birthday. In addition to pushing him into the arms of Mme de Blot, his father also urges the still greater educational benefits of a liaison with the middle-aged Mme Dupin. Why not make both affairs run concurrently?

After so much good advice of this type, reiterated year after year, was it not provoking of young Stanhope to prefer honest wedlock with Miss Eugenia Peters—and then never tell his careful father one word about it!

But though Chesterfield did not yet know of this lapse into respectability, he began in the end gradually to see that his labours were in vain. Even when Philip was only fifteen, his father already had misgivings—'As often as I write to you . . . so often I am in doubt whether it is to any purpose, and whether it is not labour and paper lost.' Seventeen years later Chesterfield's doubts were at an end. 'Enfin,' he writes to Mme de Monconseil in 1764, when Philip was now thirty-two, 'malgré tous les soins que j'ai pris pour le décrotter, il est encore trop Anglois.' Even in 1756 Chesterfield had realized that the Hamburg Residency was probably a dead end—'an obscure inefficient thing, fit for those who propose to stagnate quietly for the rest of their lives. Perhaps that may be the case of the boy, if I do not live, as I probably shall not, to shove him somewhere else.'

Indeed it is perhaps to Chesterfield's credit that, however intense his disappointment, he continued to write to Philip as 'My dear friend', to end his letters 'God bless you', to be concerned about Philip's health and Philip's career. And yet the letters seem chillingly

[1] Niece of Chesterfield's friend, Mme de Monconseil.

impersonal—Chesterfield is never intimate, he never gives himself away; and so he won little confidence in return—not even the information that he had acquired a daughter-in-law and two grandsons.

All the same Chesterfield had not wasted his paper. His son may perhaps have turned out, ironically enough, what Chesterfield had once called George Lyttelton—'a respectable Hottentot'. Yet that son's unwanted wife was to immortalize Lord Chesterfield by publishing his letters, despite his family, with considerable profit to herself.

As we have seen, the book had a remarkable sale; though there was already, as there has been since, violent criticism.[1] The letters were attacked in the *Gentleman's Magazine*; in William Crawford's *Remarks*; in a novel by one Samuel Pratt, called *The Pupil of Pleasure*, which is very small pleasure to read. One of Johnson's comments is familiar—'the morals of a whore and the manners of a dancing-master!'[2] It is less often recalled that Johnson also said, in milder mood, 'Take out the immorality and it should be put into the hands of every young gentleman'.

This seems to me a fairer summary than Horace Walpole's—'a system of education to poison youth from their nursery,' or his ironically suggested title—'The whole duty of man, adapted to the *meanest* capacities.'

Since then, the Letters have somehow kept their place, though the young Macaulay dismissed them as 'trash', and the young Carlyle denounced their 'flattery, dissimulation, and paltry cunning'. Dickens's caricature of Lord Chesterfield as Sir John Chesters in *Barnaby Rudge* remains a miserable travesty. And in recent years Chesterfield has been strongly defended by Charles Whibley, Charles Strachey, R. Coxon, Lord Carnarvon, and Professor Bonamy Dobrée (to whom we owe an admirable edition of Chesterfield's correspondence). Their apologetics, however, seem to me often excessive. Perhaps the best defence of Chesterfield, as of

[1] To ascribe this outcry merely to John Bull prejudice against a man in mind and sympathies essentially French, seems to me both over-simple, and unjust to the finer qualities of eighteenth-century France.

[2] This was too crude for the delicacy of Victorian America. 'The most epigrammatic description which Johnson gave of the Letters, for obvious reasons, we have not quoted.' (S. A. Allibone, *Dictionary of English Literature*, Philadelphia, 1859.)

Machiavelli, is that both of them have been screamed at, not so much because they were uncommonly unscrupulous, as because they were uncommonly frank. Often they have been denounced by men who thought the same without daring to say so, or did the same without daring even to think so. At all events Chesterfield's letters to his son are still alive.

But why, then, if Chesterfield to this extent succeeded with the public, did he so fail with son and godson? And what of value to us remains in his ideas?

The first reason for his failure lay, I think, in that fantastic optimism with which many educators tend to get intoxicated—that curious faith that education can turn sows' ears into silk purses, and young carthorses into Derby winners.

'I am very sure,' Chesterfield writes to his son, 'that any man of common understanding may, by proper culture, care, attention, and labour, make himself whatever he pleases, except a good poet.' By such perseverance, he repeats, 'I became a model of eloquence myself which, by care, it is in every man's power to be.' And again —'a drayman is probably born with as good organs as Milton, Locke, or Newton; but, by culture, they are much more above him than he is above his horse.'[1]

In what world, one wonders, do people live who can imagine such nonsense? I used to guess that, in making men what they become, the influence of nature and of nurture might perhaps be roughly equal; watching my children grow up—so utterly different, though under almost identical conditions—I have come to think inborn nature definitely more important than upbringing—certainly for intelligence, probably even for character. Chesterfield's belief in the omnipotence of nurture seem to me moonshine. Because of it, he wasted years in trying to enamel deal tables, to saddle and bridle young bullocks. That he could entertain such illusions is, I suppose, partly due to the generalizing tendencies of his time, whose

[1] Porson is said to have likewise maintained that anyone, by taking as much trouble, could become as good a critic as *he* was. Johnson at Dunvegan was inclined to attribute differences of ability in children wholly to differences in their education. More wisely, Hume noted how princes, though reared alike, could yet show totally different qualities; for example, Charles II and James II. (See Hill–Powell, Boswell's *Johnson*, ii, 437.) Possibly Chesterfield was influenced by the educational successes of the Jesuits, whom he found both impressive and yet repellent. (He called his dog 'Loyola', and made ungracefully disgusting jokes on the subject.)

science was too much influenced by great mathematicians. Nature's laws, it was found, were miraculously uniform; it was perhaps not unnatural, though quite irrational, to assume that Nature's products were uniform also. 'One blade of grass is like another blade of grass.' In one sense, yes; but in a preciser sense, never.

Still, though our age has long come to recognize Nature's infinite variety, I must confess that Chesterfield's view is, even now, not extinct. I have known a Cambridge educator of original mind who believed that he could mould any normal child, if caught young enough, into a scholar of Trinity. It is, no doubt, true that efficient teaching can do wonders in examinations (just as rats can be trained to negotiate labyrinths). But that is partly because the examinations are themselves, inevitably, somewhat inefficient. For one thing, they set an excessive premium on mere memory. But examinations are not life.

Surely dozens of examples from history might have warned Lord Chesterfield? Even legend, which is a part of human history, might have reminded him that from Minos, the all-righteous judge, sprang the disastrous Phædra. The Bible might have reminded him that the wise Solomon, with all his thousand wives, could breed no better heir than the foolish Rehoboam. The Stoic sage, Marcus Aurelius, had for son the monstrous Commodus. Oliver the Lord Protector produced Richard Cromwell, who could protect nothing —yet, for all that, may have been a happier man than ever his father was. Jean Racine, the poet, begat Louis Racine the poetaster, of whom Voltaire observed that not even *his* degree of nonentity could prevent his father having been a great man. As Dr Bentley consoled himself, when disappointed in *his* offspring—'Tully had his Marcus.' (The Roman orator's son was a drunkard.) Very distinguished parents have not often succeeded in rearing distinguished sons. We do not think it natural, but extraordinary, when a Chatham is followed by a William Pitt.

Secondly, I think, Chesterfield grossly mistook the effectiveness, in education, of mere preaching and admonition. Children are often less likely to do what their parents preach at them, than to do just the opposite, in natural reaction. Indeed they are liable to react, even if not preached at, from any home atmosphere that they find oppressive. The daughter of a well-to-do family may run off with the baker—not so much, sometimes, for the charms of the baker as (unconsciously, it may be) for the annoyance of her parents. I have known the son of an æsthetic and Bohemian intellectual to take refuge in working as a platelayer on a railway. And it is well-known that the sons of austere clergymen have often been particularly gay.

The essential factor, I believe, is as a rule emotional. Only if children are genuinely fond of their parents, is there much chance of their imitating them rather than reacting against them. Imitation, indeed, is far more potent than admonition; it is what parents do that matters, far more than what they say.

Chesterfield also erred fatally, in my belief, by sacrificing heart to head. This is all the more ironic because he wrote to Chenevix against sending his son to a large school precisely because 'at those great schools the heart is wholly neglected by those who ought to form it'. Yet Chesterfield strangely ignored that, to form a heart successfully, one must first win it.

In his curious way, no doubt, he loved both his son and his godson; but he did not make himself very lovable. He piqued himself too much on not being soft. He condemned Lord and Lady Blessington for spoiling their son; whereas 'I indulged no silly womanish folly for you: instead of inflicting my tenderness upon you, I have taken all possible methods to make you deserve it'. Curious word—'inflicting'! But perhaps little Philip might have deserved that tenderness a little more, if it had not been dangled above him as a sort of school-prize. This spiritual carrot failed to attract. A diplomat so distinguished might have been expected to be more diplomatic.

And there is worse. Through the letters runs a hateful undertone of threats and menaces. 'My affection for you then is, and only will be, proportioned to your merit, which is the only affection that one rational being ought to have for another.' Chesterfield would have been wiser to be less 'rational'.

Again—'as I will never quarrel with you but upon some essential point, if once we quarrel I will never forgive.' And again—'Adieu! I shall always love you as you shall deserve.'

Alas, Lord Chesterfield had forgotten Hamlet's words on the actors at Elsinore:

Polonius. 'My lord, I will use them according to their desert.'
Hamlet. 'God's bodikins, man, much better; use every man after his desert, and who should 'scape whipping?'

Unhappily, Chesterfield was nearer to Polonius than to Hamlet. And, like Polonius, Chesterfield believed that sons abroad should be well spied on. 'I give you fair warning, that at Leipsig I shall have a hundred invisible spies upon you.' And again—'I have Arguses with a hundred eyes each, who will watch you narrowly.' And again—'Remember I shall know everything you say or do at Paris, as exactly as if, by the force of magic, I could follow you everywhere, like a Sylph or a Gnome, invisible myself.' By all accounts, Lord Chesterfield was more like a Gnome than a Sylph. But he overestimated his Intelligence Service. His Arguses do not seem to have set a single one of their hundreds of eyes on Miss Eugenia Peters. Even when Philip was twenty-six, Chesterfield, asking for details of his private life at Hamburg, adds the unpleasant and ungentlemanly hint—'stick to the truth; for I am not so uninformed of Hamburgh, as perhaps you may think.' But possibly Lord Chesterfield's spies also practised, at his lordship's expense, his lordship's own maxim—'an open countenance, but thoughts well hid'.

And yet, as we have seen, Lord Chesterfield still finds fervent champions. Do they ever picture to themselves how it must have felt to be his son—to be badgered about Europe, year after year, by epistolary sermons, reproofs, and menaces, harping with mortal monotony on the same narrow range of precepts; and to suspect, in every society, the eyes of paternal spies? What a vision the old man himself gives us of his efforts to train his godson of six or seven in 'that repose Which stamps the caste of Vere de Vere'—by holding the child's head between his hands and, now and then, treading on his toes! How endearing! What shades of the prison-house for a growing boy! But Chesterfield had high standards for the young. 'I am persuaded,' he writes, 'that a child of a year and a half old is to be reasoned with.' This I count among the sublimest utterances of the whole Age of Reason.

After this, one is hardly surprised to find Chesterfield setting his godson of six[1] to learn by heart poems either absurdly erotic for

[1] It seems to me, if possible, still more extraordinary that Chesterfield, telling his

his years, like Waller's *The Girdle*, or absurdly disillusioned, like those lines from Dryden's *Aurengzebe* which haunted also the memory of Chesterfield's old enemy Johnson:

> When I consider life, 'tis all a cheat;
> Yet, fool'd with hope, men favour the deceit;
> Trust on, and think to-morrow will repay;
> To-morrow's falser than the former day;
> Lies worse, and, while it says, we shall be blest
> With some new joys, cuts off what we possest.
> Strange cozenage! None would live past years again,
> Yet all hope pleasure in what yet remain!

If Chesterfield thought such sombre wisdom appropriate for the age of six, one is hardly surprised to find him writing to his poor son on the eve of his ninth birthday (in Latin)—'This is the last letter I shall write to you as a boy. . . . Levity and childish triflings must be thrown aside; and your mind exerted towards serious objects.' Little Philip must have found his father a pretty 'serious object'.

Genuine affection, in his own queer way, the old aristocrat must have felt. 'I always made you feel the weight of my authority, that you might one day know the force of my love.' When his son had been ill, the outside of a letter directed at last in the boy's own hand 'gave me more pleasure than the inside of any other letter ever did'. Again, he looks upon the moment of Philip's return to England, 'as a young woman does upon her wedding-day; I expect the greatest pleasure and yet cannot help fearing some little mixture of pain'. (Perhaps the Graces might have found this particular image not wholly ideal for such a context.) Again, Chesterfield has bet a friend fifty guineas that Philip will become a polished man of the world—'I would most cheerfully give a thousand guineas to win those fifty.' 'When I reflect upon the prodigious quantity of manure that has been laid upon you, I expect you should produce more at eighteen, than uncultivated soils do at eight-and-twenty.' 'Manure', Lord Chesterfield? Again, what imagery! The Graces, the

son of six the tale of Troy, should relate how Apollo promised Cassandra the gift of prophecy 'pour en avoir les dernières faveurs'. To know at *six* the meaning of 'les dernières faveurs' seems pushing precocity a little far.

Graces! Did you expect so much gratitude for your 'manure'?

In fine, Chesterfield's fondness was too much the proprietary fondness of a racehorse owner for his colts; too much the possessive affection of an aggressive old patriarch; too like a sculptured marble fireplace with only cold, black embers in its grate. It lacks the one real essential—warmth. 'Gain the heart,' he had himself written, 'or you gain nothing.' Yet, quite fantastically, he goes on to explain that hearts are gained only by 'elegance'.

The Letters were not written for publication; yet they often read as if written for nothing else. They are the letters of a man who never laughed. They seem to forget that it belongs to a gentleman to be gentle, even more than to be genteel. Strangely enough, Chesterfield complains that his son's letters lack the warmth of Mme de Sévigné's. But it is hardly strange that they lacked warmth; that this polar bear should have bred for himself a polar cub. In vain he signed himself 'yours, most tenderly'; or begged his son to write to him 'not as to a father, but without reserve as to a friend'. Friends do not employ spies. Whatever Philip Stanhope's personal relations with his own friends or family, between him and that glacial father the atmosphere was almost bound to be Arctic.

Children need neither an ape-love that smothers, nor a coldness that chills—what they need is an affection that does not clutch, that is perfect freedom, that trains them to independence. Susan Miles was not thinking of this kind of love; but here, as with other kinds of love, two stanzas of hers remain vividly true.

> The wild hare of love
>   Is alert at his feet.
> O the fierce quivering heart!
>   O the heart's fierce beat!
>
> He has tightened his noose,
>   It was fine as a thread.
> But the wild hare that was love
>   At his feet lies dead.

That, indeed, is not Lord Chesterfield's kind of poetry. Nor, I imagine, would he have thought much of that strange Polish tale of the fool whose cruel mistress demanded, as the price of her love, his aged mother's heart. The fool rushed off and hacked it out; but, as he tore back with it to his trollop, he tripped on a stone and fell. And he heard the heart murmur—'My son, are you hurt?'

Some might call the tale 'sentimental'—a word so mauled and misused by modern critics that it has become almost meaningless. Lord Chesterfield might have retorted that if the old woman had not indulged in this excessive fondness, she would not have brought up her son so ill that he tore her heart out. Excessive fondness perhaps it was; but such fondness *has* existed. And from it Lord Chesterfield might have learnt something he lacked. But then, as we have seen, he believed that 'nobody was ever loved that was not well-bred'.

Because he was too rational, too ignorant of the human heart, despite all his finessing, this Machiavelli of the salons finally failed. He fussed too much. He would not let his young charges develop in their own way. He distrusted the comparative freedom of a public school, the licence of the University. He recalled his own youth—'I remember that when I came from Cambridge, I had acquired among the pedants of an illiberal seminary a sauciness of literature, a turn to satire and contempt, and a strong tendency to argumentation and contradiction. But I had been but a very little in the world, before I found that this would by no means do.' He did not wish to see his son 'illiberally getting drunk on port at the University', nor returning home from the Grand Tour, like so many young men, 'refined and polished . . . like Dutch skippers from a whale-fishing.' Mr Harte, and Lord Chesterfield's letters, and Lord Chesterfield's spies were to save Philip Stanhope from that fate. Unfortunately, in the end, the boy seems to have returned not much more polished than a Dutch skipper, after all. And surely it was a queer way of preparing a half-Dutch lad for success in English politics and the English House of Commons, to banish him for five years of his youth, from fifteen till twenty, to foreign countries, and forbid him, even there, the company of young Englishmen. Cambridge may have been 'an illiberal seminary'; but this alternative does not seem so very 'liberal'. Chesterfield forgot that young men are in many ways better educated by one another than by tutors; that even if they acquire at Universities 'a sauciness of literature, a turn to satire and contempt', after all they usually grow out of it; and that a person who has never been allowed to make a fool of himself in youth, may not make much of himself at any age. When Chesterfield writes to his son of eighteen: 'You have hitherto had more liberty than anybody of your age ever had', the unconscious irony grows almost painful.

Chesterfield's contemporary, Chatham, was less crotchety. He trained his able son; but he was not afraid to trust him to Pembroke Hall at the youthful age of fourteen. The young Pitt stayed at Cambridge till twenty-one; at twenty-four he was Prime Minister.

Nothing could have turned Philip Stanhope into a Pitt. But if a high-spirited, mischievous boy, in his childhood nicknamed 'Frisky' and in his youth recorded to have played a highly improper prank on certain grave senators of Bern, grew up into a worthy, but laconic, dull, and clumsy man, the fault may have been in part congenital, but was surely in part Chesterfield's.

One has also to remember that there may have been further psychological reasons why Philip Stanhope should defeat his father's plans.

The boy was illegitimate. And we know better, now, that illegitimate sons can nurse deep resentment against their fathers for the wrong perhaps done their mothers, and for the brand left on their own names from birth. That resentment can take its revenge by thwarting parental projects; just as Philip Stanhope turned out the opposite to what his father wished, and married a woman of whom his father would have strongly disapproved, and perhaps adopted a religion that was his father's aversion.

This, no doubt, is guessing. We know nothing of what Philip Stanhope felt towards this parent who had spent on him the labours of an educational Hercules—except for one significant trifle. On the back of a paper containing some of his father's too astute precepts, Philip wrote the ironic comment—'Excellent maxims, but more calculated for the meridian of France or Spain than of England.' That speaks worlds.

There is also a very relevant comment by Sir William Stanhope,[1]

[1] It was he who, says Walpole (to Mann, September 1, 1763), on his return from a tour abroad with his young third wife, alighted from the chaise at Blackheath to go to Lord Chesterfield's house, bowed low to the lady, and said: 'Madam, I hope I shall never see your face again.' To which the lady replied, with no less politeness: 'Sir, I will take all the care I can that you never shall.' The Graces, the Graces!

Chesterfield's brother, after Philip's long novitiate had closed in disappointment—'What could Chesterfield expect from him? His mother was a Dutchwoman, he sent him to Leipsig to learn manners, and that too under the direction of an Oxford pedant!'

Sainte-Beuve is one of the very last critics with whom I like to disagree. But I am shocked by his comment, 'Si Horace avait un fils, je me figure qu'il ne lui parlerait guère autrement.' Surely, neither Horace nor that excellent father whom Horace recalls so affectionately in his poems, could have made Chesterfield's mistake of trying to educate a son with such a lack of real warmth, such pedantry, or such menaces. And my wonder grows almost speechless when Churton Collins describes Chesterfield as 'in some respects one of the wisest men who have ever lived'.

All the pages ever penned in defence of Chesterfield's paternal preachments do not seem to me worth four words of honest old Augustine Birrell—'Ugh, what a father!'

There were plenty of repellent parents in the century of Squire Western. It was a family tradition with our Hanoverian kings to hate, and be hated by, one's heir. The great Frederick's father imprisoned his own son, and once tried to hang him. In comparison with these, Chesterfield stands high. But there are other contemporaries with whom he compares as a father less happily. There is Chatham. There is the coarse Sir Robert Walpole, who opened his gamekeeper's letters before the king's, and at the end of his life had lost the power to read anything, as Darwin lost the power to read poetry; yet in Horace Walpole he left a son who passionately championed his father's memory, and showed in his letters far more grace than Chesterfield himself. There is the Prince de Ligne, whose father had been another of the domestic tyrants of the day; so that, when his son was made colonel of a regiment belonging to himself, he wrote, 'After the misfortune of having you for son, there was nothing that could afflict me more than having you for colonel' (to which the Prince politely replied that neither was his fault, and the Emperor was responsible for the second). But of his own son, Charles, the Prince made a friend. 'We have taken Sabacz,' the young man wrote, 'I have won the cross. Well you know, papa, that it was you I thought of as we mounted to the assault.' Through all the ages I know no more touching letter from son to father, in its simple *camaraderie*. What a contrast to Chesterfield and Philip Stanhope! But why? Partly, no doubt, accident of temperament. But partly, also, because the Prince de Ligne gave a warmth of affection that was beyond Chesterfield. Chesterfield gave endless advice; but he never gave real loving-kindness; he never gave himself. However well-meaning, he rode on his son's back as mercilessly as the Old Man of the Sea on Sinbad's.

In fine, Lord Chesterfield was a less subtle psychologist than he supposed. That is nothing surprising. In no field is it easier to make mistakes. But in no field is it more fatal. Writing a character-sketch of Pope, Chesterfield more wisely confesses, for once, his own nescience—'The mind of man is so variable, so different from itself in prosperity and adversity, in sickness and in health, in high or in low spirits, that I take the effects as I find them, without presuming to trace them up to their true and secret causes. I know, by not knowing even myself, how little I know of that good, that bad, that knowing, that ignorant, that reasoning and unreasonable creature, *Man*.' Well for him had he more often remembered that Socratic doubt!

What, then, remains for the modern reader, who does not bear the burden of having Chesterfield for father? The letters have wit; wisdom; a clear and vigorous, if monotonous, style; and a certain force of personality. There are things to be learnt there. Often in them the eternal Graces become an unconscionable bore. But perhaps the Graces are often as much underestimated by the twentieth century as they were often overvalued by the eighteenth. And yet in these pages there still remains, also, much that seems repugnant.

What use in sermons on veracity and honour, when combined with that wearisome insistence on adulation and adultery? There is too much refined nagging. There is too much toad-eating; even if the toads are served, finely sugared, on silver plate. There is too much the tone of an Old Pretender to a Young.

It is, of course, the stress on gallantry—on making a ladder for ambition out of ladies' beds—that has raised the loudest storms against Chesterfield. Hence Cowper's lines:

> Thou polish'd and high-finish'd foe to truth,
> Greybeard corrupter of our listening youth.

This rings, for me, a little too rhetorically. In the queue that forms up to cast stones at the old man there are too many prim faces I dislike—too many minds whose moral indignation may be more disagreeable than the sins it denounces. I will only say that I do not much like Chesterfield's particular blend of Polonius and Pandarus. It is too cold-blooded. Especially when it comes to pushing a boy of nineteen into the arms of a girl of sixteen, only a year after her wedding to another.

Further, Chesterfield's idea of education seems absurdly narrow. It is not merely that it ignores the love of nature and the knowledge of science; it is rather that it takes as the object of life, not happiness, nor giving happiness, but 'making a figure'. Action seems replaced by mere acting. And the whole scheme remains too egoistic. Chesterfield House is built too near Patterne Hall.

His lordship, it may be remembered, took a good deal of snuff over the latter part of the *Æneid*; but in its Sixth Book,[1] there are two lines that he might perhaps have borne more in mind:

> Inventas aut qui vitam excoluere per artis,
> Quique sui memores alios fecere merendo.
>
> Those who made life more fruitful by arts they brought
> to birth,
> Those who won men's remembrance by their service and
> their worth.

Egotism, no doubt, is to be carefully banished from Philip Stanhope's conversation; but almost everything else from his thoughts. So much self-interest grows uninteresting.

In fine, there are things about Chesterfield that seem to me rather repellent; things that it is an offence in critics to defend. He is typical of one side of the eighteenth century—of what still seems to many its most typical side. But it does not seem to me the really great side of that century; and Chesterfield remains, I think, less an example of things to pursue in life than of things to avoid. Among other things, he exemplifies that *sécheresse*, that aridity of soul, which is apt to beset the spoilt and blasé aristocrat, just as vulgarity and sentimentality often beset his social inferiors. He has not yet

[1] vi, 663–4.

reached the cynicism of Choderlos de la Laclos, whose vision of life in *Les Liaisons Dangereuses* sears the eyes like the dust of some bleached Sahara; but he is on the way.

This defect of temperament leads, I think, to a certain defect in his style. It is clear, pointed, sometimes forcible; yet, for me, it remains dry, devoid of poetry, devoid of that gaiety, grace, and sympathy which win in return the reader's sympathy for Gray, Goldsmith, Hume, Walpole, or Franklin. A curious paradox—all his life Chesterfield preached the importance of charm; yet charm is precisely what, on paper at least, he lacks.

He is not very easy to like. Perhaps the best things about him are his self-command and his courage. This old Epicurean became also a Stoic. His hopes failed—he took it with dignity. Johnson flayed him—he showed the letter, and praised its style.[1] His health failed—he jested. He might become, in his own phrase, 'a deaf vegetable'—but not a broken reed.

There are even times when a glint of melancholy poetry does steal for a moment, like a ray of wintry sunset, across his grey pages—'I feel this beginning of the autumn, which is already very cold: the leaves are withered, fall apace, and seem to intimate that I must follow them; which I shall do without reluctance, being extremely weary of this silly world.' So, with an unusual touch of feeling, he wrote to his son on August 17, 1765, when he was near threescore and ten.

Vanity Fair was closing down; but at least he did not whine.

On the other hand, it does not appear that all his 'wit and wisdom' had taught him to create much happiness in life, either for himself or for others. 'I look back upon all that has passed as one of those romantic dreams that opium commonly occasions, and I do by no means desire to repeat the nauseous dose for the sake of the fugitive dreams.'

Still, he had kept faith, to the end, with his own fantastic principles. It was not unfitting that his dying words, polite to the last, should have been—'Give Dayrolles a chair.'

[1] Cf. the Rev. John Hussey's note in his copy of Boswell's *Johnson*: 'Enquiring of Dr Johnson if it were true that Ld Chesterfield had been much offended at the receipt of his letter, the Doctor replied "So far from it, his Lordship express'd himself obliged to me for it and did me the honour to say it was the letter of a Scholar and a Gentleman." ' (Boswell's *Johnson*, ed. Hill–Powell, i, 541.)

Chesterfield is an interesting host; but not a friend. One can gladly spend a few evenings with him—his speech is crisp and pointed; his stories sometimes vivid; his cynicisms sometimes amusing; his polish smooth and brilliant as the mahogany table where the wine stands mirrored. The evening draws to an end. The old man rises and goes his way with a quiet, slightly sinister dignity. One pities; but one cannot like him.

He had loved, in his queer fashion, his son and godson; he had loved Lord Scarborough—'the best man I ever knew . . . the dearest friend I ever had'; perhaps too Lady Fanny Shirley, whom he wooed as mistress (she was twenty-seven) about the time he wedded Melusina von der Schulenburg. As Sir Charles Hanbury-Williams wrote:

> There were Chesterfield and Fanny,
> In that eternal whisper which begun
> Ten years ago, and never will be done.

But Scarborough killed himself; Lady Fanny, after turning Methodist, ended in decay and melancholia;[1] Chesterfield's loves were not fortunate. And yet, in a way, Chesterfield himself was a kind of educational Methodist. Wesley thought the only destination for him was Hell; but both men alike were rigidly purposeful—enemies of laughter—Spartan disciplinarians of the young.

Did anyone honestly mourn when Chesterfield died? Perhaps poor Melusina, Lady Chesterfield? Though cattish persons like Mrs Montagu prattled that she had small cause, being an ill-used widow—'People are so disgusted at Lord Chesterfield's will that they speak slightly of his character, of which indeed he scratched the varnish at last; which is a pity, for it was the best papier-mâché character I ever knew, and with good management might have preserved its gloss a great while.' He also left £500 to Mlle du Bouchet 'as some compensation for the injury I have done her'.

[1] Finally, according to Walpole, before her death at seventy-two she lost her memory for everything else (Methodism included), and recalled only her own lost beauty—'I to be abandoned, that all the world used to adore!' (To Mason, July 16 1778.):

> Still round and round the ghosts of beauty glide
> And haunt the places where their honour died.

(And some say Pope was not a poet!)

Some might feel that such wording added insult to injury. It appears that Mlle du Bouchet indignantly refused the bequest.

But by that date Lord Chesterfield heeded such judgments or resentments no longer—as little, indeed, as if he had been alive.

After all, it is fair to remember that we have one unfair advantage over him—he is dead, and we live later. Let us not abuse it. If we find much to criticize in him, he would have found much to disdain in us—in our follies and vulgarities, in our press and our advertisements, in our literature, our art, and our society.

But he made, perhaps, one critical mistake in life. He was, in his way, a kind of humanist; yet he became inhuman—as Johnson, Goldsmith, Franklin, even Boswell, never did.

BOSWELL

Ce n'est pas le plus instruit, le mieux relationné des hommes, mais celui qui sait devenir miroir et peut refléter ainsi sa vie, fût-elle médiocre, qui devient un Bergotte.

PROUST

THE central dissension over James Boswell turns on the question—ass or genius?

The ass-view has been put most thunderously by Macaulay. 'Many of the greatest men that ever lived have written biography.' (Already, I should have thought, an exaggeration.) 'Boswell was one of the smallest men that ever lived, and he has beaten them all . . . a man of the meanest and feeblest intellect. . . . He was the laughing-stock of the whole of that brilliant society. . . .' (Yet Margaret Boswell gave him her heart, Johnson loved him, Reynolds was fond of him, the Club elected him.) 'He was always laying himself at the feet of some eminent man, and begging to be spit upon and trampled upon.' (Always? And surely his approaches to men like Rousseau and Voltaire could be more easily taxed with impudence than with servility?) 'Servile and impertinent, shallow and pedantic, a bigot and a sot, bloated with family pride, and eternally blustering about the dignity of a born gentleman, yet stooping to be a talebearer, an eavesdropper, a common butt in the taverns of London, so curious to know everybody who was talked about, that, Tory and High Churchman as he was, he manœuvred, we have been told, for an introduction to Tom Paine' (but is it not a little bigoted in Macaulay himself to imply that a Tory and High Churchman should spurn the chance of meeting a character so remarkable as Tom Paine?), 'so vain of the most childish distinctions, that when he had been to court, he drove to the office where his book was printing without changing his clothes, and summoned all the printer's devils to admire his new ruffles and sword. . . . Everything which another man would have hidden, everything the publication of which would have made another man hang himself, was a matter of gay and clamorous exultation to his weak and diseased mind. . . .' (Everything? Even poor Boswell, in the *Tour* and the *Life*, felt some things were *too* humiliating, and refused to record them.) 'All the caprices of his temper, all the illusions of his vanity, all his hypochondriac whimsies, all his castles in the air, he displayed with a cool self-complacency, a perfect unconsciousness that he was making a fool of himself, to which it is impossible to find a parallel in the whole history of mankind.' (This sentence too sounds sweeping; but here I must own that if Macaulay's ghost challenged me to produce a parallel to Boswell, I should be dumb.)

Then Macaulay points out that other good writers have made fools of themselves *outside* their books; Goldsmith, for example, or La Fontaine. 'But these men,' he continues, 'attained literary eminence in spite of their weaknesses, Boswell attained it by reason of his weaknesses. If he had not been a great fool, he would never have been a great writer. . . . He was a slave proud of his servitude, a Paul Pry, convinced that his own curiosity and garrulity were virtues, an unsafe companion who never scrupled to repay the most liberal hospitality by the basest violation of confidence, a man without delicacy, without shame' (this seems to me most untrue), 'without sense enough to know when he was hurting the feelings of others or when he was exposing himself to derision; and because he was all this, he has, in an important department of literature, immeasurably surpassed such writers as Tacitus, Clarendon, Alfieri, and his own idol Johnson.

'Of the talents which ordinarily raise men to eminence as writers, Boswell had absolutely none. There is not in all his books a single remark of his own on literature, politics, religion, or society, which is not either commonplace or absurd.' (Boswell, like Macaulay, and unlike Johnson, sympathized with the American revolutionaries;[1] Macaulay cannot have thought this 'absurd'; and it seems a little harsh to dismiss it as 'commonplace'. Again, some of Boswell's comments on Johnson seem to me quite acute.)

'Logic, eloquence, wit, taste, all those things which are generally considered as making a book valuable, were utterly wanting to him.' (But surely one should give poor Boswell some credit for the taste which selected Johnson as his principal lion, and so well selected what to record of the lion's roarings and pawings?)

'He had, indeed, a quick observation and a retentive memory. These qualities, if he had been a man of sense and virtue, would scarcely of themselves have sufficed to make him conspicuous; but

[1] In 1776 he wrote on this theme a poem even more excruciating than usual:

> On a sure basis British Empire build,
> Think not her youngest sons will ever yield
> To unconditional despotic sway.

In 1781 he was so delighted by Cornwallis's surrender at Yorktown that, for once, he 'sprung up' early in the morning. (This seems to me a little excessive.)

because he was a dunce, a parasite, and a coxcomb, they have made him immortal.' (But why, then, have countless other dunces, parasites, and coxcombs—some of whom must also have possessed 'quick observation and retentive memory'—yet failed to attain even the most modest immortality?)

'In general,' concludes Macaulay, 'the book and the author are considered as one. To admire the book is to admire the author. The case of Boswell is an exception, we think the only exception, to this rule.' (I should have thought there were plenty of others; for instance, Villon or Rousseau or Sterne may be admirable as writers, but hardly as men.) 'His work is universally allowed to be interesting, instructive, eminently original; yet it has brought him nothing but contempt.' ('Nothing but contempt' is untrue of Macaulay's own day; still more, of ours, when the tendency has become rather, I think, for Boswell to be over-idolized.)

A pity that Macaulay's brilliance was so tempestuous. For it encourages fools not to suffer him, just as he could not suffer fools. The old Seeley told G. M. Trevelyan that both Macaulay and Carlyle were 'charlatans' (a tactful remark to make to Macaulay's own nephew); yet Acton pronounced him, with all his faults, 'on the whole the greatest of all historians' (which I should have thought was running a little to the opposite extreme). Still, the other day I asked two history dons of my college—'Whom do you put highest of English historians?' And each independently replied—'Macaulay.' I was agreeably surprised—I had imagined my admiration for him out of date. (However it should be remembered that Macaulay's *History* is maturer than his *Essays*.)

Apart from his vast knowledge and his keen intelligence, Macaulay had the writer's first quality—readability. That is not common among historians or critics in any age; certainly not in ours. It is, indeed, one of the standing puzzles of existence that so many men can spend their lives communing with the angelic hosts of literature, and yet, in their own books, talk like poor Poll; so that even cultured literary journals often become like mud-flat stretching beyond mud-flat.

Secondly, Macaulay had a passionately felt standard of values. One may not always agree with it; but it is there; whereas in some modern writers the absence of any mind is matched with an equal absence of any morals. When that excellent critic Raleigh used the phrase 'a wiser man than Macaulay, James Boswell', he was, I am afraid, being tempted, like many of us, by epigram into folly. For if I am asked to think either Boswell wise, or Macaulay a fool, I can only reply that my imagination is not equal to it.

Still, I must admit that I deplore, for Macaulay's sake, much in his view of Boswell. What Macaulay would have said, had he lived to see the *Boswell Papers*, I do not know. Their bottomless pits of fatuity might have moved him to cry triumphantly, 'I told you so'; or, on the contrary, he might have felt their pathos, and done more justice to their amazing industry.

Now for some more modern estimates of Boswell, at the opposite extreme. We are told by Mr William Plomer—'I call him great, a great creative artist.' We are told by Professor Pottle, to whom Boswellians owe so much, 'Boswell was a great imaginative artist—the peer in imagination of Scott and Dickens'. We are told by Professor Abbott, to whom we also owe so much, that Boswell was 'a great writer whose skill in setting down conversations is the prose counterpart of what Chaucer so magnificently accomplished for poetry in *Troilus and Criseyde*'. 'The Dr Johnson most of us know is as much Boswell's creation as Falstaff is Shakespeare's, or Criseyde Chaucer's, or Gabriel Oak Hardy's.' And Mr Stephen Spender has compared the *London Journal* with Proust.

Now I cannot see what on earth Chaucer, Scott, Dickens, and Proust have to do with the matter. One would think Chaucer had been sitting in Criseyde's boudoir at Troy, as Boswell at The Mitre. Chaucer largely invented Criseyde; Boswell did not invent Johnson. I may be dense, but this seems to me to make a certain difference. The Recording Angel may be a most eminent angel; but he did not create the Universe.

'That a man,' says Professor Abbott, 'by nature so indolent should have submitted himself for more than thirty years to the most exacting of tasks is one of the miracles of literature. As a writer the lavishly over-rated Pepys is a schoolboy beside him.'

Now I should have thought this harsh world provided quite a number of tasks much more 'exacting' than keeping a diary. I see no need to invoke 'miracles'. Nor do I grasp why poor, charming Pepys should thus be sacrificed to the Golden Calf of Auchinleck.

'Everyone,' says Professor Abbott, 'liked Boswell.' I doubt if such a claim was ever true of any man since Adam. It is certainly not true of Boswell. And even if it *were* true? Are men's merits to be judged by Gallup polls? Not everyone liked Johnson—far from it; does that make Boswell his superior? Not everyone liked Socrates—he was given hemlock. Not everyone liked Joan of Arc—she was burnt. Not everyone liked Abraham Lincoln—he was shot.

Then there is the apologia of Lord David Cecil—'To dislike Boswell is to dislike ourselves. Alike in his strength and his weakness, his fears and desires, he is a typical example of the likeable, lamentable animal called man.'

Boswell 'typical'! I find this a strange remark for so admirable a biographer as Lord David Cecil. (Or else Oxford must be a strange place.) Does he find it 'typical' among men of his acquaintance to sit up four nights in a week recording the minutest follies of their own lives; to throw banknotes on the fire in a rage, and frugally pull them out again with tongs; to sleep in each other's beds for fear of ghosts; and to appear at Stratford festivals attired as Corsican chieftains? Boswell 'typical'!—if he were, this odd world would be a great deal odder even than it is.

However, with such an irreconcilable clash of opinions, the only course is to record the main facts and let the reader judge for himself.

The tragicomedy called James Boswell began on October 29, 1740. He was the son of Alexander Boswell (1706–82), who in 1754 became Lord Auchinleck.[1] Their ancestor Thomas Boswell had received from James IV, with whom he was to fall at Flodden Field, the lands of Auchinleck, some thirteen miles east of Ayr, and some twenty-seven south of Glasgow.

On his mother's side Boswell could claim descent still more dignified—from Robert Bruce, and from that Earl of Lennox who was grandfather of Darnley, and so grandfather-in-law of Mary Stuart.

Hence Boswell's 'feudal notions', and that family pride which made him regard himself, with constant satisfaction, as an 'old Scotch Baron'.

In 1753, at thirteen, he went to Edinburgh University. In 1757

[1] Pronounced 'Affléck'.

that streak of mental instability in the Boswell blood which should always be borne in mind (his brother John went mad, and his daughter Euphemia became queer) showed itself in a temporary nervous collapse.[1] In 1758, at eighteen, travelling the northern circuit with his father, he already kept an exact journal. Equally early began another of Boswell's lifelong pursuits—he fell in love with an actress at Edinburgh, Mrs Cowper, whom he wished to marry.

In 1760, having gone the previous year to Glasgow to study civil law, he became temporarily a Roman Catholic—just like the young Gibbon at Oxford. Much to the agitation of his parents he rode off headlong to London, covering the distance from Carlisle in two days and a half. But in London he shed his papistry, with far more ease than the young Gibbon exiled to Lausanne. Both young men were perhaps seeking escape from the dryness of the eighteenth-century atmosphere, and also from dominating fathers. But Gibbon was to find his real sanctuary, not in the Roman Church, but in the Roman Empire; Boswell was to find his, less calmly, in Johnson.

In London, Boswell was taken up by Lord Eglinton, seventeen years his senior, who is said to have rescued him from bad company, but did not perhaps bring him into company much better. At Newmarket the young Scot got introduced to the Duke of York; and wrote an asinine poem, *The Cub at Newmarket*, published in 1762 with a dedicatory epistle to the Duke, and well describing himself, at least, as a 'curious cub' from Scotland.

At this period he also added to the list of his famous acquaintances Laurence Sterne, to whom he composed a verse-epistle. One can imagine certain bonds of sympathy between the two—both were children of an age of reason and decorum, who went out of their way to lack either quality. Both were sons of whimsy. 'I took a whim,' writes Boswell later in London (December 12, 1762), 'of dining at home every day last week, which I kept exactly to. The pleasure of gratifying whim is very great. It is known only by those who are whimsical.'

None the less Sterne figures little in Boswell; this might be be-

[1] Sir Walter Scott suspected in Boswell 'some slight touch of insanity'. Euphemia, it appears, apart from other eccentricities, inserted in her will a wish to be buried in Westminster Abbey near Johnson.

cause upon 'the man Sterne' lay the implacable anathema of Johnson. And yet, when it was a question of hunting lions, or ladies, Boswell was apt to go his own way. Johnson's disapproval did not keep him from Wilkes, or Rousseau, or Voltaire. The slightness of contact with Sterne may have been mainly due to lack of opportunity. For the ailing Yorick was mainly abroad from 1761 till 1766, and died in 1768.

However, Boswell's lion-hunting had begun well. It was to go on all his life. He was a Nimrod among lion-hunters. On the other hand, it is curious that Boswell, who has added so much to literature, seems not to have felt much for it. Unlike many, he greatly preferred authors to books. His lions must be alive and roaring; not stuffed in libraries.

After three months, in June 1760, he had to return from the fleshpots of London to the dry biscuit of law at Edinburgh. But there he at least met Lord Kames, Hume, Robertson, and others; and in 1761 he added to his list Thomas Sheridan, father of the dramatist, whom Boswell was soon invoking in typical terms of rapture—'My Mentor! My Socrates! Direct my heedless steps.' 'Socrates' and 'Mentor' ring in rather incongruous contrast to Johnson's verdict on Thomas Sheridan—'Why, Sir, Sherry is dull, naturally dull; but it must have taken him a great deal of pains to become what we now see him. Such an excess of stupidity,[1] Sir, is not in Nature.'

The young Boswell, however, was an eternal disciple, in constant search of a prophet whose mantle should cover him—of guides, philosophers, and friends—in short, of father-substitutes. Indeed to the goodly family of skeletons in the cupboards of psychoanalysis one might add, in Boswell's honour, the term 'Telemachus-complex', after that son of Odysseus who found fame in seeking his lost father. Boswell would have liked to like his own father, Lord Auchinleck. Unfortunately father and son turned out to have

[1] This charge of stupidity seems not wholly unjustified when one considers, for example, the accentuation which Thomas Sheridan enjoined for Dryden's *Alexander's Feast*:

None but the brave,
None but the *brave*,
None *but* the brave deserve the fair.

Here, at least, brays a perfect ass.

opposite likings about almost every conceivable subject—about the right career for Boswell, and the right marriage for Boswell, and the right succession for the Boswell estates, and about politics, and about Samuel Johnson. Hence, just as Chesterfield looked persistently for young men to play father to, poor Boswell was driven to behave like an eternal orphan in search of a spiritual foster-parent.[1]

Towards the end of 1760 he published 'Observations' on Foote's *The Minor*, 'By a Genius' (price 3 pence). Boswell was already Boswell. In 1761 followed an *Ode to Tragedy*; anonymous ('By a Gentleman of Scotland'), but dedicated to—James Boswell. In 1762 he contributed thirty-one pieces to Volume II of *Original Poems, By Scotch Gentlemen*, including a little song on the Soaping Club, a body of that name which he had founded, with the slogan that every man should 'soap his own beard'—in other words, follow his own whim.

Boswell, of Soapers the king,
On Tuesdays at Tom's does appear,
And when he does talk or does sing
To him ne'er a one can come near;
For he talks with such ease and such grace,
That all charm'd to attention we sit,
And he sings with so comic a face,
That our sides are just ready to split.

Boswell does women adore,
And never once means to deceive;
He's in love with at least half a score;
If they're serious he smiles in his sleeve.
He has all the bright fancies of youth
With the judgment of forty and five.
In short, to declare the plain truth,
There is no better fellow alive.

Such is the writer whom modern criticism has likened to Shakespeare. 'Bright fancies of youth'—that was true enough; but 'the judgment of forty and five'!

[1] Cf. his comment after one of Lord Auchinleck's rare moments of geniality—'After breakfast, when I took leave of him, he embraced me with a cordiality which I valued more than the fond embrace of the finest Woman' (March 24, 1777).

This curious effusion, still more curiously, he thought worth publishing again a generation later, at fifty-one, only four years before he died. Boswell never grew up.

But this doggerel seems worth quoting for its picture of what one side of Boswell, the gay side, wanted to be; his life-long trouble was, however, that his gay side was matched, like Johnson's, with another alternating personality of immeasurable gloom. Boswell, like Johnson, seems an obvious manic-depressive.

In July 1762 he passed his trials in civil law. And that September he took a little excursion, recorded in the *Journal of my Jaunt*, which is already typical of so many of his journals to come—absolutely Boswellian.

> September 14, 1762. (With his cousins, the Misses Macadam at Lagwine.) 'I was here perfectly happy. As a Cousin I had their Affection; as being very clever, their Admiration; as Mr Boswell of Auchinleck, their Respect. A noble Complication.'
>
> September 19, 1762. 'At night Mrs Heron[1] read the Evening Service to us, and I beheld with delight so fine a Creature employed in adoring her Creator.'
>
> September 21, 1762. (He disagrees with Lord Kames, Mr Smith, Dr Blair and others about the author of *The Rambler*.) 'They will allow him nothing but Heaviness, weakness and affected Pedantry. Whereas in my Opinion Mr Johnson is a man of much Philosophy, extensive reading, and real knowledge of human life.'

In November 1762 Boswell was even allowed to return to his beloved London. Lord Auchinleck might growl a great deal; he might even, on occasion, threaten disinheritance; but in practice he appears a far from unindulgent parent towards a son who was a completely incompatible antithesis of himself.

In returning to London, Boswell's avowed object was to get a commission in the Guards, by the favour of some great personage like the Duke of Queensberry, or the Countess of Northumberland. He could, indeed (like his brother John, who afterwards went mad), have got a commission in a line regiment. But Boswell was not at all set on death or glory; to smell powder on the plains of Germany,

[1] Daughter of Lord Kames. Now, or soon after, Boswell seems to have become her lover (see p. 215). In 1772 her husband divorced her for adultery.

or be scalped in the backwoods of Canada, was by no means his desire; his dream was to become for life a dashing guardsman about town. His father's comment (November 27, 1762) is curtly uncomplimentary, but hardly untrue—'A man of your age to enter into the Guards on a peace and live all his days and die an ensign, is a poor prospect, which no man would be sorry to lose. The entry is shabby and the exit the same.'

However, Lord Auchinleck was less grim than his words; and James was allowed to try his luck, with an allowance, for the present, of £200 a year—two-thirds of the pension granted to Johnson after a lifetime of toil.

From this point, November 1762, till August 1763, when he left for Holland, we have Boswell's priceless *London Journal*.

Here the young Boswell reveals himself *in puris naturalibus*; though the Journal was composed, not (as its reader might well imagine) to be kept under triple lock and key, but to be posted in weekly instalments for perusal by his Scots friend, Johnston.

> November 15, 1762. (He leaves Edinburgh.) 'I made the chaise stop at the foot of the Canongate; asked pardon of Mr Stewart for a minute; walked to the Abbey of Holyroodhouse, went round the Piazzas, bowed thrice: once to the Palace itself, once to the crown of Scotland above the gate in front, and once to the venerable old Chapel. I next stood in the court before the Palace, and bowed thrice to Arthur Seat, that lofty romantic mountain on which I have so often strayed in my days of youth, indulged meditation and felt the raptures of a soul filled with ideas of the magnificence of God and his creation. Having thus gratified my agreeable whim and superstitious humour, I felt a warm glow of satisfaction. Indeed, I have a strong turn to what the cool part of mankind have named superstition. But this proceeds from my genius for poetry, which ascribes many fanciful properties to everything.'

A spectator would have thought the man mad. The interest lies in Boswell's constant self-dramatization, and the enormous admiration felt by Boswell the audience for Boswell the actor. He is the extreme antithesis to a Stoic like Marcus Aurelius with his stress on behaving ἀτραγῴδως—'*not* like a tragic actor'. Nor was Boswell particularly stoical between Stilton and Biggleswade—'I was a good deal afraid of robbers. A great many horrid ideas filled my mind.' But next day, November 19, at sight of London from Highgate, Boswell became once more Boswellissimus.

> 'I was all life and joy. I repeated Cato's soliloquy on the immortality of the soul, and my soul bounded forth to a certain prospect of happy futurity. I sung all manner of songs, and began to make one about an amorous meeting with a pretty girl, the burthen of which was as follows:
>
> She gave me *this*, I gave her *that*;
> And tell me, had she not tit for tat?
>
> I gave three huzzas, and we went briskly in.'

Cato, immortality, pretty girls—they had no incongruity for James Boswell. Doleful fears, lofty aspirations, grotesque dissipation—such was the trinity which would govern that farcical, pathetic life. November 25—'most miserable'; November 27—'I was all gentle felicity'; November 28—'In the midst of divine service I was laying plans for having women, and yet I had the most sincere feelings of religion'—so his disarming ingenuousness rambles on.[1] Among the tombs at Westminster, 'was solemn and happy'. But a meeting with some homely Scots folk in the Red Lion at Charing Cross is most mortifying—for 'I felt strong dispositions to be a Mr Addison'. (Alas, Boswell's only resemblance to Addison was to lie in fondness for the bottle.)

But a few days later comes a foreshadowing of one of those gifts that were to make Boswell far more read, one day, than Addison himself—his patiently learnt skill in recording conversation. Boswell resolved to record every Saturday some snatch of talk at Child's Coffee House. For example:

> 'Saturday, December 25, 1762:
>
> Dialogue at Child's
>
> 1 *Citizen.* Why, here is the bill of mortality. Is it right, Doctor?
>
> *Physician.* Why, I don't know.
>
> 1 *Citizen.* I'm sure it is not. Sixteen only died of cholics! I dare say you have killed as many yourself.
>
> 2 *Citizen.* Ay, and hanged but three! O Lord, ha! ha! ha!'

[1] One may recall Goldsmith's Italians in *The Traveller* (1764):

> Though grave, yet trifling, zealous, yet untrue,
> And ev'n in penance planning sins anew.

That is all. Casual, callous, stupid! And yet what a vivid slice of life!—as if the babel of two centuries were suddenly hushed, and we actually listened in for a minute to the authentic Christmas chatter of Johnson's London. So Shakespeare might have created it; and Carlyle might have groaned and stormed over such human crassness; and Dickens have chuckled over such human humours.

A moment later Boswell approaches nearer still to his future masterpieces, with an amusing snatch of dramatic dialogue between Dodsley, Goldsmith, Davies, and himself on modern poetry—Gray, Shakespeare, Johnson. And one realizes yet again how much Boswell's biographic pre-eminence was to rest simply on this gift for living talk and dramatic scenes.

But quickly the fatuous side of Boswell breaks in again. There is the vivid, grotesque, pitiful amour with Louisa Lewis. There is the incredibly fatuous letter to Lord Eglinton (February 7, 1763), with its concluding climax:

> 'Surely I am a man of genius. I deserve to be taken notice of. O that my grandchildren might read this character of me: "James Boswell, a most amiable man. He improved and beautified his paternal estate of Auchinleck; made a distinguished figure in Parliament; had the honour to command a regiment of footguards, and was one of the brightest wits in the Court of George the Third." '

One can almost hear the dry, crackling laughter of the Fates. No regiment; no Parliament; grandchildren that would blush at his very name—and yet, after all, a final blaze of glory beyond even Boswell's craziest dreams.

Then he continues:

> 'I was certain this epistle would please him much. I was pleased with writing it. I felt quite serene and happy, my mind unclouded and serenely gay. . . . All looked fine in my blest imagination.'

And again, two days later:

> 'How easily and cleverly do I write just now! I am really pleased with myself; words come skipping to me like lambs upon Moffat Hill; and I turn my periods smoothly and imperceptibly like a skilful wheelwright

turning tops in a turning-loom. There's fancy! There's simile! In short, I am at present a genius: in that does my opulence consist, and not in base metal.'

That such absurdities could make Boswell think himself a genius is fantastic enough; but what remains far more fantastic is, that for quite different reasons he had not yet dreamed of, the man almost[1] *was* a genius after all.

So the months of 1763 slipped pleasantly by. Boswell ascends the Monument, is terrified half-way up, but pride drives him to the top.

'It was horrid . . . I durst not look round me. There is no real danger, as there is a strong rail both on the stair and the balcony. But I shuddered, and as every heavy wagon passed down Gracechurch Street, dreaded that the shaking of the earth would make the tremendous pile tumble to the foundation.'

In April, 1763, may have occurred (though this is not recorded in the *London Journal*) that peculiarly Boswellian performance in the pit of Drury Lane when he won enthusiastic encores from the galleries by imitating the mooing of a cow; was rashly emboldened by success to mimic other animals 'with very inferior effect'; and was anxiously admonished by his clerical companion, Dr Hugh Blair, with 'the utmost gravity and earnestness'—'My dear sir, I would confine myself to the *cow*!'

This same month saw Boswell's newly published correspondence with Erskine[2] warmly reviewed in *The London Chronicle*, as 'a book of true genius'; the anonymous reviewer being—of course—James Boswell.

On May 16, 1763, Boswell, who had already made the acquaintance of Goldsmith and John Wilkes, at last met his destiny—Johnson. For several years Johnson had been on Boswell's hunting-list. Derrick had promised him an introduction, then Thomas Sheridan;

[1] Some would delete 'almost'; but, for me, if that maddeningly vague word 'genius' is to be used at all, it should be kept for bigger minds than Boswell's.

[2] A laborious, whimsical book. In it Erskine seems to me the less tedious of the two. The Hon. Andrew Erskine (1739–93), soldier, dramatist, and poet (Burns praised some of his songs), having lost heavily at whist, finally flung himself into the Forth.

in September 1762 we have already seen Boswell defending the author of *The Rambler* against Lord Kames and others who taxed him with heaviness and pedantry. Yet Boswell, giddy with his own affairs, met the sage only after seven months of amusing himself in London. He was to be far quicker with Rousseau and Voltaire. However, in May 1763, chance brought the first fateful meeting in the parlour of Tom Davies the bookseller. It was typical of many to follow; for Boswell incurred two resounding snubs. 'Mr Johnson, I do indeed come from Scotland, but I cannot help it.' 'That, Sir, I find, is what a great many of your countrymen cannot help.' 'O, Sir, I cannot think Mr Garrick would grudge such a trifle[1] to you.' 'Sir, I have known David Garrick longer than you have done, and I know no right you have to talk to me on the subject.' No wonder Boswell was 'stunned' and 'mortified'. But he was to become, as Horace Walpole's old fishwife said of eels being skinned alive, 'used to it'.

It is most interesting to compare the parallel passages in the *London Journal* (May 16, 1763) and the *Life of Johnson*,[2] and see how the second clarifies and amplifies the first; interesting also to see in the *Journal* how unfavourable was Boswell's first impression of his future idol's exterior—'Mr Johnson is a man of a most dreadful appearance. He is a very big man, is troubled with sore eyes, the palsy,[3] and the king's evil. He is very slovenly in his dress and speaks with a most uncouth voice.'

A week later, on May 24, Boswell called on Johnson in Inner Temple Lane, and was courteously received. But intimacy did not spring up at once. Boswell had other, sometimes less reputable diversions; and after meeting twice in May, they only met twice more in the whole of June, 1763.[4] But July brought a dozen meetings, of increasing frequency; and on August 5 Johnson, most astonishingly, volunteered to go all the way to Harwich to see Boswell off to Holland. On the way, at Colchester, the sage uttered an unerring prophecy. A moth had cremated itself in the candle.

[1] An order admitting Miss Williams to a play.

[2] Hill-Powell, i, 391 ff.

[3] Untrue, of course. Boswell was misled by Johnson's nervous tics.

[4] Not counting a chance encounter at 1 a.m. near Temple Bar, when Johnson, invited by Boswell to The Mitre, replied it was too late for admission—'But I'll go with you another night with all my heart.'

'That creature,' he said quietly, but solemnly, 'with a sly look', 'was its own tormentor, and I believe its name was BOSWELL.'

Next day—'as the vessel put out to sea, I kept my eyes upon him for a considerable time while he remained rolling his majestic frame in the usual manner.' Thus, after only two and a half months' acquaintance, they parted for two and a half years. But the foundations were truly laid.

Boswell had now submitted to his father's will. In the same month of May as saw Boswell's first meeting with Johnson, Lord Auchinleck had written fiercely from the North. His letter begins, not 'Dear James', but 'James'; catalogues Boswell's low mimicries and printed indiscretions (his giggling correspondence with Andrew Erskine); and ends with a dour threat of disinheritance 'from the principle that it is a better to snuff a candle out than leave it to stink in the socket'. However, if Boswell would turn to the law, 'I would make no difficulty, when you were a little settled from your reelings, to let you go abroad for a while'.

Whatever his narrowness, the old man shows far more Johnsonian vigour in his letters than his famous son. So now at last Boswell renounced his martial dreams; he would exchange the gorgeous regimentals of the Guards for the drab robes of the bar. From August 1763 to June 1764 he endured a Dutch exile, wrestling with Roman law under Professor Trotz of Utrecht. At first he was utterly wretched.

> 'I sunk,' he wrote to his friend Johnston, 'quite into despair. I thought that at length the time was come that I should grow mad. I actually believed myself so. I went out to the streets, and even in public could not refrain from groaning and weeping bitterly. I said always, "Poor Boswell, is it come to this? Miserable wretch that I am! what shall I do?" '

Little wonder that Boswell in the end, like so many unfortunates seeking escape, found it in drink.

Persistently these attacks of 'hyp'[1] recurred. In vain did Boswell

[1] 'Hyp' = hypochondria, *lit.* 'the parts of the abdomen under the ribs'—liver, gall, spleen, etc.; thence, the misery attributed to disordered gall or spleen.

In the eighteenth century this malady was especially associated with the English—indeed, it was called 'the English disease'. (One may suspect that over-eating, over-drinking, and too little exercise had much to do with it.) 'A celebrated French novelist,' writes Addison, 'enters on his story thus: "In the gloomy month of November, when

exhort himself, like a Roman general haranguing his legions.

> 'Learn the usage of life. Be prudent and *retenu*. Never aim at being too brilliant. Be rather an amiable, pretty man. Have no affectation. Cure vanity. Be quite temperate and have self-command amid all the pleasures. Would Epictetus or Johnson be overturned by human beings, gay, thoughtless, corrupted? No; they would make the best of them and be superior. Have real principles. You have acquired a noble character at Utrecht. Maintain it.'[1]

In vain, too, did he indulge that curious habit, long retained in his memoranda, of adjuring himself to be somebody else—'Be Erskine'—'Be Digges'—'Be Johnson'—'Set out for Harwich, like Father, grave and comfortable'—'Be Rock of Gibraltar'. In vain did he fortify his soul with that 'Inviolable Plan' drawn up on October 16, 1763, 'to be read over frequently'.

> 'Keep quite clear of gloomy notions which have nothing to do with the mild and elegant religion of Jesus.... You can live quite independent and go to London every year; and you can pass some months at Auchinleck, doing good to your tenants, and living hospitably with your neighbours, beautifying your estate, rearing a family, and piously preparing for immortal felicity.... τίμα σεαυτόν: reverence thyself.'

But all this could not conquer the 'hyp'. 'You was dreadfully melancholy and had the last and most dreadful thoughts.' Or again—'You got up dreary as a dromedary.' Or again—'You awaked shocked, having dreamt you was condemned to be hanged.'

Most of Boswell's *Holland Journal* got lost between Utrecht and Auchinleck; though notes, memoranda, and letters survive. But it is, probably, a far smaller loss than the *London Journal*, or the journal of the Grand Tour would have been. For, to be frank, Boswell's surviving records of Holland are somewhat boring—because he was himself bored.

However, in January 1764, Boswell cheered himself by courting

the people of England hang and drown themselves." ' According to Voltaire, east winds sufficed to drive us to suicide; and Diderot describes a pond in St James's Park as reserved for ladies so intending. See Matthew Green's charming poem *The Spleen* (1737).

[1] *Holland Journal*, December 19, 1763.

a pretty Dutch widow of twenty-five, Catherina Elisabeth Geelvinck, with £4,000 a year. (Boswell was apt to keep one eye on romance, the other on finance—though it was not for money that he married in the end.) But this was a brief passion. It is clear that one part of him had a haunting dread of marriage. In April he told her, 'I adore you, but I would not marry you for anything in the world. My feelings are changed'. To which she replied, as well she might, 'You are very frank'. But a more serious entanglement followed.

As early as the previous October Boswell had been struck by Madame Geelvinck's friend, another Elisabeth—Isabella Agneta Elisabeth van Tuyll van Serooskerken van Zuylen, called more shortly 'Belle de Zuylen' or, more shortly still, 'Zélide'.[1] This young lady Boswell calculated to be worth £20,000; and round her tantalizing brilliance he was to flutter intermittently for four and a half years.

Sprung from a stiff and stolid Dutch aristocracy, daughter of a worthy father with a house in Utrecht and a moated château near by, Zélide was a creature as incongruous in such surroundings as a figure by Watteau set in an interior by Pieter de Hooch. She not only wrote, she lived and felt, as if she had been a vivacious child of France. 'Ici,' she groaned, 'l'on est vif tout seul.' 'Une demoiselle, cela, une demoiselle!'—was the comment of a disapproving dowager. Why, the girl had even written a scandalous tale, *Le Noble*, about the daughter of an ancient French house who, to join her *parvenu* lover, skipped out of a window and, even more flippant than Charles Surface, used some of the family portraits to bridge the muddy ditch underneath—'she had never thought one could find so much support from ancestors'.[2]

That sentence alone should have warned off an old Scotch baron,

[1] Born 1740; began in 1760 her long correspondence (1760–75) with Constant d'Hermenches, Swiss officer in the Dutch service, bored by a wife seven years his senior; 1763, published *Le Noble*, and met Boswell; 1764–8, schemed to marry the Marquis de Bellegarde (1720–90), a Catholic Savoyard in the Dutch service; 1771, married M. de Charrière; 1784, *Mistress Henley*, *Lettres Neuchâteloises*; 1785, *Lettres de Lausanne*; 1787, met Benjamin Constant in Paris; 1788, *Caliste*; 1797, *Les Trois Femmes*; 1805, died. See P. Godet, *Mme. de Charrière et ses Amis* (Geneva, 1906), *Lettres de Mme. de Charrière à Constant d'Hermenches* (Paris, 1909); Geoffrey Scott, *The Portrait of Zélide* (1934).

[2] 'Jamais Julie n'avait cru qu'on pût tirer si bon parti des grands-pères.'

with feudal notions, like 'Boswell d'Auchinleck'. Here was no mate for him—merely a foreign enchantress as unsuited to his temperament as Suzanne Curchod to Edward Gibbon, or the Marguerite of Thun to Matthew Arnold.

Zélide was brilliant and sensitive,[1] where Boswell was naïve and obtuse; she hated cant as fiercely as Johnson, where Boswell was a son of illusion; she was free-thinking in religion and morals[2] to a degree that would have outraged Johnson, while Boswell was always yearning, though with no great success, to become respectable and *retenu*; in fine, he was bourgeois where she was an aristocratic rebel, and his ambitions were as conventional as hers were audacious. His courtship suggests a cockerel by fits and starts pursuing a dragon-fly; once caught, how she would have disagreed with him!

But how should a young couple of twenty-three be blamed for not seeing all that?

She was fascinating, and he was amorous; she was intelligent, and he had a passion for intellectual eminence, though much afraid of it in women; he was frank and vivacious, and she lived choking in a fog of dull respectability. Further, beneath their surface gaiety, both were melancholy, tormented personalities.

If it be asked how this quick-witted girl, who was one day to write delicate, yet incisive fiction, as much beyond Boswell's reach as his pertinacious chronicling of fact would have been beyond hers, could yet tolerate a lover so much less acute and sensitive than herself, the answer, I suppose, may lie simply in the attraction of his vitality and spontaneity. But I think there was more than that. Zélide was a very curious character.

Not only was she extremely versatile and capricious—'tantôt musicienne, tantôt géomètre,[3] tantôt soi-disant poète, tantôt femme frivole, tantôt femme passionnée, tantôt froide et paisible philosophe'. Not only was she fastidious—'je crains toujours d'avoir trop de tout. Une grosse portion du meilleur plat me fait peur; je ne vide presque jamais un verre; je mange la moitié de dix pêches, de dix poires, plutôt qu'une pêche ou une poire entière, essayant

1 'Vous rechaufferiez des Lapons.' (Constant d'Hermenches, November 18, 1766.)

2 'Si j'avais ni père ni mère, je serais Ninon peut-être, mais plus délicate, et plus constante, je n'aurais pas tant d'amants.'

3 She rose early to study conic sections!

toujours et ne m'attachant qu'à la perfection qu'il est si rare de trouver.' In addition, she seems obsessed by some odd impulse to marry a husband intellectually or morally beneath her. For years she used her ingenuity, and that of her confidant Constant d'Hermenches, to catch a worthy, dull Savoyard, twenty years her elder, the Marquis de Bellegarde; despite the obstacle that he was Catholic, she Protestant. Later she inclined, without having seen him, to Lord Wemyss, an exiled Jacobite, dissolute and ferocious—'No matter, a being such as I am now, deserves, at the most, a Lord Wemyss.' Marriage often becomes a penance; but it is seldom thus deliberately sought as one. In the end she gave her hand to a worthy, naïve Swiss, once her brother's tutor, M. de Charrière.

It might be supposed that she behaved thus strangely from a desire to dominate an inferior husband. Possibly. Yet it would not, one imagines, have been easy to dominate Lord Wemyss. Her tone about this last match suggests rather that she was one of those maladjusted characters whose inner sense of guilt drives them unconsciously to thwart their own lives, and nullify their own successes, in self-punishment. But we cannot know. Certainly, if unhappiness was her secret aim, she succeeded.

But all this was to come. Meanwhile, with alternate attraction and repulsion this curious pair circled about each other, from October 1763, when Boswell first appears taken with her, to May 1768, when she finally broke with him. It would be hard to find a courtship more curious, or an episode more vividly revealing Boswell. The course of this only half-true love runs far from smooth—on the contrary it hobbles grotesquely to its grotesque conclusion, while Boswell now hectors Zélide as if he were John Knox preaching to Mary Stuart, now pleads for her affection; now says he could not possibly marry her, now begs her to marry him; now denies that he loves her, now taxes her with loving him; and at intervals, as chorus to the comedy, drags in Zélide's father, Zélide's brother, his own father, his friend Temple, even Rousseau.

Two months after reaching Utrecht, in some of those appalling verses he set himself as daily task,[1] Boswell wrote (October 31, 1763):

[1] He was still spasmodically practising his 'Ten Lines a Day' as late as 1780. If persistence could make a poet. . . .

And yet just now a Utrecht lady's charms
Make my gay bosom beat with love's alarms.
Who could have thought to see young Cupid fly
Through Belgia's thick and suffocating sky?

Soon Boswell and Zélide were meeting frequently. Acquaintances began to assure him he was loved. Unfortunately he was not only attracted, he was also shocked. For Zélide, he thought, rattled too impudently. (Boswell might allow Boswell to rattle; but not women.) She 'grinned' too much. She mocked. She was metaphysical. She held views positively libertine. 'Zélide,' he records to himself, 'was nervish. You saw she would make a sad wife and propagate wretches.'

And yet? Parting, as partings will, brought a crisis.[1] For now, in June 1764, after ten months' work, Boswell was setting off for twenty months' holiday. On June 14–17 Zélide wrote him (in French) what was half a love-letter. For the last three or four days, she says, she has been thinking less of the man she may marry (the Marquis de Bellegarde). 'It is because you,[2] my philosophical friend, appeared to me to be experiencing the agitation of a lover.' 'I find you odd and lovable. I have a higher regard for you than for anyone, and I am proud of being your friend.'

Then a sudden tease. Boswell had formerly said he would not correspond with her without her father's knowledge: yet now he wants to! This she finds 'less admirable'. (Naturally she does not mention that for four years she has been secretly corresponding with Constant d'Hermenches, married and seventeen years her senior.)

Then she finds unwise the advice Boswell had given her, to choose a cold husband. In that case she would certainly have lovers.

[1] Cf. Zélide's words, in quite another context, to her married friend, Constant d'Hermenches (October 1764): 'Un ami qui part ou qui meurt devient souvent, d'un homme fort ordinaire qu'il avait toujours paru, un ami parfait, un trésor inestimable.' (One of the central ideas of Stendhal and Proust also.)

[2] Zélide had not yet even seen this gentleman. Her letters give me the impression that she wished to marry Bellegarde mainly because he was the candidate favoured by Constant d'Hermenches; who at this time really had more of her affection than anyone else. Indeed her long pursuit of Bellegarde is one of the most enigmatic actions of this enigmatic young woman. At times it puzzled Zélide herself—'Il est singulier de renverser ciel et terre, de combattre des monstres, de combler des abîmes, pour un mariage sans passion.' (To Constant d'Hermenches, August 12, 1765.)

(At this point Boswell must have bristled with disapproval.) 'But,' she adds, 'I am writing to Cato. Cato's friend is very unlike him, but loves him much.'

Then, lest Boswell-Cato be too elated by this confession, another little douche of cold water. 'Not all agitations, thank God, are infectious. . . . A few days' absence should be sufficient to enable both to forget it.'

Then warmth again. He *can* write to her secretly, through a certain bookseller—'not often, but write long letters.' 'I will send every fortnight to him to ask.' (Once a fortnight, one might think, is pretty 'often'.) Also, he had better write to her father from Berlin.

And so to the close—'Good-bye, I have said everything; or at least I have said much.'

A curious letter. Dangerous coquette, or bewildered young woman? Or both? Probably both. But it would be rash to say.

This missive she handed to Boswell on June 17, just before his departure. 'She gave me her hand at parting, and the tender tear stood crystal in her eye.'

Next day, June 18, Boswell answered, 'much flattered.' But with prudent reserves. 'I admire your mind. I love your goodness. But I am not in love with you. I swear to you I am not.' In days to come he was to unswear that often enough.

To this denial of love Zélide wrote a reply the same evening (June 18), with apparent satisfaction. 'So much the better, my friend. . . . Your friendship is more worth having than love.' Then a lot more about friendship. Then—'it would be a pleasant thing for once to think of no one, at least for a few days. But this wretched man that I love[1] does not leave me in calm for long.'

Next day she continued: 'You are very right to say that I should be worth nothing as your wife. . . . I have no subaltern talents.' (The truth of that, indeed, poor M. de Charrière was to find.) She wants Boswell for her mentor. (She can hardly have realized how much he wanted other people to be *his*.) And she explains her religious difficulties—'I hope they will not lose me a friend's esteem.'

A piquant correspondence; yet I cannot help wishing that Zélide,

[1] Bellegarde.

amusing as she is, had been a little less double-faced—I do not mean about surreptitious correspondences (after all, she was now twenty-three), but about poor M. de Bellegarde and James Boswell.

On June 18, 1764, a coach-and-four trotted out of Utrecht carrying Boswell, his friend the Earl Marischal Keith,[1] and a taciturn Turkish lady, Emetulla, Keith's protégée.[2] For three weeks silence descends between Boswell and Zélide. But on July 9 he more than made up for lost time with a letter from Berlin of no less than seventeen pages. Nor was it only a matter of size. Not even Jane Austen's Mr Collins ever penned epistle more portentous.

He apologizes for delay in writing; but sets forth in lofty tones how severely his life is planned. 'Boswell when cool and sedate fixes rules for Boswell to live by.' 'When such a man as I am employs his great judgment to regulate small matters, methinks he resembles a giant washing teacups.... There now is a pompous affectation of dignity; you must expect a good deal of this from me.'

This 'system' of his, he explains, forbade his writing till his journey was done—even if she did have to wait four weeks. He had even 'vanity enough' to enjoy picturing her anxiety 'as a friend'. 'Love is a passion which you and I have no thought of: at least for each other.'[3]

Next comes a sermon to Zélide on prudence. 'Thou favourite of Nature ... let Prudence be thy Counsellor. Learn to be mistress of thyself.' In his enthusiasm Boswell even soars into verse.

> ... The buxom lass whom you may always see
> So mighty nat'ral and so mighty free,
> A vulgar bosom may with love inspire,
> But Art must form the woman I admire....[4]

[1] 1693?–1778.

[2] She was a Janissary's daughter, captured by the Earl Marischal's brother, Marshal Keith (1696–1758), at the siege of Oczakow or Ochakov; and was now married to a M. de Froment, Colonel in the Sardinian service.

Oddly enough life brought her in the end, like Zélide, to retirement in Neuchâtel, where she died in 1820, almost a centenarian.

[3] These five words are not without point. For of course, on the journey, Boswell had flirted with the Turkish lady. 'I was pleased,' says his journal, 'with the romantic idea of making love to a Turk.' However—'I talked morality at last and thought myself a Johnson.' Who, indeed, could picture Dr Johnson making love to a Turk?

[4] Actually this lyric flight had been composed as part of his task-verses for October 3, 1763, nine months before.

(Boswell and Zélide were never to meet again. Otherwise she would have all my sympathy had she boxed his ears.)

Then a further preachment on abandoning pleasure, on following Nature, on the divine mission of Christ and his 'amiable collection of precepts'. 'My notions of God's beneficence are grand and extensive.' But let not a mere female like Zélide venture on metaphysical speculations—which 'in a woman are more absurd than I choose to express'. Much better 'embroider a waistcoat for your brother'.

The theme of prudence returns. She has a handsome fortune, and 'Zélide herself is handsome'. She should marry well. 'But take care.' She is vain. 'Do you think your *reason* is as distinguished as your imagination? Believe me, Zélide, it is not. Believe me, and endeavour to improve.'

And then her 'libertine sentiments'! 'Fie, my Zélide, what fancies are these?'

Next a demure paragraph on his own journey, with a demurely discreet reference to the silent Turkish lady. He has also seen the Comte d'Anhalt, one of Zélide's possible matches.

Then Boswell launches a sudden attack. She *was* in love when she wrote to him at their parting! 'You was pleasing yourself with having at last met with the man for whom you could have a strong and lasting passion.' But no—'I would not be married to you to be a king: I know myself and I know you.' (How little he knew of either!)

Then, suddenly, a new change of front. 'Love,' he had said in his second paragraph, 'is a passion which you and I have no thought of.' But now—'Tell me that you will make a very good wife.... Could you live quietly in the country six months in the year? Could you make yourself agreeable to plain honest neighbours? Could you talk like any other woman, and have your fancy as much at command as your harpsichord? ... Could you give spirits to your husband when he is melancholy?[1] I have known such wives, Zélide. What think you? Could you be such a one?'

[1] Professor Pottle, while granting that Boswell is here picturing Zélide as Mrs Boswell, thinks Zélide took this as referring to her possible marriage to his friend Temple—an idea he had also played with. But could she be so dense? (The 'melancholy', though Temple also suffered from it, seems particularly Boswellian.)

Then, after a brief exhortation to be a *happy* Christian—'worship the sun rather than be a Calvinist'—Boswell plunges into a postscript, which he unsealed his letter to add:

> 'If you love me, own it. I can give you the best advice. If you love another, tell me. . . . I love you more than ever. I would do more than ever to serve you. I would kneel and kiss your hand if I saw you married to the man that could make you happy.'

This seems well enough. But then he lurches back into his tactless insistence that she had been passionately in love with himself.

> 'If I had pretended a passion for you . . . would you not have gone with me to the world's end?[1] Supposing even that I had been disinherited by my father. . . . Zélide, Zélide, excuse my vanity. But I tell you you do not know yourself, if you say that you would not have done thus.'

'Was ever woman in this humour wooed?' But Zélide was not won. Strange if she had been. It is all psychologically fascinating to watch. But what frantic folly to tax a young woman with being in love with oneself, as pertinaciously as a public prosecutor indicting a prisoner in the dock!

Zélide had gone to bed, tired; but these seventeen pages with their 'seventeen thousand thoughts' (so she wrote to Constant d'Hermenches) 'made her unable to stay in bed a quarter of an hour'. But, though his interminable, havering letter might set her head buzzing, poor Boswell, on the whole, meant less to her than his vanity supposed. And he had hardly improved his chances.

> He has stretched a swift hand
> To caress the free head,
> The shy hare that was friendship
> To the covert has sped.[2]

Boswell could not know that, in this same July, d'Hermenches had brought his friend Bellegarde, for the first time, to Zélide's

[1] Cf. his behaviour to Margaret Boswell, p. 236.
[2] Susan Miles.

home; and that Zélide by now had little thought to spare for her Scots lover. 'Boswell,' she told her father, 'ne m'épousera jamais; s'il m'épousait, il en aurait mille repentirs, et je ne sais si je voudrais vivre en Écosse.' D'Hermenches, that August, was still more emphatic—'Quant à l'Écosse je frémis seulement à cette idée; c'est un pays perdu et des mœurs féroces, où je ne voudrais jamais laisser aller le plus misérable des êtres auxquels je m'intéresserais.' D'Hermenches, no doubt, was prejudiced; it seems clear that he wanted Zélide married in some region where he could easily meet her himself. But anyway, in Zélide's letters for the next three years, Boswell was to be quite eclipsed by Bellegarde.

At the end of the month, however (July 30, 1764), Boswell tried a new line of attack. From Berlin he wrote to her father (who had, of course, no suspicion that Boswell was corresponding with his daughter). He thanks Monsieur de Zuylen for his past civilities—'You had the goodness to treat me, I shall not say as though you were my father, but—as though you were my father-in-law.' Then Boswell hastily eats that bold word 'father-in-law'—he has used it merely for novelty, so as not to say 'what every one else has said a thousand times'. It must not be repeated to 'my charming friend Zélide'. (Then he decided to erase 'charming'.) For 'she would make a very different application of it from the one that I intended'. 'I like to seek novelty only in things which depend on taste, on imagination. But I am afraid that Zélide would seek novelty in serious matters. . . . My dear Sir, excuse this jocularity.' (The contortions become excruciatingly clumsy.)

Then a few details on his travels. Berlin is pleasant—including the pretty daughter of the President of Police, who plays the harpsichord and makes Boswell laugh. 'Up to now she has had a surprising influence on me. I am very curious to see how long it can last.' (It must be doubted if jealousy was a good card to play with Zélide.)

Presumably this letter was meant, despite its confidential tone, to be passed on, in whole or part, to Zélide; who might not have appreciated the comments on her imprudence. Actually she was made aware at least of the admiring parts; and amused her parents in return by relating Boswell's reasons against marrying her. But she still did not write to him. However, her father did, in a friendly tone; mentioning that he was worried about 'the marriage of a young lady for whom I ought to feel concern'. (This finessing on all sides grows oppressive.)

On September 18 Boswell replied to Zélide's father from Potsdam. Why, he asks, had Monsieur de Zuylen not said frankly that the marriage-question worrying him was Zélide's? A marriage with Baron Brömbsen? With the Comte d'Anhalt? No doubt, says Boswell, it might seem odd to consult so young a man as himself. Yet he is, after all, Zélide's 'mentor'. Perhaps he has exaggerated her faults—'your great philosophers are a little eccentric', and apt to fear too much. He hopes for her happiness. Then a postscript—he has parted with regret from the young lady of Berlin. 'She is very amiable. But alas! Sir, I shall never see her again. A traveller ought to have a great deal of friendliness, but no susceptibility.'

All this art, however, brought no reply from Zélide. On October 1 Boswell wrote to her again from Anhalt-Dessau. Why has she never answered? Is she displeased? Then out trots again that tiresome accusation that she had been really in love with him; followed by a plea for a letter, even if the last.

On December 11 Monsieur de Zuylen belatedly replied. Yes, it *was* Zélide's marriage that worried him. However, there was no more question now of Baron de Brömbsen or the Comte d'Anhalt. The letter ends with a little trivial news.

Presumably Boswell grew more and more tantalized. On December 25 he wrote back to M. de Zuylen from Geneva, welcoming this confidence—'if ever probity has existed on earth, it exists in the heart of Boswell'. 'I find her more and more charming.' (He had not had a word from her for half a year.) 'I begin to retreat from some of my prejudices towards her.' (This seems rashly presumptuous.) Yet he cannot make out how he stands. Will Monsieur de Zuylen either give her the enclosed letter, or burn it? Boswell has just seen Rousseau, and won his friendship; now he is to stay with Voltaire.[1] (In fine, he is becoming a great man; and thinks seriously of proposing to Zélide.)

Boswell's enclosed letter to Zélide yet again taxes her with her

[1] This may have impressed Zélide less than he hoped. In 1772 she refused to visit Voltaire herself—'C'est un méchant homme de beaucoup d'esprit. Je le lirai, mais je n'irai pas l'encenser.'

fond expressions to him in the past (one could scream); supporting the accusation with full quotations. Then the tone grows lofty. 'You ought to be flattered by my attachment. I know not if I ought to be equally flattered by yours. A man who has a mind and heart like mine is rare. A woman with many talents is not so rare.' Then, suddenly, the accuser's pride falters. 'O Zélide . . . I had almost come to count upon your heart. I had almost—My friend, have I been mistaken?'

Three days later, however, on December 28, 1764, his tone to Temple from Ferney becomes much more exasperated and less plaintive. 'And must I then marry a Dutchwoman? Must the proud Boswell yield to a tender inclination? Must he in the strength and vigour of his youth resign his liberty for life to one woman?' And yet . . . 'Should he not thank the Powers Above for having shown him Zélide, a young lady free from all the faults of her sex, with genius, with good humour, with elegant accomplishments? But, my dear Temple, she is not by half so rich as I thought. She has only £400 a year. Besides, I am not pleased with her conduct . . . I own that both of us are sadly undetermined. However, I hope the best.' This was hardly the way to find it.

Finally, after half a year's silence, Zélide replied on January 27, 1765, with friendly warmth in her first lines—but then with growing heat at his imputations of her being in love with him. 'I was shocked and saddened to find, in a friend whom I had conceived of as a young and sensible man, the puerile vanity of a fatuous fool, coupled with the arrogant rigidity of an old Cato.' For a moment, she admits, her senses *may* have been excited by him. But that was, at most, for a moment. 'I have not ceased to be your friend, and I shall be your friend always.'

This would have chastened most lovers. Of Boswell's answer (April 3, 1765, probably from Rome) only a postscript survives, to the effect that he will say more hereafter. 'Know then, my dear friend, that I am prepared to make you a recital which will surprise you.' But meanwhile—'Believe me, Zélide, it is you who have not sufficiently entered into the singular character of your amiable and proud Scot.' (A curious way of trying to enter the heart of this elusive and proud young Dutchwoman.) However, 'You have advanced many steps on the path. That was fine; and I know but one man who could have withstood you.' If only she had 'spoken everything out'!

To this she replied on May 25. Her father had nearly caught her writing to him. Boswell is too systematic, too fond of reasoning and preaching; though in practice he is not always so impeccable himself. Next winter she may marry Bellegarde.[1]

At this point one or more of Boswell's letters to her appear to be missing. But from Paris on January 16, 1766, after meeting there Zélide's brother, Willem, and being encouraged by him, Boswell made a more determined attempt on Monsieur de Zuylen, in a document truly amazing.

Here Boswell explains that in his days at Utrecht he had already thought of Zélide as a wife, despite 'the mistaken—and dare I say it?—licentious ideas of her imagination'. (This seems to me a caddish phrase.) She had shown a preference for him; but his lips had been sealed by her faults, his own melancholy, and his probity. 'And I swear to you that in so acting I had the pride of an heroic soul.'

But, now, does she still prefer him? And is she free? If not, 'let the blood of De Tuyll be ever fired for the sentiment of honour'. (One would have thought the De Tuylls could guard their honour without exhortations from Boswell.)

He is not in love. 'Had I that fever in my soul, I should not be thinking of a calm, conjugal engagement.' He is, also, too young to marry. Yet he is loth to miss Zélide.

But a church marriage would not be enough. Zélide must further swear before her father and two of her brothers to be always faithful; not to see or write to anyone her husband and brothers disapprove; nor to publish anything without their approbation; nor to speak against the ways of her new country.

Then follows a dream-picture of the bliss of the united families of Boswell and van Zuylen. Although Boswell has in the past attacked Holland, he now recants and sees it 'like the fields of the pious patriarchs. The amiable Belle would be my Rebecca. But she has not enough feeling for nature. To speak the truth, she has not enough feeling for anything solid or real.' (He had a queer love-hate for her.)

[1] In October 1765, she would be twenty-five, and so her own mistress—free, if she wished, to marry Bellegarde, despite her parents' objections to his Roman Catholicism.

Then another vision, of the prospective career of James Boswell Esq. 'I am singular and romantic, and such a character is made to give her infinite pleasure. . . . Since being in Corsica, since making such proofs of my talents and address, I am more proud than ever.'

But after this self-panegyric Boswell is seized anew by panic. He and Zélide are both hypochondriacs. 'My knowledge is very restricted. I have an excess of self-esteem. I cannot apply myself to study. . . . I have the greatest imaginable difficulty in overcoming avarice.' 'Judge, I beg you, if she would not be happier with Monsieur de B—.'

Finally, with another burst of tact, he taxes Monsieur de Zuylen with having himself contemplated Boswell as son-in-law. As usual with Boswell, there follows a postscript. His doubts return. 'Do not bind a worthy Scot in the chains of a melancholy regret. . . . The thought of marriage affects me with fear.' Did ever man, since Panurge consulted Pantagruel, so oscillate between the wish to marry and the dread of it?

It is piquant, and somewhat crushing for Boswell, to compare this effusion with the letter Zélide wrote Constant d'Hermenches, for transmission to her father on behalf of Bellegarde. Her conduct becomes at times distastefully tortuous; but in intelligence and finesse there can be no comparison between Boswell and her.

At this point, Boswell's mother having died, his father summoned him home (January 1766). And Monsieur de Zuylen was gently discouraging, on the ground that 'Monsieur de B's case is not settled'.

In October 1766, Zélide came to London for the winter; but she sent no word to Boswell; though her brother did. Sir John Pringle found her too vivacious. She ate roast beef and plum pudding with Hume (April 1767), whose simple honesty she liked. And Boswell wrote to Temple, piqued, 'I am well rid of her'. But he was not quite rid of her yet.

A year later, in the autumn of 1767, Boswell wrote to Zélide proposing to re-open correspondence; and in January 1768, discouraged in his courtship of Miss Blair, he wrote yet again, again professing love. This brought back some deserved taunts from Utrecht (February 16, 1768). 'Allow me to remark that you certainly take your time for everything. You waited to fall in love with me until you were in the island of Corsica; and to tell me so, you waited until you were in love with another woman and had spoken to her of marriage.... I read your belated endearments with pleasure, with a smile.' None the less she will be charmed to translate his *Corsica*.

It must be borne in mind that in January of this year 1768 Zélide had finally, after three and a half years of vain effort, abandoned hope of Bellegarde, who had shown himself hopelessly unpractical and unenterprising about getting the dispensation he needed for marriage with a heretic. He felt, he said finally, that he was unworthy of her; which means, I suppose, that he found the lady too formidable.[1]

Meanwhile Zélide's February letter was answered by Boswell within ten days (February 26, 1768). His past hesitations, he pleads, were due only to his melancholia. He is now quit of Miss Blair. What would Zélide advise? (In short, this half-hearted lover wanted to be proposed to.)

With delay, his feelings rose. 'Upon my soul, Temple,' he wrote on March 24, 1768, 'I must have her.' April brought a kind letter from his mistress, and Boswell asked his father's leave to set off for Utrecht.

But unfortunately—as if he were unconsciously resolved to leave no stone unturned to thwart himself—he also wrote Zélide a letter now lost, putting 'in the plainest light what conduct I absolutely require of her, and what my father will require.' (This concerned, in part at least, 'her levity and infidel notions'.) He also forbade her to make certain changes she had proposed in translating his *Corsica*.[2]

This was the last straw. Boswell's diary, May 2, 1768, tersely records—'Letter from Zélide—termagant.' They wrote no more. A later reference to Boswell in her letters to d'Hermenches (who was now helping, in the French service, to conquer Boswell's be-

[1] Two or three years later, at fifty or so, he married a girl in her teens, who bore him three daughters, then died in 1776, aged twenty-three. He survived till 1790.

[2] Zélide to Constant d'Hermenches, June 2, 1768: 'L'auteur, quoiqu'il fût dans ce moment presque décidé à m'épouser, n'a pas voulu sacrifier à mon goût une syllabe de son livre. Je lui ai écrit que j'étais très décidée à ne jamais l'épouser, et j'ai abandonnée la traduction.'

loved Corsicans) is bitter. She still thinks the French cause unjust: but perhaps Boswell's *Corsica* has misled her. 'Je n'étais rien moins qu'enthousiasmée de Boswell, et je voyais beaucoup de mauvais goût dans son livre, mais peut-être j'avais trop d'estime pour Paoli.'

As Landor said:

> The brightest stars are not the best
> To follow on the road to rest.

One cannot imagine her married to Boswell and enduring his extravagances with the patience of Margaret Montgomerie; much as one may wish that her rapier could have encountered the club of Johnson.[1] And so, after the brilliant matches she might have made, she settled down in stolid Swiss Neuchâtel with the excellent and reasonable M. de Charrière—simple as La Fontaine—who turned out to have, for her, the irredeemable fault of having no faults at all. *That* tragicomedy she has recorded, calmly but piercingly, in her story *Mistress Henley*:

> 'Vous avez cru,' says Mrs Henley to her Grandison of a husband, '—et qui ne l'aurait cru?—que trouvant dans son mari tout ce qui peut rendre un homme aimable et estimable, et dans sa situation tous les plaisirs honnêtes, l'opulence, et la considération, une femme raisonnable ne pouvait manquer d'être heureuse. Mais je ne suis pas une femme raisonnable, vous et moi l'avons vu trop tard.'

The eighteenth-century mind is beginning to realize that reason alone is not enough. And yet Madame de Charrière kept the faith of her age. When the passion and frenzy of the French Revolution had burst the dykes of reason, she could still advise women to study logic, and set a young woman in her circle to read Locke. For the example of the French émigrés had only deepened her conviction 'how necessary it is to have the habit of strict reasoning, in order not to fall into vulgar fallacies the moment we are tempted by any

[1] And yet at times how she and Johnson would have agreed! She had the same contempt for cant, the same stoicism; her motto was Gresset's verse:

> Un esprit mâle et vraiment sage,
> Dans le plus invincible ennui,
> Dédaigne le triste avantage
> De se faire plaindre d'autrui.

motive of pain or resentment'. That at least is still true; though Locke may not prove a wholly adequate remedy. Already when it came to signing the marriage-contract with M. de Charrière, she had trembled, shuddered, and recoiled. And yet he was so good and honourable—'le moyen de renoncer à cet homme!' All the same her less conscious mind knew better—on the wedding-night Zélide had neuralgia; and the rest of her married life was in keeping with its melancholy commencement. She loved a mediocre youth, who left her for another; and she loved, at forty-seven, the brilliant young Benjamin Constant, aged twenty, who left her in 1794 for her *bête noire*, Madame de Staël, that rising star of the new Romantic dawn.

Naturally she could not in any case have held a youth twenty-seven years her junior; but in her correspondence with him there emerges that weakness of the eighteenth-century mind, its inability ever to stop reasoning and analysing. She knew so well that the end must come, that she hastened its coming by harping on it. 'All love decays. We love. Therefore our love will decay. I will *not* be a dupe. Therefore I *will* talk of its decay'—so one may summarize the argument; and so the love does decay, sooner than it needed; or perhaps when it need not have decayed at all. It is vital, no doubt, to face facts; but it is the reverse of rational to be always facing facts, even before they are there. Minds so edged can cut the flowers of life long before they would naturally have withered. So ended Zélide, as a sharp-sighted, disillusioned, stoic character—in her own words, 'toujours mécontente d'elle-même', 'partout étrangère.' At times she recalls Madame du Deffand, who in her old age loved Horace Walpole, just as the ageing Zélide loved the young Benjamin Constant. Human love failed them both. But Zélide found, at least, a last outlet in passionate protectiveness towards the unfortunate,[1] and in novels that recall at moments the humanity of Goldsmith, at times the minute perceptiveness of Jane Austen, at times the new, romantic passionateness of Goethe's *Werther*.

She travelled in the end far from her Boswell. She grew up as he never could. Perhaps she grew up too much, into that bleakness

[1] For example, her maid, Henriette Monachon, who was with child by the coachman. The local pastor, having vainly demanded the woman's dismissal, broke off relations with Zélide in a letter signed—'Chaillet, serviteur de Jésus-Christ.' Comment by Zélide: 'On ne dira pas, "Tel maître, tel valet."'

which sees too far into life, and through it. Ten years after her old lover was laid to rest at Auchinleck, beneath the family-crest of the hooded hawk and that too ironic motto *Vraye Foi*, Zélide also died; two days after the Christmas of 1805, while in men's ears still echoed the guns of Trafalgar and Austerlitz, and Switzerland lay prostrate as a French dependency, and Zélide's own Holland was about to receive Louis Bonaparte as king. She had outlived her world. Perhaps this eighteenth-century heroine was best judged by Benjamin Constant who, for his own undoing, was torn between the analytic reason of the past age and the romantic passion of the new—'Madame de Charrière a plus d'esprit qu'il n'en faut pour faire trembler la moitié de la Germanie.' 'Comme cet esprit allait toujours tout droit son chemin, il passait sur le ventre à bien des choses, mais il avait le grand mérite d'être exempt de toute affectation, d'être pour lui-même et par lui-même sans se dénaturer pour plaire aux autres.'[1] But—'Je suis convaincu que, sans ces conversations, ma conduite eût été beaucoup moins folle. Toutes les opinions de Madame de Charrière reposaient sur le mépris de toutes les convenances et tous les usages.' Boswell's fears had come too true.

And yet this is not at all the atmosphere of her stories—which have often an idealistic and romantic tone. Zélide remains an enigma. She was that even to herself—'Plus je me vois, plus je suis surprise; plus je me regarde, moins je me connais.'

She gives the impression of a clever, but impulsive and variable person—of a character free in thought and free in language, irresistibly drawn to flirtation (the correspondence with d'Hermenches is most bizarre in its tight-rope dance between friendship and something more) and yet, one half suspects, physically inhibited towards the passion of normal lovers—with all her charm, a type of woman dangerous to others, and disastrous to herself. From this point, at all events, she was out of Boswell's life—and so much the better for both—yet not till she had drawn from him some of his most characteristic writing.

She has tempted us, seductress that she still remains, to a long digression from James Boswell. But I am unrepentant. She throws so vivid a light both on Boswell and on their century. Never, surely,

[1] Cf. her advice to a young woman-friend—'Ayez des idées nettes et des expressions simples' (the essence of the eighteenth-century spirit at its best).

did even Shakespeare conceive lover so ludicrous. Indeed Boswell as lover is too farcical for fiction. And yet when we have laughed at the comedy, something deeper and darker remains. Boswell's hopeless ignorance of life, amusing enough in youth, was to lead on hereafter to the tragic pathos of his later years. We may smile at these odd lovers whispering together above the moats of Zuylen; but those are hard-hearted, I think, who merely smile; forgetting the bitterness of both their ends.

Tragedy is true guise;
Comedy lies.

But it is time to return from the story of Zélïde, with its sombre close in after-years, to the gay young Boswell rolling eastwards out of Utrecht on his Grand Tour, under that summer sun of 1764, in company with the old Earl Marischal and the sphinx-like Turkish lady.

At Berlin Boswell resolved to add Frederick the Great to his list of lions interviewed—'I despair not to make him speak. I will let him see that he has before him a man of no common clay.' (To Temple, July 23, 1764.) He even felt an impulse at Charlottenburg to throw himself at Frederick's feet and explain. This might, indeed, have moved Frederick to speak; though Boswell might not have liked what he heard. Unfortunately for comic history, Boswell contented himself with a more modest expectation of speaking to his hero in the world to come. He was worried, however, by Frederick's unbelief. If only the hero could be converted? 'Perhaps he would be the greatest of enthusiasts, and would write a magnificent poem in praise of his faith.' Seldom did even Boswell's fantasy soar to quite such a pitch. For it is hard to say which was least likely to occur in Frederick the Great—'enthusiasm', Christian faith, or magnificent poetry.

From Berlin Boswell returned to Brunswick where he coquetted with ladies of the court. 'My mind was clear and firm and fertile. It contained in itself both male and female powers; brilliant fancies were begotten, and brilliant fancies were brought forth.'

He also worshipped in the ducal chapel. 'It was quite heaven and I adored my God, and I hoped for immortal joy. It was really grand to see the serene family of Brunswick at their devotions.' (Was there ever mind less conscious of incongruities?)

Here too he formed the scheme of writing to Johnson, asking him for 'a solemn assurance of perpetual friendship, so that I might march under his protection while he lived, and after his death, imagine that his shade beckoned me to the skies. Grand, yet enthusiastic, idea!'

Then he jaunted back to Berlin, where occurred a trivial escapade, extraordinary only for Boswell's treatment of it. He had a *passade* with a woman who came to his room selling chocolate.

> 'Bless me, have I now committed adultery? Stay, a soldier's wife is no wife. Should I now torment myself with speculations on sin, and on losing in one morning the merit of a year's chastity? No: this is womanish. Nay, your elegant mystics would not do so. Madame Guyon was of opinion that sin should be forgotten as soon as possible, as being an idea too gross for the mind of a saint, and disturbing the exercise of sweet devotion. Her notion is ingenious.'

(And this was the mind that thought it could instruct Zélide!)

At Wittenberg he had another 'most curious and agreeable idea' —of writing to Johnson from the very tomb of Melanchthon the Reformer (1498–1560). As the tomb consisted of a large metal-plate in the floor, Boswell had to lay himself prone and, in this posture, pen his letter beneath the gaping gaze of astonished Wittenbergers. Then, after all, his courage failed. Not for thirteen years did he dare lay his effusion in Johnson's hands—it was, he felt, 'too superstitious and too enthusiastick'.

At Karlsruhe, a further adventure—a young infidel courtier. 'I talked to him with firm vivacity; I showed him how inferior he was to me.'

Strasbourg—Bâle—Soleure. At Soleure they were building a church. 'When Mr Addison was here, there was a church a-building. When Mr. Boswell is here he finds the same thing. There is a stroke of real vanity.' One recalls Fluellen's discovery of 'M's in both 'Monmouth' and 'Macedon'. But even Fluellen lacked this original notion of being vain about his own vanity.[1]

[1] Cf. Temple's comment, after Boswell had been talking 'with much vanity' in

December 1764 brings us to the truly astounding interviews with Rousseau and Voltaire. But it should be recognized that if Boswell, naturally, conducted himself at them like a fool, he showed himself no mere fool in the pertinacious skill which won him admittance.

To Rousseau, now an exile at Môtiers in Neuchâtel, he had a letter of introduction from Earl Marischal Keith. But 'the proud Boswell', when the time came, decided to disdain such external aids, and to succeed single-handed with a letter of his own (which he drafted three times over).

> 'My romantic genius,' he wrote in his journal, 'which will never be extinguished, made me eager to put my own merit to the severest trial. I had therefore prepared a letter to Monsieur Rousseau, in which I informed him that an ancient Scots gentleman of twenty-four was come hither with the hopes of seeing him. . . . It is really a masterpiece. I shall ever preserve it as a proof that my soul can be sublime.'

Here are parts of the epistle in question:

> 'I present myself, Sir, as a man of singular merit, as a man with a feeling heart, a lively but melancholy spirit. . . . Forgive me, Sir, I feel myself moved. I cannot restrain myself. O dear Saint-Preux![1] Enlightened Mentor! Eloquent and amiable Rousseau! I have a presentiment that a truly noble friendship will be born to-day. . . .
>
> 'Open your door, then, Sir, to a man who dares to tell you that he deserves to enter it. Place your confidence in a stranger who is different. You will not regret it. But I beg you, be alone.'

'No other man in Europe,' he explained in a letter to Temple on December 28, 'could have written such a letter and appeared equal to all its praise.'

A few hours later he was already thumping the sick Rousseau on the back (December 3, 1764). 'I had a free air and spoke well, and when Monsieur Rousseau said what touched me more than

St James's Park: 'We have heard of many kinds of vanity, but, Boswell, you ride upon yourself.' As a boy of 17–18, Jeffrey (1773–1850), having helped to carry the drunken Boswell to bed, was rewarded next morning with a pat on the head as 'a promising lad'—'if you go on as you've begun, you may live to be a Bozzy yourself yet.'

[1] The hero of Rousseau's *La Nouvelle Héloïse.*

ordinary, I seized his hand, I thumped him on the shoulder, I was without restraint.'

On the next two days he repeated his visits; then he compiled a fourteen-page autobiographical sketch, including details of his affair with Lord Kames's daughter, Mrs Heron, added some pieces written by Zélide, dumped the lot on his victim, and threw off a triumphant letter to his friend Johnston (December 5):

> 'Johnston, I am in the village which contains Rousseau. These three days I have visited that sublime sage. He has enlightened my mind. He has kindled my soul. Yes, we are immortal.... I am to be alone on horseback in a dark winter night, while the earth is covered with snow. My present sentiments give me a force and vigour like the lion in the desert.
>
> 'Farewell, my dear friend.'

After which, the lion-like Boswell mounted and rode away, up the road towards Neuchâtel.

Nine days later, on December 14, he was back at Môtiers. Twice that day he forced himself on the sick Rousseau, and consulted him on various weighty points of morality. Might he keep a seraglio of thirty girls, who could afterwards be happily married off to peasant husbands? Might he pursue gallantries in France and Italy, where husbands were tolerant? Might he defend himself by duelling, from the 'shocking familiarity' of his own Scots countrymen?

At noon next day, December 15, he reappeared, having extorted an invitation to dine; at 2.35 Rousseau exclaimed, 'Now go away'.

> '*Boswell.* "Not yet. I will leave at three o'clock. I have still five and twenty minutes."
>
> *Rousseau.* "But I can't give you five and twenty minutes."
>
> *Boswell.* "I will give you even more than that."
>
> *Rousseau.* "What! of my own time? All the kings on earth cannot give me my own time." '

But to this Boswell archly replied that he might have come again on the two following days, for twenty-five minutes on each occasion. He was therefore saving Rousseau fifty minutes. This was irresistible. Indeed, when Boswell left at last, Rousseau 'kissed me several times, and held me in his arms with elegant cordiality'.

So the pilgrim finally took his departure for Yverdon; but not without having started a diplomatic flirtation with Rousseau's mistress and housekeeper, Thérèse Le Vasseur, 'a little, lively, neat French girl' (actually she was forty-three), who had borne to the author of *Émile* those five infants successively abandoned by him in the Paris Foundlings' Hospital. This little incident was to have its grotesque sequel thirteen months later.

After Rousseau, Voltaire. An artistic contrast. (But how Johnson would have raged, had he known![1]) Things may be briefer and clearer in chronological form.

December 24, 1764. Boswell arrived at Ferney with a letter of introduction from Constant d'Hermenches. Voltaire appeared in a slate-blue dressing-gown.

> 'He was not in spirits, nor I neither. All I presented was the "foolish face of wondering praise".
>
> 'I told him that Mr Johnson and I intended to make a tour through the Hebrides, the Northern Isles of Scotland. He smiled, and cried, "Very well; but I shall remain here. You will allow me to stay here?" "Certainly." "Well then, go. I have no objections at all." '

Boswell dined with Voltaire's niece Mme. Denis; but Voltaire was absent, and Boswell had to be back at Geneva before the gates closed at five.

December 25. Boswell has 'a noble idea' of writing to Mme. Denis, begging to sleep under Voltaire's roof. In her name, Voltaire replied favourably.[2]

[1] Cf. his comment after Boswell's return (February 15, 1766): 'Johnson said (sarcastically) "It seems, Sir, you have kept very good company abroad, Rousseau and Wilkes!" ... "Sir, you don't call Rousseau bad company...." "Sir, if you are talking jestingly of this, I don't talk with you. If you mean to be serious, I think him one of the worst of men.... Rousseau, Sir, is a very bad man. I would sooner sign a sentence for his transportation, than that of any felon who has gone from the Old Bailey these many years...." "Sir, do you think him as bad a man as Voltaire?" "Why, Sir, it is difficult to settle the proportion of iniquity between them." '

[2] Voltaire was not always so accessible, if we can trust the story of his replying to a would-be visitor from England that the sight of him cost £6—to which the Englishman answered: 'Here are £12, and I am coming again to-morrow.' On the other hand he complained in 1768 of having become, for fourteen years, 'l'aubergiste de l'Europe', and having received from three to four hundred English.

December 27. Boswell returned to Ferney. At first he was disappointed—'My hypochondria began to muse. I was dull to find how much this resembled any other house in the country.' But in the evening, wisely refusing to go to supper, he got an hour and a half alone with Voltaire, lyrically described in a letter to Temple.

'At last we came upon religion. Then did he rage. The company went to supper. Monsieur de Voltaire and I remained in the drawing-room with a great Bible before us; and if ever two mortal men disputed with vehemence, we did. . . . For a certain portion of time there was a fair opposition between Voltaire and Boswell. The daring bursts of his ridicule confounded my understanding. He stood like an orator of ancient Rome. Tully was never more agitated than he was. He went too far. His aged frame trembled beneath him. He cried, "Oh, I am very sick; my head turns round," and he let himself gently fall upon an easy chair. He recovered. I resumed our conversation, but changed the tone. I talked to him serious and earnest. I demanded of him an honest confession of his real sentiments. . . . He expressed his veneration—his love—of the Supreme Being, and his entire resignation to the will of Him who is All-wise. . . . He does not inflame his mind with grand hopes of the immortality of the soul. He says it may be, but he knows nothing of it.[1] And his mind is in perfect tranquillity. I was moved; I was sorry. I doubted his sincerity. I called to him with emotion, "Are you sincere? are you really sincere?" He answered, "Before God, I am. . . ."

'Temple, was not this an interesting scene?'

It was. And it is interesting to note the word 'scene', with its implication that Boswell was here too already aware of the importance of the dramatic. But here he has not yet reached the dramatic heights of the *Life of Johnson*, because he has not given dialogue the dominant place it holds in his masterpiece. Indeed all Boswell's life in a sense was amateur theatricals, with himself as actor, producer, reporter, and critic in one.

[1] Cf. Voltaire to Boswell (February 11, 1765): 'You seem sollicitous about that pretty thing call'd soul. I do protest you I know nothing of it. . . . Let it be what it will, I assure you my soul has a great regard for your own.' Voltaire hints similar scepticism about immortality to Mme du Deffand (*c.* 1772)—'I knew a man who was firmly convinced that the buzz of a bee did not continue after its death. . . . he compared us with a musical instrument which does not give forth another note when it is broken.'

December 28. Voltaire not well, and Boswell in low spirits.

December 29. After dinner and a short final talk with Voltaire, Boswell departs.

From these triumphs Boswell turned, at New Year 1765, to conquer Italy. 'I own,' he had told Mitchell, the British Minister in Berlin, 'that the words of the Apostle Paul, "I must see Rome," are strongly *borne in* on my mind.' 'I shall pass,' he now wrote to Temple, 'the rigorous Alps with the resolution of Hannibal.' He crossed the Mont Cenis, just eight months after his future *bête noire*, Gibbon; found at Turin John Wilkes (now thirty-eight), who the previous year had been, first, expelled from the House of Commons, then outlawed from England; and wrote him an invitation to dinner in high Boswellian terms—'Sir, I am told that Mr Wilkes is now in Turin. As a politician, my monarchical soul abhors him. As a Scotsman I smile at him. As a friend I know him not. As a companion I love him.' Was he thinking of Brutus' speech in *Julius Caesar* over the dead dictator? 'As Caesar loved me, I weep for him....' It would be rash to dogmatize.

Boswell also paid his usual attentions to three countesses at the Court of Turin. For, as he philosophically meditated, 'the women are so debauched that they are hardly to be considered as moral agents, but as inferior beings'. But the superior Boswell only gained three rebuffs.[1] Indeed one of these ladies, Madame de Saint Gilles, told him bluntly—'Réellement vous êtes un peu fou.... Vous ne devez pas faire le Métier de Gallant, ou vous serez terriblement trompé.' (On which the mortified Boswell observed to himself: 'Altho' my former Love Adventures are proof enough that it is not impossible for me to succeed with the Ladies, yet this abominable Woman spoke very true upon the whole.')

In Rome Boswell again met Wilkes; and from Naples ascended Vesuvius with this suitably infernal companion. He also visited, among other places, Venice, Florence, and Siena. Further, he laid siege at Siena to Porzia Sansedoni, a lady of thirty-five with three

[1] Boswell to the Countess Burgaretta: 'My happiness, my life, depend on you. Persist in your cruelty, and I cannot answer for the consequences of the most violent passion man ever felt.' (January 13, 1765.)

Boswell to the Countess 'Scarnavis' (Scarnafigi): 'If you accord me the supreme happiness, you will be showing yourself generous to an excellent man who would be attached by gratitude to you for the rest of his life.' (January 21, 1765.)

children, mistress of Lord Mountstuart, Lord Bute's eldest son, with whom Boswell had made friends in Rome. 'Il me paroit naturel,' he wrote to her in August (?) 1765, 'que vous pourrez m'accorder une partie de cet amour que vous sentez pour My Lord, car Je suis une partie de lui aussi bien que vous.' (My Lord was not faithful; and would not mind.) 'Quel beaux mélange de douce amitié entre nous trois!' But not even this engaging plea seems to have won the fair Porzia; and Boswell had to content himself with a certain Moma Piccolomini, also of Siena, a lady of thirty-seven, with four children, who was still writing him touching letters two years afterwards. In later years Boswell recalled 'the frame of mind I had in Italy; amorous and pious'. The piety is less conspicuous.

In such delights nine months of 1765 slipped by. And now Lord Auchinleck began to write fulminating letters (August, September, October), pointing out that the prodigal had received £460 since January. Let him come straight home. There was nothing to see in France—'I desire that . . . you don't stop in ffrance, except about ten days or a fortnight about Paris and its environs, That you may say you have been there, which is all the benefit Travellers have over others.'

But Boswell was in no hurry. On October 11, 1765, he took what was perhaps the second most important step in his life—on to a Tuscan vessel at Leghorn, bound for Corsica.

On the eve of his great adventure, he wrote to Rousseau from Lucca, on October 3, 1765, a portentous and interminable letter in French about his Italian experiences; beginning, 'Illustrious Philosopher.'

> 'I carried over the Alps ideas of the most rigorous morality. I thought of myself as a penitent who must expiate the sins which he had confessed to you in your sacred retreat; I felt like a hero of austerity in a dissolute age. But the ladies of Turin were very beautiful, and I thought that I might allow myself *one* intrigue in Italy, in order to increase my knowledge of the world and give me a contempt for shameless women.'

However, he explains, he was not a success at Turin and had to content himself with venal beauties.

'I wrote on a piece of paper, "O Rousseau! How am I fallen since I left you!" Yet my principles remained firm. . . . You told me when I was about to leave you, "Sir, all you lack is a knowledge of your own worth." Believe me, illustrious philosopher! there is a great deal in that remark.'

(One may doubt it.) Then he relates his trip from Turin to Rome. 'I had the agreeable sensation that derives from a half-knowledge of things—to many minds perhaps as great a pleasure as knowing them thoroughly.'

Then he reports his journey to Naples; and his return to Rome in Holy Week, which filled him with religious ardour. 'Let cold beings sneer; I was never more nobly happy than on that day.' Unfortunately his low amours in the Holy City had painful results; and he suffered also from his recurrent 'hyp'. Then he describes how he attached himself to Lord Mountstuart, 'a tempestuously noble soul', and continued touring Italy with him, though not without quarrels. Finally, after an account of his Sienese romance, Boswell bursts into a new apostrophe—'O dear St Preux! Yes, my soul is bound to yours. I have loved like you, I am pious like you. If we have committed crimes, we have also expiated them.' After this parallel (which Rousseau may not have much relished), the end of the letter (Rousseau must have begun to wonder if it would ever have one) is lost.

Corsica had risen against its Genoese masters in 1729; been subjugated for Genoa by the French in 1739; and risen again in 1741. In 1755 the Corsicans chose for their general Pasquale Paoli; in 1764 Genoa persuaded the French to occupy five of the chief towns; but at that point military operations ceased. In October 1765 came Boswell.

It was an enterprising step. For Corsica was little known. And there was a not wholly negligible risk of capture on the way by Turkish or Algerine pirates. Still the enterprise need not be exaggerated; it was, presumably, far less risky than Chateaubriand's and Byron's journeys in Greece and Asia Minor; and the trip to Corsica was repeated a year later by Frederick Hervey (son of Pope's 'Sporus', and one day to be renowned as the eccentric Bishop of Derry—'Gallio in gaiters'—and Earl of Bristol),[1] who on his return

[1] To whose taste for travel the infinite Hotel Bristols of the continent owe their name.

voyage to Leghorn was actually chased by a Moslem privateer.

Perhaps those autumn days among the Corsican mountains, and his other autumn days among the mountains of the Highlands, were really the two happiest periods of Boswell's life. In Corsica he could not flirt (he knew the Corsicans were ill to joke with, where their women were concerned). He could not easily drink too much (though he occasionally succeeded in the Highlands). He was healthy, excited, in the open air and among simple, unspoiled men, away from the hothouse of modern civilization. There *was* something in Rousseau's views on going back to Nature and the simple life.

In Corsica, too, Boswell was treated with kindness and hospitality; partly because the Corsicans were hospitable, partly because he was imagined an English envoy. He slept in convents; which pleased the devout side of him, with its Catholic leanings. He munched chestnuts knocked from the trees, and lapped the mountain-brooks, like a noble savage. At Corte, needing a passport, he applied to the Corsican Chancellor. That dignitary 'desired a little boy who was playing in the room by us, to run to his mother, and bring the great seal of the kingdom. I thought myself sitting in the house of a Cincinnatus'. Or again, to complete the pastoral delights of this Arcadia, Boswell flutes to the natives his Scottish tunes—*The Lass of Patie's Mill* and *Corn rigs are bonny*; or sings them *Hearts of oak*, while the cry, delighted, 'Cuore di quercia! Bravo, Inglese!' 'I fancied myself to be a recruiting sea-officer. I fancied all my chorus of Corsicans aboard the British fleet.' In fact, it was as picturesquely intoxicating as an Italian opera.

But the climax for Boswell was Paoli himself—a Corsican Johnson. Paoli had at first been suspicious. 'I was of the belief,' he related years after, in exile, as recorded by Fanny Burney, 'he might be an impostor, and I supposed, in my minte, he was an espy; for I look away from him, and in a moment I look to him again, and I behold his tablets. Oh! he was to the work of writing down all I say! Indeed I was angry.' However it would be a strange spy that openly took notes of a commander-in-chief's small talk; and so Paoli quickly warmed to his gay and simple guest. Religion, morals, politics, marriage, all kinds of topics were discussed as if they had been sitting snugly at The Mitre—even the language of animals. 'I have often since this conversation,' comments Boswell, 'indulged myself in such reveries. If it were not liable to ridicule, I would say[1] that an acquaintance with the language of beasts would be a most agreeable acquisition to man, as it would enlarge the circle of his social intercourse.' Typical Boswell! Never could he have enough 'social intercourse'. One pictures him crowding into his bulging journal the confidences of Dr Johnson's cat Hodge, or of Rousseau's dog Sultan.

By December 1765 Boswell was in Genoa; by January 1766, in Paris; whence he wrote to Monsieur de Zuylen proposing for the hand of Zélide. But his idea of rushing to Utrecht was thwarted. For, perusing the *Saint James's Chronicle*, his eye lit suddenly on the news of his mother's death. He was 'quite stunned'; then 'at six, Mme. Hecquet's[2] as in fever. Constance elegant'. Next morning he had a letter from his father. 'Wept in bursts; prayed to her' (his mother) 'like most solemn Catholic to saint. Roused philosophy, sung Italian gently to sooth'.

But 'philosophy' was soon to be forgotten again. For at this moment Hume, in his simple kindliness, had just invited the persecuted Rousseau to take refuge in England; despite warnings, from friends who knew Rousseau better, of the serpent he was taking to his bosom. And since Rousseau's mistress, Thérèse Le Vasseur, had to be forwarded after him, it was arranged that Boswell (whom we have already seen meeting her at Môtiers) should squire her to London. Thérèse seems to have been not only illiterate but almost mentally deficient. Rousseau himself, according to a letter of Hume's (January 19, 1766), 'owns her to be so dull, that she never knows in what year of the Lord she is, nor in what month of the year, nor in what day of the month or week; and that she can never learn the different value of the pieces of money in any country. Yet she governs him as absolutely as a nurse does a child. In her absence his dog has acquired that ascendant.' This remarkable damsel was now about forty-four.

In another letter (misdated January 12, 1766) the wise Hume grows actually prophetic.

[1] Typical that, however 'ridiculous', he at once proceeds to say it.
[2] A house of ill fame.

'I learn that Mademoiselle sets out post in company with a friend of mine; a young gentleman, very good-humoured' (repeatedly this comes out as Boswell's ruling characteristic), 'very agreeable, and very mad.... He has such a rage for literature, that I dread some event fatal to our friend's honour. You remember the story of Terentia, who was first married to Cicero, then to Sallust, and at last, in her old age, married a young nobleman, who imagined that she must possess some secret, which would convey to him eloquence and genius.'

This shrewd suspicion was fulfilled to the letter; though it may be doubted if Boswell was in any need of motives so literary. But this conquest made during their journey brought little satisfaction. They bored each other; and Thérèse much mortified Boswell by finding him an inferior lover to Rousseau. No doubt it was with relief that he handed over his charge to the exiled philosopher at Chiswick—'quanta oscula',[1] he records.

The same day, February 13, 1766, 'Johnson hug'd you to him like a sack.' (Johnson's welcome would have been less warm—indeed, considerably hotter—had he known recent goings-on.) A week later, Boswell called on the elder Pitt,[2] at the Duke of Grafton's house in Bond Street, to plead for the liberties of Corsica. The great man, it is recorded, 'smiled, but received him very graciously in his Pompous manner.' After all, though it would not be easy to think of two men more unlike in most ways than William Pitt and James Boswell, still both were highly eccentric characters, and highly histrionic.

At the same time Boswell had plunged into hectic journalism on behalf of his Corsican protégés.[3] He fed the *London Chronicle*, beginning even before he reached England, with a series of anonymous reports, partly true, partly fantastic, of his own adventures. January 19: 'The Genoese have been not a little alarmed.' January 11, 14: Mr Boswell said so-and-so to Paoli; Paoli gave such-and-such presents to Mr Boswell. January 23: Mr Boswell's real plan, it transpires, was to establish the Young Pretender as King of Corsica. (That was certainly a good mare's nest, to make the British public sit up on.) February 13 ('extract of a letter from Turin'):

[1] 'What kisses!'

[2] The story that he went attired as a Corsican chieftain seems, unfortunately, unfounded.

[3] See F. A. Pottle, 'The Incredible Boswell,' *Blackwood's*, August 1925.

'The Gazettes of late have talked a great deal of a certain Mr Boswell, a Scots gentleman, who has been in Corsica. It was at first rumoured that he was a desperate adventurer, whose real name was M'Donald, and who had served during the last war in North America; but it has since appeared that he is a gentleman of fortune upon his travels, a friend of the celebrated John James Rousseau.'

James the Greater and James the Less.

Evidently Boswell, had he lived later, would have been as remarkable in the rôle of advertising manager as of biographer. It now remained, after this overture of trumpets, to write his book on Corsica.

Only in March 1766 did the prodigal return, after three and a half years, to the paternal hearth in Scotland; where it may be doubted if Lord Auchinleck 'hugged him like a sack'. However in July 1766 the old man at least had the satisfaction of seeing Jamie admitted advocate.

For the next four years Boswell's main concerns were three—the Douglas law-case, Corsica, and getting married. The Douglas case turned on the claim of Archibald Douglas to the Douglas estates, on the death of the third Marquis of Douglas. The Marquis's sister, Jane, secretly married in 1746, had borne twins in Paris in 1748. One twin died; the other was Archibald the claimant. The Duke of Hamilton, the next heir, argued that the twins were spurious, as their supposed mother was fifty at the time of their birth. Hence vast litigation, into which Boswell plunged zestfully on Archibald's side. He even composed (1767) a very mediocre romance on the theme, *Dorando*, as well as two pamphlets; and became at least part-editor of Lady Jane Douglas's letters. In addition, he again flooded the press with anonymous effusions—with eulogistic reviews of his own *Dorando*, which is praised as coming 'like old Nestor, to calm the violence, and diffuse good temper and complacency of disposition', or as being, if not the work of Rousseau, 'at least the production of no ordinary genius'; with an essay in favour of Archibald Douglas, impishly arranged to be mistaken, on internal evidence, as by Adam Smith (who, in fact, was a violent opponent); and with a grotesque account of five disguised shorthand-writers, supposedly coming to report the legal proceedings in Edinburgh. One of them, he said, was descended from a sister of

Father Garnet the Gunpowder-plotter; and another was a government spy who had once taken reports of the rebels' plans at Derby in the '45, concealed in a chimney with a dark lanthorn. This prank must have amused Boswell vastly—until the Lord President cut matters short by ordering the publishers of the newspapers concerned 'to be incarcerated in the Tolbooth of Edinburgh' (though they seem to have escaped with a reprimand).[1]

Simultaneously, in this *annus mirabilis*, 1767, Boswell was not only writing his *Account of Corsica, The Journal of a Tour to that Island*; he was also keeping the public on tiptoe, and preparing his book's success, by yet more anonymous scribblings in the press.[2] He fabricated an imaginary Corsican envoy, Signor Romanzo (appropriate name), who was reported as calling now on the British Ambassador to Prussia, now on the British Ambassador at The Hague; now stalking through the Royal Exchange; now fighting a duel at Marseilles with a French prince of the blood who had insulted the English. Boswell also hatched *canards* about intervention in Corsica's favour by the Grand Duke of Tuscany; about verses composed in praise of Corsica by Frederick the Great; about envoys to Corsica from the Bey of Algiers; about six beautiful camels sent for Paoli's use by Prince Heraclius of Georgia.

He even concocted an imaginary letter, full of the wildest misspellings, from one of five fictitious English soldiers whom he pictured helping the Corsicans to storm the island of Caprera; beginning—'Dir Bob, This is to let you know I am piur and well'; and continuing with eulogies of Paoli and his patriots—'The General on him Poli is as good a man as the King himself, whom God blis'—'As we went brisely[3] on they cryd well-don Brother Inglish, well don Brother freemen.'

Thus Boswell sought simultaneously English support for Corsica and public support for his coming book. He must certainly have enjoyed 1767. Jamie was always glad, growled his father, to 'take

[1] F. A. Pottle, 'The Incredible Boswell,' *Blackwood's*, August 1925.

[2] In 1767 alone he published seventy articles in the *London Chronicle* (F. A. Pottle, *Literary Career of Boswell*, p. xxiii), while effusions of his appeared also in the *London Magazine*, *Scots Magazine*, *Public Advertiser*, *Edinburgh Advertiser*, *Caledonian Mercury*, etc.

[3] Briskly? (Cf. p.189: 'we went briskly in'.)

a toot on a new horn'; he took enough of them in this year to have demolished Jericho.

In February 1768, his *Corsica* appeared; and Boswell became a European name. 'Temple,' he wrote, 'I wish to be at last an uniform pretty man.... I am always for fixing some period for my perfection as far as possible. Let it be when my *Account of Corsica* is published. I shall then have a character which I must support.'

A 'character' he certainly did acquire; though it proved less easy to support. Corsica had become, like Poland, Greece, or Hungary later, a symbol of gallant freedom defying crushing odds. And so Boswell's book went into two editions in 1768; into a third the year following. It was widely translated—into French, Dutch, German, Italian; and it made Boswell more read in Europe at twenty-eight than Johnson at seventy-five. Mrs Barbauld celebrated the author in heroic verse. Even the sharp Mme du Deffand praised him to Horace Walpole—'J'aime l'auteur à la folie; son cœur est excellent, son âme est pleine de vertus.' He became 'Corsica Boswell'. As he later said to Paoli, 'it was wonderful how much Corsica had done for me, how far I had got in the world by having been there. I had got upon a rock in Corsica, and jumped into the middle of life.'

But, of course, not all voices were sympathetic. Lord Auchinleck disliked his son's hitching himself on to 'a landlouping scoundrel of a Corsican'; and Johnson, for once, partly agreed with Lord Auchinleck. He praised, indeed, the part of *Corsica* comprising Boswell's own journal—'I know not whether I could name any narrative by which curiosity is better excited, or better gratified'; but he had long grown impatient of Boswell's Corsicanism—'Mind your own affairs, and leave the Corsicans to theirs'; and a month after the book's appearance (March 1768), he repeated, 'I wish you would empty your head of Corsica, which I think has filled it rather too long'.

Shrewdest of all, perhaps, is the verdict of Gray:

> 'Mr Boswell's book... has pleased and moved me strongly; all (I mean) that relates to Paoli. He is a man born two thousand years after his time! The pamphlet proves, what I have always maintained, that any fool may write a most valuable book by chance,[1] if he will only

[1] 'By chance' seems a little hard. But, of Boswell, Gray here takes a view not much unlike Macaulay's.

> tell us what he heard and saw with veracity. Of Mr Boswell's truth I have not the least suspicion because I am sure he could inven[1] nothing of this kind. The true title of this part of the work is, a Dialogue between a Green-goose and a Hero.'

This judgment has been called 'obtuse'; but I do not find it so; though it is true that the Green-goose was later to lay two golden eggs.

However it is worth remembering, too, that Boswell's book was admired by one well fitted to judge, the most famous of all Corsicans—Napoleon Bonaparte.

The tour-section of *Corsica* is still pleasant reading in its simple, often artless way. Curious that it should have appeared in the same year as Sterne's *Sentimental Journey*. For Boswell's journey too was 'sentimental'—but, though it lacks the impish charm, humour, and fantasy of Yorick, still it is the product of finer feelings. With all its boyish vanity, its motives were, in part, liberal and generous.

Even after its success, Boswell did not relax his efforts. For if the year 1768 was a triumph for his *Corsica*, to the Corsicans themselves it brought disaster. In May the Genoese, despairing of reconquest, sold their rights in the island to the French; who then proceeded to reconquer it for themselves. A year later, in May 1769 they took Corte, the capital. In vain Boswell had collected in the summer of 1768 the surprising sum of £700 to provide the patriots with cannon—two 32-pdrs., four 24-pdrs., four 18-pdrs., and twenty 9-pdrs.; and had edited for publication (December 1768) *British Essays in Favour of the Brave Corsicans*. In vain at the Stratford Shakespeare-Jubilee of 1769 he appeared at midnight in Corsican dress, musket over his shoulder, with a cap bearing in gold letters the device *Viva la Libertà*, and adorned with blue feathers; so that, in his own words, 'as soon as he entered the room, he drew universal attention'. Unfortunately the forty-six-line poem he had printed to distribute on the occasion was not ready in time; nor did he succeed in reciting it. But at least he had his figure in Corsican attire engraved for four thousand copies of the *London Magazine*.

[1] Gray might have changed his mind had he known of Boswell's cock-and-bull stories in the press. But it seems, after all, true enough that though Boswell could invent audacious gossip, he could *not* have invented a character like Paoli.

Only a fortnight later, on September 21, 1769, the defeated Paoli landed at Portsmouth as a refugee. His only consolations were an audience with George III and a pension. Lord Holland had proved right—'Foolish as we are, we cannot be so foolish as to go to war because Mr Boswell has been to Corsica.'

This same year 1769 finally crowned with success Boswell's long and arduous efforts to get married. In 1766, after his return to Scotland, he had begun by falling so much in love with the gardener's daughter at Auchinleck as to dream of wedding her. Then he attached himself to a Mrs Dodds, with three children, deserted by her husband—'a pretty, lively, black little lady'—a 'dear infidel'. But unfortunately there were other moments when she annoyed Boswell, who felt jealous of her past, and found her 'ill-bred, quite a rompish girl. She debases my dignity. She has no refinement'. For some two and a half years, while still pursuing his matrimonial schemes elsewhere, he was alternately infatuated with Mrs Dodds, and unfaithful to her; now begging forgiveness of his Cleopatra, now breaking off relations, now returning to her feet—in his own words, 'feverish, Mark Anthony, quite given up to violent love'. And yet—'This evening I thought with astonishment; Is it really true that a Man of such variety of Genius, who has seen so much, who is in constant friendship with General Paoli, is it possible that He was all last winter the slave of a woman without one elegant quality?' (March 22, 1767.)

As for marriage, he havered and wavered between no less than four[1] ladies whose names, like his, all began with 'B'. 'I love my love with a B.' There was still, though in the background, Belle de Zuylen. There was Miss Elizabeth Diana Bosville in Yorkshire, who belonged to what Boswell supposed the English branch of his own clan, and who married, in 1768, Lord Alexander Macdonald, Boswell and Johnson's meanly inhospitable host in Skye. (She was, in fact—so fades romance—the unfortunate lady described by Johnson as dull and heavy enough to sink a ninety-gun ship.) Thirdly, there was another kinswoman of Boswell's, Miss Kate Blair of near-by Adamtown, a ward of Boswell's father, who would have welcomed her as daughter-in-law. Fourth and last, there was yet

[1] Not counting a passing fancy for the daughter of Sir Alexander Dick (whose life Boswell thought of writing in 1777).

another kinswoman, Miss Mary Anne Boyd, *La Belle Irlandoise*, aged sixteen and a rich heiress. But chronology alone can introduce a little clarity into this amorous chaos.

March 30, 1767. (To Temple.) 'I intend, next autumn, to visit Miss Bosville in Yorkshire. But I fear, my lot being cast in Scotland, that beauty would not be content. She is, however, grave. I shall see. There is a young lady' (Kate Blair) 'in the neighbourhood here, who has an estate of her own between two and three hundred a year, just eighteen. . . . How would it do to conclude an alliance with the neighbouring princess, and add her lands to our dominions?'

June 12, 1767. (To Temple.) Miss Blair and her mother have stayed four days at Auchinleck. 'In our romantic groves I adored her like a divinity. . . . Her children would be all Boswells and Temples, and as fine women as these are excellent men.'

But:

'I must tell you my Italian angel[1] is constant. I had a letter from her but a few days ago, which made me cry. And what shall I tell you? My late Circe, Mrs ——,[2] is with child. What a fellow am I! Come to me, Temple, and on that Arthur-seat, where our youthfull fancies roved abroad into extravagant imaginary futurity, shall we now consult together on plans of real life and sollid happiness.'

June 26, 1767. Temple shall go ambassador to the Princess. 'Give Miss Blair my letter. Salute her and her mother; ask to walk. See the place fully; think what improvements should be made. . . . Tell, you are my very old and intimate friend. Praise me for my good qualities—you know them; but talk also how odd, how inconstant, how impetuous, how much accustomed to women of intrigue.[3] Ask gravely, Pray, don't you imagine there is something of madness in that family? Talk of my various travels—German princes—Voltaire and Rousseau. . . . Consider what a romantic expedition you are on; take notes. . . .'

July 29, 1767. (To Temple.) Drinking Miss Blair's health to excess, Boswell got drunk, caught disease, and fears (rightly, it turned out) that he has infected Mrs Dodds, who is with child by him.

[1] Moma Piccolomini.

[2] Mrs Dodds, with whom he had broken.

[3] One is reminded of that strange scene in *Macbeth* where Malcolm catalogues his own failings to Macduff.

August 28–9, 1767. 'All is well between the Prince of Auchinleck and his fair neighbouring Princess.' 'Next month will probably fix our alliance.'

Autumn, 1767. Renewal of correspondence with Zélide.

November 5, 1767. (To Temple.) He has had a quarrel with the Princess (whom he suspected to be pursued by a Nabob). 'I then wrote her a strange Sultanick letter, very cool and very formal, and did not go to see her for near three weeks.' However he is staying there now. 'I am drest in green and gold. I have my chaise in which I sit alone like Mr Gray, and Thomas rides by me in a claret coloured suit with a silver laced hat. But the Princess and I have not yet made up our quarrel.'

> November 8, 1767. (To Temple.) The quarrel is still not made up. 'She did not appear in the least inclined to own herself in the wrong. I confess that, between pride and love, I was unable to speak to her but in a very aukward manner. . . . That I might give her a fair opportunity I sent her a letter of which I enclose you a copy. Could the proud Boswell say more than you will see there?'

However his letter brought the proud Boswell only a chilly answer, and a refusal of the tress he had begged. 'Wish me joy, my good friend, of having discovered the snake before it was too late.' Besides, a neighbour has told him that 'three people in Ayr agree in abusing her as a d—nd jilt. What a risque have I run!'

> 'After this, I shall be upon my guard against ever indulging the least fondness for a *Scots lass*.[1] I am a soul of a more southern frame. I may perhaps be fortunate enough to find an Englishwoman who will be sensible of my merit, and will study to please my singular humour.'
>
> 'Do you know I had a letter from *Zelide* the other day, written in English, and showing that an old flame is easily rekindled. But you will not hear of her. What say you? Ah, my friend, shall I have Miss Bosville? You see I'm the old man.'

December 18, 1767. (To Temple.) The Princess has been more benign. 'I, in short, adored her. . . . I told her that henceforth she

[1] Through Boswell's life, despite his pride in being an old Scottish baron, there runs a recurrent dislike of Scotland and the Scots; due perhaps in part to his resentment against his own father.

should entertain no doubt that I sincerely loved her—and, Temple, I ventured to seize her hand. She is really the finest woman to me I ever saw.'

December 24, 1767. (To Temple.) The Princess has blown cold again. On the Saturday he went with her to *Othello*. 'I sat close behind the Princess, and, at the most affecting scenes, I prest my hand upon her waist. She was in tears and rather leaned to me. The jealous Moor described my very soul.' Yet the following Monday she replied to his question about her feelings—'No; I really have no particular liking for you; I like many people as well as you.' For example, she liked Jeany Maxwell, Duchess of Gordon, better. But no *man* better? No. Was it possible she liked him better than other men? She did not know what was possible. (Miss Blair may have been honestly uncertain; but she was certainly also a tease.)

> '*Boswell.* You are very fond of Auchinleck—that is one good circumstance.
>
> *Princess.* I confess I am. I wish I liked you as well as I do Auchinleck.
>
> *Boswell.* I have told you how fond I am of you. But unless you like me sincerely, I have too much spirit to ask you to live with me, as I know you do not like me. If I could have you this moment for my wife, I would not.[1]
>
> *Princess.* I should not like to put myself in your offer, though....'

(It is fascinating to watch Boswell, though thus tormented, employing his vivid skill at recording dialogue.)

Since then, Miss Blair has continued to flirt; and her poor lover begs Temple's advice. 'Is it not below me to be made uneasy by her? Or may I not be a philosopher, and without uneasiness take her, if she likes me, and if not, let her alone? During her absence I have time to get a return from you.' Meanwhile he has caught a disease again. And Mrs. Dodds has brought him 'the finest little girl I ever saw. I have named it Sally'. (But he had been hoping for an 'Edward the Black Prince'.)[2]

February 8, 1768. (To Temple.) All is over. Miss Blair is rumoured engaged to Sir Alexander Gilmour, M.P. for Midlothian.

[1] Almost his exact words to Madame Geelvinck, and again to Zélide.

[2] Apparently with allusion to the mother's dark complexion.

She will not admit or deny it; but has told Boswell he has no chance. The rejected lover has composed a Crambo[1] Song on his cruel mistress, and is 'very easy and chearful'. P.S. 'You cannot say how fine a woman I may marry, perhaps a Howard or some other of the noblest in the kingdom.'

February 25, 1768. He has had a letter of 'inimitable pleasantry' from Zélide. (Next day he wrote proposing to her.)

On March 21, 1768 he was in town to enjoy the reception of his new-published *Corsica*.

> March 24, 1768. (To Temple.) 'Do you know, my charming Dutchwoman and I have renewed our correspondence; and upon my soul, Temple, I must have her. She is so sensible, so accomplished, and knows me so well and likes me so much, that I do not see how I can be unhappy with her. Sir John Pringle is now for it, and this night I write to my father begging his permission to go over to Utrecht just now. She very properly writes that we should meet, without any engagement, and if we like an union for life, good and well; if not, we are still to be friends. What think you of this, Temple?'

(Always this absurd dependence on advice. Rousseau had been quick in detecting this and warning Boswell that he relied too much on others.)

April 16, 1768. (To Temple.) Both Temple and Lord Auchinleck are against Zélide. But are they not too severe? He has once more caught disease; but is positive he will never go astray again. P.S. 'What would you think of the fine, healthy, young, amiable Miss Dick? . . . She wants only a good fortune.'

April 18, 1768. (To Sir Alexander Dick.) After various London news, Boswell makes a tactful inquiry about music to be brought back to Edinburgh for Miss Dick; and grows arch. 'She has *La Buona Figliola*.[2] But has she *La Buona Figliola Maritata*?[3] I am sure she has not *La Moglia Fedele*.[4] I beg she may tell me freely what she wants.'

April 26, 1768. (To Temple.) Zélide has written again, sensible

[1] With a recurrent rhyme. This effusion is hardly worth quoting.
[2] The Good Daughter.
[3] The Good Daughter Married.
[4] The Faithful Wife.

and tender. He has sent the letter to his father and asked to visit her, promising on his honour not to engage himself.

> 'I have written to her, and told her all my perplexity. I have put in the plainest light what conduct I absolutely require of her; and what my father will require. I have bid her be my wife at present, and comfort me with a letter in which she shall shew at once her wisdom, her spirit, and her regard for me. . . . I tell you, man, she knows me and values me as you do.'

(The same mistake as he had repeatedly made with her before. Zélide would *not* be ordered; and would *not* be taken for granted. M. de Charrière was to win her—though not for his own happiness —by doing neither.)

Unfortunately Boswell's disease is still so bad that he may not be able to go to Holland.

May 14, 1768. (To Temple.) Temple is pleased with Zélide's letters. But alas—Boswell's last letter in which 'I told her my fears from her levity and infidel notions', has brought back a thunderbolt.

> 'Read her letter. Could any actress, at any of the theatres, attack one with a keener (what is the word? not *fury*, something softer)—The lightening' (*sic*) 'that flashes with so much brilliance may scorch. And does not her *esprit* do so? Is she not a termagant or at least will she not be one by the time she is forty? . . . You may believe I was perfectly brought over to your opinion, by this acid epistle.'

One would give much for Zélide's letter. But Boswell is not downhearted. There was always himself to love. 'I am really the *Great Man* now. I have had David Hume in the forenoon and Mr Johnson in the afternoon of the same day visiting me.' (Well that they did not meet on the doorstep.)

'Pray send me a short introduction to Gray. You are wrong in being positive against Miss Dick.'

August 8, 1768. Now at last the candidate destined to success makes her entrance—Boswell's cousin, Margaret Montgomerie. On this August day she signed a jocular contract (still extant in the Malahide papers) binding herself not to wed him, or let him be engaged to her, within the year 1768, on pain of banishment from Great Britain for life. The reason—that Boswell 'is so much in love with me' and 'so inconstant that there is reason to fear that he would repent of his choice in a very short time'. (She was two years older, and poor.)

> August 24, 1768. (To Temple.) 'I am exceedingly lucky in having escaped the insensible Miss B——[1] and the furious Zelide; for I have now seen the finest creature that ever was formed, *La belle Irlandoise*.[2] Figure to yourself, Temple, a young lady just sixteen, formed like a Grecian nymph, with the sweetest countenance, full of sensibility, accomplished, with a Dublin education . . . her father a counsellor at law, with an estate of £1,000 a year, and above £10,000 in ready money . . . she, the darling of her parents—and no other child but her sister.'

Boswell had met this paragon at the house of his cousin Margaret Montgomerie, whose cousin she was. 'Upon my honour, I never was so much in love.' He is to visit her in Ireland in March. He has carved her initial on a tree and 'cut off a lock of her hair, *male pertinaci*'.[3] 'Ah! my friend, I am now as I ought to be. No reserved, prudent, cautious conduct as with Miss B. No. All youthful, warm, natural—in short, all genuine love. Pray tell me what you think.' (Always this craving for counsel.)

> 'This is the most agreeable passion I ever felt. Sixteen, innocence, and gayety make me quite a Sicilian swain. Before I left London, I made a vow in St Paul's Church, that I would not allow myself in licentious connections of any kind for six months.'

December 9, 1768. (To Temple.) Miss Blair's match with Sir Alexander Gilmour is off. Her 'wary mother' has told Boswell he missed Kate only by his own fault.

> 'Temple, to a man again in love this was engaging. I walked whole hours with the Princess. I kneeled. I became truly amorous. . . . My

[1] Blair.

[2] Mary Anne Boyd.

[3] Horace, *Odes*, i, 9, 24—of a coquette's feigned resistance. Boswell was a more ardent collector of locks even than Pope's Lord Petre; several were found among his papers; he had vainly sought one from Miss Blair; and in future years he was to extract one even from Miss Seward, the Swan of Lichfield.

relapse into this fever lasted some weeks. I wrote to her as usual the most passionate letters.... Only think of this, Temple. She might have had me. But luckily for me, she still affected the same coldness and not a line would she write. Then came a kind letter from my amiable Aunt Boyd in Ireland, and all the charms of sweet Marianne revived. Since that time I have been quite constant to her.... What should I say to Kate? You see I am still the old man. I have still need of your advice. Write me without delay.' P.S. Is he right 'to insist that my dear little woman[1] shall stay?... Is it not right I should have a favourite to keep me happy. But, alas, I love her so much that I am in a kind of fever. This is unworthy of Paoli's friend.'

April 25, 1769. Boswell set off, in company with his cousin Margaret Montgomerie, to woo his Iseult in Ireland. Two days later, drinking to the memory of Douglas under the old tower of Corsehill, he got badly intoxicated and 'behaved ill to Margaret, my own affectionate friend'. On April 30 he formed the impression that Margaret was engaged to someone. 'I was amazingly affected.[2] I cried bitterly, and would not speak to my companion.' At Ballantrae, however, Margaret reassured him that it was false. Boswell then got drunk on punch with his landlord.

In Dublin he was warmly welcomed. Oppressed Ireland sympathized with oppressed Corsica. He dined with the Lord Lieutenant, with the Lord Mayor, with the Duke of Leinster. He danced a jig with *La belle Irlandoise*, to the tune of *Carrickfergus*, played by an Irish piper.

'But,' as he wrote to Dempster on June 21, 'my Cousin hung on my *heart*. Her most desireable person, like a heathen goddess painted *al fresco* on the cieling of a palace at Rome, was compared with the delicate little Miss. Her admirable sense and vivacity were compared with the reserved quietness of the Heiress.[3] I was tost by waves and drawn by horses. I resolved to fix on nothing. My Cousin gave me that advice herself; for I had assurance enough to consult her deliberately.'

(Still the incorrigible craving for advice.)

[1] Mrs Dodds.

[2] One is reminded of Proust's hero who, having quite decided to break with Albertine, becomes suddenly fettered to her by his own jealous suspicions.

[3] It appears that Miss Boyd, abandoned by Boswell, was still ruthlessly rejecting suitors twenty years later.

Dempster replied, 'But, Boswell, why marry?' *That* advice, however, Boswell was past taking.

July 17, 1769. His next step was quite mad. He put Margaret to a test, like the lover of 'The Nutbrown Maid' so disapproved of by Johnson.[1] He asked her if she would marry him and live abroad on £100 a year, together with the interest of her own £1,000. 'This was truly romantick; and perhaps too severe a trial of a woman of so much good sense and so high a character.'

July 23, 1769. 'But while I was in church, I thought that if M. gave me a prudent, cold, evasive answer, I would set sail for America and become a wild Indian.'[2] (Boswell was furious at this time because his father, in his quieter, more resolute way, was now also bent on marriage.)

July 25, 1769. Margaret's acceptance was brought him in the Parliament House at Edinburgh. His comment is extraordinarily honest, and revealing. 'For a minute or two my habits of terrour for marriage returned. . . . But I soon recovered and felt the highest admiration and gratitude on a conduct so generous.' And he endorsed the wrapper—'The most valuable letter of my valuable friend, which does honour to both her and me. Vraye Foi.'

She was to be truer to that Boswell motto than he.

July 29, 1769. Of the complexities of his own feelings, he records: 'In short, so it is that I defy any man to write down anything like a perfect account of what he has been conscious' (*sic*) 'during one day of his life, if in any degree of spirits.' (A curious anticipation of Joyce.)

August 4, 1769. Lord Auchinleck gave his grudging consent to the marriage of James with Margaret, though he thought they would part in six months.

But Boswell was not only a happy lover, he was now also 'Corsica Boswell'. He rushed off to England, to 'clear his constitu-

[1] In Prior's tedious modernization, *Henry and Emma*. 'The experiment by which Henry tries the lady's constancy, is such as must end either in infamy to her, or in disappointment to himself.' (Johnson, *Life of Prior*.)

[2] A curious and ludicrous anticipation of *Locksley Hall*. Cf. his dialogue with Johnson two months later (September 30, 1769): '*Boswell*. "Sometimes I have been in the humour of wishing to retire to a desart." *Johnson*. "Sir, you have desart enough in Scotland." ' (And disastrously reluctant poor Boswell was to become about retiring to it.)

tion' under the care of a surgeon, to parade as a Corsican chief at Stratford, and to welcome the exiled Paoli, whom he introduced to Johnson on October 10.

'A fortnight,' Johnson wrote to him from Brighton, 'is a long time to a lover absent from his mistress. Would a fortnight ever end?' Boswell, however, endured three whole months. Only by mid-November was he at last back in Scotland; and on November 25 he was married to his cousin.[1] (He would doubtless have felt happier if his father had not also, on that same day, been married to *his* cousin, Elizabeth Boswell.) But to the very end of his courtship Boswell remained odd.

> 'Naturally somewhat singular,' he wrote in *The Hypochondriack*, twelve years later, '... I resolved to have a more pleasing species of Marriage than common, and bargained with my bride, that I should not be bound to live with her longer than I really inclined; and that whenever I tired of her domestick society, I should be at liberty to give it up.'

If this is accurate autobiography, Margaret Boswell possessed a patience almost equal to Griselda's. Certainly she was to need it. But at least, in his saner moments, Boswell did realize her worth; and after her death no one could ever replace her.

On the other hand, his moods in this winter of 1769 were not exclusively idyllic. He was exasperated with his father, not only about the old man's remarriage, but also about the succession to the Auchinleck estate. Already in 1767 he had sworn to Lord Auchinleck that he would cut his own throat if the estate were fixed on 'heirs whatsoever', when according to Boswell's own feudal notions it should go to the next heir *male*.[2] Now he knelt in the ruins of Auchinleck Castle, with a piece of the castle in his hand, to swear that if any took the estate to the exclusion of the rightful heir, he

[1] Boswell got his marriage-contract witnessed by the symbolic trio, Paoli, Johnson, and Archibald Douglas.

[2] Poor Boswell would have been damped at the time to know that his line was destined to end with his two great-granddaughters—though he might have been consoled by the fact that his own vast hoard of journals thus came before the world. Later, however, when he had daughters of his own, his views veered. On the legal aspects, see C. H. Bennett in *Times Lit. Sup.*, February 27, 1937, p. 151.

would make that stone swim in the intruder's blood.[1] After which he carefully preserved the stone.

The first two years after Boswell's marriage are nearly blank, presumably because he was happy (though still subject to 'hyp'), and his wife had steadied him. For nearly a year and a half he did not even write to Johnson. For ten years, from 1760 to 1769, Boswell had risen—erratically—but risen. Now, in 1770, he held a strikingly different position from the Newmarket 'cub' of 1760. He had found fame in Corsica; he had found—far more important for any sane individual—a good wife in Margaret Montgomerie. For five years more his career was to keep a fairly steady level. But the last twenty years, from 1775 to his death in 1795, became a dismal stagger downhill. Yet for us these are the years that matter, since they produced the *Tour* and the *Life*. Boswell had seen Johnson in 1763, 1766, 1768–9; he was to see him again in 1772, 1773 (both in London and in Scotland); and yearly from 1775–9 (twice in this last year); then in 1781, 1783, and 1784. Seven years later, in 1791, at last the *Life* appeared. The rest is wretched.

In 1773 came two great events—Boswell's election to The Club, and the Highland Journey.

The Club, founded in 1764 at the suggestion of Reynolds, was a body of formidable eminence, which came to include such members as Johnson, Reynolds, Goldsmith, Gibbon, Garrick, Sheridan, Burke, Fox, Adam Smith, the two Wartons, Malone, Steevens, Percy, Burney, the Duke of Leeds, and the Bishops of Killaloe, Peterborough, and Salisbury. To such a body election could not be easy. A single black ball was fatal; Lord Palmerston and the Bishop of Chester *were* black-balled, and even the great Lord Camden. When Garrick rashly said he would join, ' "*He'll be of us*" !' growled Johnson. 'How does he know we will *permit* him? The first duke in England has no right to hold such language.'

Clearly Boswell's chances would have been slender but for Johnson's backing. But Johnson's backing was too formidable to resist—though he was doubtless joking when he said the Club knew he would black-ball all future candidates, if Boswell were rejected. One

[1] He had a curious passion for oaths (especially with sword drawn) that makes one think of Ancient Pistol—often on the most incongruous subjects, such as being stoical despite melancholia, or never making random love without precautions.

is reminded of Rossetti's imperious intrusion of his brother William into the ranks of the P.R.B.

In the Hebridean Tour, however, Boswell is overshadowed by his master, except for occasional moments of prominence—when, for instance, he was carried away by Highland hospitality at Corrichatachin and became, in Johnson's bantering phrase, 'You drunken dog'; or when in the storm off Col, while Johnson lay in 'philosophick tranquillity' with a greyhound at his back, the terrified Boswell was bidden hold a rope attached to the mast-top, merely, as he afterwards realized, to keep him quiet (yet who but Boswell would have recorded it?); or when on Inch Kenneth he went into a ruined chapel at night 'to perform his devotions', but came back in haste for fear of spectres.[1]

In 1774 Boswell's main excitement was the case of John Reid the sheepstealer; which exhibits, if not Boswell's wisdom, at least his kindness of heart. Eight years before, Reid had really stolen some sheep, but had then the luck to get off with a verdict of 'not proven'; now, when very possibly innocent, he was condemned to the gallows, despite Boswell's frantic efforts in his defence. None the less 'being elated with the admirable appearance which I had made in the Court, I was in such a frame as to think myself an Edmund Burke—and a man who united pleasantry in conversation with abilities in business and powers as an Oratour'. 'I was much in liquor, and strolled in the streets a good while—a very bad habit which I have when intoxicated.'

Still he worked very hard for Reid's pardon. But, as the poor wretch was his first criminal client, 'I was desireous to have his picture done *while under sentence of death* and was therefore rather desireous that, in case a respite was to come, it should not arrive till he had sat his full time.' (Which seems a little hard on John Reid.)

At moments Boswell suspected Reid of lying; so that he rashly exclaimed—'If your Ghost should come and tell me this, I would not believe it.' 'This last sentence made me frightened, as I have faith in Apparitions, and had a kind of idea that perhaps his ghost might come to me.'

Yet Boswell, though grotesque, was kind-hearted. His failure to get Reid's reprieve drove him to drink and 'a state of mingled

[1] Johnson to Mrs Thrale, October 23, 1773.

frenzy and stupefaction'. He even toyed with elaborate schemes to get the victim resuscitated after hanging. Unfortunately the repercussions of this affair fell on poor Margaret Boswell. It made Boswell 'shudder' to learn that in his drunkenness 'I had cursed her in a shocking manner, and even thrown a candlestick with a lighted candle at her'. Further, a newspaper comment by Boswell on Reid's case nearly involved him in a duel with the son of the Justice Clerk; the fear of which made Margaret 'pale as a spectre'.

Seven times in his life Boswell nearly fought duels, though all of them were averted. On the other hand his son, Sir Alexander (whom one suspects of a firm resolve to differ from his father as much as possible[1]), did fight in 1822, just after the funeral of his younger brother James—and was killed.

Already, indeed, from 1775 the shadows begin to darken over the house of Boswell.

His marriage was growing less happy. Margaret complained, 'with great justice', that his talk with her was 'childish nonsense'. But this was because he had come to feel a gulf between their temperaments. 'She has no superstition, no enthusiasm, no vanity.' In fact, Margaret had too much good sense for him. Also he found her cold. 'I told her I must have a concubine. She said I might go to whom I pleased. She has often said so.' (March 8, 1775.)

But such freedoms are simpler in theory than in practice. Gloom and guilt began to sour his temper. He had fits of violence. He would throw dining-room chairs at Margaret, or break his stick and burn it on the hearth. He would hurl eggs or beer into the fire.

> 'I had a fit of gloomy passion this morning at breakfast and threw a guinea note in the fire because my Wife objected to my subscribing three shillings for a Miscellany by a Miss Edwards. I however rescued the note with the tongs before it was consumed, and, though a good part of it was burnt, I got its value from the Royal Bank. This incident shocked me, because it made me dread that I might in some sudden rage do much worse.' (February 27, 1776.)

Increasingly, as years went by, he sought that refuge of the unhappy—drink; in spite of repeated efforts to check himself, as

[1] Sir Walter Scott reports hearing that he banished a portrait of Johnson by Reynolds to an attic.

when, on a visit to the water-drinking Temple at Mamhead (1775), he swore 'under a solemn yew' to abstain. Amorous escapades multiplied. He sought to palliate his 'patriarchal extensiveness' by precedents from the Bible—'I soothed myself with old testament manners'. And, being Boswell, he had of course to enter everything in his journal. True, he adopted the feeble disguise of writing words, or groups of words, in Greek characters.[1] But it hardly needed a wife of Margaret's intelligence to penetrate such frail subterfuges as 'αμουρους δαλλιανσεσ', 'λυσχιους λιβερτιεσ', 'φοολισχ λονε φορ A.', 'πεγγι γραντ', 'πεγγι Δυνδας', or other pieces of 'μισcχιεφ' 'Ρερχαπς,' he reflects, 'I should not ωριτε αλλ θις'.[2] No, indeed, if scribble he must, lock and key would have served better. At all events, more than once, Margaret read in these precious journals and was 'σεριοσλy affected'. (Often, indeed, her quick eyes read the truth from his face alone.) 'She told me she had come to a resolution never again to consider herself as my *Wife*' (December 8, 1776—though she was too kind-hearted to keep to it).

Late in 1777 Margaret fell ill. And Boswell recorded: 'Levity of imagination about second marriage.' 'Must own had SPECULATIONS of rich matches or Lady Eg[linton] which amused fancy.' Margaret had been reading his Journal only shortly before; that he should take the remotest risk of her reading this, seems horrible.[3]

All the same one must not overload the gloom. Boswell was no Dunmow husband; yet his marriage was like many another:

> Sometimes 'my plague!', sometimes 'my darling!'
> Kissing to-day, to-morrow snarling.[4]

At heart they still loved. 'My Wife was exceedingly good to me to-night, and said, "Will you ever say again that I don't love you?" I answered that I never would' (December 24, 1779). And Boswell

[1] Like his friend Temple in his Diaries; and Benjamin Constant in his *Journal Intime*.

[2] γ = g, θ = th, λ = l, μ = m, ν = n (or v), π = p, ρ = r, σ = s, φ = f, χ = h, Δ=D

[3] By a strange coincidence, a week later he heard Lady Eglinton was dead (January 26, 1778). 'Was quite amazed; as it were My IMAGINARY δευτερογαμη' (re-marriage) 'vanished'.

[4] Prior.

in his ludicrous way, though so unfaithful, was not blind to Margaret's worth, even far off at London parties:

> 'I was in highest spirits, and called out, "I am as happy as a Prince. I resolved to be happy, and I AM happy." But I drank too much wine and too fast, and was intoxicated, and talked too openly of MYSELF and my licentious indulgences, and my Wife's goodness. And how if I was to have but ONE Woman, I'd rather have her than any one in the World.'

True, he ended the day (May 23, 1783) by having his watch stolen by a wench in St James's Street (though he had vowed at the altar of the Portuguese Chapel only the previous Sunday—'no more filles while in London'). Yet his drunken babblings of affection for Margaret were also true.

In the later seventies Boswell grew gloomy, also, about his career. 'Corsica Boswell' was coming to look like a middle-aged man with a great future behind him. Bitterly he recalled Sir John Pringle's words to him, years before—'You know nothing.' It was still so. 'I am a Lawyer. I have no system of Law. I write verses. I know nothing of the art of Poetry.' (December 22, 1775.)

But instead of setting himself to succeed in his own country, the lure of London and ambition led Boswell, early in 1775, to form that fatal dream, which was to cause him endless vexation and final failure, of success at the English Bar. He began to keep terms at the Inner Temple.

But the real root of his unhappiness lay, as so often, less in circumstances or events than in his own character—his own melancholia. It would have taxed the resources of modern psychiatry to minister to that mind diseased. Johnson, indeed, gave him good advice; but here Johnson was a physician who could not heal himself.

> ' "Sir," said he, " take a course of chymistry or a course of rope-dancing or a course of any thing to which you are inclined at the time. Contrive to have as many retreats to your mind as you can, as many things to which it can fly from itself." There was a liberal philosophy in this advice which pleased me much. I *thought* of a course of concubinage, but was afraid to mention it.' (March 22, 1776.)

One can imagine the explosion, if he had. But that remedy could not, in fact, serve Boswell's case.

And so the dark fits recurred—'indolent and gloomy'—'relished nothing'—'I recollect nothing'—'as dreary and horrible as ever'—'dreary metaphysical Wretch'. 'I saw death so staringly waiting for all the human race, and had such a cloudy and dark prospect beyond it, that I was miserable as far as I had animation' (January 24, 1777).

In the previous summer of 1776 he had been badly unnerved by his interview with the dying Hume—one of the strangest scenes on record. For it was the dying man that was placidly humorous, the visitor that was terrified; Boswell was appalled precisely because Hume was *not* appalled by the near prospect of annihilation. 'I however felt a degree of horrour. . . . I was like a man in sudden danger eagerly seeking his defensive arms.'

At moments even the beloved diary he lived for came to seem flat and unprofitable—'this dull, uninteresting journal is not worth the trouble of writing'. Boswell was ill indeed when he could feel *that*. Yet he always ended by taking up his pen again. And from October 1777 to August 1783 he further unloaded his mind in *The Hypochondriack*—essays published by the *London Magazine*. To us, who can read between the lines, these are sometimes interesting; but in themselves they appear to me usually commonplace, sometimes vapid; and one cannot wonder that the *London Magazine* tired of them, even if Boswell did not. They were not reprinted in book form till 1928.

His best chance, in these years, of shaking the Black Dog off his trail, and regaining spirits, was when he jogged south across the Border on the London road. Not even Johnson loved London more passionately; and, during these comparatively brief periods in Johnson's circle, Boswell, though as yet he could not guess it, was about his life's real business. 'I was now in that glow of good spirits which I enjoy on a fine day, walking the streets of London' (March 16, 1776). Indeed his London spirits could make him as foolish at forty as at twenty. In the coach from Woodford (April 9, 1781):

> 'I joked on everything we saw. There was "EVE'S Manufactory". That, I supposed, must be Aprons. All jokes do in a hackney coach.

> There came on a pretty smart rain. A well looked, stately woman who sat on the coachbox begged as a favour we would make room for her in the coach. I told her all the seats were filled. But if she chose to sit on my knee, and the company had no objection, she was heartily wellcome. This being agreed, in she came, and I had a very desireable armfull. She was a Widow with three children. . . . Such incidents are marrow to my bones.'

True, there was not always marrow. Even to London the Black Dog could sometimes make his way. And Boswell would invent odd causes for dissatisfaction. To 1778 belong some of the best 'scenes' of Johnson's talk; and yet 'I had a sort of regret that we were so easy. I missed that aweful reverence with which I used to contemplate *Mr Samuel Johnson*. . . . I have a wonderful superstitious love of *Mystery*, when perhaps the truth is that it is owing to the cloudy darkness of my own mind' (March 20, 1778). The real truth is, perhaps, that Boswell was a Romantic born before his time. However these jaunts usually contrived to replenish his 'stock of fine spirits'. The trouble was that London society soured and spoilt him for that of Scotland. 'Edinburgh operates like the *Grotto del Cane*[1] on my vivacity.' Yet Scotland was good enough for Hume, Robertson, or Adam Smith; Boswell would have been wiser to cultivate his own garden, instead of constantly despising 'the mere Men of this narrow country'. However his misfortune is our good luck.

With the eighties the steps of Death steal closer round him. In 1781 Thrale died; within ten days Boswell had composed his incredible *Ode by Dr Samuel Johnson to Mrs Thrale upon their supposed approaching Nuptials*. Two stanzas will be quite sufficient:

> Not only are our limbs entwin'd
> And lip in rapture glued to lip;
> Lock'd in embraces of the mind,
> Imagination's sweets we sip.
>
> Five daughters by a former spouse
> Shall match with nobles of the land;
> The fruit of our more fervent vows
> A pillar of the state shall stand.

[1] At Terme d'Agnano, west of Naples, there is a grotto, filled at the bottom with carbon dioxide, where dogs suffocated.

This rant Boswell had not only the folly to write, but also the inconceivable folly to publish, anonymously, in 1788, with a gibe at Johnson in the preface—'neither was he neat and cleanly in his person and dress'. By then, indeed, Johnson was four years dead; but Mrs Thrale was alive, and married to Piozzi. Had Johnson ever known the existence of this effusion (and Wilkes wickedly teased Boswell by threatening to show it), there would have followed such an explosion as might even have robbed us of the *Life*.[1]

In June 1782 Margaret Boswell began to spit blood (though she still had before her seven years of life—hardly of happiness). To Boswell's mania this provided an occasion for yet more journalizing —'I have a particular Journal of my Wife's illness.' 'I had even flights of fancy in the view of my being a Widower. These shocked me afterwards.' In talking with her doctor, 'there was in the midst of my anxiety and shooting pains of grief a sort of agitation that rather gave a kind of pleasure'. Boswell's intelligence was hardly outstanding; but he sometimes surprises by a ruthless honesty in observing his own emotions, that is worthy of Stendhal.[2]

Two months later, in August 1782, Lord Auchinleck sickened. He had not been showing himself very amiable—'he spoke of poor John[3] with contemptous' (*sic*) 'disgust. I was shocked and said, "He's your son, and God made him." He answered very harshly, "If my sons are idiots, can I help it?"' (August 1, 1782). Still, when the old judge lay dying at the month's end, Boswell 'wept; for alas! there was not affection between us'. 'I [had a] strange thought: "Still alive, still here! Cannot he be stopt?"' So Boswell at last was Laird of Auchinleck.

But he was no Prince Hal to become a changed man with his accession. A kind and generous landlord he always remained; but he had little zest for it. His heart, despite the advice of Johnson

[1] Cf. Johnson's shrewd warning as early as 1775: 'Your love of publication is offensive and disgusting, and will end, if it be not reformed, in a general distrust among all your friends.'

[2] Cf. his observations on visiting the home of his sister-in-law, Mrs Campbell, and her husband, both recently dead: 'It was a picture of desolation to find both Master and Mistress gone; yet I know not how, there was a sort of feeling of ease, as in barracks, and a sort of congratulating one's self on being still alive, that upon the whole I was rather comfortable. I love to mark real feelings, whatever be their causes' (March 9, 1777).

[3] Boswell's mad brother.

and his own brother David, was not in Ayr, but far away in London. 'Why, Sir,' Johnson had said in 1777, 'I never knew anyone who had such a *gust* for London as you have.' The mists on Merrick or Corserine were nothing, compared to the smoke about St. Paul's; Loch Doon or the Black Water of Dee seemed dull beside Fleet Ditch. Scott ruined himself by making too much of his Scottish home: Boswell, by making too little. On the front of his house Lord Auchinleck had inscribed the Horatian motto:

Quod petis, hic est;
Est Ulubris; animus si te non deficit aequus.[1]

Here you can find your wishes; you can find them at Ulubrae,
If your heart keeps, untroubled, its equanimity.

But, as Boswell lamented, his father's sensible equanimity was precisely what he could never attain. In the spring of 1783 he was on another of his London visits. But his records grow laxer; and Temple found him degenerated—'irregular in his conduct and manners, selfish, indelicate, thoughtless, no sensibility or feeling for others who have not his coarse and rustick strength and spirits. Sorry I came to town to meet him. . . . Seems often absurd and almost mad, I think.'

Johnson sanely discouraged Boswell's expensive dreams of a seat in Parliament. But hopes of success at the English Bar still danced and flickered before his foolish vision. He consulted acquaintances; naturally the complaisant said 'Yes', the prudent 'No'. After all, what chance had a Scot in his middle forties, with a Scotch accent, as a junior counsel on circuits among irreverent and ruthless young colleagues? But poor Boswell very humanly listened only to what he wished to hear. The pleasure of becoming Laird of Auchinleck had soon faded. All the same even he had misgivings. In a dream he saw a wretch naked on a dunghill in London, being flayed like an ox by some ruffian, with woeful laments (January 6, 1784). It is hard to doubt that this dream embodied his secret fears for his own fate. Well, for once, had he been *more* superstitious.

In June 1784, he bade farewell to Johnson for the last time. On December 13 Johnson died. 'I was now uneasy to think there would

[1] Horace, *Epistles*, I, xi. 29–30. Ulubrae was a dull hamlet in the Pomptine Marshes.

be considerable expectations from me of Memoirs of my illustrious Friend; but that habits of indolence and dejection of spirit would probably hinder me from laudable exertion.'

But he was not so indolent that he could not, at this very time, make another of his curious splashes into politics, over a proposal to reduce the number of Scottish Lords of Session. In May 1785 a letter of Boswell's resounded through the columns of the *Edinburgh Advertiser*: 'My friends and countrymen, be not afraid. I am *upon the spot*. I am *upon the watch*. The bill *shall not pass* without a spirited appeal to the justice and honour of the Commons of Great Britain. Collect your minds. Be calm, but be firm. You shall hear from me at large a few days hence.' A pamphlet followed in June.

That spring (1785) Boswell returned to London with his manuscript of the *Tour to the Hebrides*. For this, as for the *Life*, he had the luck to find a most competent and self-effacing collaborator in Edmond Malone.[1] In the autumn of 1785 the book appeared, and sold well enough to reach a second edition in December.

This should have raised Boswell's spirits. And indeed he had stood high in his own favour when he came to Court that May—'drest in my scarlet suit. Looked like a Baron, and was quite easy. Talked with Lord Cathcart, Major Arabin, Duke of Gordon, Lord Effingham, etc., etc., with a PERFECT POSSESSION of myself and SERENE GAYETY.' But unfortunately the success of his book brought fresh troubles. In it he had been far from discreet about the living. And people who had no wish to be immortalized as flies or bumble bees in Boswell's amber, began to shun him. Men and women who never said a word worth recording, none the less dreaded that this scribomaniac would record them. In particular (November–December, 1785) the *Tour* nearly brought him a duel with the furious Lord Alexander Macdonald. The interchanges between the two make ludicrous reading; but for Boswell at the time it was by no means amusing. 'Had slept not five minutes all night. The alternative of killing or being killed distracted me' (December 10, 1785).

With 1786 began five years of misery. In January Boswell was

[1] Edmond Malone (1741–1812), son of an Irish judge; friend of Johnson, Reynolds, Burke, Horace Walpole, and Mrs Siddons; editor of Goldsmith, Dryden (prose), Shakespeare, and of the third to sixth editions of Boswell's *Life*.

at last called to the English Bar. To that April belongs an anecdote told by John Scott, Lord Eldon, which cannot, however, be trusted. Scott says that at Lancaster one evening he and some other young lawyers found Boswell lying drunk on the pavement; and sent him a hoaxing brief with instructions to move in court for a writ *Quare adhaesit pavimento*,[1] together with fee. Boswell fell into the trap and duly moved in court for the writ, to the amazement of the judge—'Bless me! I never heard of such a writ. Adheres to the pavement? Pray, gentlemen, *what* is it that adheres?'

The story is full of improbabilities (so is life, for that matter). It is certainly 'not proven'.[2] But, remembering the brutal ragging of Boswell three years later at Lord Lonsdale's, one may suspect that it at least gives no very false impression of the sort of treatment that the poor victim had sometimes to put up with among his juniors at the English Bar. Certainly that summer of 1786 saw him wretched even in his beloved London—wandering in tears about streets and coffee-houses; cursing himself for neglecting his family and Auchinleck; or playing drearily for hours at draughts in his house with a young cornet of dragoons. 'I played for 100 apples a game, and felt in a degree all the Uneasiness of gaming, for I lost a great many games, he having somehow got the knack of it.' What earthly chance had the writer of such pathetic absurdities amid the brutal rough-and-tumble of English law and politics?

But now Margaret too was sacrified to his drunken ambition. In September 1786 he brought her and his family to London, and kept her there nearly two years. Her lungs suffered; she pined for Auchinleck; his own brother David urged return—'he pressed upon me the consideration how many people kept aloof from me, supposing me a man going to ruin' (June 16, 1787). But the moth could not bear to leave the candle for that 'narrow, illbred sphere'. Yet he too was ill at ease. He might flutter about the court, in a 'suit of imperial blue, lined with rosecoloured silk and ornamented with rich gold-wrought buttons' (which he could ill afford). But even such exalted circles brought their bitterness. At the Academy dinner

1 'Why he adhered to the pavement?'

2 It is worth noting, however, that Boswell's Journal (*Boswell Papers*, xvi, 182) for April 6, 1786, begins: 'Last night a feigned Brief had been left at my lodgings'; then it tantalizingly breaks off.

(April 26, 1788) 'I told Malone I was tortured to see Lord Thurlow, Lord Loughborough, Lord Amherst, and all who had risen to high situation while I was nothing; but I trusted that my being so tortured was a sign that I was made for something great, and tha· it would come. . . . I *felt* myself high above any thing in Scotland'. (If only he could have known, poor devil, that he would be, one day, far more famous than them all!) At Court, 'The King only said to me, "It is very warm weather; it is very close." I was weak though to be vexed at his indifference to a zealous Tory' (April 24, 1788). 'I found Mr Horace Walpole at home, just the same as ever: genteel, fastidious, priggish' (April 25, 1788). We know what Walpole though of 'that quintessence of busybodies'.

Even this dubious pleasure of eating inadequately sugared toads out of silver dishes, was further embittered by pangs of conscience about Margaret, much as he wriggled to stifle them.

> 'My being so much abroad appeared very unkind to her, though I was *conscious* of sincere regard. At the same time let me fairly mark the modifications of feeling by time and circumstances. I certainly had not that tenderness and anxiety which I once had, and could look with my mind's eye upon the event of her being removed by death with much more composure than formerly. This I considered as humanely ordered by Providence; yet I was not without some upbraidings as if I were too selfish, from leading what may be called a life of pleasure' (March 28, 1788).

'Just like Provvy!' Bentham would humorously exclaim when something went provokingly amiss; but even Providence can seldom have been credited with odder tasks than that of kindly dulling Boswell's affection for his wife. Silent now was that gruff voice which had growled, once, in his ears—'Sir, clear your *mind* of cant.'

Again on May 3, 1788, he rushes out to dinner.

> 'I was inwardly shocked at my rage for pleasure, which made me leave a distressed Wife, who would never have left me, even in the slightest illness. But I braved all tender checks, and truly I came to be satisfied that I had done right; for I added to my stock of pleasing

subjects for recollection,[1] and had I staid at home, should have fretted, and done my wife more harm than good. . . . It was a very pleasant day.'

Pleasant days there still were; but these were hardly pleasant years. Under their burden he even lost, at times, his faith in his ambition—'the ambition which has ever raged in my veins like a fever'. The tragic irony was that he remained fundamentally incapable of the success he craved in active life; though success beyond his dreams awaited him in literature. Constantly Boswell makes one recall '*le violon d'Ingres*'—the error of those who pique themselves on powers they lack, at the expense of those they really have. For Judge Boswell would have been extremely odd; Boswell M.P. would probably have been grotesque. However it is always hard to know oneself.

But now despair often numbed him into listless indolence. Pitt, 'insolent fellow', neglected him; the odious Lord Lonsdale,[2] whose hanger-on he had become in 1786, brought him nothing but the paltry Recordership of Carlisle (January 1788)—and bitterly he was to pay even for that. Though at times he toiled, dogged but briefless, on circuits, at other times he almost gave up—'Had not been in Westminster Hall this term' (May 5, 1788). And so he merely went there on the last day, 'but without my wig and gown'.

Similarly with the *Life* of Johnson. At times Malone's praise 'dispelled my vapourish diffidence'; yet for days or weeks he had no heart to write. On March 7, 1788 he was vexed by Mrs. Piozzi's *Letters to and from the late Samuel Johnson*—

[1] An interesting touch. His mania for recording past experiences shows that he expected to enjoy their memories; though others have found in such things 'sorrow's crown of sorrow'. But did he in fact so enjoy them? It seems hard to say.

[2] James Lowther, Earl of Lonsdale (1736–1802), known throughout Cumberland and Westmorland as 'the bad earl', possessed enormous wealth and returned nine members to Parliament—'Sir James's Ninepins'. Indeed he first brought the young Pitt into Parliament, as member for Appleby (1781). Alexander Carlyle described him as 'truly a madman, though too rich to be confined'—'a domestic bashaw, and an intolerable tyrant over his tenants and dependents'; for 'Junius', he was 'the little contemptible tyrant of the north'. He was son-in-law to Bute; but preserved at Lowther an embalmed mistress (a Cumberland farmer's daughter) with a glass pane over her face.

Wordsworth's father was Lonsdale's attorney and law-agent at Cockermouth; and suffered from his lordship's rooted objection to paying his debts.

'I was disappointed a good deal, both in finding less able and brilliant writing than I expected, and in having a proof of his fawning on a woman whom he did not esteem,[1] because he had luxurious living in her husband's house; and in order that this fawning might not be counteracted, treating me and other friends much more lightly than we had reason to expect. This publication *cooled* my warmth of enthusiasm for "my illustrious friend" a good deal. I felt myself degraded from the consequence of an ancient Baron to the state of an humble attendant on an Authour; and what vexed me, thought that my collecting so much of his conversation had made the World shun me as a dangerous companion.'

For a moment his zeal for writing Johnson's life flagged. However it was only for a moment. He found comfort in the suspicion that Mrs Piozzi had expunged from her record matter complimentary to himself.[2]

At last in May 1788 he took Margaret home to Auchinleck; and there follows a year's gap in his journal. By November he was back in London and writing to her: 'O, that I had never come to settle in London! Miserable I must be wherever I am. Such is my doom.' By February 1789, Margaret seemed near her end; in April, Boswell came home to her (and repeatedly got drunk); in May, he was dragged away by the tyrannic Lonsdale; on June 4 Boswell, with his two boys, set out post from London for Auchinleck; but that same day Margaret Boswell was at last at rest.

In the following August, 1789, Boswell was at Lowther with Lord Lonsdale. Practical jokers stole the poor widower's wig; and he had to lurk about that house of festivity a whole day in his nightcap. But protégés must smile when kicked—unless they are Johnsons. Next winter Boswell was back in London; now waking in gloom and despair of finishing the *Life*, now counting with just satisfaction that 416,000 words were finished; now wildly hoping

[1] Wildly untrue.

[2] She had. In an interesting communication to the *Times Lit. Sup.* (January 29, 1929, p. 62) R. W. Chapman describes how, in a letter written to her by Johnson from Lichfield (June 19, 1775), Mrs Thrale first erased a passage about Boswell, then pasted paper over it, then pasted over *that* a scrap cut from another letter. The suppressed passage included the sentences: 'Boswell's narrative' (*i.e.* in his Journals) 'is very natural, and therefore very interesting. He never made any scruple of showing it to me. He is a very fine fellow.'

to go to America as Ambassador's Secretary, now being 'carried to Mary Le Bone Watch-house for calling the hour in the streets'; now having a love-affair with 'C', now waking in tears from a dream of his lost Margaret. Often in these years he thought of remarriage 'with a sensible, good tempered woman of fortune'—considering his 'warm propensities' it would be 'an insurance against some very imprudent connection'. Yet Margaret haunted him; and he clung also to his liberty.

For a time, indeed, early in 1790 his volatile spirits soared again. 'Vastly well. FELT how SUPERIOUR being in Lond[on is]' (January 30, 1790). 'Floated upon life with really pleasing sensations' (February 7, 1790). 'Full enjoyment of London' (April 16, 1790). But it was a brief respite. May brought back the hyp. When he stayed with Lonsdale at Laleham, 'the Earl was violent and abusive, talking of what strange company I kept—Sir Joshua Reynolds, etc., etc., etc.... I inwardly resolved to withdraw myself from all connection with him.' (Well if he had!) 'My friend Temple told me fairly that he had never seen any body so idle as I was. I could scarcely take the necessary trouble of preparing my Book for the press' (May 29, 1790). And so the usual refuge in alcohol. That day at a Chelsea Hospital dinner 'I drank of all the liquors: cold drink, small beer, ale, porter, cyder, Madeira, sherry, old hock, port, Claret'; after which he washed down the rest with cherry-brandy.

The next twelve months were among his blackest. He felt wretched that he was now again as wretched as thirty years before, in spite of Corsica, and Johnson, and his other distinguished friends. He saw himself as a board once painted with fine figures, yet now reduced by some corrosive to its original nakedness. His last hopes of Lonsdale were dashed. He was told that the Earl had sneered at the suggestion of Boswell's becoming an M.P.—'he would get drunk and make a foolish speech'. A few days later (June 17, 1790) Lonsdale insulted him directly. Boswell, he said, was shirking his duties as Recorder of Carlisle. 'I suppose you thought I was to bring you into Parliament. I never had any such intention.'

Later that day, driving north with the Earl (who had dragged him away from Temple in London, and ordered him to his post at Carlisle), Boswell somehow irritated his patron 'almost to madness, so that he used shocking words to me. "You have kept low company all your life. What are *you*, Sir!" "A gentleman, My Lord, a man of honour; and I hope to show myself such." He brutally said, "You will be settled when you have a bullet in your belly." ' At Barnet they were on the brink of a duel: then, however, the noble bully calmly told Boswell to forget it all.

But it was not likely Boswell could forget. He brooded miserably through long days of desolation at Carlisle. He had yet again caught disease in his London escapades; and he was 'secretly struck' by hearing a Scotsman who had known Lord Auchinleck, 'regretting that I should be in the train of a tyrant'. 'What a wretched Register is this! "A Lazarhouse it seem'd." It is the Journal of a diseased mind' (July 5, 1790).

Yet, even now, he could not take Temple's sensible advice to leave the law and retire to Auchinleck—he dreaded the humiliation of admitted failure, the lonely depression, the strangely passionate disgust he felt for his own countrymen. In London, however, his spirits rose anew; and on Lord Mayor's Day 1790 he made himself more abject than ever by singing, six times over, a fulsome ballad he had composed to curry favour with Pitt—'the Grocer of London' (which he also published). Even Mr Pitt, it was observed, 'was obliged to relax from his gravity, and join in the general laugh at the oddity of Mr Boswell's character'. But such antics earned poor Boswell no advancement—only charges of servility; which he answered in *The World*. A letter to Dundas, complaining of neglect, brought him only a sharp rebuff.

Even his daughters Veronica and Euphemia, he felt, had now ceased to feel respect—'as, indeed, how could they for a sickly-minded wretch?'—and he wished them away from him.

But at last on May 16, 1791—the anniversary of his first meeting with Johnson twenty-eight years before—the *Life* was published. Yet even at this moment of triumph, when he had finally completed the circumnavigation of Johnson, the incorrigible Boswell contrived to make himself absurd. For that month, by way of puff for the *Life*, there appeared in the *European Magazine*[1] (of course, from his own pen) *Memoirs of James Boswell Esq.*; complete with quotations of his ghastly verses, 'Boswell does women adore' and 'He

[1] Articles on the *Life of Johnson*, which look as if they were also by Boswell himself, went on appearing at intervals in this periodical down to October 1792.

has all the bright fancies of youth'; with an account of his mummeries at the Stratford Jubilee; and with pompous comment on his political failure—'It was generally supposed, that Mr Boswell would have had a seat in Parliament; and indeed his not being amongst the Representatives of the Commons is one of those strange things that occasionally happen in the complex operations of our mixed Government.'

Further, even his moments of triumph were soured. That August 1791, he had a clash with Sir William Scott, because some of the other guests invited by Sir William to dinner demanded a solemn undertaking that Boswell would not record their talk. And while he rolled in his fancy various matrimonial schemes—Miss Bagnall with an income of £6–700, Miss Milles with a fortune of £10,000—at some date after August 15 he received a brusque, illiterate note from his current mistress, Mlle Divry—'Voici votre conger ne me troublé pas davantage.'

However the *Life* sold 1,200 sets by August 22; and reached a second edition in 1793.[1] By November 1792 he could record the receipt of £1,555 18*s.* 2*d.*—'very flattering to me as an Authour'.

And yet, with the appearance of Johnson's life, Boswell's own life was really over. The rest is convulsive flutterings. A few typical dates will suffice.

August 1792. Boswell, with his old kindliness, interested himself in Mary Bryant, of Fowey, and four other convicts from Australia. Mary Bryant had been transported for theft to Botany Bay, married a fellow-convict, and with him and others escaped, under fearful hardships, to Dutch Timor, three thousand miles away. Thence the survivors had been brought back to Newgate. With much labour and intercession Boswell got them eventually pardoned; and himself paid Mary a small annuity.

August–September 1792. A jaunt to Cornwall. At Wilton 'it was truly a *sight* to me, a man of *multitudinous imagination*, to behold *my daughters* Veronica *and Euphemia* sitting with the Earl of Pembroke in his immense drawing-room, under the Family Picture by Vandyck, undoubtedly the most capital Work in Portrait painting that the World has to shew. How many *Scotch Lairds* are there whose daughters could have such an honour?'

[1] Seven English editions in the twenty years 1791–1811.

He goes through old letters with Temple.

> 'My friend agreed with me that it was wonderful I had made myself the man I was, considering the extreme narrowness of my education; for he remembered me the most puritanical being, and the most timid in society; and now there was no man of more elevated eclesiastical' (*sic*) 'notions, more liberal views, and perhaps none so universally easy and of more address in social life.'

'We both agreed that I was better as the distinguished Biographer than as a Lord of Session.'

November 1792. Depression returns in London—'my *dead small-beer spirits*.'

June 1793. He plans to tour Holland and Flanders, and visit the Austro-British armies besieging Valenciennes; but coming home drunk is stunned and robbed by a footpad.

December 23, 1793. 'Was in a sad listless state, and made my son James play at drafts with me the whole day, by which I was quite stufified' (presumably 'stupefied').

March 1794. Boswell vainly writes to Dundas[1] asking to be sent to Corsica as minister or commissioner (Paoli had returned there in 1791, and in 1794 appealed to England against the French).

In the later part of 1794 he paid a final visit to Auchinleck. The following spring (1795) his fancy took one of its last flights. In the previous December the youthful William Henry Ireland (he was only eighteen or twenty) had begun his famous Shakespearian forgeries. These included legal documents; a profession of faith by the poet (pronounced by Joseph Warton to be of superior beauty to anything in the New Testament or the English Litany); letters to or from Queen Elizabeth, Southampton, and Anne Hathaway (complete with verses and lock of hair); a gift to 'mye mouste worthye and excellaunte Freynde Masterre William Henrye Irelande'[2] (because he 'pulledd off hys Jerrekyne and Jumpedd inn' to save

[1] Henry Dundas, Viscount Melville (1742–1811), Home Secretary 1791–4, Secretary for War 1794–1801. Boswell had vainly hoped advancement from this old schoolfellow; of whom he wrote, 'to be sure he has strong parts, but he is a coarse, unlettered dog'.

[2] A bad slip (apart from the almost incredible coincidence of an Elizabethan namesake); for, as Malone did not fail to point out, double Christian names were hardly known in Shakespeare's day.

Shakespeare from the Thames) of all profits from *Henry IV*, *Henry V*, *King John*, *Lear*, and *Henry III* ('neverr yett imprintedd'); a manuscript of *Lear* (expurgated and improved, to the great admiration of contemporary critics); some manuscript pages of '*Hamblette*'; and a number of old books annotated by the bard.[1]

Though a far inferior writer, Ireland was technically a better forger than the Chatterton he admired. His parchment, paper, and seals were genuinely old; his ink seemed so; only he wildly overdid his spelling, with wonders like 'dymennesyonnes', 'innetennecyonne', 'bllossommes', 'bllooms'. Still, better scholars than Boswell were duped, such as Joseph Warton and the portentous Dr Parr. And, after all, Ireland's fictitious find of Shakespeare documents, however improbable, was not in itself more incredible than the genuine discoveries of Boswell documents at Boulogne in the nineteenth century, or at Malahide and Fettercairn in the twentieth.

In February 1795, Boswell visited an exhibition of these frauds in the Norfolk Street house of the forger's father Samuel Ireland (who was himself completely hoaxed, having long regarded his son as a mere dullard). Both father and son have recorded Boswell's own exhibition—how he closely and ecstatically examined the papers; 'requested a tumbler of warm brandy and water'; exclaimed, 'with an extraordinary degree of rapture', that he could now die contented; knelt down and kissed a volume; and drew up a certificate affirming the authenticity of the papers. Next day Dr Parr snorted at this document as 'too feebly expressed', and wrote another, which was signed by twenty-one persons, including Parr, Pye the Poet Laureate, the Garter King of Arms, and James Boswell.

For poor Boswell it was a grotesque *Nunc Dimittis*. Better had he heeded his friend Malone, who remained grimly sceptical, and on March 31, 1796, buried the Irelands under a four-hundred-page volume of confutation, two days before *King Vortigern* was laughed off the boards at Drury Lane.

But Boswell was spared that last humiliation. Soon after his visit to the Irelands his health gave way. In April 1795 he was able to dictate a letter to Warren Hastings congratulating him on acquittal

[1] All these were shortly followed by two complete plays, *King Vortigern* and *Henry II*. For the whole fantastic, fascinating story see W. H. Ireland, *Confessions* (1805), and J. Mair, *The Fourth Forger* (1938).

after his seven-years trial. But on May 19, after five weeks of painful illness, Boswell found at last his own release from trials of far longer date.

> 'He was in the constant habit,' wrote Malone to Windham on May 21, 'of calling on me almost daily, and I used to grumble sometimes at his turbulence, but now miss and regret his noise and his hilarity and his perpetual good humour, which had no bounds. Poor fellow, he has somehow stolen away from us, without any notice, and without my being at all prepared for it.'[1]

Poor Bozzy! Like a great cat, huger than the Sphinx, Life plays with human mice. Not even the most prudent can escape; and for the imprudent the eyes of that Sphinx can be stony, her claws unpitying. As Shakespeare well knew, when he sent Falstaff and his merry men, his Quickly and his Doll, after all their carefree comedy, to perish so ruthlessly by halter, or sickness, or broken heart.

Boswell died at only fifty-four. Yet he was already used up and burnt out; though he had only reached the age of Johnson at their first meeting—an age when many men have still had their best work before them—the age when Churchill, for example, was still a dozen years short of his finest hours.

Wine and women, repeated drunkenness and repeated venereal infections, had sapped that vitality which had been the foundation of Boswell's youthful charm, success, and happiness. The vain lure of social, legal, and political distinction in London had wiled him away from his home in Scotland, from his wife, from his only chance of making a success of his own life as well as of Johnson's. But blame is idle. He was too abnormal. And blame is thankless. For we are immeasurably in his debt.

[1] The tone of this deserves, I think, rather more attention than it has received. Malone was kindly; he was highly intelligent; he is writing of a man newly dead; and he knew more, in many ways, of Boswell and his two great books than we can hope to know. His attitude here seems to me sympathetic, compassionate, but very much this side of idolatry. It is far from Macaulay's vituperations; but it is far also from the adulations of Boswell not uncommon in the literary or learned journals of the last twenty-five years. I suspect that Malone's view holds a very rational balance. Boswell's exuberant eulogists tend, perhaps, to forget that the astonishing is not always the admirable; and that even admirable things are sometimes done by persons not very admirable in themselves. (Cf. the obituary, attributed to Malone, in *Gentleman's Magazine*, June 1795; which credits Boswell with 'inexhaustible good humour', laboriousness, and 'considerable intellectual powers, for which he has not had sufficient credit'.)

At times Boswell's life reads as if he had been watched over, not by a guardian angel, but by a guardian goblin. Even when Boswell had died, this guardian goblin pursued his pranks with Boswell's remains. The story of Boswell's papers is as fantastic as Boswell's own.

In 1795, by a will written ten years earlier, he left his MSS and letters to Sir William Forbes, Temple, and Malone 'to be published, for the benefit of my younger children, as they shall decide; that is to say, they are to have a discretionary power to publish more or less'.[1]

In 1796 Forbes suggested to Malone that it would be wise to wait till the younger James Boswell came of age, in 1799. Subsequently, James agreed that none of the papers should be printed; and Malone advised that they should be left at Auchinleck.

In 1807 Malone, in the fifth edition of the *Life of Johnson*, referred to an original letter from Johnson to Boswell being 'burned[2] in a mass of papers in Scotland'.

In 1822 James Boswell the younger died; and, after returning to Scotland from his brother's funeral in London, Sir Alexander Boswell was challenged by a political opponent whom he had anonymously derided in the press. In the ensuing duel, he was killed, leaving his estate to his own son, Sir James.

In 1825 the library of James, Boswell's son, was auctioned, including some proof-sheets and most of the revises of the *Life* (first edition), and a commonplace book of Boswell's—'Boswelliana'.

About 1840 a certain Major Stone, buying some articles at Mme Noël's shop in Boulogne, found them wrapped in an English letter, signed 'Boswell'. Investigation was made, and a large mass of Temple's correspondence recovered from a travelling paper-merchant who used to visit Boulogne twice or thrice a year; and so, in 1856 (dated 1857), were published Boswell's letters to Temple. His long resurrection had begun; but the letters were far from resurrecting his reputation.

How had they got to Boulogne? Apparently they had been taken

[1] A codicil of December 22, 1785, left his Johnsonian material to Malone, again for the benefit of his younger children.

[2] It has been conjectured that this is a misprint for 'buried'. This seems a possibility; but no more.

there by the Rev. Charles Powlett (1765–1834), who seems to have been a grandson of the third Duke of Bolton and Miss Lavinia Fenton (the original Polly Peachum in Gay's *Beggar's Opera*); had married Temple's eldest daughter Anne; and fled to France about 1825 to avoid his creditors.[1]

In 1874 Dr Charles Rogers, publishing a collection of Boswell's jottings, as *Boswelliana*, stated that 'Boswell's manuscripts were left to the disposal of his family; and it is believed that the whole were immediately destroyed'. When Birkbeck Hill, the great Johnsonian editor, made inquiries at Auchinleck, he was repulsed. And for fifty years this myth of the papers' destruction prevailed. Members of the house of Boswell were in part ignorant, in part touchy, about its most famous member.

Meanwhile, after the death of Bozzy's grandson, Sir James Boswell (1857), the estate of Auchinleck passed to his daughter, Mrs Mounsey; after whose death in 1905 the Auchinleck papers went to her sister's son, the sixth Lord Talbot of Malahide (ten miles north-north-east of Dublin), Boswell's great-great-grandson.

In 1925, Professor C. B. Tinker, editor of Boswell's letters, having been put on the trail by an illegibly signed postcard from Dublin, was eventually allowed to see the papers at Malahide in their Ebony Cabinet; a year later he was followed by Colonel Ralph Isham, who succeeded (by dint, I have been told, of much subtle diplomacy) in buying the collection, and also further papers found later (1930) in a croquet-box (including most of the manuscript of Boswell's *Tour to the Hebrides*).

The Malahide hoard consisted of (1) letters *from* Boswell (drafts, copies, and originals), letters *to* Boswell or his wife, and letters *about*

[1] This unfortunate cleric links us for a moment with a strangely different world—Jane Austen's. Jane to Cassandra, December 1, 1798: 'Charles Powlett gave a dance on Thursday, to the great disturbance of all his neighbours, of course, who, you know, take a most lively interest in the state of his finances, and live in hopes of his being soon ruined.' (It is interesting that these charitable hopes, though unfulfilled for a quarter of a century, were excited thus early.) Jane to Cassandra, December 18, 1798: 'his wife' (*i.e.* Temple's daughter), 'is discovered to be everything that the neighbourhood could wish her, silly and cross as well as extravagant.'

Some three years before his death in 1834, Powlett received a premature obituary in the *Gentleman's Magazine* for 1830 (vol. 100, pt. 2, 471–2), which states that he left Great Dunmow in 1827, paying his creditors only 10*s*. in the pound; but that his son, also a clergyman, two years later paid up in full.

Boswell; (2) drafts of published works, MS fragments of the *Life*, the MS of the *Account of Corsica;* (3) printed broadsides and essays; (4) MS journals or notes for journals, from 1761 to 1794;[1] (5) notes, memoranda,[2] jottings, accounts, and documents.

This treasure crossed the Atlantic, and much of it has been admirably edited in eighteen volumes by Geoffrey Scott and Professor F. A. Pottle.

But another discovery quickly followed. As already mentioned, Sir William Forbes of Pitsligo (1739–1806), a member of the Club and biographer of Beattie, was one of Boswell's literary executors. His heir married in 1797 the only child of Sir John Stuart of Fettercairn House (some thirty miles south-west of Aberdeen). In 1930 Professor C. C. Abbott, who was working on Beattie, and had been informed of Beattie papers at Fettercairn, found there masses of Sir William Forbes's papers, and then of Boswell's—the *London Journal*, six other Boswell MSS,[3] drafts or copies of over three hundred of his letters, over a hundred Johnson letters, and over a thousand letters to Boswell.

In 1939 the loft of an outhouse at Malahide yielded another hoard of papers, including a large part of the manuscript of the *Life of Johnson*; and after Lord Talbot's death in 1948, further papers were found to be at Malahide, including the corrected proofs of the *Tour to the Hebrides*.

All these finds likewise joined the Isham collection; which has since passed to the University of Yale.

Apart from their intrinsic fascination, these discoveries also throw new light on Boswell as biographer. It had already been known that his habit was first to make rough notes for his journals, while his memory was fresh; then to write them up more fully. But it is quite another thing to possess the actual notes and journals.

What emerges?

[1] Including, as already stated, the original journal of the Hebridean tour.

[2] Including *London Memoranda* from December 26, 1762, to August 4, 1763. (The *London Journal* itself later turned up at Fettercairn.) These memoranda are programmes for the day and self-exhortations written before dressing in the morning. Later, Boswell's memoranda became mainly *retrospective* notes of the previous day's happenings, to be expanded in his full Journals.

[3] Including Boswell's Journal from March 20 to May 23, 1778; the ludicrous account of his last interview with Hume; and notes for a life of Oglethorpe.

First, the excessive and obsessive importance Boswell attached to keeping a journal of his own life. He even had at times the bizarre notion that he should live no more than he could record—an attitude, to me as fantastic as the ancient Egyptian feeling that what happened to one's body living mattered less than having it properly pickled for eternity.

Secondly, it becomes clear that, though Boswell says he kept constantly in view the idea of writing Johnson's life from the beginning of their twenty years' friendship, still his recordings of Johnson remained all that while only a part of the far vaster, journalized autobiography of Boswell himself. The Life of Johnson is really only an outwork of a far huger Life of Boswell.

Thirdly, the materials and methods used by Boswell become much clearer. His *London Journal* he seems to have written, as most men would, in its full form as it stands. But after leaving Holland for his tour he came to prefer the more practical method, for a hurried man, of writing notes each evening, and then writing up his full journal from these within the next three to five days.[1] At times, however, there were far longer delays, when Boswell would drop whole weeks or months behind. In 1777, for example, his April notes did not get written up till August; his May notes, not till October. Sometimes his notes never got written up at all.

Still the notes at least were there. As he remarks of journalizing in *The Hypochondriack*—'I have thought my notes like portable soup, of which a little bit by being dissolved in water will make a good large dish.'

When Boswell came to publish the *Tour to the Hebrides*, he was able to use his MS journal to provide most of the printer's actual copy. But the evidence grows of our deep debt to Malone. Most of the corrections are in Malone's hand; and 'a good third of the original record', on Professor Pottle's estimate, is cut (largely descriptions and reflections by Boswell).

The *Life* was vastly more complicated. On December 18, only five days after Johnson's death, Dilly wrote asking if Boswell could prepare four hundred pages octavo of Johnson's *conversations* by February. This suggests that Dilly, a close friend, knew, to some

[1] See *Boswell on the Grand Tour, 1764*, ed. F. A. Pottle (1953), p. 152 (October 25, 1764).

extent at least, what masses of material lay ready at Boswell's disposal, in journal-form. It may also suggest that Dilly already realized how much the liveliest thing in a life of Johnson would be Johnson's talk.

Boswell, however—most wisely—instead of thus rushing into print in six weeks, waited six and a half years—though some of that delay was due to his own paralysing indolence and lethargy.

For the parts of the *Life* where Boswell had been in Johnson's company, sometimes, it seems, he used actual sheets from a volume of his journal, which he would afterwards rebind; sometimes he wrote with his journal open before him; sometimes he had to use his remarkable memory to reconstruct the scene and talk from rough notes never written up at all—for example, the vivid meeting of Johnson and Wilkes.

How did Boswell record conversation? One may imagine him scribbling like a reporter with open notebook; but actually this crude method seems to have been the exception. True, his tablets made Paoli think him 'an espy', and Mrs Thrale criticize him as ill-bred. But though Boswell might whip out pencil and paper for special reasons—for instance, to get the exact words of a ballad-parody by Johnson ('The tender infant meek and mild . . .')—as a rule he seems to have relied on jotting down the gist of a talk as soon as possible *afterwards*, and then building up the full version later still.

At Mrs Thrale's in March 1783 Johnson was in fine form:

> 'While he went on talking triumphantly I was all admiration, and said, "O, for short hand to take this down!" Said Mrs Thrale: "You'll carry it all in your head. A long head is as good as short hand." I have the substance, but the felicity of expression, the flavour, is not fully preserved unless taken instantly.'

Boswell had trained his memory; but he realized, in his anxiety for an exact and perfect likeness of Johnson's talk, that even *his* memories needed to be quickly fixed on paper. 'As it was not taken down recently,' he records in September 1777, of a remark of Johnson's, 'it has not his rich flavour of language. To write down his sayings at a distant period after hearing them is pickling or preserving long-kept and faded fruits and vegetables.' An excellent image.

At first, indeed, he had found it difficult (so he records in the *Life*) to record Johnson's talk at all—it was too unfamiliar, too overpowering; but 'in progress of time, when my mind was, as it were, *strongly impregnated with the Johnsonian aether*, I could, with much more facility and exactness, carry in my memory and commit to paper the exuberant variety of his wisdom and wit'. Here, I think, one can trust his good faith.

Boswell had early shown a curious, indiscriminate passion for recording conversations, no matter by whom. For example, in 1762–3 he set himself to record on Saturdays snatches of quite random dialogue from Child's Coffee House.[1] But not only had Boswell trained his verbal memory by this sort of reporting. He was also a practised mimic. Hannah More once umpired between Boswell and Garrick himself, as imitators of Johnson—'I remember I gave it for Boswell in familiar conversation, and for Garrick in reciting poetry.' Now vivid mimicry involves vivid memory. The talents which had won encores at Drury Lane for imitations of a cow, were not wasted when it came to imitating the Great Bear. It is also very possible that Boswell was helped by his practice as a lawyer in court. In fine, he had justification for boasting of himself as 'one who has the power of exhibiting an exact transcript of conversations'. A most uncommon gift.

When Dr Blacklock questioned one of the remarks attributed to Johnson in the *Tour*, Boswell replied in an Appendix: 'I beg it may be remembered, that it is not upon *memory*, but upon what was *written at the time*, that the authenticity of my *Journal* rests.'

Again, his care comes out in the proofs of the *Life*. 'We may be excused,' says Johnson, 'for not caring much about other people's children, for there are many who care very little about their own children.' The proof-reader wanted to delete the second 'children'. But Boswell comments, 'The *repetition* is the Johnsonian mode.' In the proof Johnson says of Burke, 'His vigour of mind is incessant'; but Boswell corrects 'vigour of mind' to 'stream of mind'. 'I restore, I find, the exact words as to Burke.'

All this is most admirable. On the other hand, it might be very

[1] Specimen on p. 189.

misleading to exaggerate the extent to which we can trust Boswell always to give us Johnson's *ipsissima verba*. Boswell was working, after a shorter or longer interval, from short notes. He must clearly have depended a great deal on invention, as well as memory, to fill out his memoranda; which are sometimes so abbreviated as to become quite obscure, at least to us.

Take, for example, his notes of Voltaire's talk (December 29, 1764—*Boswell on the Grand Tour; Germany and Switzerland*, p. 295):

> *Boswell.* ...'Only, your *Dictionnaire philosophique*. For instance, *Ame*, the Soul—'
>
> *Voltaire.* 'That is a good article.'
>
> *Boswell.* 'No. Excuse me. Is it[1] not a pleasing imagination? Is it not more noble?'
>
> *Voltaire.* 'Yes. You have a noble desire to be King of Europe. "I wish it, and I ask your protection." But it is not probable.'

Here Professor Pottle expands 'I wish it, and I ask your protection' as meaning 'You, Boswell, say "I wish it,[2] and I ask your protection" (in continuing to wish it)'. But why should Boswell ask anybody's *protection* in continuing to *wish* something? Wishes are free.

It seems to me that there may be quite another interpretation. Voltaire can be imagined saying:

> 'You would like to fancy yourself possessed of a Soul? You think it a noble desire. But things do not become more probable just because one would like them. You might have a "noble" desire to be King of Europe. And then, indeed, I might exclaim—"My best wishes for your Majesty's accession! I beg your protection for poor Voltaire." Yet your coronation remains improbable.'

[1] What is 'it'? Professor Pottle interprets—'immortality.' But immortality has not yet been mentioned. I take 'it' to be '(the existence of) the Soul'. (Cf. Voltaire's letter to Boswell of February 11, 1765, quoted in footnote to p. 217; and, in his *Dictionnaire*, the article 'Ame', which is sceptical about the soul's very existence. Granted, Boswell's main anxiety was that the soul should be immortal: but, to be immortal, it must first *exist*.)

[2] *I.e.* immortality. But immortality has still not been mentioned. This 'it' seems to me more naturally referable to being 'King of Europe', the idea immediately preceding.

Further, in expanding or compressing Johnson's recorded words, Boswell sometimes took liberties that many of us to-day would think excessive.

Of this audacity in alteration there exists a famous example in Boswell's commonplace-book, *Boswelliana.* Johnson is ridiculing Thomas Sheridan's ideas of improving English eloquence. ' "Sir," said Mr Johnson, "it won't do. . . . He is like a man attempting to stride the English Channel. Sir, the cause bears no proportion to the effect. It is setting up a candle at Whitechapel to give light at Westminster." ' In the *Life* this becomes drastically altered—'Besides, Sir, what influence can Mr Sheridan have upon the language of this great country by his narrow exertions? Sir, it is burning a farthing candle at Dover to show light at Calais!'

Now it is, of course, conceivable that Johnson might, at different times, have uttered both versions; but it remains most improbable. It seems likelier that, in the *Life*, Boswell was deliberately compressing. He wished to keep both the Channel and the candle (which he improves to a 'farthing candle'); and so he ran the two together. This revision has been praised and admired. But I cannot see why. I do not think Johnson's words should be changed so cavalierly; and here they seem to me changed much for the worse. Dover and Calais make a contrast less apt (quite apart from the loss of alliteration) than Whitechapel and Westminster. For what is the subject? A foolish attempt to reform the English language. Westminster has associations with English at its best, Whitechapel with English not at its best; they are therefore far more pointed and relevant than Dover and Calais. In short, Boswell has here by no means bettered Johnson.

Again, as Professor Pottle has justly remarked, Boswell makes another change for the worse in the *Tour*, where Johnson says of Burke: 'If you met him for the first time in a street where you were stopped by a drove of oxen, and you and he stepped[1] aside to take shelter but for five minutes . . . you would say, "This is an extraordinary man." ' In Boswell's notes this had begun, 'If you met him for the first time in a street where there was a shower of cannon bullets, and you and he ran up a stair to take shelter. . . .' Probably Boswell thought this shower of cannon-balls too far-fetched; and

[1] 'Stopped . . . stepped' do not seem very happy in sound.

so, for bullets, substituted bullocks. But, if so, I must own I am shocked. Not only are such 'improvements' as impertinent as Bentley's improvements of Milton; but it would be a very long, or very leisurely, drove of oxen that made anyone 'take shelter' (even supposing that Johnson would have deigned to 'take shelter' from mere bullocks) for as much as five minutes. Even at two miles an hour, that would entail a column of cattle stretching nearly three hundred yards!

On the other hand, in fairness to Boswell, it must be remembered that his century was less punctilious in such matters than ours; the liberties taken by him with Johnson's conversation seem mild beside those taken by Mason, for example, with Gray's correspondence.

It would also be a foolish exaggeration to pretend that Boswell was unique in catching the authentic accent of his hero. It is a curious fact that, whereas contemporary imitations of Johnson's written style are usually feeble and futile, his spoken style is often, I think, as Johnsonian in Mrs Thrale, Fanny Burney, Murphy, Reynolds, or Cumberland, as in Boswell himself. The great difference is that Boswell gives us a continuous stream of talk, where they give only fascinating moments.

The Boswell Papers, then, seem to me to reveal, above all, two points previously far less clear: first, the strange mania of Boswell for preserving the past, above all his own past—so that his biography is, in some sense, a by-product of an immense autobiography; second, how efficiently and persistently methodical he was in this process of preservation, especially in recording conversations.

But this careful recording is only part of a larger passion for accuracy in biography which does Boswell all the more credit because the need for truth in biography or history has not always been the truism it has now become. In Antiquity Plutarch assailed the 'malignancy' of Herodotus in recording unedifying facts which would have been better left untold. Seventeenth-century biographers like Walton, nineteenth-century biographers like Stanley were similarly inclined to prefer edification to honesty. Of Boswell himself Wordsworth could primly complain that 'the life of Johnson by Boswell had broken through many pre-existing delicacies, and afforded the British public an opportunity of acquiring experience, which before it had happily wanted'.

But surely this is a little mawkish. If a man publishes books, he thereby invites publicity. If he is able to interest the public, the public will inevitably become interested in the whole truth about him—so far as that truth can be found. Such is the price of fame. If one does not wish to pay, one should avoid becoming famous—it is seldom difficult; but it is idle to aim both at being known and at being unknown.

In vain, therefore, did Wordsworth object to biographical frankness: in due time his own love-affair with Annette Vallon was disinterred. In vain did Matthew Arnold wish to have no biography at all: biographies of Arnold multiply, and scholars speculate at large on his love-affair with the Marguerite of Thun. In vain Tennyson raged about 'ghouls'. If one wishes to escape from human curiosity, one should remain securely obscure.

Our own century, no doubt, has sometimes been too much tempted to exchange hero-worship in biography for satire, reverence for impudence. At moments even Lytton Strachey yielded too much to the tempting Muse of Irony; and his camp-followers became a lamentable army. But Boswell tried, and usually with success, to hold a fair and honest balance. Just as Johnson had refused to write 'honeysuckle' lives of poets, so Boswell rejected Hannah More's plea for mitigating some of Johnson's 'asperities'—'he would not cut off his claws, nor make a tiger a cat, to please any body'.

This strong feeling of Boswell's about accuracy was, I imagine, partly ethical, partly æsthetic. It was his duty to tell the strange truth; but he also loved it. He adored oddities. He hunted lions. And of course a lion-hunter will not want to cut their claws; he is more likely to hang their heads on his wall with mouths wide agape to display their grinning fangs.

No doubt there were moments when prejudice could tempt Boswell to malice. And at other moments he carried needless candour beyond all bounds of decency. What is sport for us, was often far from a joke for his contemporaries. Johnson, indeed, had left no family to restrain Boswell in his reckless revelations; but the resentment of Lord Alexander Macdonald at Boswell's liberties in the *Tour* is perfectly understandable. And imagine the feelings of Sir John Dalrymple (1726–1810)—not to mention Sir John's amused acquaintances—in reading how, when he invited Johnson and Boswell to stay, Boswell was deliberately late, although they knew Sir John had killed a seven-year-old sheep for them (not that there seems great tenderness in a seven-year-old sheep); how Johnson laughed on the way at the thought of their host's mortification—'I dare say, Sir, he has been very sadly distressed: Nay, we do not know but that the consequence may have been fatal'—and pictured him, in a parody of Sir John's own historical style, committing suicide; how, when the travellers *did* at last arrive, Sir John was, naturally enough, in a poor humour; how his ancient bedrooms proved more suited to an Italian summer than a Scottish November; and how, finally, they thought they would find more comfort at an inn two miles off, and so removed thither next day.[1] Clearly Boswell disliked Sir John who, he says, had joined with prejudiced Scots in 'railing' at Johnson behind his back. Still, one begins to feel that the Scots had some grounds for prejudice. Hospitality accepted entails *some* decencies.

Again, there seems little excuse for publishing in the *Life* such allusions to the living as Boswell's own reflection on the hated Gibbon's[2] ugliness, or Johnson's curt comment on the Lady Diana Beauclerk[3] (who, after all, had been a friend of Boswell's)—'the woman's a whore and there's an end on't.' We cannot wonder if, as Percy records, Boswell became 'shunned and scouted' after the publication of his masterpiece.

However, the pain caused by Boswell's indiscretions is long over; and to-day we have only the amusement. Without such indiscretions he would have been a better man; but they make his book a better book.

Further, if Boswell sometimes preferred naked truth to decency,

[1] *Life*, v, 401–4.

[2] (Of Johnson's making himself agreeable to ladies) 'Sir Joshua Reynolds agreed with me that he could. Mr Gibbon, with his usual sneer, controverted it, perhaps in resentment of Johnson's having talked with some disgust of his ugliness, which one would think a *philosopher* would not mind'. (*Life*, iv, 73.) Not very prettily said.

[3] She is not named, it is true, but described as 'a lady who had been divorced from her husband by act of Parliament'. All the same, from the details given, I suspect a good many readers could identify her.

he did also take most laudable pains to be accurate. He gained much by waiting till half-a-dozen other works on Johnson had appeared. And we believe him when he tells how he would run over half London to verify a date; it is enough, for example, to note the pains he took, and the witnesses he examined, to discover who was really the prime mover in getting Johnson his pension. It would, no doubt, be absurd to compare Boswell with that amazing being, hated by him as a 'disagreeable dog', Edward Gibbon; who mastered with such ease the details, not of a single life, but of a whole empire and more than a whole millennium. Yet it remains astonishing, considering the haystacks of paper poor Boswell had to sift, and the multitude of sources, living and written, he had to consult, that so much was accomplished—even with the inspiration and instigation of the patient Malone—by a man burdened with bereavement, disappointment, melancholia, drink, and failing vitality.

This anxiety of Boswell's to report words and facts truthfully was part of a larger truthfulness. That quality may have been encouraged in him by Johnson, with his hatred of cant and his contempt for fictions and exaggerations. But it is already clear from the *London Journal* that Boswell, despite the rant and bombast of his emotional utterances, had a passion of his own for realism and minuteness in portraying life. He speaks of drawing Johnson 'in the style of a Flemish painter'. 'Every trifle must be authentick.... I am not satisfied with hitting the large features. I must be exact as to every hair, or even every spot on his countenance.' 'All I have said of the Stratford Jubilee,' he observes regretfully in his Journal, 'is very dim in comparison of the scene itself. In description we omit insensibly many little touches which give life to objects. With how small a speck does a Painter give life to an eye!' In poetry Johnson had objected to minutely counting the streaks of tulips; but in biography both he and Boswell were vividly aware of the vital importance of such 'streaks' and 'little touches'. 'The minute diversities of everything are wonderful.'

So much for Boswell's laborious veracity. But great books are not produced by mere laboriousness. The constant difficulty with history or biography is that both are partly science, partly art. And by the time a man has done his toilsome duty to scientific truth, he may easily be left barren of the vitality and inspiration needed to make his work a work of art. He may become—not like Browning's Grammarian, 'dead from the waist down'—but dead from the waist up, dead in heart and mind. One of Boswell's best qualities was his pulsating interest in human character. With his childish absurdities went a childlike eagerness and wonder at the strangeness of life and people. One can see it fading to some extent in the sadder journals of his later years, when he confesses he has lost his old art of recording conversations. But he contrived to get this eagerness into his masterpieces; and they owe much to it.

It is, then, another of Boswell's great qualities that he was not subdued by the immense bulk of his materials, but kept that zest and liveliness for lack of which the lives of dead men have sometimes become less like lives than coffins.

Again, Boswell was not content to marshal truthfully the data about Johnson; he laboured constantly to extract from Johnson more truths and new data. He anatomized, as very few biographers have been in a position to do, the living subject; even though the living subject was apt to rage and bellow under this process.

Boswell was constantly experimenting, like one of those vivisectors Johnson abhorred, to see what his Bear would do or say. How would Johnson react if introduced to his abomination, Rousseau?[1] That, alas, never came off. How would Johnson react to his other abomination, Wilkes? That was brilliantly successful.[2] How would he react to a cold sheep's head? This dish was innocently suggested by Lady Lochbuy in Mull. 'Sir Allan seemed displeased at his sister's vulgarity. . . . From a mischievous love of sport, I took the lady's part.' The trick worked. ' "No, Madam," said he, with a tone of surprise and anger . . . while I sat quietly by, and enjoyed my success.'

Similarly he incurred Johnson's wrath by rashly wishing to see him and Mrs Macaulay together—'Don't you know it is very uncivil to *pit* two people against one another?' Mrs Thrale was perfectly just when she wrote in the margin of the *Life*, 'Curiosity

[1] To Rousseau (January 4, 1766): 'Je me propose une satisfaction parfaite en vous faisant connaître M. Johnson. . . . Je suis sûr que vos grandes âmes se reconnaîtront avec chaleur.' The *chaleur*, at least, seems likely enough.

[2] In 1776. In 1770 Johnson had violently attacked Wilkes in *The False Alarm*. But it must be remembered that in 1759 Wilkes, though already at odds with Johnson, had interceded to get Johnson's negro servant, Barber, released from the Navy.

carried Boswell further than it ever carried any mortal breathing; he cared not what he provoked so as he saw what *such a one* would do.'

Above all in conversation Boswell perpetually drew his hero out and on. 'I also may be allowed to claim some merit in leading the conversation. I do not mean leading, as in an orchestra, by playing the first fiddle, but leading as one does in examining a witness—starting topics, and making him pursue them.' One is at times reminded of Socrates playing dialectical midwife to young men's unborn ideas. But even that brought Socrates to the hemlock; and Socrates was not playing midwife to a bear.

Well might Boswell say to Percy, of collecting Johnson's sayings: 'You all collect some. But I venture more than any of you. I am like the Man "who gathers samphire, dreadful trade". I gather upon the face of the rock while there is a storm.'

At times the thunderbolt hung miraculously suspended, even though the oracle was asked what it would do if it found itself alone in a castle with a new-born infant. But at other times the storm broke—and the bolt fell—'I will not be put to the *question*. Don't you consider, Sir, that these are not the manners of a gentleman? I will not be baited with *what* and *why*; what is this? what is that? why is a cow's tail long? why is a fox's tail bushy?'

Then the samphire-gatherer would take cover; but only to return, persistent as a fly.

In this aspect Boswell was a kind of grotesque anthropologist—a species of scientist. But he was also an artist. Biography, like history, remains art as well as science. Its paramount duty is truth. But though it should tell nothing but the truth, it cannot possibly tell the whole truth. It must select, or die of its own unwieldy corpulence. The thoughts of a single day might burst a whole volume of autobiography; sufficient research might swell the life of a single man to the size of an encyclopædia in thirty volumes. But it would leave the man's personality, which is the central theme of biography as of portrait-painting, swamped and blurred. To read it would be as tedious and unpractical as a walking-tour of Siberia.

Therefore selection. But with selection there comes art as well as science. What will most reliably reveal a man's personality—or his personalities? For he may have many—the name of each of us is

Legion. Are we to study a man's actions? But his actions are innumerable; and what matters to our judgment is not merely his actions, but his motives—which must often be obscure, often unknowable.

Shall we turn, then, rather to a man's writings? What a man did is often contestable; his motives in doing it, more contestable still; but with his writings we are usually certain that he did at least write them. They are often solider evidence, so far as they go. Letters, in particular, can often tell us more than deeds. Style can be extremely revealing. But letters are often insincere; even if sincere, they vary with the correspondent.

Thirdly, there is a man's talk—more spontaneous than his books or letters—but usually far less authentically recorded. None the less, where the reporting is good and the circumstances known, I do not know what reveals a man's character more vividly than his casual, unpremediated utterances. That can be seen, for example, with Wellington or Napoleon. But it is particularly true with Johnson. He came out in his talk as in nothing else.[1] Boswell was uniquely lucky in his subject.

At different times (to name only the dead) I have been lucky enough to hear Lytton Strachey and Virginia Woolf, Lord Keynes, Lowes Dickinson, and Roger Fry, H. W. Nevinson and Lawrence of Arabia, Housman and Walter de la Mare, Granville Barker and Desmond MacCarthy, George Moore, and Yeats. Often it was deeply interesting. The best was Desmond MacCarthy. The most comical was George Moore—though that was not George Moore's intention. But not one of them would have given Boswell one half the scope that Johnson gave.

Cut the talk out of Boswell's books on Johnson, and you deface them irretrievably. Without the conversations,[2] Boswell's *Johnson* would rank, I think, little above that of Hawkins and a thousand other biographies—far below the work of better critics and wiser

[1] Cf. the judgment passed by Norvins on the talk of one who was just reaching womanhood when Johnson died, Mme. de Staël—'ces conversations de salon si imprévues, si brillantes, souvent sublimes, et supérieures, je ne crains pas de le dire, à ce qu'elle écrit, qu'il eût été bien précieux de transmettre à la postérité'.

[2] Cf. the vital part played by dialogue both in the Bible and in Homer. It is seldom realized how much the vividness of *Iliad* and *Odyssey* gains by the high proportion of speeches, which have been estimated as three-fifths of the whole (*Iliad* I has 375 lines of speeches out of a total 610). The epic becomes almost drama.

men; far below Johnson's *Lives*, or Voltaire's *Charles XII*, or Lockhart's *Scott*, or Mackail's *William Morris*, or Strachey's *Queen Victoria*. These biographies succeed largely by their style and by their power of judging life and character. But Boswell was outstanding neither in his style, apart from a sometimes admirable vividness in description, nor in his judgments on life.

Clearly the credit for these priceless dialogues belongs both to Johnson and to Boswell. The ideal, no doubt, would have been for Johnson to carry a dictaphone in his pocket from the age of ten, and for the results to be edited by a Sainte-Beuve. But, as things were and are, Boswell could hardly have done much better than he did.

Not only had Boswell selected Johnson, out of the many distinguished men he knew, as his main object and subject; he had the further good sense to select Johnson's talk as the main feature of that subject. For both, he deserves full praise. If he learnt something from Mason's *Life of Gray*, he incomparably surpassed his model.

> 'Mason's *Life of Gray*,' he writes to Temple in 1788, 'is excellent, because it is interspersed with letters that show us the *man*. His *Life of Whitehead* is not a life at all; for there is neither a letter nor a saying from first to last. I am absolutely certain that *my* mode of biography, which gives not only a *history* of Johnson's *visible* progress through the world, and of his publications, but a *view* of his mind, in his letters and conversations, is the most perfect that can be conceived, and will be *more* of a *Life* than any work that has ever yet appeared.'

'It will be,' he repeats elsewhere, more strongly still, 'the most entertaining book that ever appeared.'

This confidence, though often clouded by moods of despondency, was justified. Actually, Gray was a livelier letter-writer than Johnson; if Mason's *Gray* is dead, and Boswell's *Johnson* living, it is because Johnson was a superb talker superbly reported.

For another of Boswell's merits, besides his truthfulness, his industry, and his selectiveness, is his sense of drama. Early interested in the stage, a familiar of Garrick and of lesser players, and a man only too prone to dramatize his own existence into melodrama, Boswell knew how to make his biography often as dramatic as a play. He had described his early interview with Voltaire as a 'scene';

he told Erskine in 1780, 'I must write Dr Johnson's life in Scenes.'

This dramatic effect he achieves not only by putting the names of the *dramatis personae* before their utterances, in place of the far less vivid 'said I'—'answered he'; but also by appropriate stage-directions. In his brilliant suggestion of gesture and posture, indeed, he has learnt not only from the theatre of a century of great actors, but also from the pages of a century of great novelists. Like Sterne depicting Mrs Shandy's exact pose as she eavesdrops at the door, Boswell knows the importance of making us visualize his hero's eccentric gestures and attitudes.

This dramatic effect is further heightened by the skill with which the other characters of Johnson's circle are made to play their parts, without ever masking the dominance of the great protagonist. There are moments when they remind one faintly of a Greek chorus; moments, when Boswell himself, one of the most vital figures in his own drama, dimly suggests the Greek messenger who narrates episodes in a Greek play; moments, too, when poor Bozzy recalls the Elizabethan fool who provides comic relief on Shakespeare's stage.

All these are admirable features. And it is obvious that two books so remarkable as the *Tour* and the *Life* imply remarkable merits in their author. But at this point, I think, one should grow very careful. It is easy and tempting for the critic to be drawn on into raptures and rhapsodies. But anyone who wishes to keep a sane and balanced scale of values alike in life and in literature, will beware of what Johnson called 'enormous and disgusting hyperboles'—such as comparing Boswell with Chaucer or Shakespeare, Dickens or Hardy, as a great creative genius.

Indeed I am never very happy about our happy-go-lucky use of the word 'genius'. For 'genius' becomes often rather a tiresome pomp-word, a cant-term of literary mystics, which it might perhaps be better never to use at all. The ancient Romans believed that every man possessed his 'genius', every woman her 'Juno'. The 'genius' or 'Juno' was a kind of guardian spirit. Thence in modern language 'genius' has come to denote exceptional gifts of invention or imagination. In fact, like 'inspiration', 'genius' is a dead metaphor. But even dead metaphors can be dangerous. Few of us, no doubt, believe that Homer had the *Iliad* dictated to him by a young lady in white linen called a Muse;[1] many of us suppose the 'daemon' of Socrates to have been a not uncommon type of auditory hallucination; but there remains a mystery-mongering tendency to set up 'genius' as a thing apart, separated by a great gulf from mere 'talent'. I do not believe in this gulf. From Hodge to Homer I do not believe that Nature makes a sudden leap at any point in the ascending scale of human qualities.

No doubt, in works to which we apply the terms 'genius' or 'inspiration' there is much that remains mysterious, much that makes us cry 'How the devil could he think of that!'; because a good deal of the process goes on in the Unconscious. When Archimedes leapt from his bath and ran naked through the streets crying 'Eureka!', it was simply that a problem long incubated in his Unconscious had at last found conscious solution. But unconscious mental processes are not the peculiarity of a few; they are common to all of us; it is their effectiveness that, in some minds, becomes exceptional. So it might be more useful to speak, not of genius, but of '*exceptional* creative or inventive gifts'. For I believe the difference to be one, not of kind, but merely of degree.

Boswell has produced something like a most wonderful documentary-film; but perhaps it differs more in quantity than in quality, in perseverance than in brilliance, from the scenes sketched by Hester Thrale or Fanny Burney. Johnson was an astounding subject. And I feel that Johnson was the making of Boswell, even more than Boswell of Johnson.

Accordingly Boswellians seem to me too 'enthusiastick', when they talk of his 'genius', or celebrate him as if he had gifts comparable with those of Johnson, Goldsmith, Gibbon, Hume, or Burke. His own prose style is, for me, sometimes pleasant, but often mediocre, often foolish, occasionally grotesque. His verse style is uniformly ludicrous. His imagination lacks the least poetic quality. His letters are often drivel. And neither *The Hypochondriack* nor *Dorando* suggests that he had any real creative gift. In short, outside biography and autobiography Boswell appears to me a negligible writer.

Further, it is rash to assume that the author of an admirable book must *always* be an admirable writer; still less need he be a wholly

[1] Etymologically connected with '*mania*', 'madness', 'inspiration'.

admirable human being. Sometimes it is the sick oyster that produces the pearl. Macaulay's paradox that Boswell produced a supreme biography because he was a supreme ass, extravagantly as Macaulay chose to put it, does not seem to me quite so foolish as is generally assumed. The success of Boswell's biography does partly arise, as I have suggested from real merits; but it arises also from qualities in him that seem to me defects.

First, Boswell's assiduous journalizing was the result of an enormous and abnormal interest in himself. Most of us, no doubt, regard ourselves with great—often excessive—interest; but not to the point of keeping journals for forty years, even if it sometimes involves sitting up four nights in a week to do it.

In early days Boswell sent his diary to his friend Johnston to read; later he sometimes let his wife read it—with results that did not make for domestic harmony. But on the whole he seems to have written, like Pepys, simply for himself. He may have thought vaguely of publication; at the end of his life, it will be remembered, he left that question to the discretion of his literary executors. But even Boswell can hardly have contemplated complete publication—including those compromising passages he so incompetently disguised in Greek letters.

And to the endless journals must be added an enormous amount of other record-keeping—copies of his letters, registers of letters sent and received, records of law-cases, records of guests invited and of what they had to drink. When Margaret Boswell's consumption grew acute, even that had to become the subject of a separate journal. Boswell, in short, devoted as much energy to the history of Boswell as Gibbon to that of the Roman Empire. His private archives must have acquired a bulk that might have busied, or even buried, an archivist.[1]

To Boswell's obsession with his personal records posterity is deeply indebted for both instruction and amusement. By endless self-portraiture he developed the technique for his portrait of Johnson. His indefatigable method of making immediate notes, followed by patient writing up, was the only method that could produce the *Life*. But, vastly as we have benefited by Boswell's recording mania,

[1] The index to the eighteen volumes of *Boswell Papers* alone contains the names of over 6,500 persons!

I cannot regard it, in itself, as admirable, healthy, or wise. Tastes differ. But, personally, I can neither imagine how a man could find it worth while to spend all these months writing about himself, nor how, even if he did, he could imagine it would be endurable to spend months more reading about himself.[1] The tragedy of transience seems to me so poignant that, even in a character far less hypochondriacal than Boswell, I should expect such habits to produce acute melancholia.

O Death in Life, the days that are no more.

No doubt memory is important; it may have been, in part, man's better memory that enabled him to rise above the chimpanzee; but one can easily remember far too much. The past may all be recorded in our Unconscious; but a good deal of it had better stay there. Excessive retrospection, like excessive introspection, can become perilous. The healthy mind looks a little ahead, and not too much behind—there is the present to be used, the future to be prepared, without playing Lot's wife towards the past.

In fine, to keep a diary within limits may often be sane and sensible; but journalizing on Boswell's scale seems to me a mental malady.[2] We may, in this case, have gained richly; but it still seems to me, in general, a foolish thing for any man to do.

Then again, besides Boswell's mania for self-contemplation and self-recording, there is Boswell's other itch for self-exposure. Contemporaries marvelled at the combination of so much vanity with so much indifference to humiliation. In his journals, his letters, his talk he will happily reveal weaknesses or absurdities that most men would blush to face even in their most private thoughts.[3] His wife

1 Mrs Piozzi records how, in later life, re-reading parts of *Thraliana* spoilt her sleep for a week. Even to Boswell it occurred in 1777 that if he burnt all his elaborate records of the past, he might be 'like a New being'. Luckily, however, and characteristically, instead of consigning his Journal to the flames, he merely consigned this thought to his Journal.

2 There may be a neurotic basis for this literary hoarding; which those interested in modern psychology will easily guess.

3 Dean Inge has said: 'If, however, a man writes a diary which he feels sure that nobody will ever see except himself, he is probably perfectly truthful. There is no motive for being otherwise.' This I find very doubtful. First, how many men face the full truth about themselves, even in their most private thoughts? Secondly, how can anyone possibly be 'sure' that even his most secret scribbles will never be read

told him his journal would leave him 'embowelled to posterity'. Was she wrong? In his books he has no hesitation at telling stories against himself—not merely tossings and gorings endured in the good cause of making Johnson perform, but episodes not even necessary or relevant to his subject—how he was set to pull a rope in the storm off Col merely to keep him quiet;[1] or how he was snubbed, not only by Johnson, but even by a minor figure like Colman, when Johnson was not even present. The talk had turned on second-sight. 'I avowed my conviction, saying . . . "The evidence is enough for me, though not for his great mind. What will not fill a quart bottle will fill a pint bottle. I am filled with belief." "Are you?" (said Colman), "then cork it up." '

And there the episode ends. The amused reader is grateful for being given it; but he remains a little astonished that it is given; and he may feel no disposition to admire the giver.

Thirdly, there is Boswell's passionate search, already mentioned, for guides, philosophers, and friends, for sages, Mentors, and father-substitutes, for advice at every turn of his love-affairs. In this respect, as in others, Boswell never grew up.

And so there remains, I think, this much truth in Macaulay's paradox, that some of the most admirable qualities in Boswell's works are due to qualities in his own character that are not admirable at all, but morbid; just as Johnson's picturesqueness is also due to defects as well as merits. If Boswell had not been a self-recording Narcissist, the *Life* and the *Tour* would have been mere shadows of what they are; if he had not been like Rousseau, a persistent exhibitionist,[2] these two books would have lost many of their liveliest moments; if he had not been given to hero-worship of a somewhat infantile extravagance, we should have lacked the interviews with Rousseau and Voltaire, the ardent discipleship to Johnson himself.

by others? (Even that modern neurotic who wrote poems with the tip of her tongue on the inside of her mouth in shorthand, did not evade the analyst!) The peculiarity of Pepys and Boswell is that they seem to feel far less than most men the presence of another, critical self, or of an imaginary spectator, looking over their shoulders as they write.

[1] P. 239. Naturally Rowlandson found the episode a golden subject for one of his caricatures of Bozzy.

[2] Cf. the remark in his journal: 'I have a kind of strange feeling as if I wished nothing to be secret that concerns myself.'

On Boswell the man, as on Boswell the writer, there is violent dispute. Macaulay's picture of him as an arrant idiot has been met by his defenders with whole trucks of whitewash. It appears to me that, as usual, the truth lies somewhere in between. Boswell was, at times, a complete fool; and yet this fool was not the complete Boswell.

Contemporaries had evidence we cannot have, though we on our side have evidence denied to them. We have already seen Gray's comment to Walpole on *Corsica*—'a Dialogue between a Green-Goose and a Hero'. Walpole on his side could not be expected to favour Boswell. For he detested Johnson; and he clashed with Boswell over Rousseau. 'But as he came to see me no more, I forgave him all the rest.' In short, Walpole is a much more prejudiced witness than Gray.

Then there is Goldsmith's jest—'He is not a cur, he is only a bur. Tom Davies flung him at Johnson in sport, and he has the faculty of sticking.' But Goldsmith too was doubtless prejudiced by his jealousy, as an older friend of Johnson's, towards a new rival.

Again, there is Beauclerk's suggestion that Johnson's treatment of a man's books, and Boswell's conversation, would be capable of driving any man to pack up and flee. But that is, after all, a joke. And, again, there are the attacks of Peter Pindar:

> Thou jackal, leading lion Johnson forth,
> To eat Macpherson 'midst his native North.

But that is only satire.

Hume is more indulgent and fairer—'a young gentleman, very good-humoured, very agreeable, and very mad'.

More interesting, especially when contrasted with her similar mark-sheet for Johnson, is Mrs Thrale's assessment of Boswell's character—'Religion, 5' (out of 20); 'Morality, 5; Scholarship, 5; General Knowledge, 10; Person and Voice, 10; Manners, 8; Wit, 7; Humour, 3; Good Humour, 19.' Mrs Thrale does not include marks for sense and intelligence. Like Hume, however, and Fanny Burney, she stresses Boswell's vast and disarming good humour—she gives him 19 for it, where she gave Johnson 0.[1]

[1] Cf. Johnson's statement: 'Burke says you have so much good humour naturally, it is scarcely a virtue.' (But they had not seen Boswell throwing lighted candles at his wife, and banknotes in the fire.)

Finally, one may recall the judgment of that brilliant young woman Belle de Zuylen (Zélide) on one of Boswell's letters—'the puerile vanity of a fatuous fool, coupled with the arrogant rigidity of an old Cato'.[1] To Boswell, in certain of his moods, that is, though severe, not unfair. On the other hand it is the utterance of an angry mistress. After all, there *were* yet times when this sharp-eyed young woman could think seriously of marrying him. And Margaret Boswell did. And Moma Piccolomini loved him. True, physical attraction is blind, and Titania could idealize even Bottom. But this argument cannot apply to men like Johnson, Reynolds, or Burke;[2] nor could even Johnson have forced The Club to elect a mere moron.

The chief witness against James Boswell will always be—James Boswell. There could be no clearer instance of the profound truth in Bentley's dictum that no man can be written out of reputation except by himself.

Boswell's self-portrait is indeed as remarkable as his portrait of Johnson—one of the most comic pictures in human history, and all the more comic because the comedy is so unconscious. This has been abundantly illustrated already. But if one asks, as one must, how a creature so absurd could yet be liked and even loved, I suppose the answer lies in certain engaging qualities commoner in youth than age. (Boswell remained young longer than most men of his day; and when he aged, he became a much sorrier spectacle.) There was the charm of his vitality, his eagerness, his curiosity, his flattering enthusiasm, his intellectual zest, his good humour, his good nature, his childlike simplicity. Paoli summed this side of him admirably—'I love him indeed; so cheerful, so gay, so pleasant.' In many ways his heart was better than his head. And it is only fair that he should be given credit for his practical kindness and energy in helping, now a poor sheep-stealer, now a wretched woman-convict from Australia.[3]

[1] 'La puerile vanité d'un fat jointe à la rigidité orgueilleuse d'un vieux Caton.'

[2] Even in October 1782, when Boswell had gone far downhill, Reynolds could write to him: 'Mr Burke dined with me yesterday. He talked much of you and with great affection. He says you are the pleasantest man he ever saw and sincerely wishes you would come and live amongst us.' One may discount something for friendly compliment; but it still remains striking.

[3] Cf. Charles Hay's tribute after Boswell's efforts for Reid the sheep-stealer: 'Well, God has blessed you with one of the best hearts that ever man had.'

True, Boswell's defenders have at times stressed this side of him with too little regard for another side of the truth—his monstrous treatment, at times, of Margaret Boswell; his incredible behaviour in writing (and publishing) the *Nuptial Ode by Dr Johnson to Mrs Thrale*; the callous irresponsibility which could let him make love to a girl, even if she *was* on the streets, while knowing that he had venereal disease. There were certain limits to Boswell's 'goodness of heart'. To overlook such less pretty episodes is critical cant.[1] But I suppose it is fair to add that at times Boswell seems (like his brother John and his daughter Euphemia) not sane.

Men could not agree about him then; they cannot now. But perhaps these clashing opinions are less in real conflict than they seem. Perhaps they are supplementary rather than contradictory. Different temperaments vary a great deal in their power to suffer fools gladly. There were some who could not bear, in Boswell, the gawk and gowk; there were others who felt a paternal and protective tenderness for this boyish, boisterous innocence which could never grow up; which flattered, amused, and animated them, like the old gentleman who kept company with the young Montaigne in order to imbibe his vitality.

And so, I think, one should be able to understand both those who liked Boswell, and those who loathed him.

At all events, his sins hurt no one now. The evil he did, poor devil, is buried with him; the good endures. He was, by temperament, much too mercurial; but his quicksilver has become the backing for a most magic mirror. He was an ass—in some ways, an ass unparalleled; but he also did something unparalleled by any other ass—he carried Johnson on the road to immortality better, more patiently, more sure-footedly, than many a healthier and more intelligent creature could have done.

And sure th' Eternal Master found
The single talent well employ'd.

'There are two ways,' said Johnson to Boswell, according to

[1] Cf. Lionel Johnson (in *Post Liminium*): 'In many ways a small, an undignified, a preposterous man, but never a mean, idiotic, vulgar man.' That 'never' seems to me untrue. And to call Boswell, as he does, 'a great man', while it can give no pleasure to the dead, can, I think, cheapen the standards of the living.

Fanny Burney, 'of preserving fame—one by sugar, the other by salt. Now, as the sweet way, Bozzy, you are but little likely to attain, I would have you plunge into vinegar and get fairly pickled.'

Bozzy has got fairly pickled. Some of his recent admirers have a good deal overdone the sugar. But that is probably a passing phase. Boswell's future fame is likely to be accompanied always by a good deal of vinegar. But it will long be preserved.

GOLDSMITH

Le cerveau brûlé par le raisonnement
a soif de simplicité, comme le désert
a soif d'eau pure.

RENAN

WITH Burke at Trinity, Dublin (though they seem to have been little, if at all, acquainted) there was in the later seventeen-forties a wilder, yet gentler undergraduate, less of a scholar but more of a poet, less of a thinker yet with more feeling for human nature. A quarter of a century passed. April 1774 saw Burke, already a prosperous country-gentleman, attain his full political height with the great speech on American Taxation; another quarter of a century of tireless activity was to make that once obscure Irishman a power in Europe; but April 1774 saw Goldsmith die, disconsolate and indebted,[1] in the Middle Temple. And yet, to-day, for most readers, Goldsmith, though cut off so much earlier, and so much poorer, remains far more vividly alive. Burke is famous, yet little read; but Goldsmith is still known and loved.

First, the bare facts of his career.

He was born, probably, in 1730,[2] and probably at Pallas,[3] in the heart of Ireland, fifteen miles north-east of Athlone. An ironic conjunction—for the name of Wisdom's Goddess can seldom have been linked with a man less prudent. And yet, as women sometimes do, she smiled, after all, on this truant scamp; so that, though his life ran from scrape to scrape, from his feckless lips there yet came some of the wisest sayings even of his Age of Sense.

His father was the poor rector of Kilkenny West. Being the fifth child in a needy family (especially as £400 went to dower a sister who had married above her), Oliver had to be content in 1745–9 with the humble station of sizar[4] at Trinity, Dublin; after which the

[1] £2,000, it is said. And his reported last words, to his doctor asking if his mind was at ease, were 'No, it is not'.

[2] His birthday, November 10, has been assigned to each of the five years, 1727–31. (See K. C. Balderston in *Times Lit. Sup.*, March 7, 1929, pp. 185–6, and A. Friedman in *Notes and Queries*, vol. 196 (1951), 388–9.)

[3] Local tradition said that when the house of Goldsmith's birth at Pallas afterwards fell to ruin, attempts to repair its roof were thwarted by a supernatural being in huge boots, who nightly rode the roof-ridge, and thrust his feet through tiles and upper floor. It is strange to find this roof-riding, a habit of Icelandic trolls (cf. Glam's ghost in Grettir's Saga), transferred to Ireland, and to the home of so gentle a creature as Goldsmith.

[4] Cf. his later protest, in the *Enquiry into the State of Polite Learning*, against the arrogance of college-fellows in thus taking the services of poor scholars. 'It implies a

years 1750–2 passed mainly in idling, amid spasmodic schemes for the church, for the law, for emigration to America. In 1753 a new profession came in view, and a second university—medicine, at Edinburgh. In 1754–5 followed more universities—Leyden, perhaps Louvain, perhaps Padua, and Paracelsus' university, the world of the wandering scholar, as Goldsmith tramped the roads of France, Switzerland, and Italy. In 1756 the returned exile sought fortune in London, as needy as ever. After many vicissitudes of poverty and Grub Street, in 1759 he succeeded in publishing (though himself by no means learned, and not always polite) *An Enquiry into the Present State of Polite Learning in Europe*, and the essays of *The Bee*; which was followed in 1762 by the more durable *Citizen of the World.* In that same year came the famous episode of the sale by Johnson (met in 1761) of the unfinished *Vicar of Wakefield* (not published till 1766).[1] Unfortunately Goldsmith was too free a spender to remain long a free writer. He might gain fame as a poet with *The Traveller* (1764) and *The Deserted Village* (1770); as a playwright, with *The Good-Natured Man* (1768) and *She Stoops to Conquer* (1773); but since he could not live by medicine, he had to drudge at endless reviews, articles, prefaces, revisions, translations, abridgements, and compilations—such as his English histories(1764, 1771), *Poems for Young Ladies* (1766), *The Beauties of English Poesy* (1767), *Roman History* (1769), *Grecian History* (1774), *Animated Nature* (1774). On most of these subjects, of course, he had no special knowledge—only his sense of style, and of life. When one considers the quantity of his work, and the mellow wisdom of some of it, it becomes hard to realize that, when he died in 1774, he was still only about forty-five. Impatient creature that he was, his way of putting out the light in his bedroom had been to throw a slipper at it from bed; now by equally impatient self-dosing the poor Doctor snuffed out his own brief candle.

But how colourless is mere chronology! As indispensable, but as unattractive, as the human skeleton. And how coloured, by contrast, is life! A pity that Goldsmith who wrote so much on the lives of

contradiction for men to be at once learning the liberal arts, and at the same time treated as slaves.'

[1] English editions in 1766 (three), 1770, 1774, etc. But it was not at first the striking success it later became. After the first three editions, it had still not quite paid the publishers.

men and animals, never wrote his own. *That* would have been a natural history, of an 'animated nature' indeed—as strange as the *Confessions* of Rousseau, or the *Journals* of Boswell; but far more likeable. We have to console ourselves with the many fragments of disguised autobiography scattered through his books.

Still it is worth trying to catch, through the blur of time, and the dust of scholarship, a few living glimpses of the real, charming, absurd, delightful Oliver. For one cannot know his works really, unless one knows *him*. Even his odd clothes—for the tailor becomes an important character in Goldsmith's tragicomedy—are a vital part of the real man. Without indulging in the frivolous licences of that hateful modern hybrid, fictional biography, it remains possible to reconstruct a few living scenes that may quicken that dull catalogue of dates.

First, amid the green tranquillity of the central plain of Ireland, beside the waters of Lough Ree, between the dreamy melancholy of Celtic names like Ballymahon, Glencara, Athlone, and the English bluntness of Longford, Newcastle, Edgeworthstown, there rises the rectory of Lissoy, with its orchard, and its avenue of wind-tossed ash-trees, and peals of laughter ringing from its parlour, where the Rev. Charles Goldsmith entertains his flattering cronies with anecdotes not the less mirth-provoking for their ripe and mellow age.[1] For the Rector is a man who loves learning above silver, and kindness beyond gold; but prudence, and economy, a good deal less. And under the ash trees runs a little ugly boy, disfigured for life by smallpox, and already mocked at for his uncomeliness; yet already able, with time and effort, to turn the laugh against his mockers, like the future poet of *Retaliation*. Gaiety and bitterness, simplicity[2]

[1] Cf. the *Citizen of the World*, xxvii (where the Man in Black describes his father): 'The same ambition that actuates a monarch at the head of an army, influenced my father at the head of his table: he told the story of the ivy-tree, and that was laughed at; he repeated the jest of the two scholars and one pair of breeches, and the company laughed at that; but the story of Taffy in the sedan-chair was sure to set the table in a roar; thus his pleasure increased in proportion to the pleasure he gave; he loved all the world, and he fancied all the world loved him.'

[2] Cf. his artless and unfortunate remark to Shelburne: 'I wonder they should call your Lordship "Malagrida", for Malagrida was a very *good* man.' (Gabriele Malagrida was born at Menaggio, Como, in 1689; bit his hands at school, to practise for martyrdom; became a Jesuit at 22; preached and did miracles for many years in Brazil; retired to Portugal in 1755; the Marquis de Pombal had him condemned for conspiracy; and in 1761, aged 72, he was strangled, then burnt, at an auto-da-fé.)

and genius—those are the twin threads twisted throughout Goldsmith's strand of life. Amid the harsh home-truths of acquaintances and schoolfellows may have been early sown the seeds both of his curious passion for finery and of his exasperated envy, at moments, towards those more successful in the social world—his pathetic anxiety to shine, and his dread of being eclipsed.

But if reality is already bitter, there remains the world of imagination. This ugly child, whose father shows touches of Uncle Toby, has also a schoolmaster akin to Corporal Trim—an old soldier of Queen Anne's wars in Spain, who was to live again, for ever, in *The Deserted Village*. From him, from books, from the blind harper O'Carolan, from his father's old dairymaid, the child drinks in stories of foreign lands, of the campaigns of the mad Peterborough, of banshees; or such lilting cadences of simple popular ballads as he was always to love better than all the bravuras of sophisticated opera-singers.

Next comes the schoolboy riding from home (perhaps back to school at Edgeworthstown) with a guinea hopping in his pocket; and, when benighted, asking with boyish pomp for 'the best house' in the place, only to be directed by a practical joker (for this is Ireland), not to an inn, but to Squire Featherston's mansion at Ardagh; where the Squire, another Irish humorist, amusedly took the lad's orders, without enlightening him till his morning departure. So fell out, some thirty years beforehand, the first rehearsal of *She Stoops to Conquer*.

Then comes the sizar of Trinity, in the first of his many garrets, humiliated by his menial tasks, tormented by a surly tutor with hated mathematics and loathsome logic; but compensating himself by a share in ducking a bailiff, or assaulting the Black Dog prison; glad to sell, for five shillings apiece, ballads of his own composition at a shop with the sign of the Reindeer, and already tasting a poet's triumph, as he hears them chanted by street-singers down Dublin alleys. Already he has become the reckless mixture of dissipation and compassion that he was always to remain—now being knocked down by his tutor amid a riotous party with 'idle women'; now being rescued by a friend from the mattress he had stuck inside, after crawling there for warmth, because he had given all his blankets to a beggar-woman and her children.

Then the bachelor of arts, back home again, but more inclined to become the village playboy than to seek a profession; though his father's death (1747) has left his family poorer still. He thinks of the church, unwillingly; but the bishop, says the story, had no use for an ordination-candidate who presented himself in scarlet breeches.

He tries tutoring; but he quarrels with his employer's family over cards. He thinks of America and rides off on a good horse, with thirty pounds—only to return, like Moses Primrose, stripped of horse and money too.

His generous uncle Contarine, once friend of the good Bishop Berkeley, provides fifty pounds for him to try the law, like Burke, in London; again the scapegrace returns, leaving the fifty pounds in the pockets of a Dublin cardsharper.

Neither church, nor teaching, nor law. What next? Medicine? Long-suffering relations peer again in their purses, and pack him off to Edinburgh. His very arrival beneath those bleaker skies provides a new picture—Goldsmith, having rushed from his new lodging to see the city, has forgotten his own address. Outcast again! Luckily he meets at last the porter who had carried his baggage there. Then the reek of Edinburgh closes round him, lodged with 'hardly any other Society but a folio book, a skeleton, my cat, and my meagre Landlady'. But by the help of tailors' bills we catch glimpses of a homely youth colouring the grey Scottish streets with all the splendours of silver hat-lace, 'Sky-Blew Shalloon', 'white Fustian', 'white Allapeen', or 'best superfine high Clarett-colour'd Cloth'. And already the letters home of this born writer, though ill-punctuated and ill-spelt, show some of the charm of the *Citizen of the World*.

He decides on further studies in France; only to be arrested at Newcastle (supposing we can believe him) on a suspicion of recruiting Scots for the French service—most luckily, since his ship (so he *says*) subsequently perished with all hands off the Garonne. But Holland will do as well as France—perhaps, like George Primrose, he had rosy plans for teaching English to the Dutch, forgetting that this could hardly be done without knowing Dutch himself. Anyway, 1754 sees him at Leyden; only to wander off a year later,[1]

[1] By one account, after winning heavily at play, despite advice to tempt fortune

like his Irish fellow-countrymen who had roamed the Europe of the Dark Ages, nearly a thousand years before. (He may have been following the example of his admired Holberg, the Danish dramatist (1684–1754), whom he describes in his *Polite Learning* as wandering over Europe singing for a supper.) But, at the moment of departure, some rare bulbs in a florist's garden catch his eye—what a present for good Uncle Contarine, who loves such things! So off go the bulbs to Ireland; and off goes Oliver into Europe, with a clean shirt, a guinea, and a flute. Flanders, France, Switzerland, Italy, Tyrol, perhaps Germany[1] saw this strange vagabond trudge by, now playing to the poor, now gaining a supper (we are told) by theological debate in the local monastery—fluting and 'disputing his passage through Europe'.

> Remote, unfriended, melancholy, slow,[2]
> Or by the lazy Scheld, or wandering Po;
> Or onward, where the rude Carinthian boor
> Against the houseless stranger shuts the door;
> Or where Campania's[3] plain forsaken lyes,
> A weary waste expanding to the skies.

A sombre picture; and yet one may suspect that Goldsmith, like Johnson and Boswell, Rousseau and Gray, really passed his happiest days as a rambler on the road.

At last the *Wanderjahre* end. The prodigal returns; but to no fatted calves. In February 1756 he lands at Dover, penniless still. London swallows him (as, a few years later, it swallowed Chatterton and Crabbe)—to pound drugs for an apothecary; to doctor the

no further he soon returned to the gaming table, and lost so much that he had to leave Leyden.

[1] It has been suggested that his route may have run: Louvain—Brussels—Maestricht—Flanders—Paris—Strasbourg—Baden—Bâle—Geneva—Florence, Verona, Mantua, Milan, Padua, Venice—Carinthia (see A. L. Sells, *Sources Françaises de Goldsmith*).

[2] It will be recalled that Goldsmith, asked if 'slow' meant 'tardiness of locomotion', replied vaguely 'Yes'; and was corrected by Johnson—'No, Sir . . . you mean that sluggishness of mind which comes upon a man in solitude.' But why should Goldsmith not have meant both?—steps literally slow, but also the forlornness of mind they can betray?

[3] Probably Goldsmith meant 'the Roman Campagna'; not the fertile Campania near Naples.

Southwark poor; to read proofs for Samuel Richardson, printer and novelist; to endure the humiliations of a school-usher; to devil for a journalistic bookseller, who mauled his articles, while the bookseller's wife helped to maul his articles, and also skimped his meals; to dream of practising medicine on the coast of Indian Coromandel, or as a hospital mate—and be disappointed yet again. For at Surgeons' Hall (December 21, 1758) he was 'found not qualified'.

Slow rises worth by poverty depressed.

And yet it rises. Strange magic of style. Goldsmith was not erudite. He was not strikingly original. He was not mystically imaginative. He offered no new creed to interpret life. He was content with common sense, common humanity, gaiety and grace. Yet his pen had some touch that the dozens of his fellow-hacks had not. Somehow in that London of 1759–60, amid the excitements of the Seven Years War and the bells clashing out, month after month, for the victories of Pitt, men began to notice the bitter-gentle charm that passed from Goldsmith's personality into Goldsmith's style.

In March 1759, Percy of the *Reliques*, the future bishop, climbs the stairs of the ironically named 'Green Arbour Court', above 'Breakneck Steps'. In that dirty room Goldsmith offers his guest the single chair, and seats himself in the window. A knock, and a little ragged girl enters with a curtsey—'My mamma sends her compliments and begs the favour of you to lend her a chamberpot full of coals.'

Not here, O Apollo,
  Are haunts meet for thee.

Yet sometimes Apollo came.

And after Percy climb others. Our glimpses grow clearer and wider (thanks largely to Boswell), as they near their end. There heaves into view the snorting bulk of Johnson, alternately helping and snubbing, baiting and praising, his 'Goldy'; and Sir Joshua Reynolds, affectionately leaning his ear-trumpet towards the pocked face and bulging forehead at his side; and the small figure of Garrick, capering and mincing about the room, with mingled irritation and admiration for the playwright he has so often baulked and disappointed; and the busy Boswell himself, no less jealous than he taxes Goldsmith with being, towards his rival next Johnson's throne.

And still on Goldsmith's small person costume follows costume —now he strolls by, in medical state, with purple-silk small-clothes, scarlet roquelaure (cloak), great wig, sword, and gold-headed cane; now in that famous bloom-coloured coat of which Johnson mischievously observed that its tailor was doubtless proud to show 'how well he could make a coat even of so absurd a colour'; now half-drawing his sword on two coxcombs in the Strand who had jeered at his little figure, with its long weapon, as 'that fly with a long pin stuck through it'.

Goldsmith has now improved his lodgings also, thanks to £500 brought by *The Good-natured Man.* In Brick Court, Middle Temple, the good-natured poet throws parties, sings, kicks his wig at the ceiling, or plays blind man's buff, while in the rooms beneath there groans the great Professor Blackstone, trying to labour at his massive *Commentaries on English Law.*

But there is also the quieter Goldsmith, retired to lodgings in a farmer's house six miles out on the Edgware Road; wandering about the hedgerows to meditate, 'with a most tragical countenance', the jests of *She Stoops to Conquer*; or scribbling on the walls of his room fragmentary descriptions of beasts, for his *History of Animated Nature.*

On the other hand, there is the passionate Goldsmith, 'irascible as a hornet'[1] with the fighting blood of Ireland. The miserable Dr Kenrick had written in the *London Packet* (March 1773) an offensive letter jeering not only at 'Goldy's' 'monkey face and cloven foot', but also at his affection for Miss Mary Horneck—'was but the lovely H——k as much enamoured, you would not sigh, my gentle swain, in vain'. This insult to a lady was too much. The little poet appears in Paternoster Row at the shop of Evans, publisher

[1] Cf. the anecdote recorded by Mrs Le Noir, Christopher Smart's daughter, of Goldsmith's habitual irritation when defeated by Mrs Fleming at cribbage or piquet during his visits to Canonbury House, Islington. 'Once after losing 15 games running he rose in a pet, crying out that with his knowledge of the game to be beaten by a fool was insupportable. She was however no fool, but a woman of good sense and some reading.'

of the *London Packet*, and lays his cane across the bookseller's back, as he stoops to pick up the guilty article. A scuffle—a broken lamp, which rains oil impartially on Tweedle-dum and Tweedle-dee—the combatants are separated, and Goldsmith sent home in a coach. It proved an expensive adventure; for he only avoided an action for assault by paying £50 to a charity; and wits were not slow to make jests about 'stooping to conquer'.[1]

Or there is the kindly Goldsmith of a child's memories. One evening, drinking coffee with George Colman, the theatre-manager, Goldsmith takes on his knee Colman's small son of five and begins to play with him—only to be slapped hard in the face. The indignant father locks up the urchin to howl and kick in a dark room—till the door opens and there appears Goldsmith himself, candle in hand and cheek still red. 'He placed,' says the younger George Colman in his *Random Records*, 'three hats, which happened to be in the room, upon the carpet, and a shilling under each: the shillings he told me, were England, France, and Spain.' A minute later—'hey, presto, cockalorum!'—all three shillings were magically congregated under one hat. Tears were forgotten; the boy and the wizard became friends till death.

But this innocent of the imaginary world had a perilous hand at real things. In vain, when Goldsmith talked loftily about prescribing medicine 'for his friends', had the ironic tongue of Topham Beauclerk retorted by begging him to prescribe only for his enemies. The day came when he prescribed for himself the famous, but dangerous powders of Dr James of Lichfield.

And so to the last scene of all—that death in debt, melancholy, and disquiet of mind; when Burke burst into tears at the news, and Sir Joshua, the ceaseless worker, for one day threw aside his brushes, and outcast creatures sat weeping on the dead man's stair.

They are pretty tragic, the ends of these great Irishmen of the eighteenth century—the mad Swift mopping and mowing at his mirror; the lonely Sterne watched in his last agony by a Highland servant in a Bond Street lodging; the mulberry-faced, degenerated Sheridan pursued by bailiffs to his deathbed, and even beyond; Burke weeping on the neck of his dead son's horse at Beaconsfield.

Goldsmith, as we have seen, was only about forty-five. He had

[1] See Johnson's comment in Boswell (April 3, 1773).

gaily wasted years. We tend to think of him as an easy-going Irish idler. But look at the list of his productions (the hackwork included)—it is staggering, appalling. How he must have toiled![1]

And even the hackwork has quality, as well as quantity. His 'book-building', as he called it, was not mere jerry-building. There have, of course, been plenty of jokes about it. 'Tell me,' said Goldsmith to Gibbon, 'what was the name of the Indian king who fought Alexander?' 'Montezuma,' replied the mischievous Gibbon; then, as the guileless Goldy started to write it down, 'But stay! I mistake. 'Twas not Montezuma. 'Twas Porus.' And generations have smiled at the brown savage of Tibet nesting in the branches of the spreading pomegranate, or the 'insidious tiger' that haunts the backwoods of Canada.

'Poor fellow,' wrote Cumberland, 'he hardly knew an ass from a mule, or a turkey from a goose, but when he saw it on the table. But publishers hate poetry, and Paternoster Row is not Parnassus.' And similarly Johnson—'If he can distinguish a cow from a horse, that, I believe, may be the extent of his knowledge of natural history.'[2] Yet Johnson stood up, also, for Goldsmith's merits: 'Sir, he has the art of compiling, and of saying everything he has to say in a pleasing manner. He is now writing a Natural History and will make it as entertaining as a Persian Tale.' Certainly it was no ordinary hackwork that went on being reprinted fifty years later. Indeed, parts of *Animated Nature* are readable to-day.

For even in his pot-boiling Goldsmith remains himself—a man

[1] According to Prior, for example, the two hundred and forty octavo pages of the *Life of Nash* occupied five weeks, and earned only fourteen guineas. However things mended. Eight hundred guineas for *Animated Nature* seems not illiberal.

[2] All the same I suspect that Goldsmith's ignorance of animal life has been exaggerated by anecdotal friends, and too uncritically swallowed by later critics. After all, Goldsmith was, like Shakespeare, a country boy who had hunted otters; a man who had wandered Europe with interested eyes, noting such things as the woodcock he flushed in the Jura; and who carefully watched the rooks from his Temple window, or the spiders in his room. He was no expert; but hardly such a complete ignoramus. He did, however, copy from Buffon the myth that cows shed their horns; and believed that we eat by raising our upper jaws.

On the other hand, it now appears that *Animated Nature* was based on wider and more conscientious reading than commonly supposed (see W. Lynskey, 'Scientific Sources of Goldsmith's *Animated Nature*', in *Studies in Philology*, xl (1943), 33–57). And Goldsmith's American 'tiger' is simply the puma, which was quite commonly given the grander name.

who, unlike many more learned, has a feeling for living facts; and, with it, the gift of living speech. When Johnson wrote that famous epitaph which all the entreaties of the Club could not coax him to turn from Latin to English, he put his blunt old finger on the vital truth—'There was hardly one branch of literature he did not touch; none, that he touched and failed to adorn.'

For example, how delicately, in his *Animated Nature*, Goldsmith touches the squirrel!

> 'What I am going to relate, appears so extraordinary, that were it not attested by numbers of the most credible historians, among whom are Klein and Linnaeus, it might be rejected, with that scorn with which we treat imposture or credulity: however, nothing can be more true[1] than that when these animals, in their progress, meet with broad rivers, and extensive lakes, which abound in Lapland, they take a very extraordinary method of crossing them. Upon approaching the banks, and perceiving the breadth of the water, they return as if by common consent, into the neighbouring forest, each in quest of a piece of bark, which answers all the purposes of boats for wafting them over. When the whole company are fitted in this manner, they boldly commit their little fleet to the waves; every squirrel sitting on its own piece of bark, and fanning the air with its tail, to drive the vessel to its desired port. In this orderly manner they set forward, and often cross lakes several miles broad. But it too often happens that the poor mariners are not aware of the dangers of their navigation; for although at the edge of the water it is generally calm, in the midst it is always more turbulent. There the slightest additional gust of wind oversets the little sailor and his vessel together. The whole navy, that but a few minutes before rode proudly and securely along, is now overturned, and a shipwreck of two or three thousand sail ensues. This, which is so unfortunate for the little animal, is generally the most lucky accident in the world for the Laplander on the shore; who gathers up the dead bodies as they are thrown in by the waves, eats the flesh, and sells the skins for about a shilling the dozen.'

It may be doubted if this is very sound biology.[2] And the style is not Goldsmith at his best. It is wordy; perhaps because it would have taken him longer to make it shorter. Yet there is about it a

[1] This seems going rather far!

[2] Sir James Gray has kindly confirmed my guess that this cock-and-bull story about squirrels is ultimately based on the migratory habits of the lemming.

charming sympathy with the little squirrels; far more genuine, for instance, I feel, than Coleridge or his Mariner really felt for albatrosses, or for water-snakes (not, it must be admitted, very sympathetic creatures).

Still, like Sheridan, Goldsmith recklessly squandered both his money and his genius. The money both men wasted does not matter now; but the time and energy they flung away may at times still wake our regret. With Dryden, it can be argued that the thousands of couplets he scribbled in often futile productions, yet trained that facility which in the end produced his best translations and his *Fables*. But the prose of Goldsmith does not seem to offer even that consolation. Between his first published book, the *Polite Learning* of 1759, and his death there elapsed fifteen years; it may be doubted if his style improved during the last dozen. He never bettered—it would be hard to better—the easy flow of the *Citizen of the World* or *The Vicar*. However the world has far more good literature than human life can cope with. We need not regret too much, where regret in any case is vain. To-day, for most readers, Goldsmith is *The Vicar of Wakefield*. All his essential qualities are there—the reckless extravagance (for its plot remains preposterous); but also the charm of personality, the gentle poetry, the goodness saved from relaxing mawkishness by a keen breeze of irony, the wisdom all the deeper because so full of gaiety and humour.

Perhaps the finest and most interesting praise of the book and its author comes from Goethe, who loved it in youth and, after re-reading it at eighty, wrote to Zelter (December 25, 1829):

> 'It would be impossible to grasp the effect on me, just at the critical point of my development, of Goldsmith and Sterne. That lofty and benevolent irony, that fairness in all views of life, that gentleness in all contrarieties, that equanimity in all vicissitudes, and all their kindred virtues, call them what you will, gave me the most admirable education; and, when all is said, it is dispositions like these that bring us right again after all false steps in life.'[1]

[1] So elsewhere—'To Shakespeare, Sterne, and Goldsmith, my debt has been infinite.' *The Deserted Village*, again, 'has been one of my most decided passions'. (For details of Goldsmith's influence on Goethe, see C. Hammer in *Journal of English and Germanic Philology*, xliv (1945), 131–8.)

Cf. too Taine's comment, in a letter: 'Olivier Goldsmith a fait plus avec son *Vicar* que cent prédicateurs avec cent sermons.'

In *The Vicar*, of course, the plot creaks. What more conventional, yet impossible, than this story of an eighteenth-century Job vexed by Satan in the shape of a wicked young squire, who seduces his elder daughter under pretence of a sham marriage; kidnaps his second daughter; steals his eldest son's betrothed; and then has the son arrested for murder, the old Vicar himself for debt; till finally this stage-villain is defeated by his disguised and benevolent stage-uncle, who becomes both *deus ex machina* and the Vicar's son-in-law? What a barrow of chestnuts!

And then the coincidences. By accident the Vicar goes to a theatrical performance and sees on the stage his own son, turned strolling player; by accident he meets his lost daughter in an inn; by accident he encounters in prison the sharper who had duped, first him, then the wicked Squire. Even the merchant who absconded with the Vicar's wealth is, of course, to complete the happy ending, caught at Antwerp and compelled to disgorge.

But though one wishes the story less fantastic, one does not read the story for the story. Despite Aristotle, I believe that first-rate characters even with a second-rate plot succeed far better than a first-rate plot with second-rate characters. And yet though—or perhaps even because—the plot is melodramatic, *The Vicar of Wakefield* is one of the few exceptions I have seen to the general rule that novels filmed or dramatized are usually horrible. I can recall a dramatization of Goldsmith's tale that proved quite charming on the stage. Even at this date Goldsmith had already a dramatist's sense both of character and of dialogue.

Still, to the reader, the best part of *The Vicar* is before the action has really begun to move, while we are merely being introduced to the characters; once the melodrama starts, the comedy fades.

For what matters most in a novel, or play, is people, people, people. And foremost among the characters here is Goldsmith himself—the shy smile, the mellow wisdom, the loving-kindness that yet is never soft. It is a healthy book, healthy as an apple out of a hayloft; not like the maggoty cheese, or game high to putrefaction, that more sophisticated modern tastes are apt to demand. Its influence-value is as sound as its pleasure-value is lively. A good deal of water has run down the Liffey between Goldsmith and

Joyce. Even Tolstoy could have included *The Vicar* among the few books he approved.

Beside Goldsmith, Richardson (apart from his suffocating prolixity) seems to me too canting—a pornographic prude. Even the saner, healthier Fielding is apt to be coarse-grained. And where Sterne, that livelier jester, too often has only sentiment, Goldsmith has feeling. It is, no doubt, dangerously easy to exaggerate such antitheses; the Sterne who created Uncle Toby must also have possessed goodness himself; but too often he used his heart like a baby's rattle. Sterne shakes his heart as freely as other men shake their heads. He was cleverer than Goldsmith; but less good and less wise.

In a way, many good novels might share the title *Sense and Sensibility*. For there are few conflicts in life so constantly recurrent as the clash between these two qualities; and a good writer needs both of them himself. *The Vicar* lacks the careful artistry of Jane Austen's work; and yet beside Goldsmith she seems to me, at times, a little chilly, a little flat, a little dry. Further, though her style is excellent for conversation, in narrative it is sometimes prosy. And not only, I think, does Goldsmith narrate events more charmingly, though he constructs them far more carelessly; he also gains enormously by putting his tale into the mouth of Dr Primrose. The use of the first person in fiction has drawbacks and dangers; but here one cannot imagine any other technique being adopted without ruining the book. Dr Primrose is, among other things, one of those excellent comic characters whose comedy depends on their unconsciousness; who are amusing, not so much by trying to say amusing things, but by saying things they do not realize to be amusing at all.

Dr Primrose is supposed to be based on Goldsmith's father, as Mr Micawber on Dickens's; though the Rev. Charles Goldsmith, one imagines, might have enjoyed his own portrait a good deal better than Mr John Dickens. But of course the Vicar has also a good deal of Goldsmith himself—the same mixture of simplicity and shrewdness, gentleness and irony. 'As some men gaze with admiration at the colours of a tulip, or the wing of a butterfly, so I was by nature an admirer of happy human faces.' (This has sweetness; but, lest it grow sickly, a pinch of pepper is quickly added.)

'However, when any one of our relations was found to be a person of a very bad character, a troublesome guest, or one we desired to get rid of, upon his leaving my house I ever took care to lend him a riding coat, or a pair of boots, or sometimes a horse of small value, and I always had the satisfaction of finding he never came back to return them.[1] By this the house was cleared of such as we did not like; but never' (the sweetness returns) 'was the family of Wakefield known to turn the traveller or the poor dependant out of doors.'

Surely it is such touches of genial irony and unembittered realism that make the most striking and charming feature of the book. What, after all, does the ordinary reader remember?—not the fantastic twists of the story, but such things as the Vicar's epitaph for his wife, framed on the mantelpiece and celebrating her as the *only* wife of Charles Primrose, and obedient till death. 'It admonished my wife of her duty to me, and *my* fidelity to her; it inspired her with a passion for fame and constantly put her in mind of her end.' How perfect!

Or there is the Vicar's sardonic reply, after their impoverishment, to his wife and daughters overdressing for church—'Call our coach'; or his tipping their saucepan of brewing cosmetics, by careful accident, into the fire; or the family-portrait, with the young Squire as Alexander the Great, at Olivia's feet, which symbolically proves too grandiose to get into any room but the kitchen; or the Vicar's innocent stratagem for assuming prophetic powers:

' "Aye," returned I, not knowing well what to think of the matter, "heaven grant they may be both the better for it this day three months!" This was one of the observations I usually made to impress my wife with an opinion of my sagacity; for if the girls succeeded, then it was a pious wish fulfilled; but if anything unfortunate ensued, then it might be looked on as a prophecy.'

What a contrast with the irony of Swift—as different as a west wind from an east!

'But we could have borne all this, had not a fortune-telling gypsey

[1] The only weakness is that, in real life, there are plenty of characters who would have come back *without* returning them.

> come to raise us into perfect sublimity. The tawny sybil no sooner appeared, than my girls came running to me for a shilling apiece, to cross her hand with silver. To say the truth, I was tired of being always wise, and could not help gratifying their request, because I loved to see them happy.'
>
> 'Michaelmas Eve happening on the next day, we were invited to burn nuts and play tricks at neighbour Flamborough's. Our late mortifications had humbled us a little, or it is probable we might have rejected such an invitation with contempt; however, we suffered ourselves to be happy.'

'We suffered ourselves to be happy'—on those six words a man might write a whole book. I doubt if any other writer of the time could have put so much into a simple phrase, clear as water, yet full of unlooked-for reflections—unless it were Johnson.

Later in his tale Goldsmith has said the same thing again as simply, though less briefly—'I passed among the harmless peasants of Flanders, and amongst such of the French as were poor enough to be very merry.'

Often contemporary readers may get more from a work than posterity—they may see nuances that time quickly blurs; but in other ways posterity may sometimes see more of the game. *The Vicar* is an example of what biography can add to understanding. For we can discern far better, now, than the ordinary reader of 1766, how much of himself Goldsmith has put into his book. The wanderings, and the literary teethings, of George Primrose draw visibly on Goldsmith's own experiences; so do the mishaps of the blundering Moses. When the Vicar records, 'all our adventures were by the fireside, and all our migrations from the blue bed to the brown', he is quoting, word for word, a phrase from a letter (1757) of Goldsmith's own; when we watch Mr Burchell, to rescue the abducted Sophia, 'come running up by the side of the horses, and with one blow knock the postillion to the ground', this may go back to an actual feat of Goldsmith's surly tutor at Trinity, the Rev. Theaker Wilder, who once showed similar agility in chastising a Dublin cabman that had accidentally flicked him with his whip. And if Goldsmith's father lives again, to some degree, in Dr Primrose, in Mrs Primrose there remains perhaps something of the writer's less congenial mother.

On the other hand the Vicar's sage admonitions about sober prudence and quietness in dress gain, for us, a new, unconscious irony from Goldsmith's own passion for finery; and the irony is hardly unconscious when we are told how Mr Burchell 'in his own whimsical manner, travelled through Europe on foot, and now . . . his circumstances are more affluent than ever'. Goldsmith's affluence after his own Grand Tour could have been counted in halfpence.

Into his novel the author has also packed some of his own most cherished beliefs—his own distrust of Venetian oligarchies such as the great Whigs aimed at, where the rich tenaciously upheld their traditional liberty—of battening on the poor; his own hatred of the absurdly multiplied death-penalties that disgraced eighteenth-century England; his own contempt for æsthetic jargon, and artificiality, and the foolish complications dear through the ages to the over-clever. ' "However that be," cried I, "the most vulgar ballad of them all generally pleases me better than the fine modern odes,[1] and things that petrify us in a single stanza; productions that we at once detest and praise." '

Long before Wordsworth, Goldsmith defended the value of simplicity, both in creation and in criticism. Unlike most critics, authors, and philosophers, he was not at all inclined to exaggerate the importance of his own calling; and gaily laughed, through George Primrose, at its comic side.

> 'Upon asking how he had been taught the art of a connoscento[2] so very suddenly, he assured me that nothing was more easy. The whole secret consisted in a strict adherence to two rules: the one always to observe the picture might have been better if the painter had taken more pains; and the other, to praise the works of Pietro Perugino.'

> 'Like the porcupine, I sat self-collected, with a quill pointed against every opposer.'

> 'I began to associate with none but disappointed authors, like myself, who praised, deplored, and despised each other.'

(How many literary circles are summed up in those three verbs!)

[1] An allusion to Gray?

[2] 'Conoscente', 'conoscitore' would, of course, be more correct.

It is an easy transition from Goldsmith's novel to his essays; as it is from *Rasselas* to *The Rambler*. Johnson's was a more masculine and a gloomier mind; superior to Goldsmith in criticism, and far superior in talk, but inferior in the more imaginative fields of fiction, poetry, and drama. Yet both men thought and felt so intensely and personally about life, and what is worth while in it, that their personal values stamped whatever they wrote—whether drama, fiction, or essay. Both had a healthy hatred for abstractions; yet neither was content to draw the details of life without drawing from them, also, universal conclusions. They sought the general principles of living; yet such generalities would have seemed to them too shadowy, unless often embodied in concrete forms and actual instances. Hence their fiction shows some characteristics of their essays; and their essays include fictitious characters.

The *Enquiry into the Present State of Polite Learning* is thin.[1] Yet it is interesting to see how, even at his thinnest, Goldsmith can still interest.

Take him, for example, on the Germans—perhaps, of all European nations, the nation furthest removed, by temperament, from Goldsmith's Irish lightheartedness.

> 'If criticism could have improved the taste of a people, the Germans would have been the most polite nation alive. . . . But, guilty of a fault too common to great readers, they write through volumes, while they do not think through a page. Never fatigued themselves, they think the reader can never be weary; so they drone on, saying all that can be said on the subject, not selecting what may be advanced to the purpose. Were angels to write books, they never would write folios.
>
> 'But let the Germans have their due; if they are dull, no nation alive assumes a more laudable solemnity, or better understands all the decorums of stupidity. Let the discourse of a professor run on never so heavily, it cannot be irksome to his dozing pupils, who frequently lend him sympathetic nods of approbation.'

Here Goldsmith the essayist seems recalling memories of Teutonic

[1] It is hard to imagine Goldsmith as learned. He possessed neither the temperament nor the memory. 'He had indeed,' said Johnson (whose memory, in contrast, was abnormally tenacious), 'been at no pains to fill his mind with knowledge. He translated it from one place to another; and it did not settle in his mind; so that he could not tell what was in his own books.' Even so, it is a little extraordinary to find him writing such pigeon Greek as 'παντα γηλως'.

lecture-rooms that Goldsmith the vagabond had once himself witnessed. No doubt, he is being culpably superficial, and ignorantly frivolous. He is blind to all that German doggedness had done and, still more, was yet to do, for science and learning. And yet.... How much of what he says was true, and has remained true, for two centuries since, both of German pedantry, and of pedantry not German! Thousands of Germans have known more than Goldsmith, and have added more to knowledge than Goldsmith could have in a thousand years; but, though this passage is far from Goldsmith's best writing, how few Germans could have written it! Such lightness of touch is no light matter to attain.

In France, however, Goldsmith shows things being ordered with typical contrast.

> 'A man of fashion at Paris, however contemptible we may think him here, must be acquainted with the reigning modes of philosophy, as well as of dress, to be able to entertain his mistress agreeably. The sprightly pedants' (typical phrase!) 'are not to be caught by dumb shew, by the squeeze of a hand, or the ogling of a broad eye, but must be pursued at once through all the labyrinths of the Newtonian system, or the metaphysics of Locke. I have seen as bright a circle of beauty at the chymical lectures of Rouelle as gracing the court at Versailles.'

(Again Goldsmith the wanderer rises for an instant from the past.)

Then he turns cursorily to England, lamenting (as well he might) the discouragements that here beset the creative writer. And again there flashes out that scorn which Goldsmith, though—or because—a critic himself, felt for average criticism. Already at the beginning of his essay he had attacked critics as 'studious triflers', and charged them (quite excessively, I should have thought) with being the main cause that ancient literature declined. Now he returns to the attack—'from this proceeds the affected security[1] of our odes, the tuneless flow of our blank verse, the pompous epithet, laboured diction, and every other deviation from common sense, which procures the poet the applause of the month.' Exaggerated? No doubt. Yet how strangely apposite some of this sounds, not to 1759, but to 1959! Frivolous, superficial, even downright foolish,

[1] Obscurity?

Goldsmith can often be. But every now and then he strikes out something of lasting interest and value, because he was convinced that nothing can give happiness, or even content, but the lasting emotions of the healthy human heart; while affectations, artificialities, and crazes can leave only the grey, acrid ashes of a bonfire of straw. And this, unfortunately, is something that civilized men need perpetually to re-learn. Subtlety is precious; but simplicity remains vital. The two may be happily combined; but the first alone can become poisonous.

Then, as further examples of the evil influence of criticism, Goldsmith attacks that dread of 'lowness' which had driven mirth from the English stage, and that pedantic classicism which had banished rhyme from much of English poetry. (But Goldsmith's own critical views can best be dealt with later, as a whole.)

At times, of course, his essay becomes childish. One may wish that he had paused before writing that mathematics 'seems a science to which the meanest intellects are equal'; or that Dante owed his glory to the obscurity of his barbarous age, 'as in the land of Benin a man may pass for a prodigy of parts who can read'. And yet can one really regret even this? Without them, our picture of Goldsmith would be less lively. And if he was childish at times, he kept, in compensation, the sharp-eyed directness of a child.

What qualifications, for example, had Goldsmith for criticizing universities? And yet immediately after that inane remark on mathematics comes an observation about lectures which, to me, was new, and has ever since seemed worth remembering:

> 'The most methodical manner of lecturing, whether on morals or nature, is first rationally to explain, and then produce the experiment.[1] The most instructive method is to show the experiment first; curiosity is then excited, and attention awakened to every subsequent deduction.'

There is excellent sense in that.

The Bee, also of 1759, seems something of a drone—or, perhaps, a worker-bee dulled by overhurried labour. Being Gold-

[1] He means here 'instance' or 'illustration' from actual experience. Cf. Bacon: 'And it hath much greater life for practice when the discourse attendeth upon the example, than when the example attendeth upon the discourse . . . examples alleged for the discourse's sake . . . carry a servile aspect towards the discourse which they are brought in to make good.' (*Advancement of Learning*, ed. A. W. Pollard, 353.)

smith's, it could not be wholly without honey. Yet it remains rather sticky; and one cannot wonder that this periodical soon failed. But Goldsmith grows a different creature—far more himself—in the *Citizen of the World*, which started appearing in *The Public Ledger* at the beginning of 1760, and became a volume in 1762.

Here, with the adventures of Goldsmith's Chinese, as with Addison's Sir Roger in *The Spectator*, the essay swings back towards the novel. The device of criticizing the West through the eyes of the East was, even then, an old one. It had been adopted, amongst others, by Montesquieu in his *Lettres Persanes* (1721), by D'Argens in his *Lettres Chinoises* (1739), and by Horace Walpole in his *Letter from Xo Ho* (1757); it was to be done again by Lowes Dickinson in his *Letters of John Chinaman*. It is an old way of making familiar things new. Yet it wears well, for it is based on an eternal truth—the relativity of ethics, customs, and values—of which it is useful for all ages constantly to be reminded; and particularly useful for the eighteenth century, with its mania for rash generalizations about mankind from China to Peru.

There is much to be said for reading the oriental letters of Goldsmith and Montesquieu together. Montesquieu is, of course, a far deeper and more thorough thinker—a man who strangely combined elements of Goldsmith, Gibbon, and Burke. One can never get used to the idea that the writer who threw off those seemingly pert and frivolous *Lettres Persanes* should have gone on to labour twenty years like a galley-slave at *L'Esprit des Lois*—much as if Oscar Wilde should have produced, in the end, *The Origin of Species*. None the less, behind the gay impudence of the *Lettres Persanes* there lies already a profound sense of human relativity and subjectivity; while, on the other hand, the grave pages of *L'Esprit des Lois* are still lit up at moments by a wit as ironic as Gibbon's.

Montesquieu's treatment of religion and morals is, of course, much more daring than Goldsmith's. Goldsmith, though hardly a pious figure, was yet the son of a Rector, and the creator of a Vicar: Montesquieu, though a prudent deist, seems to me without any real religious instinct. And it is, after all, usual for French minds to be less prudent, or less timid, than English in following logic to its extreme limits.

Similarly with morals. The *Lettres Persanes* are enlivened by the growing anarchy that invades the harem of the absent Usbek; with details of a laughing impropriety that shock even some French critics (I own that they seem to me amusing). But Goldsmith remains much more English. On such subjects he kept a certain reserve, which foreigners might call 'English cant'; but it is really part, I think, of a less simple quality—reticence. Goldsmith found *Tristram Shandy* 'obscene and pert'. Yet, by conventional standards, he may well have been a more immoral man than Sterne; who, if he flirted day in and day out, appears to have done little more than flirt; whereas Goldsmith, being ugly and poor, pursued 'venal beauties', such as that Iris in one of his poems:

Say, cruel Iris, pretty rake,
  Dear mercenary beauty,
What annual offering shall I make,
  Expressive of my duty?

And then, too, there are Garrick's significant lines:

With the love of a wench, let his writings be chaste...
That the rake and the fool o'er all may prevail,
Set fire to his head, and set fire to his tail.

Nor do I see cause for throwing stones about this. Poor Goldsmith's indulgences seem to me probably much preferable to the neurotic mixture of prudishness and obscenity in Swift, who made life a hell for Vanessa and none too heavenly, I should imagine, for Stella. But, whatever the licences of his life, Goldsmith preferred to keep them out of his books.

Again, the very first words of Montesquieu are an audacious mockery unthinkable in Goldsmith—'Nous n'avons séjourné qu'un jour à Com. Lorsque nous eûmes fait nos dévotions sur le tombeau de la vierge qui a mis au monde douze prophètes, nous nous remîmes en chemin.' How, one wonders, did Montesquieu dare publish that? In 1721, the very year of the *Lettres Persanes*, nine men and eleven women, says Michelet, were burnt alive at Granada in Spain, in furnaces shaped like figures of prophets. The Most Christian Majesty of France, with his dubious financial devices, escapes no better from the satirist's irreverent smile:

'D'ailleurs ce roi est un grand magicien; il exerce son empire sur l'esprit même de ses sujets; il les fait penser comme il veut. S'il n'a qu'un million d'écus dans son trésor et qu'il en ait besoin de deux, il n'a qu'à leur persuader qu'un écu en vaut deux, et ils le croient. S'il a une guerre difficile à soutenir et qu'il n'ait pas d'argent, il n'a que leur mettre dans la tête qu'un morceau de papier est de l'argent, et ils en sont aussitôt convaincus. Il va même jusqu'à leur faire croire qu'il les guérit de toutes sortes de maux en les touchant, tant est grande la force et la puissance qu'il a sur les esprits.'

Then comes the turn of the Holy Father:

'Il y a un autre magicien plus fort que lui . . . le magicien s'appelle le pape: tantôt il . . . fait croire que trois ne sont qu'un; que le pain qu'on mange n'est pas du pain ou que le vin qu'on boit n'est pas du vin, et mille autres choses de cette espèce.'

Next the priests—'Les libertins,' writes Usbek from Venice, 'entretiennent ici un nombre infini de filles de joie, et les dévots un nombre innombrable de dervis.' Two simple statements, of undeniable truth. Who could object? And yet. . . .

Love? Jealousy? The French take the first frivolously; the Italians take the second with deadly earnest. For Montesquieu, both are comical. All is relative.

The French think 'qu'il est aussi ridicule de jurer à une femme qu'on l'aimera toujours que de soutenir qu'on se portera toujours bien, ou qu'on sera toujours heureux. Quand ils promettent à une femme qu'ils l'aimeront toujours, ils supposent qu'elle, de son côté, leur promet d'être toujours aimable, et, si elle manque à sa parole, ils ne se croient plus engagés à la leur.'

At Leghorn, on the other hand, Usbek considers that, by Persian standards—

'les femmes y jouissent d'une grande liberté: elles peuvent voir les hommes à travers certaines fenêtres qu'on nomme jalousies; elles peuvent sortir tous les jours avec quelques vieilles qui les accompagnent; elles n'ont qu'un voile.[1] Leurs beaux-freres, leurs oncles, leurs neveux, peuvent les voir sans que le mari s'en formalise presque jamais.'

[1] 'Les Persanes en ont quatre.'

All is relative. Even that 'presque' is charged with irony.

Or finally there occurs perhaps the most crushing epigram ever pronounced against the literature of a whole nation, in the glance shot by this eighteenth-century Frenchman across the Pyrenees at romantic Spain—'Le seul de leurs livres qui soit bon est celui qui a fait voir le ridicule de tous les autres.'[1]

Montesquieu and Goldsmith are as different as that sun of the Midi which flashes down on the dryness of pointed limestone and darting lizard, from the sun of Leinster that silvers fitfully the flow of Shannon, and turns only greener the fields of Clonmacnois where the memories of Erin sleep. Montesquieu is more brilliant, but more cynical; less human and less constructive (his constructive side was to come with *L'Esprit des Lois*, which proved solid enough to provide in part a foundation for the constitution of the United States). Yet both books transport me with pleasure and admiration, as examples of human intelligence humorously contemplating the world with a vision clear, clean, and unfuddled by 'enthusiasm' or mysticism.

Goldsmith's Chinese, then, are less sharp and hard than Montesquieu's Persians. He has caught some of the quizzical humanity of the real China—as in that genuine piece of Chinese wisdom he quotes, about the old sage who argued that soft and gentle things are, strangely enough, in the end the strongest. For, though he had lost all his teeth, he still had all his tongue.

Throughout the *Citizen*, even at its most satirical—and it is largely occupied with satirizing shams—Goldsmith relies on his own charm of tongue; not, like Swift, on gnashing of teeth. Vague as may have been his knowledge of China through du Halde, he was curiously close in this at least to Confucius' ideal of the gentleman, who is like a breeze blowing along the Way, while common men are insensibly swayed by him in the same true direction, just as grass is swayed.

For example, there is the perennial sham of clap-trap about freedom (indeed 'Wilkes and Liberty' were shortly to turn London upside down). Goldsmith did not undervalue freedom; its praises were to form the climax of his *Traveller*. But he realized that some of those who shout loudest for freedom, are themselves the most

[1] Of course, *Don Quixote*.

enslaved by words; that political freedom is for many a mockery, when it goes with economic bondage (just as the modern dream of economic welfare in political bondage remains a selling of man's birthright for a mess of pottage). But with what smiling calm, what an absence of screams, does Lien Chi Altangi observe his English hosts!

> 'A few days ago, passing by one of their prisons, I could not avoid stopping, in order to listen to a dialogue, which I thought might afford me some entertainment. The conversation was carried on between a debtor through the grate of his prison, a porter, who had stopped to rest his burthen, and a soldier at the window. The subject was upon a threatened invasion from France, and each seemed extremely anxious to rescue his country from the impending danger. "*For my part,*" cries the prisoner, "*the greatest of my apprehensions is for our freedom; if the French should conquer, what would become of English liberty? My dear friends, liberty is the Englishman's prerogative; we must preserve that at the expense of our lives; of that the French shall never deprive us; it is not to be expected that men who are slaves themselves would preserve our freedom should they happen to conquer.*"
>
> "*Ay, slaves,*" cries the porter, "*they are all slaves, fit only to carry burthens, every one of them. Before I would stoop to slavery, may this be my poison*" (and he held the goblet in his hand), "*may this be my poison . . . but I would sooner list for a soldier.*"
>
> The soldier, taking the goblet from his friend, fervently cried out, "*It is not so much our liberties as our religion that would suffer by such a change; ay, our religion, my lads. May the Devil smite me into flames*" (such was the solemnity of his adjuration) "*if the French should come over, but our religion would be utterly undone.*" So saying, instead of a libation, he applied the goblet to his lips, and confirmed his sentiments with a ceremony of the most persevering devotion.'

Now it is a shock to find that this delightful passage is, in essentials, lifted from John Byrom's *Tom the Porter*. For Goldsmith, like Shakespeare and Webster, Molière and Sterne, could be an unblushing thief. He was too genuinely original to fuss about originality. On the other hand, he has so improved what he stole that the theft becomes far more than justified.

Then we turn to literary shams—the publisher who, like some more modern press-barons, has found success in merely following the popular opinions he seems to guide.

'Others may pretend to direct the vulgar; but that is not my way; wherever popular clamour arises, I always echo the million. For instance, should the people in general say that such a man is a rogue, I instantly give orders to set him down in print a villain; thus every man buys the book, not to learn new sentiments, but to have the pleasure of his own reflected.'

Or, again, Goldsmith attacks one more of his lifelong abominations, the æsthetic snob. The simple pawnbroker's widow has accompanied Beau Tibbs and his wife to Vauxhall; the widow, poor soul, would revel in it all, were she not perpetually snubbed by a couple whose chief pleasure consists in being displeased.

'By this last contradiction, the widow was fairly conquered in point of politeness. She perceived now that she had no pretensions in the world to taste; her very senses were vulgar, since she had praised detestable custard, and smacked at wretched wine; she was therefore content to yield the victory, and for the rest of the night to listen and improve. It is true, she would now and then forget herself, and confess she was pleased, but they soon brought her back again to miserable refinement.... She once praised the painting of the box in which we were sitting, but was soon convinced that such paltry pieces ought rather to excite horror than satisfaction; she ventured again to commend one of the singers, but Mrs Tibbs soon let her know, in the style of a connoisseur, that the singer in question had neither ear, voice, nor judgment.'

It might have been written yesterday; though few pens in any age possess this deadly ease. 'Miserable refinement'!—it could serve as motto for much of our loftier academic criticism. And my memory goes back to the phrase of a modern Irishman with much of Goldsmith's gaiety and grace—Desmond MacCarthy's description of English spectators wandering about a picture gallery, in a state of 'elevated depression'.

Depression of any kind, indeed, is one of the qualities most absent from Goldsmith's work; though even he must have found depression enough in life. He might write to his brother (1759)—'I have thought myself into a settled melancholy, and an utter disgust of all that life brings with it.' He might hope that his nephew would never be allowed to touch novels, because they 'describe happiness that man never tastes'. He might speak of having lived through miseries that would have driven many 'to the friar's cord, or the suicide's halter'. But he was not one of the many writers who have asked the world to pay them gratefully for deepening the gloom of nations. And so it is typical that one of the most light-hearted pieces in the *Citizen*—the story of the Prince of Bonbobbin, the Princess Nanhoa, Barbacela Queen of Emmets, and the white mouse with green eyes—should apparently be associated with a trick on Goldsmith himself which to most penniless writers would have seemed cruel beyond a joke—the fraud devised by the worthless Pilkington, who persuaded the good-natured Goldsmith to pawn his watch, so that Pilkington might buy a cage (so he pretended) for two white mice wherewith to court the favour of a mouse-collecting duchess. An enemy might indeed have said that the moral of the fairytale—'they who place their affections on trifles at first for amusement, will find those trifles at last become their most serious concern'—applied only too shrewdly to much of Goldsmith's own literary career. But I think the enemy would be unfair. Real goodness like Goldsmith's is none too common in literature; just as common sense is none too abundant in life. And if he is often a flippant writer, has he not himself wisely said—'It is remarkable that the propagators of false doctrines have ever been averse to mirth, and always begun by recommending gravity, when they intended to disseminate imposture'? Gaiety, he points out, is compatible with all the virtues (though prigs have denied this); but with some of the vices it is *not* compatible.

Perhaps Goldsmith never wrote anything better than the best parts of the *Citizen of the World*. His *Essays*, collected in 1765, are, I think, much slighter stuff; yet they too share that admirable lightness of touch. Beside the author of *The Rambler*, Goldsmith seems, to adopt his own image, a little, agile, silvery fish beside a majestic whale. In the *Essays* he again shows himself a light-fingered and light-hearted borrower—one of their best things, the story of the strolling player (Essay VI), is lifted from the *Spectateur Français* of Marivaux[1]; but, as usual, Goldsmith vastly betters what he steals.

[1] From whom Goldsmith borrowed also in the *Citizen of the World*, no. lxv (the poor cobbler); in *The Vicar of Wakefield*, ch. xx (George Primrose and the lord); and in his plays.

Like Chaucer, to whose French gaiety, intelligence, and good humour he approaches far nearer than most English writers, Goldsmith too was a *grand translateur*. This does not lessen—it heightens—the irony of the preface to these very *Essays*, where Goldsmith complains how others have pirated *him*; yet complains with a most typical gaiety.

> 'It is time, however, at last to vindicate my claims; and as these entertainers of the public, as they call themselves, have partly lived upon me for some years, let me now try if I cannot live a little upon myself. I would desire, in this case, to imitate that fat man whom I have somewhere heard of in a shipwreck, who, when the sailors, prest by famine, were taking slices from his posteriors to satisfy their hunger, insisted, with great justice, on having the first cut for himself.... However, whatever right I have to complain of the public, they can as yet have no just reason to complain of me. If I have written dull essays, they have hitherto treated them as dull essays. Thus far we are at least upon par....'

Criticism of life interested Goldsmith far more than criticism of literature, and even his literary criticism was concerned mainly (as I think it should be) with the relation of books to life. But though he was not, and did not wish to be, pre-eminently a critic, the critical views of any creative writer are usually interesting—and chiefly interesting, very often, for the light that they throw upon himself.

For criticism in general, as we have seen, Goldsmith felt an even deeper contempt than most creative writers. He satirized its pedantries in the 'polite' Germans, in George Primrose with his Pietro Perugino, in the Tibbses and the poor widow at Vauxhall. He hated its tendency, on the one hand, to pour supercilious cold water into other people's soup; on the other, to be fulsomely servile where adulation might pay.

> 'In reading the newspapers here, I have reckoned up not less than twenty-five great men, seventeen very great men, and nine very extraordinary men, in less than the compass of half a year. These, say the gazettes, are the men that posterity are to gaze at with admiration; these are names that fame will be employed in holding up for the astonishment of succeeding ages. Let me see . . . forty-six[1] great men,

[1] It is typical of Goldsmith that the addition should be wrong.

in half a year, amount just to ninety-two in a year. ... I wonder how posterity will be able to remember them all, or whether the people in future times will have any other business to mind, but that of getting the catalogue by heart.'

Amid all the changes of two centuries, this at least seems little changed. Our literary columns still resound with similar facile Alleluias. On the other hand, Goldsmith seems to me to go too far, when he says: 'The ingenious Mr Hogarth used to assert, that every one, except the connoisseur, was a judge of painting. The same may be asserted of writing.' Surely to say a work, or a woman, is 'beautiful', means 'beautiful beyond the average'; and to know what the average is, needs experience. Sensibility, again, though partly innate, is partly also trained (though, of course, it may be and often is, overtrained). Taste (like greatness, in Malvolio's letter) is sometimes born; sometimes, alas, thrust upon us; but in part it has to be achieved.

However, despite his contempt for critics, Goldsmith himself was driven, for a livelihood, to criticize. Yet here too he remains, at least, spontaneous and genuine. A simple, gay, happy-go-lucky Irishman, he inevitably rebelled against the academic, the pedantic, the snobbish, the priggish, and the solemn. He was indeed the very opposite, by temperament, of that Lord Chesterfield who had ruled in Dublin as viceroy when Goldsmith shivered there as a poor sizar. Chesterfield piqued himself on never laughing: Goldsmith's philosophy is precisely the opposite—'The wise bustle and laugh as they walk, but fools bustle and are important; and this, probably, is all the difference between them.' In short, let us laugh—*vive la bagatelle!* Chesterfield thought it beneath any gentleman to perform on a musical instrument; Goldsmith fluted through Europe. Chesterfield was concerned to avoid the low; Goldsmith raged against snobs who were so afraid of the low that they never reached any true heights. Better a heartfelt ballad of the people than all the bravuras of opera, or nightingales chirruping in petticoats. Since Richardson and the *comédie larmoyante* of the French theatre, sentiment had shrouded English comedy in wet handkerchiefs. And against such mawkishness Goldsmith, both in theory and in practice, passionately revolted. What should comedy be, if not comic? If laughter was 'low', then Shakespeare and Falstaff, Vanbrugh and Miss Hoyden were 'low'. Better be 'low' than frozen on icy altitudes. Goldsmith put into *The Good-Natured Man* a scene with bailiffs that had to be dropped because it was so 'low'; but he was unrepentant and printed it. And now we wonder what on earth there was to object to.

> 'By the power of one single monosyllable our critics have almost got the victory over humour amongst us. Does the poet point the absurdities of the vulgar; then he is *low*: does he exaggerate the features of folly, to render it more ridiculous, he is then *very low*. . . . On my conscience, I believe we have all forgot to laugh in these days.'

(This may have been true enough; on the other hand, could Goldsmith have listened to the B.B.C., he would have seen that drama can suffer from other things besides an excessive dread of being 'low'.)

Similarly in poetry, when Goldsmith objects to blank verse, it is partly because he thinks its rhymelessness mere classical pedantry; but partly, also, because it brings 'a disgusting solemnity of manner into our poetry'. He allowed (no doubt, with Milton in mind) that blank verse might succeed on the heights of the sublime; just as Johnson held that, if blank verse were not 'tumid and gorgeous', it was merely 'crippled prose'—and thereby implied that, when 'tumid and gorgeous', it *might* succeed. Both men, in fact, are fighting on the same side; but on opposite flanks. For one may question if Goldsmith really felt much enthusiasm for the 'tumid and gorgeous' anywhere; whereas Johnson objected to blank verse as often low, and unmusical, what Goldsmith hates is its 'disgusting solemnity'. A typical objection for Goldsmith. I cannot recall its being made by anyone else.

Both Johnson and Goldsmith seem to me partly right, partly wrong. Much eighteenth-century blank verse—say in Thomson, Young, Akenside—recalls the churchyard sculpture perpetrated by monumental masions, in Carrara marble of a whiteness as stiff and dead as those it commemorates. And, again, reading the duller blank-verse passages of Cowper, Wordsworth, or Browning, one feels that Goldsmith was absolutely prophetic. They *can* be 'disgustingly solemn'. On the other hand, Landor was to write blank verse of a delightful grace and simplicity; and things like *Michael*, or *Tithonus*, or *Sohrab and Rustum*, or Browning's Bishop of St Praxed's, prove that, even for themes less exalted than *Paradise Lost*, blank verse has powers that Goldsmith and Johnson little guessed.

None the less, blank verse remains as difficult as it looks easy. And I find myself remembering Goldsmith when I read the cataracts of translations from Greek Tragedy that now tumble upon us. Their authors, with their studiously bleak blank verse and their still duller unrhymed choruses, seem to imagine that all Athens went clothed in sackcloth and ashes. The marble of Æschylus they exchange for brick; the ivory of Sophocles, for bone. And they do it with 'disgusting solemnity'. Anyone who attempts blank verse will be wise, even now, to remember Goldsmith's warning.

Again both Johnson and Goldsmith disliked Gray, particularly the *Odes*. But again Goldsmith attacks from a different flank. He is more mindful of the viewpoint of simple men—'We cannot behold,' he says, 'this rising poet seeking fame among the learned, without hinting to him the same advice that Isocrates gave his scholars, *study the people*.' (Gray's learned poetry, one may note, is attacked with a learned allusion.)

Even the *Elegy in a Country Churchyard*, for Goldsmith, was 'a very fine poem, but overloaded with epithet'.[1] Perhaps it is. Certainly what one may call 'epithetitis' is a besetting disease of much verse, and especially of eighteenth-century verse. Goldsmith, with his rooted hatred of artificiality, felt so strongly on this point that he dragged the question of epithets even into *The Vicar of Wakefield*. ' "It is remarkable," cried Mr Burchell, "that both the poets you mention" (Ovid and Gay) "have equally contributed to introduce a false taste into their respective countries, by loading all their lines with epithet." ' One is reminded of Voltaire's wise and witty adage that though the adjective agrees with the noun in number and gender, it yet remains its greatest enemy.

Probably Goldsmith is again thinking of Gray and his school when he writes, in his life of Parnell:

'These misguided innovators have not been content with restoring

[1] In conversation Goldsmith is said to have proposed amending it 'by leaving out an idle word in every line'. This seems a good deal too strong. In general, he seems to have felt (like Tennyson—and, I think, rightly) that most poems are too long. Thomson is 'verbose'; Pope's *Eloisa*, 'drawn out to too tedious a length'; Parnell's *Hermit* is praised as 'concise'.

antiquated words and phrases, but have indulged themselves in the most licentious transpositions, and the harshest constructions, vainly imagining that the more their writings are unlike prose, the more they resemble poetry. They have adopted a language of their own, and call upon mankind for admiration. All those who do not understand them are silent, and those who make out their meaning are willing to praise, to show they understand.'

(How modern this too sounds!) Goldsmith might have liked Gray better, could he have read those letters where the Cambridge poet allows the humour of his sunnier moments to make April-play with the clouds of his melancholia.

'Study the people.' Goldsmith did not love blank verse with the fondness of Cowper and Wordsworth (who might perhaps have done well to love it a little less); but in this other respect—of going back closer to the unspoiled people—Goldsmith is curiously prophetic of Cowper and, still more, of Wordsworth.

One suspects that a similar tendency to prefer simple nature lies behind Goldsmith's comment on Milton's *Il Penseroso*, and *L'Allegro*—'I have heard a very judicious critic say, that he had an higher idea of Milton's style in poetry from the two following poems, than from his *Paradise Lost*.' So too with his remark on Dryden's *Alexander's Feast*: 'This ode has been more applauded, perhaps, than it has been felt' (though he adds, 'however, it is a very fine one'). I must own, indeed, that I have doubts even about that—*Alexander's Feast* seems to me as brassy as the most strident of military bands. Perhaps the noise of military bands may be appropriate to Alexander. But a little of it goes a long way.

Again, Goldsmith did not like Sterne—'a dull fellow',[1] whose fiction he called 'obscene and pert'. At first sight this may appear surprising. To-day one can see both Goldsmith and Sterne as a pair of lively squirrels who come frisking across the Ha-ha into the formal eighteenth-century garden—untamed creatures of the wild woodland that skip mischievously across shaven lawn and decorous parterre. In their simple goodness Uncle Toby and Dr Primrose seem not far apart. And Goldsmith and Sterne have in common a certain Irish whimsicality; true, Sterne was Irish only by his birth

[1] To which Johnson replied, 'Why, no, Sir!'

at Clonmel; yet if it comes to that, what name more English than Goldsmith?[1]

However I suppose the explanation of Goldsmith's antipathy for Sterne may be partly that writers are apt to like writers quite unlike themselves, writers who do not compete; as Milton liked Euripides, or as Kipling adored Jane Austen. But it was still more, I imagine, that Goldsmith suspected Sterne, with all his sentiment, of being a Joseph Surface. When Sterne died in Bond Street, no outcasts sat weeping on *his* stairs. Sentimentality was Goldsmith's aversion on the stage; why should he be more tolerant of it in the novel? *Tristram Shandy* and the *Sentimental Journey* are more original, more brilliant, more effervescent than *The Vicar of Wakefield*. But Sterne's sincerity is less above suspicion, his mind less healthy. All the same there is one respect in which Sterne and Goldsmith stand close together—both of them loved the grace and gaiety of a France as yet undarkened by Revolution.

> To kinder skies, where gentler manners reign
> I turn; and France displays her bright domain.
> Gay sprightly land of mirth and social ease,
> Pleas'd with thyself, whom all the world can please,
> How often have I led thy sportive choir,
> With tuneless pipe, beside the murmuring Loire!
> Where shading elms along the margin grew,
> And freshen'd from the wave the Zephyr flew;
> And haply, though my harsh touch, faltering still,
> But mock'd all tune, and marr'd the dancers' skill;
> Yet would the village praise my wondrous pow'r,
> And dance, forgetful of the noon-tide hour.

This is strangely near to that scene in *Tristram Shandy*, 'in the road betwixt Nismes and Lunel, where there is the best Muscato wine in all France', and where Sterne dances with Nannette in her slit petticoat to the 'Gascoigne roundelay:

> Viva la joia!
> Fidon la tristessa!'

[1] His ancestors are said to have come from Kent; but it was noted centuries since that settlers in Ireland easily become 'ipsis Hibernis Hiberniores'—'more Irish than the Irish themselves'.

And yet even here it is perhaps typical, that Goldsmith stays wistfully piping, but Sterne frisks gaily into the dance himself.

Happy age when the Channel was so narrow, and the two finest literatures of modern Europe could interact! The influence of France on Gibbon and Walpole, Sterne and Goldsmith (so extensive that a whole book has been written on Goldsmith's French sources)[1] seems to me a good deal happier than that of Germany in the next century on Coleridge, or Carlyle, or Arnold. It helped Goldsmith, I suspect, to become less ponderous and thick-ankled and insular than Johnson, or Richardson, or Fielding, or Smollett. And he was doing something to repay his own debt to France when he rebuked Reynolds, with unwonted severity, for painting that allegorical picture of Dr Beattie and the Angel of Truth putting to flight the demons of Sophistry, Falsehood, and Infidelity, where Sophistry was given the familiar features of Voltaire. 'Dr Beattie and his book,' Goldsmith protested, 'will not be known in ten years; but your allegorical picture on the fame of Voltaire will live for ever to your disgrace as a flatterer.'

It would be difficult to say how far Goldsmith, who drew so largely at times on French writers for what he had to say, was also influenced by French style in his way of saying it. He seems to have learnt French early and fluently—perhaps from Irish Catholic priests (who were mostly trained in France). In spite of geography, the Scots for political reasons, and the Irish for reasons both political and religious, have often stood closer to France than the English. But on the whole I suspect that a certain French quality in Goldsmith's prose—a simplicity that suddenly sparkles, an ease that suddenly strikes—is due less to influence than to similarity of temper. Goethe complained of the Germans that 'alles über ihnen schwer wird, und sie über allem schwer werden'; it would be hard to find a better description of what Goldsmith is not.

Some styles show a continuous tension—and the strain becomes unpleasant; some are permanently relaxed—and the effect is lazy or dull; the happy compromise comes with an easeful relaxation that can yet, when occasion comes, suddenly tighten to intensity and force. It was not without reason that, at a dinner party of (probably) 1783, where the dead writer was disparaged by the future Lord

[1] A. L. Sells, *Sources Françaises de Goldsmith.*

Eliot, Johnson burst out—'Is there a man, Sir, now who can pen an essay with such ease and elegance as Goldsmith?'

True, in his careless Irish way, he can at times be a strange sloven—'after thus grieving through three scenes, the curtain dropped for the first act'. But this air of indolence only makes his sudden pounces the more pleasantly startling. In these effortless sentences there comes, all at once, some word, or phrase, or image, that flashes out and lives in the memory; as in the level green of an alpine meadow the sudden colour of a gentian; or amid the flow of some quiet, limpid stream, a sudden eddy glinting in the sun.

> Where the broad ocean *leans* against the land.

> On the stage he was natural, simple, affecting;
> 'Twas only that when he was *off*, he was acting.

'Not a curtsey or nod that was not the result of art: not a look nor a smile that was not designed for *murder*'—'the Squire would sometimes fall asleep in the most pathetic parts of my sermon, or his lady return my wife's civilities at church with a *mutilated* courtesy'—'fine modern odes, and things that *petrify* us in a single stanza'—'an old woman may be miserable now, and not *be hanged for it*'—'the *tawny* sybil'—'I readily therefore gave my bond for the money, and testified as much gratitude *as if I never intended to pay*'—'Romeo was to be performed by a gentleman from the Theatre Royal, in Drury Lane; Juliet, by a lady who had never appeared on any stage; and I was to snuff the candles: *all excellent in our way*'—'all the nightingales that ever *chirruped in petticoats*'—'triflingly sedulous in *the incatenation of fleas*'—'a tiger *of common sensibility* has twenty times more tenderness than I'—'wheedle *milk from a mouse*.' It may be noted that in this enlivening imagery a large part is played by animals; as, again, when he describes a lady trailing a train of glory—'if ever she attempts to turn round, it must be in a circle not smaller than that described by the wheeling crocodile, when it would face an assailant'. Or there is the hopeful young author—'like the porcupine, I sate self-collected, with a quill pointed against every opposer'. And when Goldsmith would express the loneliness and provocations of his own London exile, amid a society often rough and heartless, it is still by an animal figure—'to fret and scamper at the end of my chain'.

Many another writer, of course, has delighted in animal imagery—Goldsmith's formidable friend Johnson, for one. But, characteristically, Goldsmith's animals are more creatures of sympathy than Johnson's 'stately horse', or his milked bull, or the packs of 'dogs' he kept at constant call; Goldsmith's mouse is 'wheedled', his squirrels are 'little sailors'; even his crocodile remains lady-like, his tiger is a tiger of 'sensibility', his Johnson has 'nothing of the bear but his skin'.

Indeed there is no more typical, or more charming, tale of Goldsmith than Reynolds's account to Miss Horneck, the 'Jessamy Bride', of a friend who found Goldsmith at work—teaching a dog to beg, with solemnly raised forefinger, while on his desk there lay, with ink still wet, the lines:

> By sports like these are all their cares beguil'd,
> The sports of children satisfy the child.

Or again when he writes homesick to that Ireland he was so often to talk of seeing, but was never to see again, how Goldsmithian is the phrase—'and if there is a favourite dog in the family, let me be remembered to him'!

And so the animals came very happily to the flutings of this ugly little Orpheus. Even the clods of earth rise up at his beck and dance, when another typical sentence describes, with one of Goldsmith's nearest approaches to really bitter irony, the mercenary, loveless marriages of high society—'the gentleman's mortgaged lawn becomes enamoured of the lady's marriageable grove; the match is struck up, and both parties are piously in love . . . according to act of parliament'.

For producing poetry on a large, or lofty, scale one may doubt if Goldsmith had the temperament. If one believed in 'Celtic magic', one might have expected him to become a pre-Romantic like Gray, Chatterton, Macpherson, or Burns. But Goldsmith was too sociable a person to brood like the lonely, melancholy Gray in country churchyards, or among the untrodden ways of northern hills; too fond of the balanced sense and ironic laughter of eighteenth-century

France to share the medieval nostalgia of Chatterton (though he was taken in by the sham antiquity of the Rowley poems). His biographer, indeed, the worthy Prior, thought Goldsmith's *Edwin and Angelina* 'the most beautiful ballad in our own, or perhaps in any language'. Yet how could he!

> And when beside me in the dale,
> He carol'd lays of love,
> His breath lent fragrance to the gale,
> And music to the grove.

It is enough to contrast for a single moment the genuine ballad-ring:

> 'Betide me weal, betide me woe,
> That weird shall never daunten me.'
> Syne he has kissed her rosy lips,
> All underneath the Eildon tree.

The two styles are as far apart as honeysuckle from heather. *Edwin and Angelina* may have pleased Percy's patroness, the Countess of Northumberland; it may be less insufferable than Mat Prior's murder of *The Nutbrown Maid* in *Henry and Emma*. But 'Angelina'! The very name is enough. For civilized minds like Goldsmith's the best thing about the Middle Ages was, really, that they were over. 'An old woman may be miserable now, and not be hanged for it.' That prose sentence of Goldsmith's comes nearer than anything in his ballad to the tragic savagery of those bygone centuries.

Again, he had too much gaiety and sense of measure to abandon himself to misty moanings and moonings like *Ossian*; and to write lyrics like those of Burns I doubt if he had the intensity.

Goldsmith, I suppose, might have replied: 'It is because you are sickened and surfeited with civilization that you hanker after savage scenery, primitive brutalities, hyperbolical emotions. It is *you* that are unhealthy; as it was already something unhealthy in the effeminate Mr Gray that made him go wandering off into Highland glens and Norse ferocities.' And perhaps Goldsmith would not have been wholly wrong. But of course it is also true that eighteenth-century polish was in some ways strangely narrow, while we have learnt far wider knowledge and emotions far more versatile.

In any case, Goldsmith's Muse was a gentle, wistful, humorously ironic creature, far removed from that elephantiasis of the ego often found in Romantics; who were apt to wear on their sleeves models of their hearts several times larger than life, and not always as natural. In Wordsworth or Byron, Chateaubriand or Hugo, Goldsmith would have found a touch of the monstrous.

Typically eighteenth-century verse seems to me happiest when it forgoes the heights of imagination, and is content to be either satirically bitter or wittily gay. But Goldsmith had neither the hornet's venom of Pope, nor the fierce gloom of Johnson, nor the gay sparkle of Prior. Goldsmith's *Elegy on the Death of a Mad Dog*, or that on *Mrs Mary Blaize* are gay, but trivial; winning a smile of indulgence rather than delight. Only three of Goldsmith's poems, for me, leave their mark on the memory. One is a satire too gentle to be very satirical—*Retaliation*. The other two are, in a sense, political poems—but like no other political poems that I can think of. Perhaps the chief charm of all three is that they are full of Goldsmith's own personality.

Byron, I admit, judged Goldsmith far more emphatically. 'Where is the poetry of which one half is good? Is it the *Æneid*? Is it Milton's? Is it Dryden's? Is it anyone's except Pope's and Goldsmith's?—of which all is good.'[1] But this seems to me partly poetic licence, and partly due to a desire on Byron's part, to strike—and wound—detested contemporaries. But though Goldsmith might have enjoyed this tribute, it is not the type of exuberance he would have allowed himself to indulge in.

The Traveller embodies a thesis. But it may be questioned how many, even of those who recall its best passages, can remember its argument; so perhaps it may be briefly outlined here. After a prologue to his brother Henry, the wandering Oliver seats himself on a mountain-eminence with Italy to his right, Switzerland to his left, and France behind. Which is the happiest of earthly lands? Each man thinks, his own. Yet all have their special blessings.

[1] This seems even more fantastic to say of Pope than of Goldsmith; parts of Pope's less-known verse are, for me, lamentable.

Tho' patriots flatter, still shall wisdom find
An equal portion dealt to all mankind.

(A benevolent optimism; which I doubt.) The trouble comes, Goldsmith continues, when a country pushes its own particular blessings too far:

'Till, carried to excess in each domain
This favourite good begets peculiar pain.

Thus Italy, perfect in beauty, is yet degenerate in manhood.

Here may be seen, in bloodless pomp array'd,
The paste-board triumph and the cavalcade;
Processions form'd for piety and love,
A mistress or a saint in every grove.
By sports like these are all their cares beguil'd,
The sports of children satisfy the child.

Next, Switzerland—'where rougher climes a nobler race display'.

No product here the barren hills afford,
But Man and steel, the soldier and his sword. . . .
No Zephyr fondly sues the mountain's breast,
But meteors glare, and stormy glooms invest.

Yet, though hardy, frugal, resolute, the Swiss remain crude and gross as the bears of Bern.

Some sterner virtues o'er the mountain's breast
May sit, like falcons cow'ring on the nest;

but (this I should have thought a monstrous libel)—

But not their joys alone thus coarsely flow,
Their morals, like their pleasures, are but low,
For, as refinement stops, from sire to son
Unalter'd, unimprov'd the manners run,
And love's and friendship's finely pointed dart
Fall blunted from each indurated heart.

It would have been interesting to hear the comments on this, of the passionate Rousseau, visited in that same December 1764 by Boswell, or of Mlle Suzanne Curchod, so docilely dropped by her English lover, Gibbon, only seven years before.

Next there is France, 'gay, sprightly land of mirth and social ease'; and yet debased by too much frivolity and vain display.

Here vanity assumes her pert grimace,
And trims her robes of frize with copper lace,
Here beggar pride defrauds her daily cheer,
To boast one splendid banquet once a year.

The Dutch, again, are industrious and ingenious; but, by excess, they grow commercial and money-grubbing.

Then, at last, the wandering Goldsmith turns his thoughts home to England, and to that praise of her freedom which Johnson himself was one day to quote, tears in his eyes, far off among the Hebrides.

Stern o'er each bosom reason holds her state,
With daring aims irregularly great,[1]
Pride in their port, defiance in their eye,
I see the lords of human kind pass by,[2]
Intent on high designs, a thoughtful band,
By forms unfashion'd, fresh from Nature's hand;
Fierce in their native hardiness of soul,
True to imagin'd right, above controul,
While even the peasant boasts these rights to scan,
And learns to venerate himself as man.[3]

[1] The first line of this couplet embodies our traditional view of the eighteenth century: but its second line our traditional view tends too often to forget.

[2] It is worth recalling that this was the year after the Peace of Paris; the next twenty were to see that pride considerably humbled.

[3] It is not without interest to compare—and contrast—the judgment of the old Clemenceau (1928): 'Elle a été une très grande dame, l'Angleterre . . . fermée, cruelle, mais qui avait de l'allure. L'Angleterre est peut-être de tous les peuples celui qui a voulu le plus longuement. Malheureusement il se produit chez elle comme une espèce d'affaissement, de lassitude. Le conquérant ne répond plus tout à fait à sa conquête. Que voulez-vous? Leur histoire dure depuis très longtemps. . . . Les Anglais d'aujourd'hui luttent moins que ceux d'il y a cent ans. Il y a quelque chose qui est en train de s'abandonner.' (The challenge met in 1940 may seem to belie this judgment. Yet it provokes thought.)

But—we see Goldsmith's moral approaching—freedom too has its excesses—arrogance, faction, anarchy, and (as in Holland) an egoistic greed of gold.

> When I behold a factious band agree
> To call it freedom when themselves are free;
> Each wanton judge new penal statutes draw,
> Laws grind the poor, and rich men rule the law;
> The wealth of climes, where savage nations roam,
> Pillag'd from slaves to purchase slaves at home;
> Fear, piety, justice, indignation start,
> Tear off reserve, and bare my swelling heart;
> 'Till half a patriot, half a coward grown,
> I fly from petty tyrants to the throne. . . .
> Have we not seen, at pleasure's lordly call,
> The smiling long-frequented village fall?
> Beheld the duteous son, the sire decay'd,
> The modest matron, and the blushing maid,
> Forc'd from their homes, a melancholy train,
> To traverse climes beyond the western main;
> Where wild Oswego spreads her swamps around,
> And Niagara stuns with thund'ring sound?

Here, on the horizon there rise already the roofs of *The Deserted Village*.

And so to the conclusion of the whole argument, where Johnson lends his robust arm to 'Doctor Minor'.[1] We squabble idly about constitutions. Happiness lies within us.

> How small of all that human hearts endure,
> That part which laws or kings can cause or cure!

It is one of Johnson's most triumphant couplets. It stands a perpetual warning to hysterical reformers of the not uncommon type which thinks that, with enough red tape of a new model, mankind can be legislated into everlasting bliss. And yet our age at least should have learnt how far from truth Johnson's dictum remains—how unendurably human hearts can suffer from laws and rulers—in total war, or in a Third Reich, or behind an Iron Curtain. And

[1] Of the poem's five closing couplets, all are by Johnson except the last but one.

Goldsmith too might have remembered how many villages, even while he wrote, lay deserted and destroyed from Calcutta to Quebec, largely because a fame-thirsty young monarch had once seized a Naboth's vineyard in Silesia. A few years yet, and similar devastation was to be caused, in another seven years of war, civil and foreign, largely by the follies of that very throne where Goldsmith here seeks shelter. And beyond that lay the further havoc of French Revolution and Napoleon.

For that matter Goldsmith himself had elsewhere complained bitterly and justly enough of the misery inflicted by English laws, with their countless capital offences.

And the black gibbet glooms beside the way.

Indeed, with different laws *The Deserted Village* itself need not have been deserted.[1]

As political argument, then, *The Traveller* rambles too much. Goldsmith's and Johnson's Tory democracy was not democratic enough. 'Put not your trust in princes.' The English poor were to find shelter, not in the House of Hanover, but, after slow generations, in their own votes. Benevolent monarchs, like benevolent oligarchies, are a dream; since no one has ever found how to make them benevolent, to keep them benevolent, or to ensure the benevolence of their successors.

The Traveller, published in December 1764, had three more editions in 1765, and five others before Goldsmith's death in 1774. Johnson judged it 'a poem to which it would not be easy to find anything equal since the days of Pope'. His modesty omitted himself; his hostility, Gray. His verdict witnesses, I think, to the general poverty (despite its modern defenders) of eighteenth-century poetry; for I cannot believe that *The Traveller* would have thus stood out in the seventeenth century, nor yet in the nineteenth.

Goldsmith's best poem seems to me *The Deserted Village* (pub-

[1] Had Johnson merely stressed that the proportion of unhappiness caused by public measures was *relatively* small, one must agree. Cf. for example, Mme de Boigne's story of Castlereagh announcing to George IV, when Napoleon died: 'Sire, je viens apprendre à Votre Majesté qu' Elle a perdu son plus mortel ennemi'—to which the King replied, 'Quoi, est-il possible! elle est morte!' (Caroline was more in his mind than even Bonaparte.)

lished May 1770, with at least nine further editions the same year); partly because, like *The Vicar of Wakefield*, it contains so many of Goldsmith's own personal recollections. For he stands half-way between amazing creators, like the inventor of Pickwick, and exact copyists like the Boswell who painted himself complete with every wart and freckle. Goldsmith remelts and remoulds his own memories into fiction. And so *The Village* suited him; for he remained always something of a countryman caught in the iron cage of London. But here at least he escaped. Here, in his village-schoolmaster, he could recapture Thomas Byrne, the old quartermaster of Lissoy; in the village-parson (a gentler successor of Chaucer's), his own dead father, and his dead brother Henry.

Macaulay has treated Auburn as more fictitious than it is—as a mixture of a village in Kent and an ejectment in Munster. 'By joining the two, he has produced something which never was and never will be seen in any part of the world.' Even if it 'never was'—which seems pretty dogmatic—how could Macaulay think himself so sure it never would be? An age which has seen six million Jews liquidated, and ten million Germans flee west of the Elbe, may well wonder at such certainty.

But even about the eighteenth century Goldsmith is, as he himself protested, by no means so far wrong. In origin, the village is Goldsmith's native Lissoy, whose present counterpart has long since changed its name in his honour to Auburn. There, in Goldsmith's boyhood, a certain General Naper or Napier seems to have ejected cottagers to enlarge his domain. However, Goldsmith has transplanted Auburn to England, before making its rustics migrate to America.

And why not? He could justly have pleaded that Scotland and England, as well as Ireland, had seen similar tyrannies. Boswell and Johnson found plenty of depopulation, thanks partly to grasping lairds, going on in the Highlands; as it has gone on since.[1]

[1] In the Highlands, between 1861 and 1870, the natural increase was 37,000, but 46,000 emigrated; in 1921–30 the natural increase had dropped to 3,000, but the emigration was still 28,000.

> From the lone shieling on the misty island
> Mountains divide us, and the waste of seas;
> But still the heart is strong, the blood is Highland,
> And we in dreams behold the Hebrides.

In England, again, between 1760 and 1774 the Enclosure Acts numbered no less than seven hundred. And the process long continued, despite the angry roars of Cobbett and the laments of Clare, whose native Helpstone was enclosed by an Act of 1809. The modern research of the Hammonds in their *Village Labourer* treats Goldsmith as a much more serious witness than Macaulay had in 1856, or Goldsmith's biographer, Prior, in 1837. Nor has his protest lost all its force even yet, while the 'great wens' of London and our other giant cities still continue their cancerous growth.

No doubt the enclosers could justly claim increased production; but not even that excuse was always thought necessary. In 1786 Joseph Damer, future Earl of Dorchester, objected to the village of Milton (near Blandford) being in sight of his mansion. He removed the whole place—a hundred houses, a brewery, a grammar-school that had bred Nelson's Hardy, almshouses, inns, even the very tombstones. Even so, it is recorded that Mr Damer was much annoyed because the bones of past Miltonians kept turning up as he laid out his gardens.[1]

True, he was at least considerate enough to resettle the exiles half a mile away in a charming eighteenth-century model village—alternate cottages and horse-chestnut trees that still climb its wooded hill. But, once again, the incident illustrates the monstrous power of eighteenth-century magnates.

Similarly one hears of a village near Swaffham (Norfolk) where in 1773 the houses were tumbling, the farmers dead or reduced to labourers, because a gentleman of Lynn had bought the locality and reduced twenty farms to seven; of Foston (Leicestershire), dwindled after enclosure from some thirty-five houses to a parsonage and two herdsman's cottages; of Wiston in the same county, and about the same size, where only the squire's house remained.

[1] R. S. Crane pointed out in *Times Lit. Sup.*, September 8, 1927, p. 607, that Goldsmith wrote anonymously in *Lloyd's Evening Post*, June 14–16, 1762, an indignant description, curiously anticipating his poem, of a happy village evicted to make way for a *pleasure-seat* designed by 'a Merchant of immense fortune in London'. This is a similar case to Mr Damer's, in that the motive was not agricultural productivity, but a lordly residence. (See R. S. Crane, *New Essays by Goldsmith* (1927), 116–24.)

On the other hand, in the introduction (which seems Goldsmith's) to *Goody Two-shoes*, Sir Timothy Gripe and Father Graspall are concerned to merge a number of farms in one.

Defenders of the slave-trade, according to Whitbread, argued that West Indian Negroes were treated better than English villagers. And Arthur Young, who had himself supported enclosures, concluded in 1800: 'I had rather that all the commons in England were sunk in the sea, than that the poor should in future be treated on enclosing as they have generally been hitherto.'

Perhaps a sounder criticism of *The Deserted Village* would be that, though English villagers were only too often evicted, mass-migration to America seems to belong, rather, to Scotland or Ireland. But this point does not seem to have worried Goldsmith's contemporaries.

Crabbe's criticism, it will be recalled, was quite a different one—not that the sufferings of Goldsmith's villagers were exaggerated, but, on the contrary, that their happiness was overdrawn, in too honeysuckle style. And that was probably just—though one should still remember Clare's happy memories of Helpstone:

> Oh happy Eden of those golden years
> Which memory cherishes, and use endears.

It is hard to say anything new of a poem that has long become a national possession; and little new needs to be said—it is better to reread it. Perhaps the strangest thing about *The Deserted Village* is the way that Goldsmith has contrived to breathe into the heroic couplet (often a somewhat brassy instrument) a gentler sweetness all his own.

> The hawthorn bush, with seats beneath the shade,
> For talking age and whispering lovers made.

> Sweet as the primrose peeps beneath the thorn.

Contrast that companion piece, the *Country Churchyard*, where Gray achieved his supreme success by doing for once what Goldsmith once urged him to do—'study the people.' (Gray, indeed, seems to have liked Goldsmith's poetry better than Goldsmith liked his. Goldsmith thought even the *Elegy* 'overloaded with epithet': but Gray, hearing Nicholls read *The Deserted Village*, observed 'That man is a poet'.) To pass from the *Elegy* to the *Village* is like hearing a wistful flute after some deep organ—

> Where through the long-drawn aisle and fretted vault
> The pealing anthem swells the note of praise;

as Gray had heard it in King's Chapel, as Wordsworth was to hear it there after him. No doubt this is partly because, though its line-length remains the same, the decasyllabic quatrain differs mysteriously from the decasyllabic couplet. Its movement seems far slower. The rhymes are content to wait, unhurried, for twice as long before their echo comes. The effect is graver, more processional. But here the difference depends, not only on instrument, but also on temperament. Gray, with his melancholy, prefers to lose himself in the owl-haunted dusk, among the graves of the village-dead; remembering the greater dead whom they might have equalled, and who are equalled with them now; remembering, too, that far-off voice of Lucretius proclaiming the adamantine finality of death itself.

> For them no more the blazing hearth shall burn,
> Or busy housewife ply her evening care:
> No children run to lisp their sire's return,
> Or climb his knees the envied kiss to share.[1]

To this Dead March the flute of Goldsmith replies in tones less grand, yet more alive—alive with humanity's eternal alternation between grave and gay, between laughter and tears. Not to Goldsmith belongs that mournful sublimity of Gray; as Dante's dark mantle could never shadow Chaucer's quick, amused, ironic eyes.

> The noisy geese that gabbl'd o'er the pool,
> The playful children just let loose from school—

imagine a goose escaped into Gray's churchyard! Goldsmith's

[1] Cf. Lucretius, iii, 894–6:

> Iam iam non domus accipiet te laeta, neque uxor
> Optima, nec dulces occurrent oscula nati
> Praeripere et tacita pectus dulcedine tangent.

village-schoolmaster is no 'mute, inglorious Milton'; he is a not unvainglorious Holofernes:

> Full well they laugh'd with counterfeited glee
> At all his jokes, for many a joke had he; . . .
> And still they gaz'd, and still the wonder grew,
> That one small head could carry all he knew.

Gray's work, no doubt, is finer literature, and purer art—great poetry miraculously made out of undertakers' commonplaces. And yet, in a way, though Goldsmith's village lies deserted—as dead as Gray's villagers—his poem remains more alive, more human, with its passionate indignation against the tyrants of the living world, with its mingling of joy in life, and laughter at it, and pity for it. Between the two pieces, in two words, lies the difference between sublimity and charm. Gray, I suppose, was the better poet; but it seems to me a good deal healthier to be Goldsmith. 'Let the dead bury their dead.' Gray too had a very pretty humour; but for him (as not for Goldsmith) there was something that 'froze the genial current of the soul'.

But though Goldsmith was light-hearted, he did not take his art as poet lightly. He used to begin, we are told, with a prose plan; then versify; then correct. 'If sometimes,' says William Cooke, 'he would exceed his prose design by writing several verses impromptu, he would take singular pains afterwards to revise; lest they should be found unconnected with his main design.' Both *Traveller* and *Village* were written with wide interlineations, for corrections so extensive that, it is said, scarcely a word escaped unaltered. Their author may have been a feckless Irish Bohemian; but he remained the child of an age that left even Ireland's capital splendid with streets classic in their architecture.

After all, *The Deserted Village* itself, with all its Irishness, preserves a classic tradition. It is hard to associate anything that seems often so artless with anything so artificial as pastoral. But a pastoral it is. Indeed Virgil's *First Eclogue* is likewise a lament for country-folk evicted by the military colonies of Augustus.

On the other hand, as I believe writers are always wise to do, Goldsmith freely mingles with this classic element both the realistic and the romantic. He may not have been realist enough for Crabbe: but he could write, at times, verse that Crabbe might have signed.

Here while the proud their long-drawn pomps display,
There the black gibbet glooms beside the way.

Beside yon straggling fence that skirts the way,
With blossom'd furze unprofitably gay.

A window, patch'd with paper, lent a ray
That dimly shew'd the state in which he lay,
The sanded floor that grits beneath the tread,
The humid wall with paltry pictures spread . . .
With beer and milk arrears the frieze was scor'd,
And five crack'd tea-cups dress'd the chimney board.[1]

But such things in Goldsmith are only momentary realisms. Of these two poet-doctors, Crabbe was far the more thorough, with a sombre Anglo-Saxon doggedness; one cannot picture the Irishly truant Goldsmith laboriously botanizing weeds, or dissecting dead dogs cast up on Aldeburgh beach. Crabbe put Truth before Beauty; Goldsmith, Beauty before Truth. Yet each poet has his share of either quality; let us be grateful for them both.

There appear also, on the smooth waters of Goldsmith, cats-paws here and there of the Romantic storm to come. Already the Alps loom up in the distance with a grandeur that is no longer merely 'horrid'.

No vernal blooms their torpid rocks array,
But winter ling'ring chills the lap of May;
No Zephyr fondly sues the mountain's breast,
But meteors glare, and stormy glooms invest.

We may smile at the idea of Zephyrs 'suing the breast' of the Jungfrau; but, even so, the atmosphere has begun to change.

There are, too, 'Romantic' attempts to catch the haunting mystery of transatlantic wildernesses.

[1] *Description of an Author's Bedchamber*; partly reproduced in *The Deserted Village.*

On Torno's[1] cliffs, or Pambamarca's[2] side.

Where wild Oswego[3] spreads her swamps around
Or Niagara stuns with thund'ring sound.

Through torrid tracts with fainting steps they go
Where wild Altama[4] murmurs to their woe.

As some tall cliff that lifts its awful form
Swells from the vale, and midway leaves the storm,
Though round its breast the rolling clouds are spread,
Eternal sunshine settles on its head.

This image of the village-pastor's soul was thought by Gilbert Wakefield 'perhaps the sublimest simile that English poetry can boast'. (So tastes alter!) It may be indebted to Homer's Olympus, by way of Claudian, to Chapelain, Chauileu, or Young, and to Ulloa's travels in South America. But the 'eternal sunshine' does not suggest much knowledge of real mountain-tops, whether in Alps or Andes.

Yet such passages as these, though historically interesting, never seem to me the true Goldsmith—in them one feels that he is straining his voice to a slight falsetto. Auburn is the 'loveliest village of the *plain*'; to its quiet landscape belong neither Alps nor Andes. Its author is not at home by 'Niagára', as Chateaubriand was to be; the Alps reach very different heights in Wordsworth, Byron, or Arnold. Goldsmith remains like the shepherd in Tennyson's Lauterbrunnen idyll:

nor cares to walk
With Death and Morning on the silver horns.

Goldsmith, too, might have cried to his Muse—

Come down, O maid, from yonder mountain height;
What pleasure lives in height (the shepherd sang),

[1] Tornea, or Tornio, in Finland?
[2] In Ecuador.
[3] River flowing into Lake Ontario.
[4] Altamaha, river in Georgia, U.S.A.

> In height and cold, the splendour of the hills? . . .
> But come; for all the vales
> Await thee; azure pillars of the hearth
> Arise to thee; the children call, and I
> Thy shepherd pipe, and sweet is every sound,
> Sweeter thy voice, but every sound is sweet.

At Byron's praise of his verse as 'all good' Goldsmith might have smiled with pleasure, but also with doubt. I suspect that he would have been more touched by a crazier tribute from an obscurer brain. At Oxford, once, the younger Colman met a half-mad poet called Harding, topped by a hat curiously embellished with bits of thatch and a huge broken brick—'Sir,' said the eccentric, 'to-day is the anniversary of the celebrated Dr Goldsmith's death; and I am now in the character of his Deserted Village.'

When Prior published his *Goldsmith* (1837), the rectory of Lissoy was now a roofless ruin. The words of the poet had been fulfilled:

> There, where a few torn shrubs the place disclose,
> The village Preacher's modest mansion rose.

Its orchard and garden were weeds, its avenue of ashes felled. The Bishop of Ardagh had meant to cut down the hawthorn too; but when told by one of his clergy that it was Goldsmith's hawthorn, he replied (unlike the clerical murderer of Shakespeare's mulberry)—'Ma foy![1] Is *that* the hawthorn-bush? Then ever let it be sacred from the edge of the axe, and evil to him that would cut from it a branch!' But, despite this pious curse, pious travellers had destroyed it by 1820, carrying off bits of its boughs, even of its very roots, as relics. The inn had been repaired, named 'The Three Jolly Pigeons', and equipped with new copies of 'the twelve good rules, the royal game of goose'. Even Goldsmith's 'broken tea-cups wisely kept for shew' had been represented by specimens embedded in mortar; though these too had been mainly carried off, also by pilgrims. This, I suppose, is true fame. No doubt if Goldsmith's *Traveller* and *Village* appeared for the first time to-day they would be greeted with hoots of derision, or with silent contempt. *We*

[1] As noted above, the Irish Catholic clergy came from French seminaries.

are not so simple. And yet, minor poet though Goldsmith may remain, it would not be wholly surprising if his verse were still read hereafter, long after most of the poems of our age have been abandoned by all but the fanatic researcher.

Oliver Elton was a very level-headed person, and his *Survey of English Literature* stands high, I think, among literary histories. But when he writes, of Goldsmith's plays, 'they are his best work', I must confess astonishment. For it seems to me idle to devote much time to *The Good-Natured Man* (Covent Garden, 1768). This half-farce (based partly on *Le Legs* of Marivaux), with its impersonations and coincidences, its misunderstandings and miscarried letters, seems mainly of historic interest as a revolt against the school of sentiment in eighteenth-century comedy, typified by the very title of Kelly's rival piece at Drury Lane—*False Delicacy*. Plot, indeed, was never Goldsmith's strong point.

His hero, the gentle Honeywood, who can never say 'No' to the beggings of distress, loves, but dare not woo, the rich heiress, Miss Richland, who is ward of the gloomy Mr Croaker and can inherit her estate only if she weds Croaker's son, Leontine; if she refuses, she forfeits half her heritage. But Leontine is in love with a lady from Paris. He was sent to bring thence his own sister Olivia, educated since childhood in France; but returns, instead, with this other Olivia, pretending to his father that she is his own sister. A stage-uncle has Honeywood arrested for debt. Leontine, after pretending to propose, as his father orders, to Miss Richland, unsuccessfully tries to elope with his Olivia. Finally, all is straightened out by the *deus ex machina*, Honeywood's uncle.

In fine, it is one of those theatrical plots so inconceivable outside the theatre that one wonders how any theatre could ever endure them. Indeed one of the most really comic things about the play is the quite unconscious humour of Johnson's preposterously sombre prologue, like a skeleton ushering in a feast.

> Prest by the load of life, the weary mind
> Surveys the general toil of human kind.

Did ever comedy have such a Dead March for overture?

No doubt there is also, for *us*, a certain humour in seeing Goldsmith satirize his own good-natured weaknesses in his good-natured hero, Honeywood—'how,' as Honeywood's uncle observes, 'can I be proud of a place in his heart, where every sharper and coxcomb find an easy entrance? ... He calls his extravagance, generosity; and his trusting everybody, universal benevolence.'

There is humour, too, in the character of the melancholy Croaker (compared with whom the Melancholy Jaques was almost an optimist). There comes occasionally a happy repartee—'An only son, sir, might expect more indulgence'—'An only father, sir, might expect more obedience.' Or there is Mrs Croaker's rebuke to her husband's talk of 'our bad world'—'Never mind the world, my dear; you were never in a pleasanter place in your life.' All the same, Sheridan could have given us far more wit in far less space.

In short, I cannot believe in what happens to the characters; nor care whether it happens or not. No doubt comic extravaganzas can succeed better on the stage, where the actors and the scenery, if nothing else, look comparatively real, than in the cold light of the study. But it is not surprising that *The Good-Natured Man* has proved too unnatural to keep the theatre since.

Of *She Stoops to Conquer* (Covent Garden, 1773) the *Evening Post* generously observed, 'the plot is exceedingly probable and fertile'. Now it is true that the mistaking of a house for an inn appears to be based on a real incident in Goldsmith's youth. But real incidents are often far too improbable for fiction; and the *Evening Post* seems to me excessively indulgent; just as Horace Walpole's comment is excessively unkind—' "Stoops" indeed! So she does—that is, the Muse. She is draggled up to her knees, and has trudged, I believe, from Southwark Fair.' Walpole's rather hoity-toity attitude recalls Lockhart on *Pickwick*—'all very well, but damned low'. And a satire on such squeamishness is already provided in the play itself, by Goldsmith's tipplers at *The Three Jolly Pigeons*:

First Fellow. The 'Squire has got spunk in him.

Second Fellow. I loves to hear him sing, bekeays he never gives us anything that's *low*.

Third Fellow. O damn anything that's *low*, I cannot bear it.

Fourth Fellow. The genteel thing is the genteel thing at any time. If so be that a gentleman bees in a concatenation accordingly.

This later work is, at least, a vast advance on *The Good-Natured Man*. After all, how many other English comedies are there, apart from Sheridan's, in the space of nearly two centuries between Vanbrugh and Wilde, that are ever acted now? With a spirited cast, *She Stoops to Conquer* still passes pleasantly enough; though not perhaps with very high honours. But, having enjoyed it once, I must admit that I am in no tearing hurry to enjoy it again.

Tony Lumpkin has, in his humble way, become a stock type in current speech; and Kate Hardcastle lives. The rest, if not high thinking, is at least high spirits. But I cannot call it one of the world's great plays; nor rank Goldsmith as playwright with his countrymen Sheridan, Shaw, Wilde, or Synge.

However, to dissect this butterfly longer would be to expose oneself to Goldsmith's humorous criticism of critics in the *Citizen of the World*.

> 'If then a book, spirited or humorous, happens to appear in the republic of letters, several critics are in waiting to bid the public not to laugh at a single line of it, for themselves had read it; and they know what is most proper to excite laughter. Other critics contradict the fulmination of this tribunal, call them all spiders, and assure the public, that they ought to laugh without restraint. Another set are in the mean time quietly employed in writing notes to the book, intended to shew the particular passages to be laughed at; when these are out, others still there are who write notes upon notes: thus a single new book employs not only the papermakers, the printers, the pressmen, the bookbinders, the hawkers, but twenty critics, and as many compilers. In short the body of the learned may be compared to a Persian army, where there are many pioneers, several sutlers, numberless servants, women and children in abundance and but few soldiers. Adieu.'

None the less this lovable Irishman lives, for me, in English literature not so much as a dramatist, not so much as a poet even, but rather by the fiction and the essays where he could be most clearly his good-natured yet ironic, wise yet unassuming self.

In April 1774 Goldsmith was laid to rest in the Temple (not in that Poets' Corner of Westminster where he had once stood with Johnson, and where Johnson was ten years later to be laid); still exiled, far from the white Atlantic clouds sailing across the green fields of Lissoy. But ninety years later, when it was debated which of Ireland's worthies should have statues by College Green in the heart of Dublin, though the list held also the names of Swift, and of Berkeley, it was Oliver Goldsmith who received that honour first, five years before Edmund Burke himself. The stone that the builders rejected, was become the head of the corner.

Goldsmith remains an example of what goodness, good sense, grace, gaiety, and simplicity can do, even in a harsh world preoccupied with many meaner things. Even more than by the characters he put into *The Vicar of Wakefield* and the *Citizen of the World*, he lives by his own.

To-day, as one drives through industrial cities, on every side rise forests of television masts—as if in our new termitaries the very houses, like ants, had grown antennae. I doubt if they find much time for Goldsmith. He was no aristocrat; but, champion of the poor though he was, the taste that came to value him was not untouched by aristocratic standards. But now it is that odd, somewhat pathetic being, the commonplace man, the '*pauvre Pécus*' of Anatole France, who most pays our pipers and most calls our tunes. And *Pécus* likes cruder fare than Goldsmith offered. And yet—

> The heart distrusting asks, if this be joy.

Had Goldsmith lived to-day, he might have changed one word in his *Deserted Village*—

> Ill fares the land, to hastening ills a prey,
> Where *Science* accumulates, and men decay.

I have no wish to gird indiscriminately at science. Without science our civilization could no longer even eat; yet one may be allowed at times to wonder what sort of civilization the scientific future holds in store. And the ghost of Johnson answers: 'Sir, you *may* wonder.'

EPILOGUE

THESE four lives are strange and fascinating enough in themselves, without any need to squeeze conclusions from them. 'L'ineptie,' thought Flaubert, 'consiste à vouloir conclure.' Yet even that was a conclusion. And if one thinks at all over what one reads, it is hard not to draw *some* conclusions, however provisional. Here are mine—very possibly wrong—but perhaps, even so, not wholly without use to readers in arriving at views of their own.

'Men are tired,' said Mussolini, 'of liberty.' He did not foresee how much more tired, in a few years, men would be of *him*. Yet to some extent he spoke true. For many, Liberty *had* become a disappointing bore; and despotism, not for the first time, seemed better at all events than anarchy. It was left for Hitler and the Kremlin to cure that dangerous disillusion—to teach at least a large part of the world that, if political rights can become a mockery without economic rights, and freedom from tyrants futile without freedom also from want, yet the converse too is true.

Similarly many in the modern world are tired of reason. This, indeed, is an older form of weariness—old as Solomon—old perhaps as the Pyramids. St Paul adjured the Galatians not to grow 'weary in well-doing': men are no less liable to weary of clear thinking. Our present fit of this really began with Romanticism—with Rousseau cursing civilization; with Blake railing at Newton and Locke, Johnson and Reynolds; with Keats drinking confusion to the cold philosophy that plucks the glory from the wings of seraphim.

Later critics may often have mocked at the Romantics; realist and naturalist writers may have reacted against them; but, despite temporary checks, that Romantic retreat from good sense has persisted. Arnold, protesting a century ago against contemporary lack of sanity, little guessed what strange monsters the further ebb in the tide of reason was yet to leave wriggling and ramping in the sight of day—pragmatism, Futurism, militarism, nationalism, Marxism, Fascism, Nazism, Dadaism, Surrealism, Existentialism, and how many -isms more! We may have reached, here and there, a century of the common man; but who cares about anything so dull as a century of common sense?

It has been propounded by an authoritative critic of our day that 'there may be a good deal to be said for Romanticism in life, there is no place for it in letters'. But I wonder if the exact opposite is not truer. One may surely hesitate to deny a place in literature to Scott or Chateaubriand, Keats or Hugo; yet feel that, from Nero to Hitler, the world has suffered hideously from Romantic unreason in real life. Even as private persons, Romantic living hardly brought Byron or Musset what they dreamed.

In 1860 the Goncourts lamented the depressing reasonableness and lack of extravagance in contemporary history; they sighed for 'quelque grand toqué de gloire ou de foi qui brouille un peu la terre et tracasse son temps à coups d'imprévu'. They had not long to wait—only ten years. The result proved not very agreeable. Since then we have gone on from strength to strength, with plenty of 'grands toqués de gloire ou de foi'. Yet even in 1913 an intellectual could observe—'La guerre, pourquoi pas? Ce serait amusant.' To-day, at last, the romance of war, at least, has paled. Even the most romantic find unappetizing the prospect of being conveniently cremated alive on the most masterly scale. And so cold war has replaced hot on the menu. Yet the romance of power, the romance of nationalism, the romance of communism retain, for much of mankind, a deadly glamour that laughs at dull reason.

Now of course it is true that in our demented period Science has yet risen to unimagined triumphs by the logical use of reason, observation, and experiment. But at this new master the world looks with mixed feelings—with exaltation, but also with apprehension; with hope, but also with dread. And, in reaction, some are driven by these too overpowering feats of reasoning still further along the road to the irrational.

Further, though Wells might dream of a world ruled rationally, at last, by scientific minds, others note with dismay that even scientists, once emerged from their laboratories, though often delightful and admirable persons, can prove strangely unscientific—

far from stable compounds themselves. They can swallow queer philosophies; they can be duped, one after another, by the most transparent frauds of Marxist pseudo-science.

This is surprising; and not very reassuring. Yet it may be less paradoxical than it seems. The scientist, as a rule, pursues knowledge in an atmosphere comparatively insulated from emotions, (except for curiosity and the love of truth); but outside his glass-doors, exposed to a very different air full of passions and prejudices, he may succumb to these with a curious helplessness, as unimmunized races can succumb to so mild a virus as measles. Again, most scientists deal much less with people than with things; but few things have the incalculable complexity of people. Sense may be the basis of science in the laboratory; but science, unfortunately, seems no guarantee of sense outside it.

Indeed one of the most vital discoveries of scientific reason in our time has been the frailty of reason itself—how easily it is intoxicated and distorted by fears or wishes from the dimmer depths of consciousness. Never before had it been so clear how hard it is to think clearly.

The eighteenth century, we can see now, monstrously underestimated the difficulty of being rational. It was as if a man should attribute disturbances in his cellar to a few rats; when beneath his foundations flowed really a subterranean river, full of strange forms of life far less easy to control. It does not, indeed, seem to me very intelligent to talk, as some delighted persons now do, of a rediscovery of 'original sin'. For that idea is too much mixed up with primitive beliefs in collective and hereditary guilt. But man *has* discovered, as never before, his own persistent and perverse irrationality.

Yet if reason turns out to be like a little candle on an ocean-raft, that need not make it, as some have rushed to suppose, less precious; it makes it only the more vital to use every effort to keep its light dry and unextinguished. Still it also becomes understandable that Freud was no optimist.

He had lit up the hairy arms of Caliban, shaking the polished cage-bars of civilization. We have watched the bars bend in our time. No one can be quite certain they will not break. And meanwhile science is less successful at taming Caliban than at pushing within his reach new toys and tools; compared with some of which dynamite was a squib.

Some might expect that in the face of this we should develop ten times the passion of the eighteenth century for sense, for intelligence, for understanding; ten times its enthusiasm against what they called 'enthusiasm', and we, 'fanaticism'.

Yet this has not happened. Men patch up international machinery. But it creaks. The old passions and prejudices get between the wheels. Men cry that the world needs 'a change of heart'. No doubt. But that cry has been reiterated for thousands of years by now. The results seem hardly adequate. True, the human race has become in some ways more humane; yet our age has seen calculated atrocities on a vaster scale, perhaps, than ever before; it has seen the civilized restraints of whole nations dissolve like snow in the lava of fanaticism.

If men are too emotional, it is not clear that the cure lies in appeals to emotion. The need is not only for a change of heart. The need is also, perhaps more, for a change of mind—for clearer thinking. But amid the voices calling for a revival of religion, little is heard of a revival of reason.

No doubt that is natural. Most men have always had misgivings where reason might lead. The beasts know neither Time nor Death—only the blind urge to cling to life, and to reproduce it. But when man discovered that grim Trinity, the Past, the Present, and the Future, he discovered also the need to escape them by intoxication. Having learnt to remember, he sought also to forget. Having learnt to foresee, he sought also how not to see. Knowing so little, he must dream that he knew much. Only so could he blot out the bleakness of the Universe that widened round him. Perhaps there have only been two ages when even a sizeable minority in any society developed a definite cult of reasonableless, a passion for seeing things as they are—for what Heraclitus called 'dry light'. The first of those ages was Greek antiquity; but the Greeks, too passionate and excitable, destroyed themselves. The second was the eighteenth century; but there too the minority was too small, the problems too difficult, the strain too great.

Dionysus, Lord of Intoxication, is a formidable god. He has filled the earth with dreams, the heavens with visions, the future with Utopias. He enraptures lovers with the illusion that they, and their passion, are unique. Literature, art, music are full of him. He has raised the Pyramids and the Gothic Cathedrals. He brought the armies of 'fanatic Arabia' to the Atlantic, the hordes of Genghiz from the Great Wall to the Adriatic, the columns of Charles XII, Napoleon, and Hitler to the heart of Russia.

To those who question him, he is quick and deadly in answer; against those who oppose him, endlessly resourceful. Against the reason of the Hellene he set the fervour of the Hebrew; Luther he raised up beside Erasmus, Calvin beside Montaigne; Rousseau beside Hume, and Robespierre beside Franklin; beside Darwin, Marx, and Strindberg beside Ibsen; beside Freud, D. H. Lawrence, and Hitler beside Einstein.

For to many minds, perhaps to most, the nescience of Socrates, the scepticism of Hume, the refusal to believe without fuller evidence, the acceptance of the pillow of doubt, seem intolerable. They picture the world of reason as a dusty desert where Newton dismisses poetry as 'ingenious nonsense', sculpture as 'stone dolls', or Bentham despises verse as no better than pushpin, the *Iliad* as inferior to solitaire. They cry out with repugnance—as Charlotte Brontë and Alice Meynell at Jane Austen; or Carlyle at Mill—'sawdust to the masthead'. They imagine themselves reduced by doubt to the melancholy impotence of Hamlet, or the desolate ennui of Mme du Deffand. They exclaim like Benjamin Constant: 'J'aime mieux la folie de l'enthousiasme, si ce qui rend heureux est folie, que cette funeste sagesse.' With too much passion wrong things may be done; but with too little passion, they argue, nothing gets done at all.

Now of course these dangers exist. The poetry of the eighteenth century, except where it is gay or sardonic, is often pompously and prosaically dull. Machiavelli and Chesterfield *do* seem often cold as serpents. Amiel and Clough *were* paralysed by excessive scruples about intellectual honesty.

But these drawbacks need not be inevitable. They may come from excess of rationality; Apollo was wiser, who gave Dionysus a share—though a lesser share—in his own Delphic shrine. They may come from defects of temperament, from lack of vitality. A searching keenness of intellect did not dry up the poetry of Euripides or

Horace, Goethe or Hardy. Socrates and Montaigne, Hume and Franklin, active and buoyant to the last, were no Hamlets.

Imagine, for instance, a Hamlet with the character of Hume or Franklin. He would have doubted the ghost; and even if unable to doubt his father's murder, he would have doubted the value of vengeance. Claudius, seemingly, was a tolerable king: would Denmark be any happier for regicide and civil war? Such a Hamlet would have gone philosophically back to the world of ideas in Wittenberg; ready if Denmark needed him, to do his part as prince (Hume and Franklin were no cloistered pedants); but equally, or even more, content with obscure usefulness, since well-being lies ultimately in states of mind alone. The world would have been the poorer for a fine tragedy: but whatever else the world may be short of, it is not tragedies.

For ages men have lamented over the Fall. But few seem to consider that the fault of Eve might have been less fatal, had the Apple itself not been a fraud. It was to give knowledge of good and evil: but that 'knowledge' has remained most fallible and contradictory. Who shall say whether more misery has been caused on earth by the presence of sin or the absence of sense? For the rigid moralist, Charles I was doubtless a better man than Charles II; George III that George IV; Louis XVI than Henri IV. But their wrong-headed good intentions cost their subjects a good deal dearer than the vices or indolences of their less virtuous counterparts. Catherine of Russia was a good deal frailer than poor Queen Gertrude in Elsinore; but well for the world if Russia had never had worse rulers than Catherine.

And if the irrational stupidity of the good causes needless suffering untold, so does the irrational stupidity of the wicked. True, civilization, such as it is, might not have survived at all but for the strange fact that the wicked seem almost automatically to become stupid—so that a Hitler, for example, is blinded into invading Russia, or a Stalin into producing Marshall Aid and a closer union of the West than might otherwise have been possible (we have given men grateful statues for benefits far less). But, unfortunately, the stupidity of the wicked fills the earth with pointless havoc also, because they are so bad even at judging and compassing their own bad ends. Often the unscrupulous succeed; but their enjoyment of that success seems rarely such as any sane being would covet. (Who could envy Henry VIII, or Peter the Great?) Diogenes in his tub must have been happier than most of them.

And yet the religions of the world, with rare exceptions, have generally concentrated on dubious metaphysics, questionable emotionalism, and exhortations to often unintelligent patterns of behaviour. They have talked constantly of strait gates; seldom of straight thinking. They might have served human happiness better, had they thought and taught more about sense, and less about 'sin'.

There have, indeed, been partial exceptions like Apollo of Delphi with his 'Know thyself' and 'Nothing too much'—yet his wisdom became adulterated with corruption and fraud; or like Confucius, who somehow contrived to make men passionate for moderation—yet Confucius was less a religious thinker than a sage. There is, too, some superb wisdom literature in the Old Testament; but it often seems somewhat avoided by the orthodox, as embarrassing rather than admirable.

All this may be natural enough. Men at large are far more attracted by emotion than reflection. Antony can generally beat Brutus out of the Forum. Even so-called Ages of Reason have only faintly deserved their name—they were merely, for a small minority, rather less unreasonable than other periods. Not a chapter in the history of the fifth century B.C. or the eighteenth A.D. that is not blotted with follies and crimes. None the less when, for a while, it became a tradition to try to be intelligent, and unfashionable to glorify the irrational, the results, though perhaps slight, were perceptible. Let me illustrate. And because women are commonly supposed less rational, more emotional, than men, let the examples be taken from women.

'The next time I see her, I believe I shall say: "O Common Sense, sit down; I have been thinking so and so; is't not absurd?" '

(Horace Wálpole, of Mme Geoffrin.)

'L'esprit de Mme du Deffand est un bel esprit amateur du vrai, du noble, du simple, ennemi de la prétention, de l'affectation, et de tout ce qui a l'air de contrainte ou de grimace ou de vouloir briller au dépens de la justesse ou du naturel.'

(M. du Châtel, father of the Duchesse de Choiseul.)

'Il faut, ma reine, vous resoudre à vivre avec moi avec la plus grande vérité et sincérité.... Vous serez charmante tant que vous vous laisserez aller à votre naturel et que vous serez sans prétention et sans entortillage.'

(Mme du Deffand to Mlle de Lespinasse.)

'Lucinde, spirituelle Lucinde, en attendant les Clitandre, vous n'avez rien de mieux à faire que de devenir parfaite. Ayez des idées nettes et des expressions simples.'

(Mme de Charrière—Boswell's Zélide—to Mlle L'Hardy.)

Germaine Necker, the future Mme de Staël, to her mother (it is interesting to watch Romanticism already on the way): 'Oui, maman, quand je vivrais mille ans pour vous contempler, si vous retourniez un instant la tête, il me semble que j'en serais encore jalouse.'

Mme Necker, in reply: 'J'aimerais bien que tu n'exagérasses rien, méme en matière de sentiments. Tu sais qu'il faut toujours faire sa cour à cette bonne raison que j'aime tant.... Quand on a plus vécu, on s'aperçoit que la véritable manière de plaire et d'intéresser est de peindre exactement sa pensée sans charge et sans emphase.'

'To be rational in anything is great praise.'

(Jane Austen.)

Very few moderns talk like that. Not because they can take good sense for granted; but because they have ceased to think, or care, so much about it. To hear, amid contemporary chatter, a still, clear voice like Mme de Charrière's, seems to me like passing from the frantic, hooting traffic of a modern metropolis to the keen, quiet air of the Jura, where the Weissenstein, above her own Neuchâtel, looks across the plain of Bern to the mountain-wall—calm, relentless, immutable—of the distant Oberland.

No doubt the 'Age of Reason' could be stupid, or silly, or bored, or bad; just as the Age of Chivalry could be gross and cruel. Life seldom rises to the height of ideals: but without them it sinks far lower. This passion for sense, sincerity, and simplicity appears to me not only far more admirable (that is personal), but also far wiser, saner, and safer than the obscurantism and oddity so often dear to modern minds.

So with Johnson and the rest. If Johnson remains to-day more than a grotesque or picturesque eccentric, it is largely because, though often swept into nonsense by passion, prejudice, or pride, he wrestled perpetually with himself for honesty of mind. If Boswell is more than a pathetic figure of fun, it is largely because, though so often senseless himself, he tirelessly pursued good sense and intellectual distinction in others. If Chesterfield, too prone to mistake cleverness for wisdom, is more warning than example, still the positive value of his writing lies in its effort to see realities unclouded by convention or cant. And Goldsmith—to Hawkins, 'this idiot'; to Walpole, 'an idiot, with once or twice a fit of parts'—may yet seem to others in some ways the wisest of the four. For he was more sensitive, and yet the astringent good sense of his age helped to preserve his sentiment from growing too sweet.

With all four, the quest for happiness hardly ended happily—less happily than with the four other figures that I hope to deal with in a later volume—Horace Walpole, Hume, Burke, and Benjamin Franklin. Walpole was luckier in circumstance and temperament. Burke, indeed, does not seem to me a very happy person; but the wiser part of his thought seems highly important for the happy government of mankind. And Hume and Franklin got as much, I think, from life as any reasonable person can expect; partly perhaps because they thought less of happiness, and more of a disinterested pursuit of reason and truth; so that happiness, or content, came more to them, in the way it often does, as a by-product.

It is idle guessing the future of the world. A Third War? A relapse to barbarism? A world of ant-states, with aristocracies of bureaucracies, in control of inarticulate masses mechanically tending machines? A world of welfare-states, inhabited by orderly hordes of Philistines, largely preoccupied with physical enjoyment and sport, 'telly' and belly? Or—perhaps the likeliest—something unlike any of our dreams? (After all our sun, it appears, might always boil over, as suns do, into a *nova*, and roast all life—even the oceans—from the face of the earth. A conceivability hardly worth dwelling on; but perhaps worth sometimes recalling.)

Luckily we do not have to guess. It seems to me that those who think of the matter at all, have simply to make up their minds on an issue difficult enough, but at least less difficult. Is it desirable that human life should become more or less rational? That it should tend towards more suspension of judgment, or more unhesitating fanaticism?

Many writers and thinkers in the last century and a half, still more in the last half-century, have chosen, whether consciously or not, the side of the irrational—*mauvais clercs*, in my belief, if ever there were. Many men of action have done the same. And in general it seems a common assumption to-day that stress on reason is unnecessary, or unimportant, or undesirable, or unoriginal, or unexciting. The consequences of this have certainly been exciting; but dubiously desirable.

Those who take the other side, the side of reason—who try to believe nothing unless there are rational grounds for it, and otherwise to be content with probabilities, or frank uncertainty, may be wrong—or they may be right, yet destined to defeat. None of them can live long enough to know. But at least they will not have frivolously undermined the foundations of their own civilization. They will not be like a recent critic who complacently wrote, 'I have little or no idea where I am going'. No one, of course, can know. But he meant, apparently, that he had no values whatever—that he did not know what he stood for. Not very enviable; not very useful. I prefer Chekhov, who wrote to Suvorin, about a similar indifferentism in Suvorin's son: 'He looks on at the cock-fight like a spectator, and has no fighting-cock of his own. And one ought to have one's own fighting-cock, else life is without interest.' Chekhov had.

Those who urge, in the eighteenth-century way, more passion for reason and less glorification of hysteria, may easily be destined, like eighteenth-century reasoners, to fail. They may be like ants nibbling at a mountain. Very well, nibble. But there is perhaps one ground for not being quite so pessimistic. Circumstances have changed. They have grown more dangerous. And in the history of evolution it has often been the challenge of necessity that called out the qualities to meet it. In his remote past, man survived the struggle with animals physically more powerful by being more intelligent: to-day in the struggle with the beasts within him, in the new jungle he has created for himself, his own survival may depend on becoming more intelligent still. For ages he has had, as a species, no enemies that could wipe him out but the bacillus. To-day, once more, as in remote prehistory, he is perhaps less secure.

Now men never know what they can do till they are faced with destruction. Death is a remarkable stimulant. A large part of the world seems living on an emotional intoxication beyond its means; but it might still be sober enough to grasp that, while there is still time.

All this may be fantasy. It is hard even to discuss such things without sounding sombre and sensational. At worst, one can only say, like Skarphedinn in *Njal's Saga*, 'If it is my father's humour that we should all be burnt in his house, very well.' In any case, though there are many other issues in the infinite complexity of living, none seems to me more important than this question of reason, intuition, and emotion. And my conclusion is to suggest that twentieth-century minds can gain from those of the eighteenth not merely amusement, not merely culture, but also a stronger conviction that, even if there may be other qualities more engaging, or valuable, in the individual, there is yet (especially if we think of the common good) no substitute for good sense. None. Our age suffers from too much knowledge, too much frenzy, too little judgment. 'To be rational in anything is great praise.'

INDEX

9781334976148

WS - #0026 - 280623 - C0 - 229/152/20 - PB - 9781334976148 - Gloss Lamination